The Price of Wealth

A volume in the series

Cornell Studies in Political Economy

EDITED BY PETER J. KATZENSTEIN

A full list of titles in the series appears at the end of the book.

The Price of Wealth

Economies and Institutions in the Middle East

Kiren Aziz Chaudhry

Cornell University Press

Ithaca and London

First published 1997 by Cornell University Press

Library of Congress Cataloging-in-Publication Data

Chaudhry, Kiren Aziz.
The price of wealth : economies and institutions in the Middle East / Kiren Aziz Chaudhry.
p. cm. — (Cornell studies in political economy)
Includes index.
ISBN 0-8014-3164-6 (cloth : alk. paper)
1. Saudi Arabia—Economic policy. 2. Yemen—Economic policy. 3. Middle East—Economic conditions. 4. Saudi Arabia—Politics and government. 5. Yemen—Politics and government. I. Title. II. Series.
HC415.33.C49 1997
338.953—dc21 97-1536

Printed in the United States of America

This book is printed on Lyons Falls Turin Book, paper that is totally chlorine-free and acid-free

Cloth printing 10 9 8 7 6 5 4 3 2 1

For Aden and Rem

Contents

Acknowledgments

After winning a Pulitzer for *Pilgrim at Tinker Creek*, Annie Dillard wrote a short book called *The Writing Life* in which she cautioned would-be writers against showing their readers what she called the "price tag" on their work. Dillard meant that writing should be lean. But, fresh from my work in the Middle East, I took it to mean also that the reader should be spared the suffering and anxieties of the writer. That was some years ago. This book has been so long in the making that it has become therapy. I have no price tag to display, only warm thanks for those who helped me.

The early support of Samuel Huntington, David Landes, and Stephan Haggard, who gave me the intellectual freedom to shape my own research agenda, was critical in initiating the field work on which the book is, in large measure, based. Over time colleagues read all or parts of the manuscript. Suggestions, criticisms, and encouragement offered by Chris Ansell, Sheila Carapico, Ruth Berrins Collier, David Laitin, Elizabeth Perry, Robert Powell, Robert Price, Suzanne Rudolph, Charles Schmitz, and John Zysman have been enormously helpful. David Collier supported this project in countless ways and well beyond the call of duty. The manuscript also benefited from the detailed comments of an anonymous reviewer for Cornell University Press.

Two colleagues, Peter Katzenstein and David Woodruff, put themselves "in" the manuscript, so to speak, and, more than alerting me to what was wrong with it, helped me make it a better version of what it already was. For their care and empathy I am grateful. In the company of my former student David Woodruff, I developed many of the arguments and sifted through much of the evidence. His intellectual companionship was indispensable in freeing me to pursue arguments that initially appeared heretical. Others at Berkeley shaped my thinking and gave me courage by subjecting my ideas to the kind of scrutiny that only graduate students can offer. I owe thanks to the students who, as part of my political economy seminar since 1991, have sustained me in an intellectual landscape that appeared, at times, strangely parched. In particular, I acknowledge Regina Abrami, Anne Marie Baylouny, Arthur Burris, Melani Cammett, Julie Lynch, Khalid Medani, and Lauren Morris. Ken Dubin and Evan Leiberman gave me excellent research assistance and many substantive suggestions that improved the work. Arthur McKee prepared the manuscript for publication and in the process thoroughly confirmed my high opinion of historians.

Through the various incarnations of this project my friends Muhammad Alwan, Robin Einhorn, Naomi Rustomjee, Peter Sahlins, Shannon Stimpson, and Michael Watts have offered general advice about how to survive as well as candid, sometimes scathing, evaluations of the style or substance of the arguments I was contemplating. John and Lois Young and Anwar and Kathleen Chaudhry helped in numerous ways, practical and otherwise, both in the Middle East and in the United States.

In my ambition to understand two countries I had known only through books, I have had excellent guides. My debt to Samir Anabatawi, Saleh Toaimi, Husayn al-Saqqaf, ʿAli Salami, ʿAbdalqawi Humaiqani, Mansur ʿAbdallah Yasin, and Hussein al-Hubaishi cannot be summarized in any neat way. The reasons for their generosity during my stay in Arabia are still mysterious to me, but their efforts on my behalf came closer to a pure quest for knowledge than much of what goes on in the American academy. Without their help, their courage, and their patience the best parts of this book could not have been written. I could not have done research in Saudi Arabia without the support of ʿAbdulaziz al-Dukheil. His friendship, generosity, insight, and sheer unfounded belief in my ability to put it together brought vividly to life the most venerable traditions of Arabia. Because of him, several organizations gave me access to the unusual information, archives, and data on which my analysis of Saudi Arabia is based.

With some initial mixture of suspicion and curiosity and, later, genuine interest, the staffs of the Jeddah, Riyadh, Sanʿa, and Taiz Chambers of Commerce and Industry and the director and librarians of the Institute for Public Administration in Riyadh put up with me for months, giving generously of their time, their institutional memory, their data, and their advice. The American Institute for Yemeni Studies under the directorships of both Jeffrey Meisner and David Warburton facilitated my research in countless ways in 1986–87 and in 1992. My field work and writing were generously funded by the Fulbright-Hays Commission, the Social Science Research Council, the Kukin Fellowship at the Harvard Academy for International and Area Studies, and the Institute for International and Area

Studies at Berkeley. Deans Henry Rosovsky and Al Fishlow, both institutions in themselves, were particularly supportive of my efforts. Finally I thank Roger Haydon for good advice and good cheer; for living up to the legend. With all this help I wish I could attribute the remaining inadequacies of my work to someone else as well; but they, and the views and interpretations expressed in this book, are mine alone.

It is probably not unusual that the most important influences on my work have been people not directly involved in its actual production. Three people, each in very different ways, have been enormously important, largely by example, in shaping my ideas about what it is we do and why. With hope that if not this, then my next book will reflect some of what I learned from them, I thank Michael Burawoy, Stephen Holmes, and Michael Rogin.

K. A. C.

Glossary of Saudi Archival Documents

These documents are in the Saudi National Archive, in the Institute for Public Administration, Riyadh.

Amr Malaki	Royal Ordinance
Amr Sami	Royal Decree
Diwan al Malaki	King's Office
Khitab	Letter (followed by name of issuing body)
Majlis al-Shura	Consultative Council
Majlis al-Wukala'	Council of Deputies
Majlis al-Wuzara'	Council of Ministers
Marsum Malaki	Royal Decree based on the recommendation of the Council of Ministers. (Usually the king's approval of legislation passed by Decree of the Council of Ministers)
Qarar	Decree (followed by name of issuing body)
Qarar Malaki	Royal Decree
Qarar Ri'asah al-Majlis al-Wuzara'	Decree of the president of the Council of Ministers (Since the end of King Saud's reign, the council president has also been king)

The Price of Wealth

Chapter One

Oil and Labor Exporters in the International Economy

In 1973 the international price of oil quadrupled, precipitating the largest and most rapid transfer of wealth in the twentieth century. In the magnitude of the changes they wrought in the global economy, the oil shocks of the 1970s and early 1980s were comparable to the crises of the 1920s and 1930s. They created severe pressures for adjustment in the advanced industrial countries, triggering changes in economic policy and fundamentally altering macroeconomic relationships that had stabilized over the preceding three decades. In the developing world, sovereign and private borrowers gained access to recycled petrodollars, generating a host of economic dependencies that culminated in the debt crisis of the mid-1980s. The oil shocks transformed international financial markets, initiating a trend that assumed institutional form in the liberalization of major financial centers in the 1980s.

At the epicenter of these systemic changes—the Middle East—the deluge of oil revenues flooded a region whose countries had skewed but complementary national factor endowments. What decades of Pan-Arab sentiment had failed to achieve, the oil boom accomplished effortlessly: through the prosperous years of the 1970s and early 1980s, the economies of capital-scarce labor exporters and labor-scarce oil exporters became tightly linked through massive flows of labor and capital across national borders.

Shared resources made shared history. From Morocco to Iraq, the countries in the regional economy experienced three identical episodes of change: the oil boom (1973–1983), the recession leading up to the Gulf War (1984–1990), and the aftermath of the Gulf War. Between 1973 and 1983 the regional economy was characterized by unprecedented levels of interdependence between capital and labor exporters. In some instances—Tunisia and Libya, for example, or Yemen and Saudi Arabia—this interdependence was bilateral.[1] Other labor-abundant countries, such as Jordan, Palestine, Syria, and Egypt, exported workers to many destinations. Oil revenues and labor remittances were supplemented by bilateral aid from the oil-rich Gulf states, Europe, the United States, and the Soviet Union. Aid constituted a substantial portion of government revenues for capital-scarce Middle Eastern countries; even for major labor exporters, aid at times outstripped remittance earnings.[2] Oil revenues, aid, trade, remittances, and borrowing grew in tandem in the 1970s, reinforcing interdependence (as Figures 1.1–2 illustrate).

Quick to emerge, the regional economy was also short-lived. When oil prices plummeted in the 1980s, a severe regionwide recession ensued. From a 1980 high of $243 billion, oil revenues for major exporters fell to $67 billion in 1988.[3] The economic downturn had an almost immediate impact on labor exporters, as government contracts in oil exporters were terminated and state spending dropped. Workers' remittances declined, generating severe balance-of-payments crises.[4] Similarly, Arab bilateral and multilateral aid declined from a high of $10.9 billion in 1981 to $2.5 billion in 1987. By 1989 there was a net *outflow* of $2.2 billion from labor exporters in repayment of Arab nonconcessional loans. Other debt payments simultaneously came due for many of the region's heavy borrowers.[5] The decline of region-specific capital flows and the rise of debt repayments in the mid-1980s coincided, roughly, with the termination of much of the bilateral aid that the Arab states had been receiving from the Soviet Union and the United States (see Figure 1.3).

The Gulf War formally severed links that had been weakening through the late 1980s and signaled the unqualified end of the regional economy. The Iraqi invasion of Kuwait, as well as the positions taken by different

[1] Before 1978 Libya relied on Tunisian labor; later, Egypt replaced Tunisia as Libya's main source of labor. Similarly, three-fourths of Yemen's labor force was employed in Saudi Arabia during the oil boom, when labor remittances constituted over 150 percent of Yemen's official GNP.

[2] In 1978 and again in 1990, for example, Egypt's aid receipts exceeded labor remittances.

[3] The figures include value of fuel exports from Algeria, Ecuador, Gabon, Indonesia, Kuwait, Libya, Nigeria, Saudi Arabia, the United Arab Emirates, and Venezuela; see *World Tables, 1991* (Baltimore: Johns Hopkins University Press/World Bank, 1991).

[4] It is generally accepted that government and World Bank figures on labor remittances are inaccurate, as they reflect only earnings sent through formal banking institutions. The rise in remittances at the end of the 1980s (Figure 1.2) reflects one-time repatriations of savings at the termination of contracts and different reporting conventions in labor-exporting countries. For a review, see Gil Feiler, "Migration and Recession," *Population and Development Review* 17 (March 1991): 133–55.

[5] Pierre van den Boogaerde, "Financial Assistance from Arab Countries and Institutions," *Middle East Executive Reports,* April 1992.

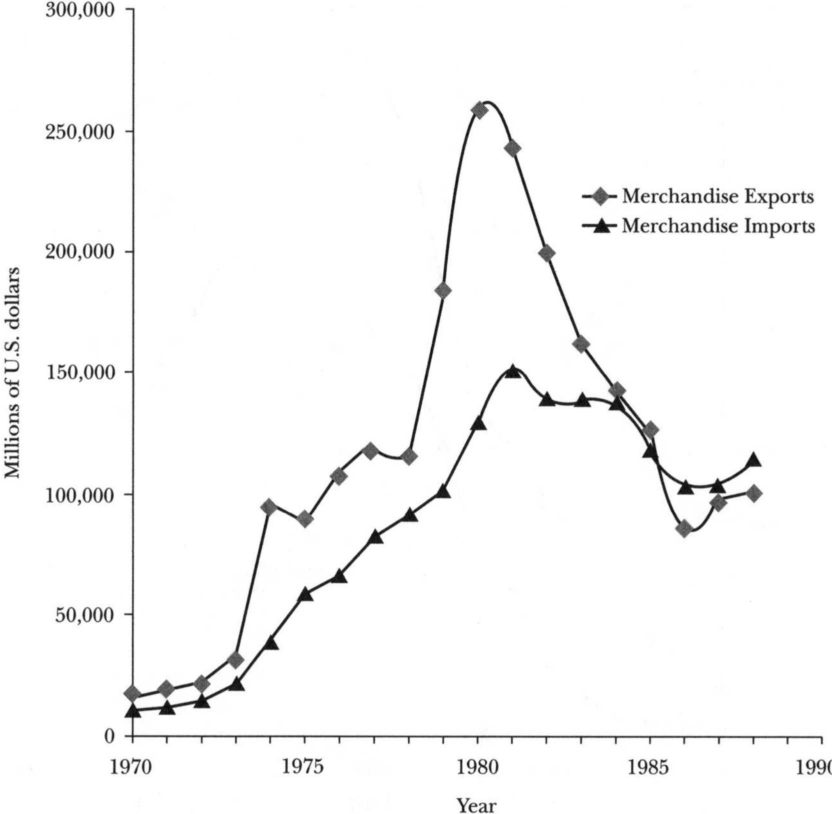

Figure 1.1 Middle East / North Africa: Merchandise exports and imports. (Sources: *World Tables,* 1991; 1989, 1990 figures for Libya and all figures for Iraq and Qatar calculated from International Financial Statistics, various years. Totals rounded to nearest million.)

Arab governments during the conflict, reflected varying domestic economic crises. The rift between rich and poor took institutional form briefly in 1989, when the Arab Cooperative Council was created by Iraq, Egypt, Yemen, and Jordan as a counter to the oil-rich members of the Gulf Cooperative Council. By the end of the war these conflicts had become largely superfluous: in 1990, when the Gulf states placed themselves directly under the security umbrella of the United States, they dissolved the political and military foundations of the regional economy.

The boom decade did not change a single political regime in the Arab world: indeed, in the vast majority of cases, the same political leaders who ushered in the boom were still in charge in 1996. Yet the capital flows of the 1970s reshaped the domestic institutions and economies of each constituent country: whole classes rose, fell, or migrated; finance, property rights, law, and economy were changed beyond recognition.

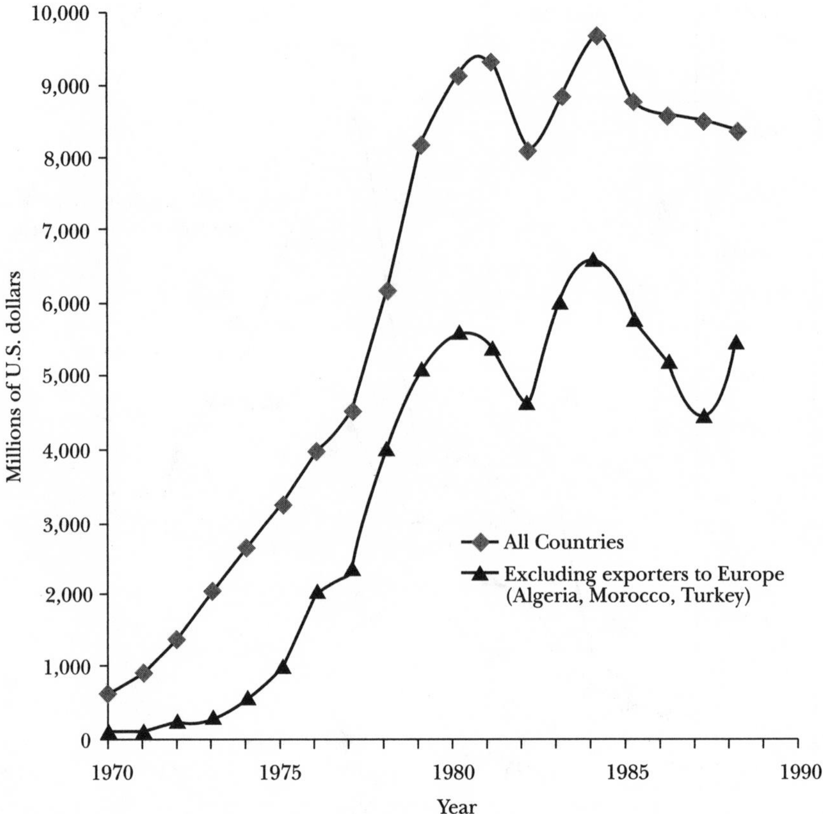

Figure 1.2 Middle East / North Africa: Officially recorded workers' remittances. (Sources: *World Tables,* 1991; Alan Richards and John Waterbury, *A Political Economy of the Middle East* [Boulder, Colo.: Westview Press, 1990]. Figures rounded to nearest million.)

The transmutations of the boom years rested on what an observer of sixteenth-century Spain once called "money made in air." When the recession of 1986 hit, the foundations of the boomtime political economy crumbled, subjecting institutions and political relationships to new pressures. The recession thrust each country in the region back onto domestic endowments utterly transfigured over the preceding decade. In both labor and oil exporters, the project of constructing viable national economies began anew in an international economy radically different from that of the 1970s and early 1980s.

This book examines how the exogenous shocks of the 1970s and 1980s transformed the domestic political economies of two countries embedded in this regional system. Yemen and Saudi Arabia are extreme cases of dependence on, respectively, labor remittances and oil, the two dominant forms of capital inflows in the Middle East. Tracing these cases from their

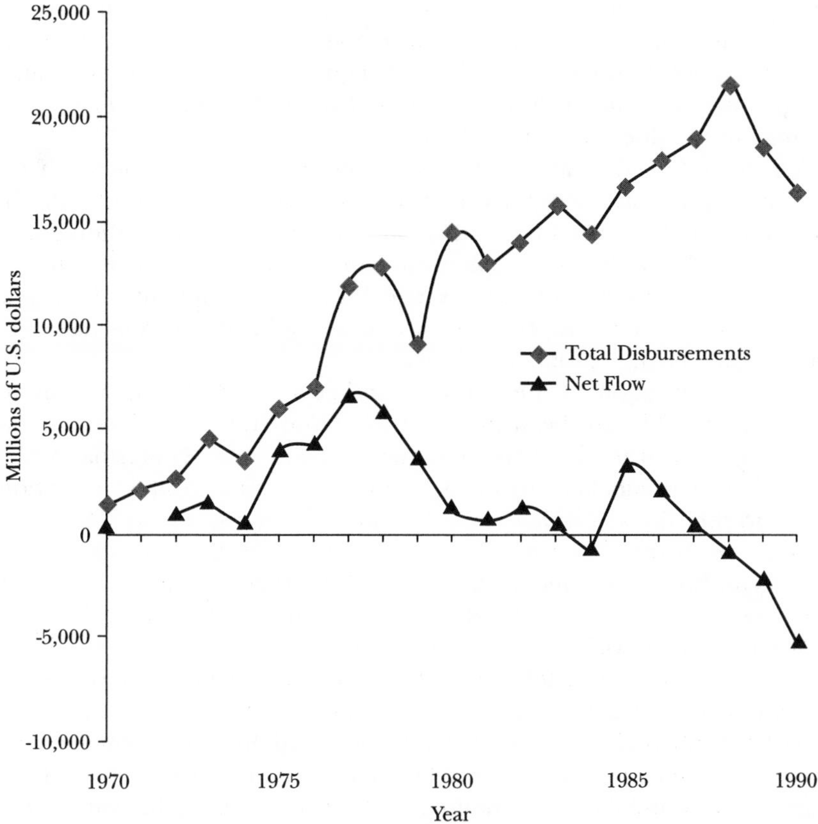

Figure 1.3 Middle East / North Africa: Debt flows. (SOURCES: *World Debt Tables,* 1979, 1983, 1989–90, 1991–92. Numbers rounded to nearest million.)

relative insularity in the interwar period, through the dramatic economic changes of the 1970s, 1980s, and 1990s, I explore the changing links between international and domestic political economies in late developers. In doing so, I expose the process by which exogenous shocks transform domestic interests and institutions at one juncture only to undercut the foundations of these accommodations at another. Clearly defined economic cycles (connected to oil prices) reveal contours of change and conflict that remain hidden in more stable environments.[6] The "boom" pattern (1973–1983) exposes responses to soaring external capital inflows, whereas the "bust" pattern (1986–1996) demonstrates how institutional

[6] For the special utility of studying politics in times of economic crises, see Peter Gourevitch, *Politics in Hard Times* (Ithaca: Cornell University Press, 1986). G. John Ikenberry echoes the importance of focusing on crises in "Conclusion," *International Organization* 42 (Winter 1988): 233–36. See also Charles P. Kindleberger, *Manias, Panics, and Crashes* (New York: Basic Books, 1978).

and political relationships forged in the boom break down in times of crisis, conditioning institutions, organizations, and policy outcomes in unexpected ways. In these clearly defined sequences we can test the relative weight of international, institutional, and interest-based explanations of change in the domestic political economy.

Yemen and Saudi Arabia had similar beginnings: neither country had a colonial legacy, and the oil boom of the 1970s coincided in both with the construction of a central bureaucracy and the creation of a national market. Two different types of capital flows thereafter shaped state structure and capacity, national integration, and business-government relations in divergent ways, revealing the discontinuous, highly contingent nature of institutional change in late developers.[7]

Before unification of the national market in Saudi Arabia and in Yemen, one would have been hard put to identify what "the international economy" meant for local communities in the Arabian Peninsula. Arabia existed in a Braudelian world of international trade routes, migration, and currency flows in which major international events—World War I, the dissolution of the Ottoman Empire, the collapse of the gold standard—had significant local effects. The communities that experienced these effects, however, had yet to be defined at the national level, and mechanisms for coping with economic change were local. The very institutions that separate the national from the international, a national market and a state, did not exist. Nevertheless, in this period of relative isolation and poverty, substantial institutional change occurred: in quite dissimilar ways, between 1916 and 1973, a central bureaucracy and army were forged, the currency was unified, and a national market was created in both Yemen and in Saudi Arabia.

The boom rapidly transformed each of these fundamental institutions. In the 1970s, almost unnoticed, the tax and regulatory bureaucracy was dismantled, the financial system was completely restructured, and new institutions arose in response to the influx of oil revenues and labor remittances. These new institutions, born of a sudden connection to the international economy, in turn reshaped society. Through the institutionally mediated flow of remittances and oil revenues, economic and ascriptive

[7] I define *state-building* as the elimination or cooptation of existing forms of authority and exchange that might challenge the existence of the state and the expansion and centralization of the fiscal, legal, and regulatory instruments of the state. *State structure* is the differential capacities and development of coercive, extractive, distributive, redistributive, regulatory, and participatory institutions. *Financial institutions* refers to the relative mix of state, commercial, informal, and other agencies and to the way the regulatory agencies of the state influence the allocation of finance. *State capacity* varies across organizations. It is measured by the ability of the government to formulate and implement policies and includes an institutional and a political component. By *national integration* I mean the use of resources, incentives, force, and assimilation to depoliticize ascriptive (regional, ethnic, and sectarian) cleavages and to create national institutions that, at least formally, create excludable economic, political, and social goods for nationals.

categories, on the wane in the 1960s, realigned. Then, in the bust, political relationships forged in the boom years broke down, generating intense conflicts over the future shape of domestic institutions. Scarcity bred a new politics centered explicitly on who would design the institutions that governed the national market. Conflict reentered the two systems, engaging groups constituted during the boom.

In the 1980s, policy goals were identical, but outcomes diverged. Starting in 1983, plummeting oil prices precipitated a severe economic recession in Saudi Arabia, which rapidly affected the Yemen Arab Republic, Saudi Arabia's southern neighbor and the main source of its imported labor force. The dimensions of the crisis are legendary. Saudi Arabia's oil revenues declined from a high of $120 billion in 1981 to $17 billion in 1985. Yemeni labor remittances dropped by about 60 percent, and development aid, which had covered the entire current budget of the Yemeni government, dropped to only 1 percent of the state budget. Both countries experienced severe fiscal crises that prompted wide-ranging economic reforms in 1986–87 designed to cut government outlays of foreign exchange, increase domestic taxation, and regulate what had been two of the most open economies in the world. Reform efforts produced different outcomes in the two countries. The Yemeni government's thoroughgoing package included heavy, retroactive taxation, foreign trade reforms, and a host of economic regulations that restricted the activities of its powerful private sector. In contrast, private elites in Saudi Arabia forced the Saudi government to withdraw most reforms within days of their enactment.

If economic power produces political power—if autonomous states are "strong," and independent groups are efficacious—this outcome is exceedingly puzzling. Oil revenues had accrued directly to the Saudi government over the boom decade—making government spending virtually the sole engine of domestic economic growth and freeing the state from reliance on domestic sources of revenue—whereas privately controlled labor remittances had bypassed the Yemeni state altogether. Entering the country through informal banking channels, remittances had expanded an already powerful domestic commercial and industrial elite. Paradoxically, in neither Yemen nor Saudi Arabia did the wealth of the boom translate into efficacy in the bust: the financially autonomous and affluent Saudi state could craft but not implement austerity measures; the Yemeni private sector could not resist the draconian reforms of a government that was poor, administratively weak, and politically isolated.

The economic reforms of the 1980s open a window on the way that oil revenues and labor remittances had transformed the political economy of Saudi Arabia and Yemen, revealing the radically different nature of their interactions with an international economy that was itself experiencing fundamental change. Going back through the 1970s, to Yemen and Saudi

Arabia as they were before the oil boom, this book traces the genealogy of three fundamental institutions—the national market, the central bureaucracy, and business-government relations—to explain the processes through which institutional change occurs.

I develop three main arguments. First, the analytical tasks of explaining institutional origins and institutional change in periods of isolation and of immersion in the international economy are not identical. Moreover, specifying the mechanisms of institutional change in periods of relative isolation from exogenous forces is critical, not only to appreciate the impact of the international economy but also to delineate the explanatory scope of theory. The unification of the national market under the aegis of the modern state was a historically specific process. That process actually created the geographical and political boundaries of community which form the unit of analysis commonly used in studying the effects of international change on national institutions. The creation of a system of states and national markets demarcated the boundaries between the international and national arenas: they created the categories that subsequently defined the nexus of institutional change. By focusing on the same institutions through several conjunctures of international and local time, one can appreciate the empirical limits on theorizing institutional change.

Second, the mechanisms through which international forces shape domestic institutions vary, depending *both* on forms of integration into the international economy and on broad sea changes in the organization of the international economy itself. Neither the international economy nor any society's experience of it is constant; sources of institutional origination and change vary according to the dominant mechanisms through which international and domestic actors and organizations interact. Sea changes in the international economy exert relatively uniform constraints on domestic possibilities, but national-international links vary substantially with the specific ways in which any particular country is connected to the international economy. I demonstrate this point by illustrating the simultaneous workings of shared systemic change *and* the divergent domestic effects of different kinds of capital flows.

Third, these two levels of variation have implications for how we study institutional change. Locating sources of institutional change in the same set of forces, actors, or motives, for all cases and for all times, and using identical frameworks to study them is at least empirically indefensible. A methodological eclecticism grounded in substantive differences in international organization can encompass broad similarities in institutional responses. Within systemic conjunctures if we disaggregate different kinds of capital flows as different experiences of the global economy, and separate "the state" into its regulatory, distributive, extractive, and redistributive organs, we permit ourselves a more concrete evaluation of differences in the impact of international economic change. In its methodological eclecticism and its critical examination of the constructs "the international economy" and "the state," this book does not promote pure description. Rather it builds a case for a broader dialogue between disparate branches of political economy, kept apart by methodological debates that more often than not overshadow the substance of the empirical puzzle.

To develop and defend these claims, I begin with theories of institutional change in closed systems, focusing on the work of historically oriented neoinstitutional economists (NIEs). Challenging the assumptions of the NIEs with insights from the Marxist tradition, I emphasize the historical specificity of the state and the national market, and outline a framework for examining institutional change in isolation. The second section of this chapter focuses on the impact of international economic change on domestic institutions and then discusses the implications of broad systemic changes for method. The third section illustrates what is meant by specific forms of insertion into the international economy. The fourth uses these frameworks to present a narrative of the two cases across three different periods of institutional change.

Theories of Institutional Change

How does international change influence domestic institutions? and how do institutions shape outcomes? These twin issues are central to contemporary debate in the social sciences. Recent scholarship, focused on advanced industrial states, explores the extent to which domestic institutions are shaped by international economic pressures, echoing the questions asked earlier by dependency theorists. Not surprisingly, the picture of domestic political economies buffeted by foreign pressures is no more agreeable to academics and policy-makers in industrial states than it has been to their counterparts in the Third World.

The neoinstitutionalists rightly criticize their neoclassical and behavioralist predecessors. Yet beyond their rejection of the idea that interests aggregate without friction, economists and political scientists with institutionalist predilections share very little except a belief in the relative longevity and stability of institutions and in the ability of institutions to shape outcomes. This emphasis on stability may be responsible for the fact that the new institutionalisms have generated few theories of institutional change. Longevity and stability were defining characteristics of institutions for earlier theorists as well, with much the same result.[8] Samuel Huntington's famous observation that the difference between developed and developing countries was not the form but the degree of government captured the chimerical nature of political authority in the developing

[8] This is true, for example, of Samuel P. Huntington, *Political Order in Changing Societies* (New Haven: Yale University Press, 1968).

world. Yet his "organizational imperative" offered institutions as the solution to political decay—as though stable political parties and functioning central bureaucracies could be willed into existence outside of social conflict.

The NIEs have been most concerned with constructing general, microfoundational theories of institutional change in closed systems. As a result, their contributions are an appropriate point of departure for discussing the genesis of institutions in isolated contexts.[9] In correcting the neoclassical belief in the institution-free market, NIEs have focused more on describing what institutions do (specify the rules of competition and cooperation, provide a structure of property rights, maximize rents to the ruler)[10] than on where they come from. Their useful analysis of the institutional prerequisites for functioning markets gives few hints about how institutions arise. In directly confronting the question of institutional origins, Douglass North solves the analytical problem through an act of definition. He approaches the question of institutional change by first distinguishing between institutions and organizations. "Institutions" are the fundamental set of property rights at a given time and place; they include a bundle of ideational, economic, political, and social assets that cannot be separated and as such are akin to old-fashioned notions of "power." Institutions "dictate" the framework for organizational construction, and institutional change shapes the "evolution" of organizations. But organizations, which, North concedes, can embody class interests, themselves

[9] Note that the NIEs have a very broad definition of "institutions." According to Douglass North, "Institutions are the rules of the game in a society or, more formally, the humanly devised constraints that shape human interaction. . . . They structure incentives in human exchange, whether political, social or economic" (*Institutions, Institutional Change, and Economic Performance* [Cambridge: Cambridge University Press, 1990], 3–4). By this definition, anything from social convention (e.g., the social acceptability of male hand-holding in the Indian subcontinent) to the criminal justice code of twentieth-century America is an institution. Surely any theory that could explain the origins and evolution of both these institutions would be so general as to be meaningless. Efforts to distinguish between organizations and institutions have clarified matters somewhat, but they are not relevant to the categories of institutions I propose to analyze here. North defines organizations as including "political bodies (political parties, the Senate, a city council, a regulatory agency), economic bodies (firms, trade unions, family farms, cooperatives), social bodies (churches, clubs, athletic associations), and educational bodies (schools, universities, vocational training centers). They are groups of individuals bound together by some common purpose to achieve objectives" (*Institutions,* 5). For my purposes, separating institutions and organizations is not particularly useful. The tax bureaucracy of the central state, for example, is clearly an organization, but it also embodies and defines a fundamental set of relationships between state and citizen which go beyond the workings of the actual organization. Although it is possible conceptually to disconnect the institution of taxation as a set of rules from the organizational characteristics of the coercive and information-gathering arms of the tax bureaucracy, in practical terms the two are too closely related to separate, for the "humanly devised constraints" of taxation have no meaning apart from the actual functioning of the organization. This inseparability is perhaps responsible for the fact that NIE theorists most fond of making the distinction conveniently collapse the two categories every time they discuss an empirical case.

[10] See Douglass North, *Structure and Change in Economic History* (New York: Norton, 1981), 24.

shape institutions. In closing the circle, he writes: "Moreover, it is the bargaining strength of the individuals and organizations that counts. Hence only when it is in the interest of those with sufficient bargaining strength to alter the formal rules will there be major changes in the formal institutional framework."[11]

In this tautological account, the origins of institutions and organizations can be known *only* through an empirical description of both and a clear understanding of the social structure of society. If North explicitly called for empiricism and history, his position would hardly be objectionable. In fact, however, NIE accounts of institutional change claim the status of general rules that transcend historical context: their methodological individualism fuels their search for universals, but their actual analyses promote only description. This search for universals ultimately makes it impossible for the NIEs to explain institutional variation across time and place.

One might suggest that dynamic, politically grounded models of institutional origination are problematic for NIEs because such accounts must confront issues of aggregation that methodological individualists prefer to bypass. Most NIE accounts start with the purposive actions of individuals who create "the rules of the game": state institutions and organizations are the creatures of individual "rulers" seeking to maximize revenues. Who controls state institutions? The answer is murky, for although neo-institutionalist constructs always begin with an individual ruler, the ruler's representational characteristics are unclear. In contrast to Margaret Levi, who claims that rulers usually rule in coalition, North suggests that some rulers represent particular classes, whereas others do not.[12] The NIEs focus on the efficiency of institutions for the economy in aggregate, making the representational character of rulers irrelevant. Either institutions are efficient or they are not. Economic outcomes are unrelated to the coalitional base of rulers, who all appear to have identical aims. If history has no telos except efficiency, and efficiency is by definition achieved through the aggregate actions of rational self-interested individuals, then world-historical time is irrelevant and historical periodization unimportant. When states fail to meet their technological production horizon, it is because they are "predatory"; when they succeed, it is because they have minimized transaction costs in perfect accord with their endowments.[13] Past choices embodied in institutions and organizations create "path dependencies" that constrain the actions of individuals, but there is no discoverable pattern to history apart from variation introduced by the NIE's

[11] North, *Institutions,* 78, 3, 73, 4–5, 68.

[12] Margaret Levi, *Of Rule and Revenue* (Berkeley: University of California Press, 1988), 44; North, *Institutions,* 32.

[13] See Thrainn Eggertsson, "Mental Models and Social Values," *Journal of Institutional and Theoretical Economics* 149, no. 1 (1993): 24–28.

catchall variable of "cultural difference." The NIE version of "structure" is thus little more than a layering of choices made by individuals who had strong bargaining power at earlier junctures.

The progression from methodological individualism to ahistorical analysis takes explicit shape in Levi's work. For Levi, all rulers have identical goals. If *all* rulers are "predatory" (within constraints) and "design" institutions to achieve their aims, then one can use ancient Rome and contemporary Scandinavia to support the same proposition. But even if the theorem that the cases support *were* true for all times and places, and it is not, this generality captures commonalities at a level that is more philosophical than analytical. The approach can explain neither different trajectories of institutional change nor different outcomes. If the institutions of the tax state were drafted by omniscient rulers who knew the limits of their subjects' tolerance, why—in the now famous observation of Charles Tilly—did such a minute fraction of modern nation-states survive? Why did they take the diverse forms they did?

The NIEs' rejection of historical specificity flows not from their rationalist proclivities but from their emphasis on choice and efficiency. Marxists also have a rationalist theory of interest formation, but for them institutions emerge from social conflict engendered by historically specific changes in the mode of production. Explaining the origins of the national state and the national market requires a sociology of interest aggregation that accounts for the distinctiveness of these institutional constructs: an appreciation of the difference between local fairs and the national market. Such a sociology directly contradicts the NIEs' aim of discovering universal and timeless rules of human cooperation. In institutional terms, is the ability of two individuals to use a common measure of value to exchange goods, long distance trade in the preindustrial era and a seasonal market *really* identical to a national market in which millions of producers, distributors, retailers, consumers, and capitalists participate in multiple economic transactions under the auspices of a central state and a uniform legal system? More, since institutions do not spring up in a vacuum, but always displace existing institutions, a single, decontextualized theory of institutional origins will not suffice for it could not explain this process of displacement.

The problem of aggregation—the reluctance to move beyond the individual—is critical to explaining the NIEs' inability to generate a theory of state and market institutions. It is common sense that low transaction costs promote gains from trade. Yet it is not at all clear in whose interest it is to promote aggregate growth. The NIEs tell us that it is not useful to think of social actors in class terms, but they fail to explain how individuals discover their interest in supporting institutions that are "good" only when considered from the perspective of the entire community. How and why are problems of collective action overcome for goods that are general? This issue of aggregation becomes even more problematic in situations where the boundaries of economic communities are unformed or, worse, in bitter dispute. Before institutions emerge to cut transaction costs, and delimit the new economic unit, how can we measure efficiency? To be fair, some neoinstitutionalists concede that gains can be distributed unequally. But how can we discover the particular set of individuals with a common interest in cutting transaction costs? Who pays to maintain the institutions and organizations that provide collective goods shared by the entire community, particularly when high transaction costs (in the form of barriers to exchange) so often constitute the core advantages from which economic elites benefit? Without class-based conceptions of institutional formation, and in the absence of an understanding of structural constraints, how can we begin to explain variations in the form and content of institutional outcomes?

Some of these questions become accessible though class analysis, which emphasizes conflict and specifies a clear causal relationship between economic change, aggregate interests, and institutions. It is by now well established that Karl Marx did not view the state exclusively as the administrative handmaiden of capital, but the state's ability to act outside dominant class interests still gives few hints on who "the state" is. For orthodox Marxists, when and how the modern national state emerged remain critical questions, for the state's genesis signals the birth of modern capitalism.[14] Whatever their disagreements, Marxist analysts concur that conflict is the dominant motor of change in political organization. Conflict predates the full-fledged construction of capitalism; in Maurice Dobb's account, for example, bourgeois interests prevail in tandem with the destruction of restrictive precapitalist monopolies. In subsequent struggles between emerging merchant capital interests and the trade guilds, the triumph of the former was marked by its control of municipal government.[15] Struggles between town and country, between guild and merchant, ever resulted in the victors' control of administration and law and the political fora through which they were publicly controlled. Even in pre-industrial contexts, in short, economic ascendancy coincided with wresting control of the institutions that governed the market. The class basis of administrative authority and the specific ways in which dominant interests are expressed by, or mediated through, public institutions are not artifacts of modern capitalism alone, even though for Marx himself capitalism was a distinctly industrial phenomenon. Exploitation is constant, but Marxists perceive tensions between different forms of economic organization.

[14] For the lines of debate on this important issue, see Keith Tribe, *Genealogies of Capitalism* (London: Macmillan, 1981), 1–34.

[15] Maurice Dobb, *Studies in the Development of Capitalism* (New York: International, 1947), 25, 91–104.

This formulation is intuitively appealing: it exemplifies the holistic analytical approach that distinguishes the Marxist tradition, and it erects conceptual categories that can be brought to bear on a variety of economic-political junctures. These conceptual continuities, however, foreclose the possibility of pinpointing the moment when economically dominant classes develop an interest in maintaining the bureaucratic apparatus that governs the modern nation-state and the national market. Precisely because exploitation is a permanent feature of social life, the construction of the national market and the centralized state is not the break of primary significance. Much more important is the rise of the working class as the transformative historical actor of the industrial age.

The NIE and Marxist perspectives come close to a dynamic account of institutional change, but neither recognizes the creation of national markets as a distinct conjunctural moment in the emergence of the modern state. The national unit is implicitly used in NIE accounts to pass judgment on the efficiency or inefficiency of institutions. Yet historically oriented neoinstitutional economists recognize neither the specificity of these institutional constructs nor the fact that their microfoundational accounts of institutional genesis ultimately support a macroeconomic vision of efficiency. Where the NIEs have no theory of the origins of institutions,[16] for orthodox Marxists the emergence of the national economy and the state is not imbued with particular analytical relevance because exploitation is constant.

Karl Polanyi identified the creation of unified national markets as a distinct revolutionary event. The unified national market was a radical disjuncture in human history because it redefined the boundaries of the economic community. National markets were necessary preconditions for industrial capitalism, constructed on the ruins of precapitalist local economies, but they also created a set of generalizable goods that linked individuals to the new centralized authority. Far from being cost-less, the destruction of local mechanisms that cut transaction costs—the guilds, customs, monopolies, and monopsonies—was necessary for the construction of national-level mechanisms, whose benefits were hardly apparent to those experiencing the Great Transformation. Polanyi viewed this process not as an incremental progression but rather as a radical disjuncture in how human society and the economy interact.

Dysfunction and unintended consequences were at the core of Polanyi's analysis. Like North and Robert Bates, Polanyi saw institutions as more often than not inefficient, if not perverse. But unlike North, Polanyi had no difficulty identifying the losers; unlike Bates, Polanyi rejected the

[16] This point is made by both Robert Bates, "Macropolitical Economy in the Field of Development," in James Alt and Kenneth Shepsle, eds., *Perspectives on Positive Political Economy* (Cambridge: Cambridge University Press, 1990), 31–54; and Thrainn Eggertsson, *Economic Behavior and Institutions* (Cambridge: Cambridge University Press, 1990), 247–358.

empirical possibility of a neutral, institution-free market. For Polanyi, societies were never "efficient" or "inefficient" as a whole.[17] The productive superiority of the national economy was built on the smashed remains of local economies, stripped of their material foundations and robbed of the ideational constructs that gave them meaning. Efficiency and growth may be desirable outcomes, but they obscure the internal workings of economic systems as they experience rapid transformation.

The construction of central bureaucracies, territorial states, and national markets are historically bounded, mutually enforcing, and usually violent processes. Bureaucracies that make authoritative decisions over a given territory are necessary for the expansion of a national market and the elimination of barriers to exchange within it. The expansion of the borders of the economic and political community (and perhaps their contraction too), so often dressed up in the language of collective efficiency, actually strips individuals of their economic life-blood. When the boundaries of the social aggregate are in flux, overall efficiency and specific efficiency rarely match.[18] As different scales of production redistribute transaction costs within a constituted economic community, the community *as a whole* may not benefit from gains in trade and specialization. Different groups within economic communities have radically different reactions to economic change and institutional shifts, depending on their specific location in prior socioeconomic exchange networks. To call the expanding territory of exchange an "efficient" outcome is a political act. It presents the enhanced fortunes of a small minority as an aggregate good.

The building of states and markets cannot be apprehended without reference to the social coalitions that emerge to support or oppose these institutions. Living local communities rarely if ever agree on whether and how to cut transaction costs, let alone on which transaction costs should be cut and who should pay to facilitate freer trade over larger territory. In the move from local to national economies (and vice versa, for that matter), the boundaries of economic community are redefined, and new notions of the common good are constructed. When in the institution-exchange nexus do sufficient aggregations of interests emerge with a common stake in cutting transaction costs? The coalition for the national market and the state that governs it need not always be led by the same groups. Dominant class interests in maintaining a strong, rich, interventionist state are impermanent; they vary at different junctures of capitalist accumulation.[19] State-class connections are fluid by nature. Analyzing the

[17] Karl Polanyi, *The Great Transformation* (Boston: Beacon, 1944).

[18] Jean Ensminger, *Making a Market,* (Cambridge: Cambridge University Press, 1992), esp. 25–28. Gary D. Libecap also makes this argument in "Politics, Institutions and Institutional Change," *Journal of Institutional and Theoretical Economics* 149, no. 1 (1993): 29–35, in response to North's essay "Institutions and Credible Commitment," in the same volume, 11–23.

[19] Writing of an earlier juncture of European history, Rudolf Goldscheid identified "one of

construction of the institutions that first destroy local economies and then create and govern unified national economies thus becomes an empirical question.

Studying the origins of institutions prompts us to examine the processes of political "decay" that Huntington sought to forestall through institutional innovation; it takes us directly into the thicket of social conflict. Institutions are not formed out of the bland abrogation of freedoms in return for property rights and liberty, or from the voluntary associations of consent struck in Rousseau's bucolic state of nature. They do not flow effortlessly from the design tables of omniscient rulers, nor do they evolve as efficiency-maximizing rules to govern the clear-eyed exchanges of rational self-interested agents. Rather, the creation of the national market requires a state capable of destroying local economies and the legal, economic, and social relationships they were based on. Force sufficient to reveal potential benefits to segments of the economic elite lodged in these local economies is the cement that binds the coalition for the national market. There was nothing automatic about the balance of forces that tipped in favor of the national option, for in specific cases economic elites fought centralization tooth and nail. Institutions not only liberate exchange and protect the members of the newly constituted unit; they also proscribe and limit the actions of groups. The aggregate groups in favor of a national market rarely include the old economic elite as a whole. It is in this deeply violent and fundamentally political process, in all its historical specificity, that we can observe the interlinked origins of the national state and market.

National Institutions and the International Economy

The task of explaining institutional change is difficult enough in contexts conceptually or actually bereft of exogenous influences; it becomes even more complex when the independent or mediated effects of the international economy are endogenized. In contrast to the NIEs, historical institutionalists have dealt explicitly with the impact of international economic change on the domestic political economy. Until recently, analytical positions on the relative importance of domestic institutions and international economic forces in shaping outcomes tended to vary with case selection. Accounts of advanced industrial countries tend to emphasize the importance of domestic institutional structures, coalitions, and organi-

---

the most interesting chapters in the history of the evolution of the State [as] the transition phase when the ruling classes' best interests began to be served by a poor rather than a rich state" in Rudolf Goldscheid, "A Sociological Approach to Problems of Public Finance," in Richard Musgrave and Alan T. Peacock, eds., *Classics in the Theory of Public Finance* (London: Macmillan, 1964), 204.

zations in shaping responses to identical or similar systemic pressures.[20] Studies of late industrializers or countries vulnerable by virtue of size or international placement, on the other hand, have emphasized the important ways the international economy shapes domestic institutions and power relations.

Dominant views of how late developers interact with international economic forces have undergone substantial change. Early research posited direct links between the international economy and economic change in developing countries, prompting the familiar observation that traditional dependency formulations obscure the independent role of the state as a mediator between domestic and foreign capital.[21] Recent studies, in contrast, differentiate between domestic actors and organizations, stressing the specificity of the links between them and international forces.[22] Although they have gone far in undoing the teleologies of both modernization and dependency theory, the "new historical institutionalists"[23] use institutional differences to explain variation, focusing less on how institutional variations are created and more on their effects on policy and performance.[24] Although sensitive to international pressures and placement, they take state bureaucracies and stable borders as a point of departure: their focus has been on the ways that institutional structures influence policies or regenerate the conditions for their existence, broadly neglect-

[20] A good example is Peter Katzenstein, ed., *Between Power and Plenty* (Madison: University of Wisconsin Press, 1978). For exceptions see Michael Loriaux, *France after Hegemony* (Ithaca: Cornell University Press, 1991); and Robert Reich, *The Work of Nations* (New York: Knopf, 1991).

[21] The scholarship of Raul Prebisch, Samir Amin, Fernando Cardoso, Enzo Faletto, and Arghiri Emmanuel exemplifies this literature. For reviews of the numerous works of classical dependency theory see Tony Smith, "The Underdevelopment of Development Literature," *World Politics* 31 (January 1979): 247–88; J. Samuel Valenzuela and Arturo Valenzuela, "Modernization and Dependency," *Comparative Politics* 10 (July 1978): 535–57; Thomas Biersteker, *Distortion or Development?* (Cambridge: MIT Press, 1978), 1–27, 49–69; Richard Newfarmer, "International Industrial Organization and Development," in Newfarmer, ed., *Profits, Progress and Poverty* (Notre Dame: University of Notre Dame Press, 1985), 13–61.

[22] See Peter Evans, "Reinventing the Bourgeoisie," in Michael Burawoy and Theda Skocpol, eds., *Marxist Inquiries* (Chicago: University of Chicago Press, 1982); David Becker, *The New Bourgeoisie and the Limits of Dependency* (Princeton: Princeton University Press, 1983); Michael Shafer, "Capturing the Mineral Multinationals," in Theodore Moran, ed., *Multinational Corporations* (Lexington, Mass.: Lexington Books, 1985).

[23] Theda Skocpol, "Bringing the State Back In," *Items* 36 (June 1982); Skocpol, *States and Social Revolutions* (Cambridge: Cambridge University Press, 1979); and Skocpol, "Political Response to Capitalist Crisis," *Politics and Society* 10 (1980): 155–202; Eric Nordlinger, *On the Autonomy of the Democratic State* (Cambridge: Harvard University Press, 1984). On what the "statist school" has in mind, see Stephen Krasner, "Approaches to the State," *Comparative Politics* 16 (January 1984): 223–46; Joel S. Migdal, *Strong Societies and Weak States* (Princeton: Princeton University Press, 1988), 3–45; and David Held, "Central Perspectives on the Modern State," in Held et al., eds., *States and Societies* (New York: New York University Press, 1983).

[24] See, e.g., the otherwise excellent analyses in Alice Amsden, *Asia's Next Giant* (New York: Oxford University Press, 1989); and Stephan Haggard, *Pathways from the Periphery* (Ithaca: Cornell University Press, 1990).

ing the confluence of exogenous and endogenous forces that *forge* bureaucracies to begin with or that fundamentally shape structure and function.[25] In studies of business-government relations in advanced industrial societies or growth in the East Asian NICs (Newly Industrialized Countries) for example, institutions are the departure point for the causal chain through which difference becomes comprehensible.[26]

Using institutions as an explanatory variable stalls the analysis precisely where it links up to the critical issue of how exogenous resources affect institution-building itself. The new historical institutionalism allows us to say, for example, that "autonomous" states are better able to implement economic policy; or that particular kinds of financial systems adjust best to exogenous shocks; or that domestic institutional arrangements shape responses to common experiences of the international economy. But it does not tell us how and why some states become "autonomous" while others are "captured"; why financial systems assume their particular forms; or why domestic structures differ. By focusing on institutions as independent variables, historical institutionalists privilege analyses of processes where the role of constituted institutional arrangements is observable. Taking institutions as given obscures the social and economic interests they embody. Not only does this approach foreclose the possibility of making political judgments about what "autonomy" or embedded autonomy means; it also fails to specify how changing interests and coalitions reconstitute established institutions or create new ones. Historical institutionalists begin with outcomes—growth, industrial adjustment, liberalization, debt management—and then read institutional variation back into the case: thus institutions are discovered only through outcomes they presumably produced.

Contemporary studies of development combine the neoinstitutionalist penchant to reify "the state" as an undifferentiated entity with an undertheorized sense of structural junctures in the international economy.[27] On

[25] G. John Ikenberry, "The Irony of State Strength," *International Organization* 40 (Winter 1986): 105–37; Ikenberry, "The State and Strategies of International Adjustment," *World Politics* 39 (October 1986): 53–77; Peter Hall, *Governing the Economy* (New York: Oxford University Press, 1986). Stephen Skowronek's *Building a New American State* (Cambridge: Cambridge University Press, 1982) is a notable exception.

[26] John Zysman, *Governments, Markets, and Growth* (Ithaca: Cornell University Press, 1983); and Richard Samuels, *The Business of the Japanese State* (Ithaca: Cornell University Press, 1987). On the NICs, see Miles Kahler, "Orthodoxy and Its Alternatives," in Joan M. Nelson, ed., *Economic Crisis and Policy Choice* (Princeton: Princeton University Press, 1990), 33–62. See also Tony Killick and Simon Commander, "State Divestiture as a Policy Instrument in Developing Countries," *World Development* 16, no. 12 (1988): 1465–79; Tariq Banuri, "Introduction," and Albert Fishlow, "Some Reflections on Comparative Latin American Economic Performance and Policy," both in Banuri, ed., *Economic Liberalization, No Panacea* (New York: Oxford University Press, 1991), 1–29, 149–70; and Amsden, *Asia's Next Giant.*

[27] In the term *structural junctures in the global economy* I am trying to capture the kind of broad contextual grounding that typifies the world-systems approach. Arguments to this effect are made in W. Rand Smith's review essay "International Economy and State Strategies," *Comparative Politics* 25 (April 1993): 351–72.

one hand, state attributes—"autonomy" or "capacity"—do not vary across agency, task, or time in line with the specificities of national-international ties; on the other, the new international political economy stresses contingency and diversity at the expense of common experiences of broad structural changes in the international economy. Responses to the call to "bring the state back in" promoted a monolithic view of "the state" as actor, entirely missing that part of the neostatist agenda which sought, conceptually and empirically, to dissect the state. The monolithic state was resurrected at a historical moment when both the international and domestic roles of the national state were being redefined by unprecedented levels of economic interdependence. None of this would be particularly troublesome if we lived in a world of institutional stability, where institutional attributes smoothly predicted outcomes. But no one witnessing the near-universal deconstruction of the welfare state and the reorganization of the industrial work force can believe in institutional continuity. Institutions change, and sometimes they change very quickly. If explaining institutional genesis in closed systems requires a sociology of aggregation that is sensitive to historical context, institutional change in response to international economic pressures and opportunities must begin with the question of what the international economy *is*.

In emphasizing the diverse ways that countries interact with the international system, Michael Loriaux rightly observes a tendency to "conceive of the 'international system' as a coherent whole—as an 'ether-like' entity." The multifaceted nature of the international economy is accurately reflected in studies of national-international linkages which portray the international economy variously as a "net" on which countries are located by size or geography, as a set of systemic events, as a switch that is on or off, or as changes in relative "prices."[28] Although they reflect different perceptions of how the international economy shapes domestic politics, these images are equally valid. Does this mean that the international economy itself is the sum of these relationships, devoid of identifiable structural changes?

Despite the lack of agreement on the motive forces of change in the international economy, there is considerable consensus on a broad periodization of systemic change, usually presented in the form of "system-opening" episodes around which particular research questions are posed and answered.[29] Political economists generally agree that the interwar period, the postwar reconstruction, and the weakening of the Bretton Woods regime in the early 1970s demarcated periods of systemic change.

[28] Respectively, Peter Katzenstein, *Small States in World Markets* (Ithaca: Cornell University Press, 1985); Loriaux, *France after Hegemony*; Ronald Rogowski, *Commerce and Coalitions* (Princeton: Princeton University Press, 1989); and Jeffry Frieden and Rogowski, "The Impact of the International Economy in National Policies" (manuscript, University of California at Los Angeles, 1994).

[29] Gourevitch, *Politics in Hard Times*, 22.

Similarly, recent studies have argued that the tighter organization of international capital, prompted by the oil shock of 1973 and the subsequent deregulation of banking in major financial centers, has introduced fundamental changes in the international economy, with important implications for the fortunes of domestic coalitions and for the ability of national governments to control international transactions.[30] Whether they stress changes in production technologies, the communications revolution, the sheer mobility of capital, or the enhanced power of firms as international actors, observers broadly agree that the contemporary, deregulated environment is a distinctive episode in international economic organization.

The systemic changes of the 1970s and 1980s were reflected in the flow of resources to and then from the developing world. The decade 1973–1983 was distinguished by an enormous inflow of wealth in the form of aid, loans, oil revenues, labor remittances, and investment.[31] In the 1980s, capital flows to the developing world fell dramatically. From an inflow of $33 billion in 1978, net transfers on LDC (less developed countries) debt in 1989 was an astonishing *outflow* of $42 billion. From a 1980 high of $243 billion, oil revenues for major exporters fell to $67 billion in 1988.[32] Direct foreign investment, which actually declined from 1981 to 1986, had surpassed all other forms of lending as a source of foreign capital for developing countries by 1988.[33] Similarly, the end of the Cold War reduced the facility with which developing countries could barter allegiance for cash; at the same time, competition for plummeting levels of aid, foreign investment, and loans became fierce.[34]

[30] On tax capacity, see Hugh Ault and David Bradford, "Taxing International Income: An Analysis of the U.S. System and Its Economic Premises," in Assaf Razin and Joel Slemrod, eds., *Taxation in the Global Economy* (A National Bureau of Economic Research Project Report), (Chicago: University of Chicago Press, 1990), esp. 16, 19, and 38; Joel Slemrod, "Tax Principles in an International Economy," in Michael Boskin and Charles McLure, Jr., eds., *World Tax Reform,* (San Francisco: International Center for Economic Growth, 1990), 11–25. More generally, Jeffry A. Frieden, "Invested Interests," *International Organization* 45 (Autumn 1991): 425–51; Gourevitch, *Politics in Hard Times*; Ethan Barnaby Kapstein, "Between Power and Purpose," *International Organization* 46 (Winter 1992): 265–87; Reich, *Work of Nations*; Susan Strange, "States, Firms, and Diplomacy," *International Affairs* 68 (January 1992): 1–15; Michael C. Webb, "International Economic Structures, Government Interests, and International Coordination of Macroeconomic Adjustment Policies," *International Organization* 45 (Summer 1991): 309–42.

[31] Barbara Stallings, "The Role of Foreign Capital in Economic Development," in Gary Gereffi and Donald L. Wyman, eds., *Manufacturing Miracles* (Princeton: Princeton University Press, 1990).

[32] For the 1978 figure, *World Debt Tables, 1982–83* (Washington, D.C.: World Bank, 1982), xii; for the 1989 figure, *World Debt Tables, 1990–1991,* 126. The 1980 and 1988 oil revenues include value of fuel exports from Algeria, Ecuador, Gabon, Indonesia, Kuwait, Libya, Nigeria, Saudi Arabia, UAE, and Venezuela; see *World Tables, 1991.*

[33] *World Development Report* 14 (1991): 95.

[34] Laura D'Andrea Tyson, "Debt Crisis and Adjustment Responses in Eastern Europe," in Ellen Comisso and Laura D'Andrea Tyson, eds., *Power, Purpose, and Collective Choice* (Ithaca: Cornell University Press, 1986), 63–110; Joan M. Nelson, "The Politics of Economic Transformation," *World Politics* 45 (April 1993): 433–63.

These two periods can be described as distinct phases of international change. For late developers they first presented a common set of opportunities and then exerted a common set of pressures, representing qualitatively different forms of international interdependence. "Internationalization" is often used to describe the level of interaction between the domestic and international economies, but international relations experts generally conflate two different meanings of "internationalization."[35] One measures the sheer volume of cross-border exchanges; the other measures the extent to which domestic and international prices converge. For students of international relations the distinction may be trivial; they often assume that more transactions *imply* a more open economy. But the assumption does not always hold, conceptually or empirically. International interaction and price convergence actually promote different roles for national institutions as mediators between the national and international economy. A single domestic economy can be at once very internationalized in its volume of transactions *and* heavily protected from international prices through the regulatory and distributive acts of government. Conversely, openness (in the form of deregulation that allows international prices to be reflected in domestic markets) can coincide with minimal levels of international transactions, if the country in question has nothing to offer investors, or no foreign exchange with which to buy foreign goods. For much of the Third World, the 1970s was a period of intense internationalization when measured in capital flows but of low internationalization when measured in price convergence. In the 1980s and 1990s the reverse was true. The first phase coincided with high levels of étatism in the developing world, usually in the service of industrialization; the second, with a virtually universal shift to economic liberalism and increasing levels of price convergence.

These two different forms of internationalization suggest different intersections between international economic forces and domestic actors, organizations, and institutions. The central difference concerns the extent to which governments mediated the domestic impact of international economic changes. In contrast to the 1970s, when government organizations were critical in shaping the domestic impact of the international economy, the 1980s and 1990s saw more direct linkages between international economic forces and domestic actors. Unmediated international prices were experienced directly through mechanisms and in arenas distinct from the state-mediated interdependence of the 1970s.

The difference between the domestic effects of internationalization in the 1970s and in the 1980s can be grasped through consideration of what the étatism of the 1970s actually meant. The capital flows of the 1970s,

[35] See Kiren Aziz Chaudhry, "Prices and Politics," paper presented at the Annual Meeting of the American Political Science Association, New York, 1994.

combined with higher state capacity to control them, and relatively high transportation costs, allowed governments to mediate domestic prices on a broad scale. Through subsidies, import restrictions, tariffs, exchange rates, direct production and retailing, and pure distribution, governments manipulated prices to achieve a host of goals; industrialization for the national market figured prominently. Through the same mechanisms they also cemented political relationships that were based on their capacity to protect domestic constituents from flux in international prices. These protective measures undergirded domestic coalitions, buttressed state legitimacy, and defined the life chances of regimes. At the border between the national and the international, the state used these instruments to define entitlements and shape society. With the systemic changes of the 1980s and 1990s, not only these policies but the instruments through which they were enforced were, in varying degrees, abandoned. In many cases governments not only stopped mediating prices, deregulated, devalued, and privatized, but they also began to develop domestic sources to sustain themselves in response to fiscal crises, thereby reinitiating conflicts over who would pay to achieve collective goods.

This crude account of shifts in the "international economy" is clearly only a starting point. Recognizing the existence of sea changes in the international economy, measured both by quantitative criteria and by common policy shifts among LDCs, need not obscure specificity: case-level differences are necessary building blocks for understanding international change.[36] In many labor exporters, indeed, private-sector organizations grew in tandem with state interventionism. Such recognition does, however, suggest that explaining domestic institutional change over time and in different international contexts requires alternative analytical frameworks. One key difference is the number of domestic arenas where the national and the international economy intersect. In the étatist 1970s, the organizations that deployed capital flows domestically were the mediators of institutional and social change. In the deregulated 1980s and 1990s, by contrast, the international economy in some measure directly influences the daily decisions, transactions, and life chances of individuals. Just as the creation of the national economy meant the elimination of local monopolies and barriers to exchange, so cutting transaction costs at the international level mandates the destruction of the national institutions that stand between global prices and national constituencies: the national state, in its intrusive guise, creates barriers to entry and manipulates exchange in ways conceptually analogous to the role guilds and estates played before the unification of the national market. Thus, although one important nexus for examining the impact of the new internationalization comprises the organizations and agencies of the state itself, unmediated

[36] Gourevitch makes this point in *Politics in Hard Times,* 34.

contacts between international economic forces and local actors cannot be neglected. Financial sectors in LDCs are tightly linked to international markets and impervious to old-style regulatory efforts. Moreover, joint ventures between local agencies and multinationals, nonunion employment in transnational corporations (TNCs), aid from governments or private groups directly to local nongovernmental organizations, the direct sale of raw materials by local firms on international markets, and the prevalence of international prices in a host of domestic markets exemplify new arenas of local and international interaction. Here international economic forces can generate new interests at the sectoral, industry, local, or regional level and precipitate the collapse of formerly robust class-based, nationally focused coalitions. New aggregative influences set in motion by price convergence and attendant efforts to redefine the borders of economic community suggest that deductive frameworks using the assumptions of rationalist individualism are the safest starting point for locating the struggles attending institutional change *in the contemporary context.* Neoclassical economics, despite its robust lineage of inaccuracy, may yet emerge as a starting point for a new sociology of institutional origination because although such frameworks simulate the mechanism through which interests aggregate, they do not prejudge the form that politically relevant groups will take.

Different conjunctures of local and global time can be said to distribute different "weights" in institutional genesis and change. The genesis of the foundational institutions of the modern state and the national market can be studied through a modified class analysis that does not prejudge the specific form of the social coalitions that support them. In the first episode of internationalization after 1945, the presence of these institutions and the dominant role of the state in mediating international-domestic links, tilts analysis to the constituent parts of the state. In the second episode of internationalization, which started in the early 1980s, more direct links between international and local economies prompt a dual focus: on changes in the organization of the state, and on microlevel rationalist analyses that redeploy the question of interest aggregation as an empirical one.

The Links: International Capital Flows Compared

Systemic changes exert broadly definable pressures on domestic political economies, but experiences of the international economy are not identical. Comparing different kinds of capital inflows allows us to examine how international changes shape domestic possibilities at a middle level of generality. Distinguishing the effects of different kinds of capital flows on specific state institutions is one way to bridge the divide between excessively ethereal and completely descriptive accounts of domestic-international interactions. It provides another lens through which to examine how clusters of countries fare within sea changes in the international economy.

Development aid, borrowing on the international market, labor remittances, oil rent, direct foreign investment (DFI), and revenues from foreign purchases of government bonds and equity are all examples of exogenous capital flows. External capital inflows differ on a variety of counts important to the domestic system, but analysts have focused narrowly on aid, debt, and DFI.[37] Oil and labor remittances, the main sources of capital inflow in the Middle East, are not included in contemporary accounts and have rarely if ever been used even to frame general discussions of development.[38] The study of oil revenues and labor remittances has been the preserve of area specialists who, with few exceptions, prefer single case studies.[39] As a result, analytically important distinctions among different types of capital inflows, and the role of intervening variables such as levels of bureaucratic and entrepreneurial development in mediating their effects, remain obscured.

Primary distinctions among types of capital inflows involve variations in the degree of *control* that different public- or private-sector groups exercise over their allocation, and the extent to which that control is dispersed or centralized within those groups. Labor remittances accrue directly to millions of migrants, often tenant farmers or landless peasants, through informal banking systems invulnerable to state control.[40] At the

[37] In a 1993 volume, international capital flows to developing countries were grouped into two categories: borrowing, and direct foreign investment. See Barbara Stallings, "International Influence and Economic Policy," and Stephan Haggard and Robert Kaufman, "Institutions and Economic Adjustment," both in Haggard and Kaufman, eds., *The Politics of Economic Adjustment* (Princeton: Princeton University Press, 1993), 41–88, 3–40.

[38] For a more detailed discussion, see Kiren Aziz Chaudhry, "The Middle East and the Political Economy of Development," *Items* 48 (July–September 1994).

[39] A notable exception is Jill Crystal, *Oil and Politics in the Gulf* (Cambridge: Cambridge University Press, 1990).

[40] Placing recipients of labor remittances in a single category is difficult, since labor-exporting countries usually receive some form of developmental aid or borrow on the international market. But for Egypt, Yemen, Pakistan, India, Jordan, Tunisia, Turkey, Sudan, Somalia, and others, labor export is the largest earner of foreign exchange. In countries with strong regulatory institutions, remittances can be controlled through management. South Korea, for example, harnesses remittances by providing preferential investment opportunities to labor in exchange for foreign currency earnings and integrating labor export with Korean contractors in the Middle East. See Sooyong Kim, "Contract Migration in the Republic of Korea," ILO Working Paper (Geneva: International Migration for Employment Branch, 1982); *Proceedings of the ILO/ARPLA Inter-Country Symposium on Overseas Employment Administration* (Pattaya, Thailand, May 1984). See also J. S. Birks and C. Sinclair, "Migration for Employment among the Arab Countries," *Development Digest* 17 (1979); Nazli Choucri, "The New Migration in the Middle East" (manuscript, Migration and Development Study Group, Center for International Studies, MIT, 1977); Nader Fergany, "The Impact of Emigration on National Development in the Arab Region," *International Migration Review* 16 (Winter 1982): 757–80; Fred Halliday, "Migration and the Labor Force in the Oil Produc-

same time, however, exporters of temporary labor tend also to have access to state-controlled capital inflows, in which aid typically figures prominently. At the opposite end of the spectrum, oil rents and revenues from government bond sales to foreigners are highly centralized and accrue directly to the state, which then distributes or invests them. Other forms of external capital, such as development aid, borrowing, and DFI, fall somewhere between, apportioning control among government decision-makers, transnational actors, and domestic entrepreneurs.[41]

A second distinction is between capital inflows that involve a transnational *third actor,* in the form of multinationals, donors, or lending institutions, and those that are regulated exclusively by international market forces. Capital inflows regulated by market forces are subject to different levels of flux than those mediated by bargaining. Market-regulated inflows such as oil revenues, labor remittances, and portfolio investments are highly volatile, whereas aid, DFI, and borrowing tend to be more stable because they are subject to periodic review and negotiation. Market-regulated capital inflows elicit institutional responses different from those involving a transnational actor. The administrative problems of dealing with transnational actors require institutions qualitatively different from those created by attempts to manage impersonal market forces. Aid, foreign investment, and international borrowing are types of capital that favor a large state role in negotiating, administering and allocating resources—particularly in integrated nation-states that have strong, entrenched bureaucracies.

A country's *level* of dependence will also affect the domestic impact of capital flows. The absolute level of global capital flows and the number of recipients have grown with time, but extreme cases are a distinct category.[42] In Israel, Saudi Arabia, the Yemen Arab Republic, Kuwait, the United Arab Emirates, Libya, and Iraq, international capital inflows comprise 50 percent or more of gross national product. The newly industrialized countries rely less on inflows: cumulative disbursed foreign debt was about 25 percent of their 1980 GNP and constituted only 40 percent of investment capital for that year.[43] Major oil exporters, such as Libya, Saudi Arabia, the UAE, and Iraq, are obvious test cases for the hypothesis that state-controlled international capital augments state strength, autonomy, and capacity. Major oil exporters are financially autonomous from their citizenry and raise fascinating questions: how and why do bu-

ing States of the Middle East," *Development and Change* 8, no. 3 (1977): 263–91; and Paul Streeten, "Migrant Workers in the Arab Middle East," *Third World Quarterly* 4 (July 1982).

[41] Freiden estimates that 80–90 percent of international lending among the largest debtor nations was to the public sector or the central banks; see his "Third World Indebted Industrialization," *International Organization* 35 (Winter 1981): 441.

[42] See Everett E. Hagen, *The Economics of Development* (Homewood, Ill.: Irwin, 1968).

[43] *World Tables,* various years.

reaucracies develop and change when they have no revenue-gathering motive?[44] Unlike welfare states, which are "redistributive," rentier states do not exist by extracting surplus from the local population.[45] Institutional development in distributive states is thus likely to diverge from classical patterns of state-building as their bureaucracies emerge in response to the need to allocate rather than to appropriate revenue.[46]

Furthermore, class stratification in distributive states is likely to be an exclusive function of state spending patterns; in this extreme form of corporatism, the state not only reorganizes or promotes, encourages or disbands, existing occupational groups but actually *creates* entire sectors.[47] Oil exporters give new meaning to the word state autonomy: oil revenues enable governments to stop taxing altogether. They empower the state to create new social groups from whole cloth. A fall in capital inflows later will necessarily mark a juncture of radical change in the domestic political economy.[48] Access to inflows alters not only the resources that different domestic groups bring to bear on struggles for political and economic power but even their ability to engage in such contests.

In major labor exporters, economic transactions take place in an informal market without state regulation. Through these markets, private-

[44] See, e.g., Hazem Beblawi, "The Rentier State in the Arab World," Giacomo Luciani, "Allocation vs. Production States," and the other articles in Luciani, ed., *The Arab State* (Berkeley: University of California Press, 1987). See also Richard Auty and Alan Gelb, "Oil Windfalls in a Small Parliamentary Democracy," *World Development* 14, no. 9 (1986): 1161–75; Cyrus Bina, "Some Controversies in the Development of Rent Theory," *Capital and Class* 39 (Winter 1989): 82–112; Patrick Conway and Alan Gelb, "Oil Windfalls in a Controlled Economy," *Journal of Development Economics* 28, no. 1 (1988): 63–81; George W. Grayson, "Oil and Latin American Politics," *Latin American Research Review* 24, no. 3 (1989): 200–210; Terry Lynn Karl, "Petroleum and Political Pacts," *Latin American Research Review* 22, no. 1 (1987): 63–94; Otwin Marenin, "The Nigerian State as Process and Manager," *Comparative Politics* 20, no. 2 (1988): 215–32.

[45] H. Mahdavy, "The Patterns and Problems of Economic Development in Rentier States," in M. A. Cook, ed., *Studies in the Economic History of the Middle East* (London: Oxford University Press, 1970). The implementation of extractive, redistributive, and distributive policies requires regulatory and administrative institutions whose tasks may or may not overlap. Extractive policies and institutions may perform redistributive functions (e.g., through progressive tax schedules), and redistribution implies the prior extraction of resources. Distributive policies do not involve redeploying resources that were extracted from the domestic economy. Theodore Lowi's useful typology of regulatory, distributive, and redistributive "coalitions" are actually all encompassed in my "redistributive" category, since they exist within the context of an extractive state; see his "American Business, Public Policy, Case-Studies, and Political Theory," *World Politics* 16 (July 1964): 677–715.

[46] Jacques Delacroix, "The Distributive State in the World System," *Studies in Comparative International Development* 15 (Fall 1980): 3–21.

[47] Philippe Schmitter's classification of "exclusive" or "inclusive" corporatism does not quite capture the quality of the links between oil states and their populations. Still, if modified to include the patrimonial/clientelistic aspects of state spending in oil exporters, it appears the most appropriate framework for describing these relationships. See Schmitter, "Still the Century of Corporatism?" *Review of Politics* 36 (January 1974): 85–131.

[48] I borrow the term *juncture* from Ruth Berins Collier and David Collier, although I use it to refer to conjunctures of domestic and international change. See their *Shaping the Political Arena* (Princeton: Princeton University Press, 1991), esp. 27–39.

sector elites have access to virtually unlimited amounts of foreign exchange for investment, imports, and hoarding, which enable them to thrive without the protection and supervision associated with capitalism in late developers.[49] Remittances guarantee the financial independence of the private sector. They also generate local resources that enable rural communities to suspend reliance on the state for the provision of basic infrastructure: roads, electricity, water, clinics, schools.

Finally, countries are distinguished by the institutional relationships in existence before they are integrated into capital flow networks. As Alexander Gerschenkron observed decades ago, timing matters.[50] Moreover, timing has both international and local dimensions. The local effects of external capital flows are mediated by ongoing conflicts, national endowments, and the existing strength of regulatory institutions and entrepreneurial groups. These factors determine the state's ability to allocate resources in the service of coherent economic policies, national integration, and development. Degrees of bureaucratic and entrepreneurial development were crucial in determining the success or failure of European colonial powers in taking advantage of capital inflows and overseas markets in the eighteenth and nineteenth centuries.[51] The experience of modern recipients is similar. If even advanced industrial states with entrenched bureaucracies and relatively stable sources of revenue are today experiencing difficulty in controlling highly mobile international capital, countries still forging central institutions can potentially evolve almost solely in response to capital inflows, generating bureaucracies that are direct products of the international economy. Where capital inflows coincide with the birth of the bureaucracy, institutions are especially vulnerable to fluctuations in the international market, and bureaucratic elites must overcome both institutional obsolescence and domestic opposition in times of economic recession. In contrast, where strong institutions are in place, as in the East Asian cases that have provoked so much scholarly inquiry,

[49] The classic argument on the financial burdens of late industrialization is Alexander Gerschenkron's *Economic Backwardness in Historical Perspective* (Cambridge, Mass.: Belknap Press, 1963). See also Rondo Cameron et al., eds., *Banking in the Early Stages of Industrialization* (New York: Oxford University Press, 1967); Cameron, ed., *Banking and Economic Development* (New York: Oxford University Press, 1972). Bureaucratic-authoritarian models draw heavily on these arguments to explain regime change in late developers.

[50] Gerschenkron, *Economic Backwardness.*

[51] With the exception of Japan, foreign capital inflows have played a major role in the economic development of every industrialized country. See Henry Rosovsky, "What Are the 'Lessons' of Japanese Economic History?" in A. J. Youngson, ed., *Economic Development in the Long Run* (London: Allen & Unwin, 1972); David Landes, "Japan and Europe," in William W. Lockwood, ed., *The State and Economic Enterprise in Japan* (Princeton: Princeton University Press, 1965), 93–182. The relationship between capital inflows and the Industrial Revolution has been explored in Patrick O'Brien, "European Economic Development," *Economic History Review*, 2d ser., 35 (February 1982): 1–18; David Landes, *The Unbound Prometheus* (Cambridge: Cambridge University Press, 1967); Immanuel Wallerstein, *The Modern World System* volume *II* (New York: Academic Press, 1980), 144–241.

international capital is more likely to be used to promote economic goals. In communities embroiled in constructing central bureaucracies and national economies, international economic forces and agents can shape fundamental processes of state-building and national integration.

In this typology of financial flows, Saudi Arabia and the Yemen Arab Republic are similar in all respects but one. Apart from the temporary effects of the Organization for Petroleum Exporting Countries (OPEC), both oil and labor remittances are regulated only by exceptionally volatile market forces. Transnational actors such as banks, multinational companies, and international organizations play little part in mediating the entry and use of oil revenues and labor remittances in the domestic economy. As a result, traditional dependency arguments concerning the undue influence of international actors do not apply. Nor does the possibility arise of linkages between international and domestic organizations except, of course, in the case of oil companies. Moreover, both Yemen and Saudi Arabia are partially tribal societies that are divided along sectarian and regional lines. Both countries were at early stages of state-building and national integration at the onset of the oil boom in the early 1970s. Neither country has a long history of bureaucratic development, and both avoided being colonized. The absence of a colonial experience is important, since much of the literature on the Third World rightly attributes the structure and behavior of local bureaucracy to colonial legacies.[52]

At the onset of the boom period, both countries were in the early stages of national integration. The sudden rise in external resources meant a dramatic shift in the power of the social groups that controlled the sector into which external capital flowed. In most of the period I cover, neither Yemen nor Saudi Arabia was troubled by the experience of formal representative government, and both embraced capitalist economic principles. Since 1973, oil rent and labor remittances have made up well over 80 percent of the GNPs of Saudi Arabia and Yemen. Aid constituted the entire current budget of the Yemeni government between 1973 and 1983, making the Yemeni state fiscally autonomous from society. Yet compared with the volume of remittances, its aid receipts were negligible. Saudi Arabia and Yemen are, then, extreme cases of dependence on market-regulated capital flows, differing primarily in the domestic groups and organizations that controlled them.

To present cases as "extreme" examples of anything carries attendant risks; it is an enduring legacy of modernization theory that a conscious

[52] For the ongoing debates in the radical literature, see W. Ziemann and M. Lazendorfer, "The State in Peripheral Societies," in Ralph Miliband et al., eds., *The Socialist Register* (London: Merlin, 1974). In *The State and Social Transformation in Tunisia and Libya, 1830–1980* (Princeton: Princeton University Press, 1984), Lisa Anderson uses similar arguments for the importance of the colonial experience in shaping outcomes in Libya and Tunisia.

rejection of the notion of a "modal" case often coexists with an unconscious belief in a master pattern from which all other experiences deviate (to greater or lesser degrees). With England at its spiritual center, this belief has shaped the rich historiographical traditions of the Continent and especially of Germany.[53] Revived modernization theory and contemporary rationalist efforts to resuscitate the quest for the universal laws of history and human behavior currently exemplify these impulses. Readers familiar with the conventional terrain of comparative studies may rightly question the relevance of Saudi Arabia and Yemen to general discussions of political economy. The Middle East and North Africa have rarely animated debates in the political economy of development; and even in an area studies tradition marked by an astonishing paucity of empirical research, Saudi Arabia and Yemen qualify as two of the least studied cases on record. Moreover, this book is *really* about Yemen and Saudi Arabia. For these reasons, it is desirable that I articulate explicitly the claim to generality on which this study is based.

For analytical purposes the question of whether the processes of institutional genesis and change in Yemen and Saudi Arabia were more or less like the processes in other, self-evidently "important," cases is an empirical one that cannot be answered conclusively absent an uncontested account of each case in the available universe of cases. Thus, although it is customary to privilege national cases on any number of other criteria—power, location, cultural affinity, the sheer number of specialists who have devoted their careers to studying a particular country—the task of defining the representational scope of any case for the purposes of theory-building is, in fact, exactly identical. Saudi Arabia and Yemen are no more and no less "unique" than France and England; their capacity to inform theory is not circumscribed by their location on the Arabian Peninsula.

Yet it is clearly desirable to escape the self-evident observation that each case is unique: this terminus deprives us of the ability to separate pattern and contingency and to understand the relationship between them; in its service to equality, it clouds our ability to think politically by obliterating the distinction between what is shared and what is particular. Typically, categories allow us to get as close as possible to defining the representational character of an event or a case. Categories are constructions that need not stem from conclusions about the modal character of an event or case, and categories can be constructed in more or in less convincing ways.

If Saudi Arabia and Yemen were unique, their responses to the economic disruptions of the last three decades would enlighten us about diversity in national experiences of the international economy. Yet in at

[53] For a revisionist account of the German *Sonderweg*, see Geoff Eley, *From Unification to Nazism* (Boston: Allen & Unwin, 1986).

least three ways, they can tell us about a broader range of national experiences. The first point is pedestrian: Saudi Arabia and Yemen are comparable, in their reliance on oil revenues and labor remittances as primary sources of foreign exchange, to at least fifteen other oil exporters and eleven other exporters of temporary labor.[54] In geographical spread, and certainly in the number of people whose daily lives are shaped by the exigencies of international labor and oil markets, these categories are larger than Europe and the United States put together. Second, as I have argued above, neither the Middle East nor these two cases are unique in their experience of the international economy over the last three decades. Finally, as institutionally weak and deeply divided societies, Saudi Arabia and Yemen illustrate pressures common to an increasingly large number of countries which, immersed in a volatile and changing international economy, confront the task of creating institutions in a domestic context where there is no agreement as to how individual and collective goods ought to be weighed, let alone how these goods should be achieved. If, as recent studies suggest, liberalization, decentralization, and deregulation are global responses to the expansion and tighter organization of international capital in the 1980s and 1990s, then the question of how deeply divided societies craft new institutions while buffeted by international economic forces becomes an issue of general interest, if not deep concern.

TWO COUNTRIES IN THREE ACTS

In the pre-boom days of what would become Saudi Arabia and Yemen, the forging of state and market institutions was a deeply conflictual process in which social forces fought tooth and nail to define economic institutions. The vast majority of the population neither wanted nor benefited from the emerging tax state. Moreover, the state-builders were socially and culturally distinct from the economic elites. Only after organizations to protect property had been built did economic elites lodged in fragmented local markets throw their weight behind builders of the nascent state. Nor were the benefits of the national market immediately apparent to commercial elites, whose profits flowed from high transaction costs. In sequence, a coercive force able to extract surplus from an expanding territory, a unified army loyal to the centralizing elites, and the promise of protected larger markets were prerequisites for forging the coalition for the national market. The promise of the national market, built on a credible capacity to coerce, exclude, and restrict, fed elite appetites for a

[54] Oil exporters: Nigeria, Venezuela, Mexico, Malaysia, Indonesia, Iraq, Iran, Algeria, Libya, the UAE, Qatar, Kuwait, Tobago, Trinidad, and Brunei. Labor exporters: India, Pakistan, Bangladesh, the Philippines, Sri Lanka, Egypt, Jordan, Palestine, Morocco, Tunisia, and Sudan.

strong state; though only a small portion of the old economic elite survived to benefit from more open exchange across a larger territory. The vast majority of the population—the tribes, the guilds, the agriculturalists—fought and lost their struggle against centralization.

During this violent process of institution-building, economic policy rarely took the form of industry- or firm-specific contests, but rather as fundamental struggles over the rules of the game.[55] The central institutions of the territorial state emerged from violent, historically specific battles in which the composition of the community, the borders of the political unit, and the elements of political identity were contested. In Yemen and Saudi Arabia, as in other societies where ethnic, regional, tribal, religious, or sectarian cleavages overlap with socio-economic ones, economic policy entwined with the political exigencies of state-building. The "imperatives" of unifying the market and building the state commingled with cultural, regional, and economic differences: *Shiʿa* or *Sunni*, northerner or southerner, tribal or nontribal, cosmopolis or hinterland.[56] And policy often had, or was perceived to have, the dual and conflicting aim of nurturing a domestic base of support and destroying forms of political and eco-

[55] Huntington views the rise in violence in developing countries as a result of the government's inability to respond to demands from social groups (see his *Political Order,* 39–59), whereas Clifford Geertz, Youssef Cohen, and others argue that in both late and early developers it is a predictable response to state penetration, representing efforts to resist taxation or to capture the newly independent state. See Geertz, "The Integrative Revolution," in his *The Interpretation of Cultures* (New York: Basic Books, 1973), 255–310; and Cohen, "The Paradoxical Nature of State-Making," *American Political Science Review* 75 (December 1981): 901–10.

[56] In most Middle Eastern, Asian, and African countries tribal, sectarian, ethnic, and regional groups tend to be concentrated either in the bureaucracy and the army or in the private sector. In Syria the army and bureaucracy are dominated by the Alawi minority, the private sector by *Sunnis* from Damascus and Aleppo. In Iraq the state is dominated by the *Sunni* minority of the north; the commercial class was predominantly from the southern *Shi'a* areas until oil wealth precipitated the emergence of a new state-created *Sunni* industrial class through state contracts, loans, and subsidies. Similar patterns are found in Pakistan, India, Hong Kong, Taiwan, Lebanon, Kuwait, Nigeria, Guinea Bissau, and the UAE. See Hanna Batatu, "Some Observations on the Social Roots of Syria's Ruling Military Group and the Causes of Its Dominance," *Middle East Journal* 35 (Spring 1981): 331–44; Nikolas van Dam, "Sectarian and Regional Factionalism in the Syrian Political Elite," *Middle East Journal* 32 (Spring 1978): 201–10; Michael van Dusen, "Political Integration and Regionalism in Syria," *Middle East Journal* 26 (Autumn 1972): 123–36; Donald Reid, "Syrian Christians," *International Journal of Middle Eastern Studies* 1 (October 1970): 358–67; Batatu, *The Old Social Classes and the Revolutionary Movements of Iraq* (Princeton: Princeton University Press, 1978); Fuad Khuri, *Tribe and State in Bahrain* (Chicago: University of Chicago Press, 1980); George Lenczowski, ed., *Political Elites in the Middle East* (Washington, D.C.: American Enterprise Institute, 1975). Class analyses are relatively rare except for Egypt: Leonard Binder, *In a Moment of Enthusiasm* (Chicago: University of Chicago Press, 1979); a more general argument is Arnold Hottinger, "How the Arab Bourgeoisie Lost Power," *Journal of Contemporary History* 3 (July 1968): 111–28. The implications of such divisions are explored in Chaudhry, "The Myths of the Market and the Common History of Late Developers," *Politics and Society* 21 (September 1993): 245–74. On the implications of such divisions for economic policy, see Chaudhry, "Economic Liberalization and the Lineages of the Rentier State," *Comparative Politics* 27 (Winter 1993): 1–25.

nomic organization that could rise to challenge the nascent central state. Nevertheless, the ethic of the state-builders and their supporters was universalistic: it held out a future in which the national community would subsume ascriptive groups.

The story of institutional genesis in pre-boom Saudi Arabia and Yemen after 1918 was one of deep conflict, in which whole communities staked their survival and mostly lost—a story that becomes comprehensible only in terms of the dynamically reaggregating interests of state-builders, potential beneficiaries, and taxpayers. Surprisingly, institutional change and obsolescence in the boom period was a smooth, uncontested process embedded in public and private organizations that were not objects of social scrutiny. The economic changes of the 1970s intruded on and reshaped existing political coalitions and institutional structures, shifting nodes of conflict. Yet because the first shock was positive, the massive institutional changes of the 1970s occurred in a context of previously unimaginable prosperity (and previously unthinkable political apathy). The capital inflows of the 1970s fundamentally reshaped the very institutions that had earlier been at the core of social conflict. This time, hardly anyone noticed. Not only was social struggle conspicuous by its absence, but the sites where changes played out were seemingly benign, lodged in the organs of the state and the self-help associations of migrants.

They were, nevertheless, changes at the foundation. The capital flows of the 1970s transformed the tasks that bureaucratic organizations were required and able to perform; they fundamentally reshaped the institutions that governed the economy. Labor remittances and oil revenues precipitated the decline of the regulatory and extractive institutions of the state. The tax and regulatory bureaucracies were dismantled, and other methods of governing economic life arose in their stead. Beyond this basic similarity, the effects of labor remittances and oil revenues diverged. In Saudi Arabia, as in other oil exporters, capital flowed directly into the state treasury. The decline of extractive institutions was matched by the overnight emergence of a huge distributive and productive bureaucracy designed exclusively to allocate oil revenues domestically. State-controlled capital inflows enabled the government to shelter itself from the political and social conflict that accompanies taxation and centralization by simply abandoning the project. In Yemen, as in other labor exporters, revenues entered the economy through informal banks fed by millions of migrants and rapidly flowed into the hands of private-sector elites involved in a host of commercial and industrial projects. The Yemeni fisc, already afloat on aid, replaced domestic taxes with customs duties and jettisoned its extractive bureaucracy. Duties were low by international standards. But the sheer volume of private-sector imports, combined with aid, easily replaced direct taxes.

At a superficial level, relief from the need to tax looks like an administrative and political bonus. In light of the uses to which most governments put their tax receipts, it is difficult not to view such relief as a general good. Yet the decline of a tax bureaucracy has unintended consequences that bode ill for the long-term development of all parts of the bureaucracy. Extractive institutions are the base of administration; without them, regulation and redistribution are impossible. Setting up an extractive apparatus is the first—and the most intrusive—economic act of the state, involving the centralization of the fiscal apparatus, territorial control, political and economic decisions about entitlements, the acquisition of information, and the design and implementation of collection mechanisms and enforcement procedures. The political dimensions of the process include setting long-term economic and fiscal priorities and codifying legal obligations.[57] Institutions for taxation foster related agencies, leading to a diversification of the tools available to decision-makers. In developing countries in which there are large parallel markets in goods and currencies and in which monetary tools are limited, taxation and the data collected through the process are among the few means to regulate the private sector and to permit the functioning of the national market.

Further, the various functions of the bureaucracy require different types of information. Thus the fiscal needs of the state affect not only what the government does but also what it knows. To tax subjects, the state must build a case for doing so; it must construct an account of who is part of society and of that society's collective goals. To distribute revenues, however, the government need only pass some baseline threshold of legitimate expenditure. Without taxation, the principles informing state spending need not be specified. As I show in Chapter 4, unusual criteria can fill the void. The absence of basic data about the economy has negative effects on the quality of local investments, particularly when there are many new and inexperienced entrants into the business community. Needless to say, taxation policies condition the practices of the private sector in important ways. Commercial and investment taxes have a ripple effect, forcing entrepreneurs and merchants to adopt uniform management techniques and accounting procedures.[58] In this realm, taxes *cut* transaction costs. Besides directing investment and consumption patterns, taxation is crucial in delineating the parameters of what society expects from govern-

[57] The European variant of the process is explored in Charles Tilly, ed., *The Formation of Nation-States in Western Europe* (Princeton: Princeton University Press, 1975); Perry Anderson, *Lineages of the Absolutist State* (London: Verso, 1974); Charles Kindleberger, *A Financial History of Western Europe* (London: Allen & Unwin, 1985), 158–76. This argument finds ample support and documentation in Carolyn Webber and Aaron Wildavsky, *A History of Taxation and Expenditure in the Western World* (New York: Simon & Schuster, 1986), esp. 228–489; and in Harold J. Berman, *Law and Revolution* (Cambridge: Harvard University Press, 1983), chaps. 13, 14, and Conclusion, esp. 510, 533–34.

[58] Lowell Harris, "Property Taxation and Development," in N. T. Wang, ed., *Taxation and Development* (New York: Praeger, 1976), 1–64.

ment. To the extent that they enhance accountability, there is a normative argument to be made for governments supported by direct domestic taxes; demands for political participation have more often than not been a response to taxation. However potentially perverse the political consequences of an efficient and well-informed bureaucracy may be, the actions of an unaccountable, inefficient, uninformed, but all-powerful bureaucracy have even more sinister potential.

Over the boom years, oil revenues and labor remittances created very different balances of economic power between state and society and within society itself, directly shaping organizations and institutions in government, economy, and society. In Saudi Arabia, as elsewhere, oil revenues bred large, fiscally autonomous distributive organizations that undercut the development of political and economic institutions in the private sector by displacing old economic groups and creating whole new classes of entitlement groups through state spending. Remittances also weakened state institutions, forcing them to contract their extractive apparatuses to nodes on the border. Saudi Arabia saw the virtual elimination of an independent social sphere; in contrast, as state institutions receded from the Yemeni countryside, remittances provided resources and incentives for the emergence of strong local participatory institutions from below. In Yemen, remittances provided funds to support the activities of hundreds of local cooperatives, which were vital participatory civil institutions led by democratically elected leaders. Through migrant donations and collective efforts, the cooperatives took over the provision of basic government infrastructural and social spending projects.

Finally, labor remittances and oil rents had opposite effects on the composition, vitality, and political character of entrepreneurial groups and capital accumulation in the private sector, producing business-government relations that differed radically both from each other and from what each country had known in the past. By the eve of the recession, not only had the tax and regulatory bureaucracies atrophied and the basic structure of financial systems been utterly changed, but the social bargain between business and state had been renegotiated in a frictionless environment of plenty.

The oil price plunge of the 1980s created severe fiscal crises in both Yemen and Saudi Arabia, generating new efforts to cut spending, to tax, and to regulate. Conflict reentered two systems that had grown unaccustomed to it. Since neither country had a politically significant domestic labor force, the conflict occurred in a direct face-off between business and government. Despite the common source of crisis, and despite their equally ravaged extractive and regulatory bureaucracies, the two governments faced somewhat different sets of constraints. The Saudi government needed to cut government spending and withdraw the robust set of subsidies it had distributed to consumers and producers alike. The suddenly bankrupt Yemeni government needed to tax to survive. Ultimately, consumers paid for whatever adjustment occurred, in Yemen through inflation, in Saudi Arabia through cuts in consumer subsidies and hikes in user fees. But before this final outcome, policy went through several renditions.

Both governments started out by trying to reinstitute taxation—with different results. The Yemeni government implemented a heavy new tax program specifically targeting the independent and autonomous Yemeni business elite. The Saudi government, in response to business protest, withdrew its new proposed taxes three days after they were announced and initiated a series of pro-business policies designed to stem the effects of the recession on the private sector.

"Autonomy," as an attribute of social groups or the state, has been seen as a symptom of or prerequisite for strength.[59] Unfettered by narrow class interests, "autonomous" states are deemed capable of making decisions that favor the long-range vision of technocrats over the short-term interests of "dominant" social groups. Even democratic regimes, we are told, wield the power to base policies on an agenda set in the inkwells of the bureaucracy; authoritarian regimes, for their part, suppress demands for participation and equity in the interest of capitalist development.[60] Similarly, "autonomous" social groups spearhead revolutions, transforming the system by will[61] or circumstance.[62] These widely accepted attributes of autonomy make us expect different outcomes in Yemen and Saudi Arabia. In Saudi Arabia a financially autonomous state should have been able to withstand the opposition of the weak and dependent private sector. In Yemen an ineffective and poor state should have been incapable of taxing the independent and affluent private sector and harnessing the vibrant local institutions. Yet Saudi Arabia's "autonomous" state failed in implementing austerity reforms, whereas Yemen's "weak" state succeeded: the dependent, state-created Saudi private sector first forced the oil state to withdraw austerity reforms and then extracted a plethora of highly favor-

[59] Theda Skocpol, "Bringing the State Back In," in Peter Evans, Dietrich Rueschemeyer, and Skocpol, eds., *Bringing the State Back In* (Cambridge: Cambridge University Press, 1985), 4; Stephen Krasner, *Defending the National Interest* (Princeton: Princeton University Press, 1978), 55–57. For an exhaustive chronicle of what state autonomy means, see Nora Hamilton, *The Limits of State Autonomy* (Princeton: Princeton University Press, 1982), 4–25. For two exceptions, see Ikenberry, "Irony of State Strength"; and Peter Evans, Dietrich Reuschemeyer and Theda Skocpol, "On the Road toward a More Adequate Understanding of the State," in *Bringing the State Back In*, 354.

[60] Nordlinger, *Autonomy of the Democratic State*; David Collier, "An Overview of the Bureaucratic Authoritarian Model," in Collier, ed., *The New Authoritarianism in Latin America* (Princeton: Princeton University Press, 1979).

[61] Skocpol, "Rentier State and Shi'a Islam in the Iranian Revolution," *Theory and Society* 2 (May 1982): 265–83.

[62] Skocpol, *States and Social Revolutions*; and Skocpol, "What Makes Peasants Revolutionary?" *Comparative Politics* 14 (April 1982): 351–75.

able concessions from the government, whereas Yemen's independent bourgeoisie was powerless to influence policy.

These events become comprehensible when we consider how the sectoral distribution of remittances and oil revenues interacted with existing ascriptive groups. In both cases, the flow of external resources into the domestic economy had combined with the existing sectoral distribution of ascriptive groups, aligning tribal and regional cleavages tightly with occupational ones. In Saudi Arabia, the government used oil revenues to eliminate the old economic elites of one region and create in another an entirely new class of entrepreneurs directly dependent on the favor and financial support of the government. By contrast, private-sector elites in Yemen were independent of the state, relying on a robust, informal, unregulated financial market for foreign exchange. Over the boom years, Yemeni business had become exceedingly independent: autonomy from protection, funding, regulation, and even the practice of getting permits for imports and industrial investments during the 1970s, weakened ties between the private sector and state elites to the point of virtual nonexistence.

In the recession, the lines of communication and access atrophied, making Yemen's private-sector elites the easiest political target.[63] Where the political will existed, state organizations were strikingly resilient. Unconstrained by personal and kinship ties, and perhaps even freed by sectarian difference, the state taxed Yemeni business with impunity. The central offices of economic ministries in the Yemeni capital were swiftly reorganized. Local associations fed by remittances were harnessed to the state's ends, permitting the central government to establish a local presence in the hinterland without incurring the heavy financial and administrative burdens associated with building an entirely new institutional structure. State capacity was, initially at least, enhanced rather than diminished by strong institutions in civil society. By contrast, the task facing the Saudi government involved the dismantling of distributive agencies and the complex web of economic links that these agencies had created between bureaucrats, princes, and entrepreneurs. Strong ties—financial, familial, tribal—between the state-created business class and the Saudi government precluded implementation of a mild set of economic reforms that aimed not so much to tax or regulate as merely to prune existing subsidies. The Saudi state's distributive measures had bought peace, but they also entangled the government in mediating between various economic and social groups.

The historical artifact of sectoral control at the onset of the boom, subsequent recruitment patterns, and the mechanisms through which oil rev-

[63] This pattern is the opposite of the African one described by Robert Bates, where state policies squeeze the agricultural sector for the benefit of the modern one. See his *Markets and States in Tropical Africa* (Berkeley: University of California Press, 1981).

enues and labor remittances entered the economy generated strong connections between the Saudi public and private sectors and disconnected the Yemeni bureaucracy from business. In both cases, the politics of ascription flowered and assumed institutional form, embedding regional and religious differences in the very structure of economy and administration. In the Saudi case, the end of the boom found Nejdi business and Nejdi government united. In Yemen, recruitment into the poorly paid bureaucratic and military cadre continued to favor the northern *Shiʿas*, while the control of southern *Sunnis* over private economic activity both broadened and deepened.

State capacities and political access did not function in identical fashion for all sectors of the economy. In both cases, the financial sector circumscribed the logic of business-government relations in the realm of taxation and regulation. From almost identical starting points, remittances and oil revenues had spawned completely different financial systems, the latter almost completely state-dominated, the former completely free of state regulation. Both systems, however, were intimately tied to the international banking system and so were relatively unconstrained by the exigencies of state policy. These direct links between domestic actors and the international economy were powerful enough to stem the logic of domestic economic policy in both cases. In avoiding regulation, informal bankers made it impossible for the Yemeni government to maintain control over the foreign trade sector it had wrested from private hands; Saudi joint venture banks put limits on the concessions the government wanted to give its client merchant classes. The Yemeni government's political willingness to tax permitted it to appropriate fixed assets, but the success of its heavy-handed reforms soon stalled when it failed to gain control of the informal banking system that was the sole mechanism through which foreign exchange entered the domestic economy. Within months, the lack of hard currency forced the government to abandon direct control over imports. Finance also demarcated the limits of the Saudi government's support of its client private sector. By 1988, commercial banks forced a reversal of Saudi Arabia's heavily pro-business stance on defaults by ceasing to lend and calling into question the credibility of the government in international financial markets. Stemming the predations of the Islamic courts, the government revived and expanded an independent secular court to hear financial cases. Subsequently, of course, Saudi Arabia used this new reputation for fair play to borrow heavily on international markets.

Businessmen are closely attuned to economic policy and tend to respond with alacrity to policy signals. The organizational strategies of business groups in response to policy differed in the two cases. In Saudi Arabia, business as a whole won significant concessions at first but soon fragmented: importers argued for low tariffs, industrialists demanded protection from imports, contractors pressed for relief from foreign partners and local creditors, and farmers demanded sustained input subsidies and government-guaranteed purchasing prices. As the recession wore on, huge segments of the new Saudi business classes disappeared into the ranks of consumers. In Yemen, business remained largely united, first in opposition to tax policies and then in support of unification with South Yemen, a former socialist outpost of the Soviet Union. To be sure, in both countries economic decline hit the bulk of the population: consumers. Yet the organizational capacities of consumers are notoriously weak in any context. Neither country had a politically significant labor force to spearhead popular demands; Yemen's previously strong labor unions had disappeared with the boom, and labor organizing was strictly prohibited in Saudi Arabia. Moreover, with three-fourths of Yemen's labor force in Saudi Arabia, and a predominantly foreign labor force in Saudi Arabia, consumers had few fora for agitation. The significance of labor as a social force is nevertheless apparent in the observation that the expulsion of Yemeni labor from Saudi Arabia in 1991 precipitated the Yemeni civil war.

The histories of Yemen and Saudi Arabia give us insight into the origins and transmutations of the basic bureaucratic institutions that govern the domestic economy at specific junctures of the global economy. They suggest that the parallel processes of state-building and national integration, embodied in the expansion of the fiscal and monetary instruments of the state, are reversible and that they covary. Both systemic economic change and the specific form of national-international linkages profoundly influence patterns of institutional change.

The Plan of the Book

The material is presented in three paired case studies, corresponding to the pre-boom, boom, and recession periods. I use a comparative framework to explore the confluence of domestic and international factors that shaped processes of institutional change between 1916 and 1995. The book is based on a close examination of history, but it is not a history book. In negotiating a balance between evidence and analysis, I have sought to reach two distinct audiences that, at least in the Middle East field, have remained separate. Although the book uses heretofore unexamined archives and is based on two years of field work, area specialists seeking detailed historical description will probably be disappointed. This same level of historical detail, on the other hand, will probably jar the spartan sensibilities of theorists accustomed to studying countries with well-known and better established histories. My negotiation, in short, is an uneasy one, but one that I believe yields substantial rewards.

Each chapter includes an analytical and an evidentiary component. Using a modified class analysis, Chapters 2 and 3 focus on the pre-boom years, outlining the process through which institutional change took place in Saudi Arabia and Yemen in a period of relative isolation. These chapters examine the formation of the central bureaucracy and the construction of the national market prior to the oil boom, explaining the process by which ascriptive divisions became embodied in the public and private sectors.

Chapters 4 and 5 analyze the impact of labor remittances and oil revenues on the domestic political economy in the boom period of the 1970s, focusing on changes in the organizations, both public and private, that mediated the influx of capital and influenced the domestic uses to which it was put. Chapter 6 presents a comparative case study of finance in Saudi Arabia and Yemen to illustrate the dramatic ways in which remittances and oil transformed the structure of the financial systems during the 1970s, generating different outcomes by the onset of the recession. However different they were in form, these two financial sectors were intimately tied to international markets impervious to state regulation. In the 1980s, the financial sector was immune from the logic of business-government relations as reflected in the realm of taxation and regulation. The autonomy of finance from regulation is a systemic change in the international economy of the 1980s and 1990s.

Chapter 7 analyzes policy responses and institutional developments during the recession of the 1980s, charting the way that interests fragmented and reaggregated in response to policy changes, producing the social movements of the 1990s. A short concluding chapter revisits the analytical concerns of the project and makes the analytical thrust of the cases explicit.

Part I

INSTITUTIONAL ORIGINS IN ISOLATION

Chapter Two

The National Market Unified

In 1916 it would have been inaccurate to describe Yemen and Saudi Arabia as national entities. In both, a multitude of political, juridical, and military authorities vied for control of overlapping economic and monetary networks that were, themselves, in flux. The collapse of the Ottoman Empire and subsequent regional developments jostled the boundaries of political and economic exchange, undoing modes of interaction between urban, agricultural, and tribal communities. These changes rearranged the terms on which political entrepreneurs competed. Everywhere in the Arabian Peninsula, the end of the Turkish Empire and the beginning of the European Mandate expanded the fiscal appetite of local leaders. When the Europeans drew national borders in Palestine, Iraq, and the Levant, they created an entirely new set of possibilities for competing elites in Arabia. Arabia was believed to be a backwater, relevant to haute politics only to the extent that its borders rubbed up against the richer Arab lands to the north. For the Arabians, however, the changes set into motion after World War I were momentous: once borders were drawn, the possibility of controlling them presented theretofore unavailable opportunities for stable sources of revenue and the establishment of permanent control over territory. Contests over the shape and control of borders, in turn, spurred the formation of standing armies. The fiscal appetite of state-builders fed the expansion and centralization of legal, administrative, and economic instruments, generating local resistance. In simple terms, the end of World War I fueled the process of state-building and the unification of the national market in what was to become Saudi Arabia and the Yemen Arab Republic.

This chapter and the next present an empirically based account of the origins of state and market institutions in Saudi Arabia and Yemen before the oil boom of 1973. This account has a dual aim. The first is to examine processes of institutional origination in periods of relative international isolation. The second is to explore the tensions and synergies between the twin processes of state and market building as a base against which to evaluate patterns of institutional change in the 1970s, when both countries were immersed in the international economy.

The general argument is simple: in the pre-boom period, as in the boom years, the forms and functions of state institutions were shaped by sources of revenue. Changing modes of domestic taxation, and the social struggles attending them, influenced the construction of the state bureaucracy and the national military. Underpinning each major turningpoint in institutional change were different renditions of business-government relations. In both Saudi Arabia and Yemen, military-political elites initially formed the vanguard for centralization of state and market institutions against the opposition of economic elites. These efforts generated resistance from economically dominant classes, as well as other groups—the guilds, the tribes—that stood in the way of state and market centralization. Ultimately, the creation of a stable coalition in favor of the national market and in support of the central state rested, in both countries, on a progressive narrowing of protagonist groups. Taken together, Saudi Arabia and Yemen before 1973 reveal the origins of national institutions in local social conflicts in which majorities lost and minorities won.

Within a broad context of similarity, the cases illustrate markedly different patterns of state and market creation. State-building and the creation of a unified national economy are usually mutually reinforcing processes. Through the construction of a standing army, a centralized bureaucracy, a uniform legal system, and the unification of currency, state institutions support the establishment of property rights and a common set of rules of exchange within a contiguous territory. Under some circumstances, however, the construction of central administrative and extractive institutions can undermine the unification of the national market. In these cases, the prerogatives of state-building so widen fissures in economic exchange systems that fiscal and administrative centralization results in the fragmentation of markets. Public finance is a window on the contingencies that produce these different outcomes. Underlying public finance, however, is a sociology of the shifting coalitional basis of the modern state and the national market.

The pre-boom account of state-building in Saudi Arabia and Yemen offers a glimpse into the relationship between state- and market-building in divided societies. Starting from a common condition in which the monopoly on violence was held by an ascriptive group entirely separate from the economic elite, two very different outcomes ensued. In Saudi Arabia the relationship between state-building and the creation of a national market was one of symbiosis and reinforcement. Success in the former realm eventually attracted the participation of commercial and financial elites in the latter project. In Yemen, by contrast, state-building processes, undertaken by a ruler who lacked a monopoly on violence and could not prohibit exit, undermined the possibility of creating a national market. Extraction took a form that created incentives for economic elites to support a monetarily, institutionally, and geographically fragmented economy. A coalition in favor of a national economy emerged only after the profit-generating capacities of these fragmented enclave economies were exhausted.

The cases support three main claims. First, minimum cuts in transaction costs (public goods in the form of order and security), performed in the service of revenue extraction, *precede* the formation of a national market. Second, although it is impossible to measure transaction costs with any accuracy, particularly when the borders of the economic community are uncertain, it is easy to show that transaction cost cutting is far from costless for many members of society. This hardly leaves us with a standard Marxist story, for elite interests in the creation of a unified national economy cannot be assumed; what appears to be an obvious "good" from the perspective of transaction-cost theorists who think in aggregate terms is not necessarily perceived as such by actors who make choices based on the proverbial short-term calculation. In particular, the benefits of low transaction costs across unified national economies are not immediately evident to economic elites functioning profitably in enclave economies, using cost-cutting mechanisms appropriate to their profit niches. Stable coalitions in support of national markets emerge only through struggles that produce winners and losers. As exemplified by the Saudi experience, the participation of economic elites in the state-building project *followed* the successful completion of a rudimentary military and institutional infrastructure. In short, the class basis of the state is not always visible in its genesis. Sustaining institutional gains, however, soon requires the support of economic elites. Thus, although the initial construction of state institutions cannot automatically be traced to the purposeful acts of the economically dominant members of society, their support is necessary for the stabilization of market institutions at the national level.

Third, opportunity structures are critical in determining whether efforts to provide basic public goods will generate a successful coalition for the creation of a national market or lead to the fracturing of the domestic economy along geographical or sectoral lines. The conditions under which economic elites develop or fail to develop an interest in a national market and a stable set of property rights are contingent on the available alternatives at any given time. These alternatives, in turn, are directly related not just to local and national conditions but also to regional and global opportunity structures, including opportunities to exit. The process through which the institutions that forge and govern national markets are created is a symbiotic interaction of the extractive prerogatives of the bureaucracy, the goal of maintaining power, and the interests of economic elites.

The case material presented here answers questions inaccessible through the level of generality and random case selection typical of rationalist accounts. It shows that how state bureaucracies emerge and whether they survive are questions linked to who creates them, when, and under what circumstances. These historically specific accounts explain the connection between revenue sources, changes in the form and functions of the bureaucracy and, ultimately, changes in the social support base of the bureaucratic state. State-building is always violent, and the organization of coercion precedes other forms of institutional change; but, in opposition to the neo-institutionalist denial of historical specificity and world-historical context, late development deeply shapes the process.[1] Because they neglect this fact, different patterns of institutional genesis cannot be explained using the evidentiary tradition of the neo-institutionalists.

A REVISIONIST HISTORY SUMMARIZED

The historiography of the Saudi state is dominated by retrospective interpretations that place the Al Saud at the center of a constant, indomitable, military-religious energy that periodically burst forth from the desert with the aim of establishing a unified nation-state in northern Arabia. A powerful romance holds the conventional narrative together, knitting contingency into a neat teleological account: three times in the last three centuries, Nejdi tribal confederations, motivated by religious zeal and led by the Al Saud, attempted to construct a unified political authority. The first two attempts failed as a consequence of Turkish, Egyptian, and British intervention. The last one, initiated by Ibn Saud in 1902, succeeded, and the Kingdom of Saudi Arabia—latent in the religious-military alliance struck in the mid-eighteenth century between the Al Saud and the Hanbali reformer Muhammad Ibn ʿAbd al-Wahhab—was born.

The narrative is powerful. It ends with the right actors in the right positions, but it is factually indefensible. Until World War I not only were the indicia of a nascent central authority absent from the scene, but the very idea that there was an Arabia to unite was utterly fantastic. At the turn of the twentieth century even the possibility of a single, lasting military-administrative authority in the Nejd was remote. Of the "Three Saudi

[1] Charles Tilly, "War Making and State Making as Organized Crime," in Peter Evans, Dietrich Rueschemeyer, and Theda Skocpol, eds., *Bringing the State Back In* (Cambridge: Cambridge University Press, 1985), 169–91, esp. 184–86.

Kingdoms," as they are called, only the eighteenth-century conquests stand somehow outside the pattern of Nejdi political history. Until the borders between Iraq, Kuwait, and the Nejd were drawn at the Uqair Conference in 1922 and Ibn Saud was proclaimed sultan of the Nejd by the British, any number of Nejdi factions could have triumphed over the Al Saud and constructed equally coherent genealogies of their historical right to rule Arabia. For until the onset of World War I the Al Saud and their followers were but one group among a host of contenders for ascendance in the Nejd.

The extractive and regulatory state that was dismantled in Saudi Arabia in the 1970s had been forged over the preceding fifty years in a violent and fitful process that repeatedly reshaped the fundamental political economy of the region. Before 1915 there was nothing resembling a central bureaucracy in the disparate areas that would later constitute the Saudi kingdom. By 1952, institutions that governed a national market had been formed with authority over a very large contiguous area.

Examining the origins of the institutions of the Saudi state exposes both the causal sequence through which its central bureaucracy and national economy were forged and the social struggles that underlay each successive rendition of the emerging bureaucratic and military state. Before the oil boom, the centralization of the Saudi bureaucracy was driven by the expanding appetite of the state fisc. In fits and starts, the quest for ever increasing tax revenues generated an extensive and increasingly efficient extractive and regulatory bureaucracy. The story of Saudi state-building is, to an unusual extent, an internal one. In the Arabian Peninsula, unlike surrounding territories and particularly the Mandate states, colonial interference was minimal. Nevertheless, exogenous events did remove longstanding barriers to the construction of such a state, enabling the Al Saud to overcome the scarcities that had prohibited the formation of a central authority in the Nejd, their home region. The history of European state-building is almost completely irrelevant to understanding the process under way in the first decades of twentieth-century Arabia, when the majority of the population was organized in nomadic tribal confederations subsisting on the outskirts of agricultural enclaves. It is surprising, therefore, that the impetus behind the Saudi process—a quest for taxes and a unified army—matches that of Europe more than that of post-colonial states where the bureaucracy, the tax system, and the military were created by European powers.

At the turn of the century the territory we now call Saudi Arabia spanned four distinct political economies that had never been united under a single administration (see Map 2.1). In Al-Hasa, the eastern province where oil was later found, coastal oasis communities and towns had longstanding links to the Persian Gulf and the Indian Ocean. Asir, a Yemeni province annexed in 1934, was a rich agricultural producer on the Yemen-Iraq trade axis. An important source of taxes in the early years, and the most heavily populated region in Saudi Arabia, Asir has nevertheless been the most politically marginal. Figuring most prominently in this story are the central province of Nejd, largely arid desert land dotted with the important oases of Hail, Qasim, and Riyadh; and the rich commercial enclaves of the Hijaz on the Red Sea, based on the ancient pilgrimage site of Mecca and connected to cosmopolitan Islamic centers in Egypt and Turkey. From the Nejd arose the Al Saud and their new tribal military; in the Hijaz lived what would become the first national commercial classes of unified Arabia.

None of these regions had experienced direct European colonization, and each entered the twentieth century with a unique cultural, political, and economic history. Information costs, methods of coercion and control, and the role of intermediaries varied according to regional economic endowments. These variations created different forms of revenue generation, which yielded divergent state structures at the local level, reflecting the balance of political power between regional elites and the Al Saud. The formation of borders was an exceedingly important fiscal event, for their political and military control spawned the possibility of collecting indirect taxes, which are administratively easy and virtually costless.[2] Agricultural and livestock taxes on mobile nomadic populations have much higher information costs and require among other things a uniform measure of value. The transportation of livestock across inhospitable expanses of desert was not an option, and local markets only infrequently had sufficient demand to fetch attractive prices for the king's take of the surplus.

The creation of a central bureaucracy and national market were mutually reinforcing processes that went through three distinct transitions, each marked by the destruction of the social groups that had supported the previous rendition of the tax state. The tribal confederations of the Nejd, the guilds and the smaller merchants of the Hijaz, and eventually the big commercial houses of Jeddah participated, in turn, in their own destruction by helping to eliminate one another from the political arena. Ultimately, state centralization was a fitful process in which groups that challenged the emergence of a national market were either eliminated or reorganized under the aegis of the state. The means through which they were reorganized were crucial to their loss of political relevance.

The key protagonists in this story were the commercial and service communities of the Hijaz and the political-military elites of the Nejd. In Saudi Arabia, where no colonial state existed and no national commercial class formed until the 1950s, a business-state coalition stabilized only after the rudiments of a national legal, financial, and regulatory system were in

[2] For the importance of the establishment of borders in the English case, see John Brewer, *The Sinews of Power* (New York: Knopf, 1989).

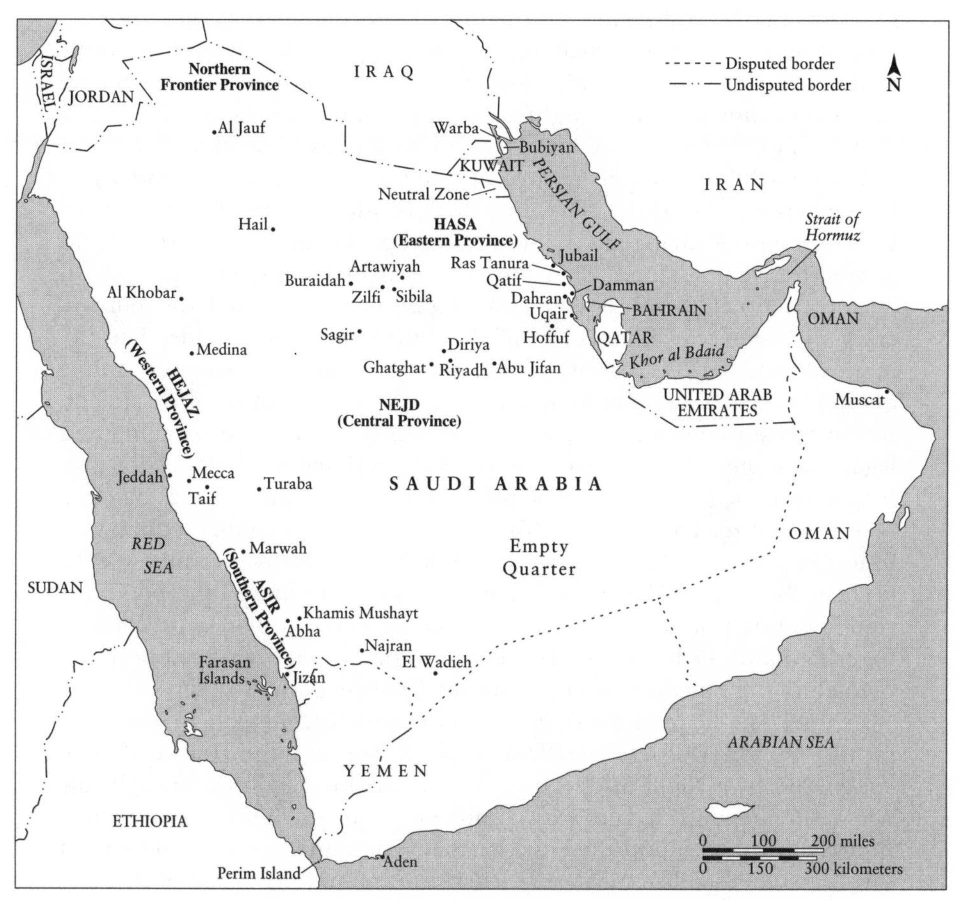

Map 2.1 Saudi Arabia, 1990

place. Only then was sufficient social support for a unified national economy generated among business elites with national aspirations. The control of territory, a uniform legal code, the destruction of internal barriers to exchange, and the creation of a national currency preceded the construction of a powerful alliance between the commercial elites of the Hijaz and the Al Saud. There was nothing automatic about the unity of interests that underlay the alliance, nor did the alliance precede the construction of the rudimentary structure of the national market and the central state. Rather, the coalition emerged out of a slowly evolving unity of interests that was not understood as such until political and would-be national economic elites recognized their common interest in eliminating claimants to resources based in precapitalist modes of organization.

These coalition relations changed three times between 1925 and 1960. In the earliest period the state, heavily dependent on the Hijazi elite for tax collection, exchanged autonomy and representation for revenue and administrative assistance. Then, in the crisis of the interwar period, an alliance between political elites and consumers supported the bureaucracy's incremental elimination of the restrictive Hijazi guilds. The numerically smaller but wealthier commercial elite that survived subsequently formed a national developmentalist alliance with the government. In this transition, commercial elites exchanged political participation and legal autonomy for access to an expanding national market and for protectionist policies; only at this point did the coalition for a national market stabilize. The terms of this alliance for a national market had profound implications for subsequent patterns of business-government relations in the 1970s. The Hijazi merchant elite that entered the boom period was not just numerically small and isolated; it had systematically bargained away its legal and economic independence for the support of a regulatory bureaucracy that soon stopped needing allies.

In 1902, the head of the Al Saud clan returned from exile in Kuwait to capture Riyadh. By 1932 the Nejd, Al-Hasa, Asir, and the Hijaz had been conquered by a Nejdi army led by Abdul-ʿAziz ibn-Saud and brought under a single political authority. Confronting much more cosmopolitan subjects to the west and the east, the Saudi state managed, by the end of the 1940s, to establish a national market with a uniform legal system and a single measure of exchange. In less than two decades a centralized bureaucratic administration had been forged. What happened?

THE NEJD AND THE HIJAZ RECONFIGURED

The Nejd, with its expanses of desert and its scattered agricultural communities, was the perfect arena for a protection racket.[3] Before the per-

[3] Tilly, "War Making and State Making."

manent consolidation of power by the Al Saud in 1922, the main conflict in central Arabia was between the urban areas and the much more numerous nomadic and seminomadic populations. Labor and arable land were scarce, and only an intricate balance between nomadic and sedentary communities prevented massive depopulation through migration. Power in the Nejd was contested by several fluid urban-nomadic alliances of relatively equal strength. With the exception of the Saudi-led coalition with the eighteenth-century religious reformer Muhammad ibn ʿAbd al-Wahhab, no alliance was dominant for long.

The production of insecurity and order was the economic lifeblood of the nomadic tribal confederations. Alternatively, through raiding or tribute, economic resources flowed from the urban to the nomadic communities. Military contests centered on acquiring and keeping protection contracts for the urban areas. Politics was the art of maintaining a coalition of warriors strong enough to guarantee the contract but not so large as to put unsustainable material demands on urban tribute payers. The families that brokered these fragile and impermanent contracts had always come from urbanized segments of the large tribal confederations. The Al Saud, with their base in Dirriyah and later in Riyadh, were such a family.[4]

Tribal affiliations spanned the sedentary and nomadic realms, but the urban areas were tribally heterogeneous, and on balance the dominant urban interest in security and safe trade routes trumped tribal allegiances. Unconverted to coercive power, the relative wealth of the settled communities translated into vulnerability only; the nomadic ability to coerce, in contrast, underlay a complex system of forced redistribution. Sometimes with but often without the support of their immediate kin, urban families built coalitions with the nomadic confederations to protect trade routes and settlements in return for the right to collect and allocate tribute. These brokerage families were rarely the actual leaders of the tribal confederations. The Al Saud of the Bani Hanifah, for example, came from a kinship group only tangentially related to the great north Arabian ʿAnizah confederation, and were far from its tribal chieftaincy.

The urban and nomadic communities were two distinct institutional realms that valued wealth, physical prowess, generosity, and security very differently. However symbiotic their historical existence, individuals within them acted on markedly different sets of incentives and rationalities. Thus it becomes impossible to describe the system in which both the urban and the nomadic communities were located through the language of individ-

[4] I am grateful to ʿAbdul Aziz Al-Fahad for pointing out the importance of the urban-tribal rift in the Nejd, the central role of the Al Saud as an urban clan representing urban interests, and the exit from the "steady state" of the Nejd to a central authority as a decisive victory of the urban communities in general and those of the Qasim and Riyadh oases in particular. Parts of Nejdi history would have been incomprehensible without his insight.

ual rationality, for the mechanisms that made the Nejd a "whole" were located in the nexus of economic, social, and ecological *difference* that was the basis for their co-existence. In the Nejdi scheme of things, the urban communities alone had an interest in a unified political authority; neither the nomadic tribes nor the brokering families sought the long-term ascendance of any one protection coalition. Coalitions that lasted too long or covered too much territory were anathema to the nomadic economy as a whole, which was heavily dependent on raiding as a means of economic redistribution. Complete or permanent exclusion of any one confederation was counterproductive because it encouraged the rise of a rival coalition. Tribal alliances too were ephemeral; they required constant tinkering and manipulation. No single coalition was able, for any length of time, to gain enough military edge to monopolize protection rents, for there were limits to what the urban populations would pay for protection.[5] The scarcity of labor empowered urban communities with credible threats of "exit," and one protector could always be exchanged for another.

The expansion and consolidation of the Saudi state in the first half of the twentieth century was made possible by complex external and internal changes that weakened the nomadic economy and permitted the formation of a permanent tribal army. In the normal pattern of Nejdi political history, this expansion would have been rolled back by rival tribal coalitions. The expansion of the Al Saud, however, coincided with the collapse of the Ottoman Empire, which spurred the British to define and defend borders in contiguous states. This exogenous event made territorial expansions permanent, bringing larger and more stable sources of revenue under Saudi control. Thus, although the initial growth of the Saudi-controlled territory occurred within the established parameters of military and political competition in the Nejd, the new permanent resources funded an ever larger military force able to ban tribal raiding in an expanding contiguous territory.

The social base on which the Saudi extractive bureaucracy was subsequently built emerged out of the disruptions that World War I wrought in both the Nejdi and Hijazi political economies. The collapse of the Ottoman Empire and the imperial struggle that followed undid standing relationships between the settled and nomadic populations in the Hijaz as well as the Nejd. Out of this fissure was born a unity of interest between the Hijazi and Nejdi urban centers for a single, stable administrative and legal authority stretching from the Gulf to the Red Sea. The conquest of the Hijaz in 1924–25 guaranteed the nascent Saudi state a steady source of income that funded the national bureaucracy. Through the legislative

[5] For one instance in which mass migration was used as a political weapon, see Jill Crystal, *Oil and Politics in the Gulf* (Cambridge: Cambridge University Press, 1990), chap. 3.

acts of the Saudi ruler, a national economy emerged. The stable support of the only group with national commercial aspirations, the Hijazi merchant elite, followed.

The initial impetus for rapid expansion of the territory controlled by the Al Saud coalition was largely internal, driven not by religious zeal but by the more mundane motive of revenue. Expanding armies extracted increasingly regular taxes, which fueled a military force and, when territories became large enough, generated a bureaucracy to administer them and collect taxes. To avoid imposing direct taxes that would test the loyalties of the Nejdi urban areas he already controlled, Ibn Saud conquered the Turkish garrisons stationed in the rich oases of Al-Hasa with the explicit goal of gaining access to customs revenues from the ports of Jubayl, Qatif, and Ujayr.[6] Customs offered a steady and administratively simple source of revenue but required the existence and control of borders. The Al Saud subsequently became involved in a series of international conflicts, including a protracted customs war with Kuwait[7] and a lasting conflict with Sheikh Isa of Bahrain, from whom the Al Saud sought to wrest tariffs on the inland Nejdi trade.[8] In 1915, international political changes allowed these territories to be consolidated. That year, the Darin Pact between the British government and Ibn Saud demarcated the eastern borders of the expanding Nejdi coalition. Designed to guarantee the sovereignty of Kuwait, Qatar, and the Emirates against the Al Saud, the pact had the unintended effect of legitimating Saudi control in contiguous areas.

The pact was a unique event in Nejdi history, for it introduced the idea of negotiated borders into a political economy premised on their absence.

[6] "Major Dickson's Report," 1920, PRO, FO vol. 5062, E 6289/9/44.

[7] In 1922, Ibn Saud requested permission to collect customs dues in Kuwait on goods reexported to Nejd; see 16 June 1922, PRO, FO vol. 7723, E 6092/5372/91. To the embarrassment of the British (". . . the Sheikh [of Kuwait] is a feeble and stupid creature, [who] but for our protection would be swallowed alive by Ibn Saud," Kuwait Conference, February–March 1924, PRO, FO vol. 9997, E 1877/4/91), the tariff dispute remained unresolved at the Uqair Conference (1922) and the Kuwait Conference (1924), resulting eventually in a blockade of goods from Kuwait which by 1929 had reduced Sheikh Al Sabah's revenue by 70 percent. "Letter from Ahmad Al Jabir As [Al] Sabah to Dickson," 3 August 1929, PRO, FO vol. 15292, E 4032/91. By 1931, the trade was successfully rerouted to Bahrain, Uqair and Huffuf, in conformity with the interests of the Nejdi merchants and Ibn Saud alike; see "Questions Connected with Koweit [*sic*], Record of Foreign Office Meeting" 12 August 1931, PRO, FO vol. 15292, E 4267/230/25.

[8] Before 1916, goods entering Uqair, Qatif, and Jubayl ports from Bahrain were taxed 5 percent by the Sheikh of Bahrain and 10 percent by the Turkish forces stationed on the mainland. After 1916 the Bahraini customs duties were raised to 7.5 percent and the rate on the mainland lowered to 8 percent by Ibn Saud. Even though Bahrain was a British protectorate, Sheikh Isa so annoyed the British that they eventually supported Ibn Saud and the majority of merchants servicing the Nejdi and Al-Hasa markets. See "Customs Dispute Between Bin Saud and Sheikh of Bahrain on Transit Duties to Najd, Memorandum from the Office of the Civil Commissioner, Baghdad, Major H. R. P. Dixon to the India Office," 14 March 1920, PRO, FO vol. 5265, E 7255/44; the merchants' grievances are summarized in the same memorandum.

A year later the Al Saud announced and enforced a ban on raiding in the Nejd and initiated a program of settling the now economically disenfranchised bedouin tribes on agricultural lands. This newly created social structure, initially held together by a mixture of ideological and material incentives, became the source of manpower from which Ibn Saud drew his conscripts.[9] The Uqair Conference of 1922, which recognized the Saudi capture of Hail and fixed the borders between the Nejd, Kuwait, Iraq, and the Gulf sheikhdoms, continued the pattern set in motion by the Darin Pact. Borders thus came before the development of an administrative arm in central Arabia, making permanent the territories that had been conquered by an increasingly large standing tribal army in search of stable sources of revenue.

The exogenous event of the collapse of the Ottoman Empire had quite divergent local consequences in Arabia. The same international forces that allowed the urban to triumph over the nomadic in the Nejd and Al-Hasa precipitated the collapse of the urban economy in the Hijaz; the same rupture that allowed the Al Saud to fund a standing army, caused the Hashemite king's army to disintegrate. The commercial enclave of the Hijaz was based almost exclusively on the *haj*, the annual Muslim pilgrimage. As such, it was vulnerable not only to global politics that affected the Muslim world and their respective colonial administrations but also to intra-Arab intrigue.[10] In 1916, when King Hussein declared the independence of Hijaz from the Ottoman Empire, he brought a severe fiscal crisis upon himself. Independence meant the withdrawal of Turkish soldiers, scribes, administrators, and subsidies. At the same time, Hussein's fiscal needs grew in tandem with his Pan Arab aspirations to rule a unified Transjordan, Syria, and Iraq. He met these needs by taxing the Hijazi merchants, guilds, and pilgrims in increasingly brutal and arbitrary ways, using seigniorage, confiscation, forced loans, and direct taxes.

Hussein's strategy produced the desired fiscal effect: his treasury grew rich.[11] Moreover, the budget surplus he attained by the early 1920s was

[9] John Habib, *Ibn Sa'ud's Warriors of Islam* (Leiden: Brill, 1978), and Christine Moss Helms, *The Cohesion of Saudi Arabia* (London: Croom Helm, 1981), are the two most authoritative texts on the Ikhwan settlements.

[10] Disagreements concerning the leadership of the Arab world in its dealings with colonial powers and, more generally, who would replace the Ottoman khalif as the paramount religious leader of the Muslim world often resulted in the cancellation of the Turkish *waqf* payments that had defrayed the major costs of hosting the *haj*. The next largest contributor was Egypt; Malaysian and Indian religious establishments also made significant contributions. Among broader international forces, British policy was a key determinant of both the number of pilgrims and the size of the British subsidy, which provided a significant portion of Hussein's resources.

[11] From a severe deficit in 1916, Hussein's treasury was in considerable surplus by 1923. Annual revenue from customs and other *haj*-related fees had grown threefold. Revenues in 1919 were estimated at £180,000 ("Memorandum from the Acting Civil Commissioner in Mesopotamia to the Secretary to the Government of India in the Foreign and Political Department, Delhi," 22 December 1919, PRO, FO vol. 5177, E 1746/318/44). By 1923,

achieved not through administrative reform but by substituting private economic organization for a bureaucratic and coercive apparatus. The *haj* economy was run by a highly stratified business community divided into self-regulating service guilds and business associations that served as tax farmers. Direct pilgrim dues, customs duties, taxes on health and other services, fuel, and produce were negotiated annually in an auction.[12] Each year the service, transportation, and pilgrim guide guilds contracted directly with the *Sheriff* for the season.[13] Even the new 1923

---

counting only the 74,667 pilgrims who came by sea, Hussein's profits were £520,000 from direct taxes alone. The expenditures of the wealthy group of 30,389 Javanese pilgrims in the Hijaz during the 1923 season were the equivalent of £3 million gold, much of which was recaptured by taxing the merchants; see "Report on Economic and Financial Conditions in the Hedjaz," by Consul Bullard, to the Marquess Curzon of Kendleston, 31 October 1923, PRO, FO vol. 10006, E 289/298/91 (hereafter cited as "Economic and Financial Conditions").

[12] Pilgrims: See "Jeddah Report," PRO, FO, E 9280/653/91; "Jeddah Report," 31 December 1922–15 January 1923, PRO, FO, E 653/653/91. Hussein regularly inflated the official estimate of the number of pilgrims in order to increase the sum of fees payable to him by the pilgrim guides and merchants and to extract a large British subsidy. In 1922, for example, the British estimate of total pilgrims from land and sea was approximately 65,000. Hussein's figure for the same year as published in *Al-Qiblah,* the official gazette (no. 608, reprinted in PRO, FO, E 9524/656/91) was 200,000. See "Jeddah Situation Report," 11 July–10 August 1922, PRO, FO, E 8630/656/91.

Customs: Local notables offered Hussein £40,000/month (gold) for control of the Jeddah customs office in 1922; see "Jeddah Situation Report," 21 June–10 July 1922, PRO, FO vol. 7718, E 7618/91.

Auction: "Arrangements for the 1921 Pilgrimage," 27 January 1921, PRO, FO vol. 6285, E 1525/97/91; "Letter from General Haddad Pasha to Major Young regarding Hijaz pilgrim dues" and "Letter from British Agent, Jeddah," 2 February 1921, PRO, FO, E 1385/97/91; "Jeddah Situation Report," 1–31 January 1923, PRO, FO vol. 8946, E 2477/653/91; and "Jeddah Situation Report," 31 December 1922–15 January 1923, PRO, FO vol. 8946, E 653/653/91.

[13] The powerful guild of *mutawwifin* (pilgrim guides) was organized by country. Sub-sections specializing in Indian, Javanese, Malaysian, Syrian, and other foreign pilgrims spoke their language and made all their arrangements: transportation, accommodations, food, and money exchange. Government tariffs and the guides' rates varied according to the resources of the pilgrims, constituting indirect income taxes on nonresidents. The prices were highest for Javanese and Malaysian pilgrims, who spent as much as three months in the Hijaz before, during, and after the pilgrimage; those for Indian pilgrims were about in the middle; Arabs paid the least—mostly because they spoke the local language and were able to do some purchasing on their own.

At the beginning of the season the head of the *mutawwifin* guild estimated the number of pilgrims they expected that year and submitted a bid of revenue to be remitted to the king. In 1922, for example, Yusuf Qahtan, the *sheikh* in charge of Javanese pilgrims, began the bargaining by offering to pay the king £200,000 (gold); in response the king made his own (usually inflated) estimate of the number of pilgrims expected; the final tax rates were the result of such bargaining between the guild *sheikhs* and Hussein. Thus, the administrative responsibilities of the central authority were reduced to bargaining and agreeing on revenues with about a dozen guild leaders, each of whom was in turn responsible to the *shaykh shuyukh al-mutawwifin* (the *sheikh* of all *sheikhs* of the *mutawwifin*), who guaranteed the bargain to both the guild masters and the king. Costs were passed on to retailers and importers through the guilds after they had made their commitment to the *sheriff,* thereby distributing the burden among all members of the business community. See "Jeddah Situation Report," 1–20 January 1922, PRO, FO, E 371/7718.

income tax for the cities of Jeddah and Mecca was farmed out to the guilds.[14]

Revenues were put not to founding an efficient military but to Hussein's broader regional ambitions. Thus higher taxes coincided with progressively fewer services, eroding the security of the urban enclaves against the Hijazi tribes. The balance between the tribes and the cities of the Hijaz was precarious, and its destruction precipitated the end of the Hussein's tenure, for as in the Nejd, the tribes controlled the transportation and security business. Transportation was vital to the *haj* economy, and tribal subsidies were a fixed cost to any caretaker of the holy cities. Indeed, the tribal nomads were more numerous than the city dwellers: of the total population of the Hijaz estimated at 650,000–750,000 in 1923, no fewer than 500,000 were bedouin.[15] More important, the seminomadic tribes immediately surrounding the cities were critical to the functioning of the *haj* economy itself. Organized into caravan guide, transportation, and insurance guilds that interacted vigorously with the urban economy during the *haj* season, the tribes linked the urban communities and provided crucial services to the pilgrims. Off season, they constituted the permanent market for Hijazi goods and services. Seasonal migrations brought many tribes from the Nejd and the northern areas surrounding Hail to the Hijazi market. Wages plus the sale of livestock, dates, and other produce to the cities were the bedouin's only source of cash. And the exchange of subsidies for peace was the critical accommodation between the cities—whoever ruled them—and the tribes.

This system was utterly disrupted in 1921 when Hussein terminated the tribal subsidy that guaranteed the security of the cities and the trade routes linking Mecca, Medina, and Jeddah. This act wrecked the urban-tribal balance, and generated an escalating series of hostilities between Hussein and the tribes, that grew into a veritable war between the cities and the hinterland. Finally Hussein banned all economic transactions with the bedouin and simultaneously raised taxes on the transportation guild they controlled.[16] Quickly enough, the transporters' guild members

[14] ". . . the president of the Jeddah Municipality summoned the shopkeepers, artisans and workmen and informed them that a new tax was to be introduced. The tax varies from 25 piasters for, e.g., water-carriers, to 200 piasters for the more prosperous callings. The tax is to be collected by the *sheikhs*, one to be elected by the members of each calling, who will receive 10% of what they collect. It is supposed that higher rates will be fixed for merchants, shipping agents and the like." ("Jeddah Report," 28 September 1923, PRO, FO vol. 8946, E 11151/653/91).

[15] "Economic and Financial Conditions."

[16] The sale of goods to certain tribes was forbidden absolutely. Grains were rationed, and the bedouin were not allowed to enter the city gates with more than a certain amount of produce. To assure that the merchants did not sell to the tribes secretly, goods were signed for by merchants at the destination and checked by the guards. If discrepancies arose between the amount that left one city and what arrived in another, retribution followed; see "Jeddah Situation Report," 1–20 January 1922, PRO, FO, E 371/7718. Hussein profitted: Camel dues were raised in March 1922 to £2 per camel journeying between the three cities.

turned from protectors to bandits: the transportation and insurance system so vital to the *haj* economy collapsed.[17] The war between the tribes and the king effectively severed the economic links between the cities and the hinterland, cutting off the inland trade from the Jeddah port and the merchants from their markets.[18] Hussein had tried to fight a war without an army, for his troops, despite being his biggest local expenditure, were a ramshackle collection of forcibly conscripted Sudanese and West African pilgrims who were paid irregularly and who made ends meet by collaborating with the Hijazi bedouin in extracting protection money from the pilgrims.[19]

Under the strains of Hussein's revenue drive, the Hashemite enclave began to implode: the population of Medina declined from at least 40,000 (possibly 70,000) before the war to between 7,000 and 8,000 in 1923.[20] Starting in 1922, the impossibility of communication and transportation led to the withdrawal of Hashemite officials from secondary Hijazi cities and even from strategically important port towns on the Red Sea.[21] Growing lawlessness in the cities, corruption in the criminal courts, and the increasing levels of brutality used in conscription had brought the Hijazis to the verge of revolt. In both Mecca and Medina, rumors of rebellion and scattered bombing incidents were commonplace by the latter part of 1922. Growing nostalgia for the relative security of the pre-1916 Ottoman administration generated a strong pro-Turkish sentiment, par-

---

In April alone, 2,054 camels departed from Mecca to Medina. See "Jeddah Report," 11–31 March 1922, PRO, FO, E 4085/656/91; and 1–20 April 1922, PRO, FO, E 4651/91.

[17] A caravan of 2,000 camels from Jeddah to Medina was held up by tribes for a toll of £1/camel; and a 500-camel caravan of wealthy Indians paid a passage tax of £15/camel but "after much bargaining the demand was reduced to £9/camel, the Badawin saying with some humor that the pilgrims could surely afford that since they had paid £9 to the chief robber at Mecca." See "Jeddah Report," June 1922, PRO, FO, E 11149/46/91; 30 April 1923, PRO, FO, E 5175/653/91; and 21 April–10 May 1923, PRO, FO, E 5426/656/91. One tribe, the *Ahamda*, fixed their tax at 16 majidis/camel, but most tribes levied their taxes according to the apparent wealth of the pilgrims. One Persian caravan of 400 camels, for example, paid £3,000, but the Indians among them were asked to contribute only 30–50 Rupees each; see "Jeddah Report," 11 July–10 August 1922, PRO, FO, E 8630/656/91.

[18] "Economic and Financial Conditions."

[19] See "Letter from Major Batton," 10 April 1925, PRO, FO, E 4927/455/91; and "Memorandum from Acting Civil Commissioner in Mesopotamia to the Secretary to the Government of India," 22 December 1919, PRO, FO vol. 5177, E 1746/318/44; "Economic and Financial Conditions"; and "Jeddah Report," 10–28 February 1922, PRO, FO vol. 7718, E 4085/656/91. Appeals to Mecca's four quarters to send sixty men each for the army in November 1920 were ignored. "Jeddah Reports," 1–20 January 1922 and 10–28 February 1922, PFO, FO vol. 7718, tell of Indian subjects being conscripted through "brutality." See also the "Jeddah Report," 21 January–10 February 1922, vol. 7718; "Jeddah Situation Report," 30 August–19 September 1922, PRO, FO vol. 7718, E 9524/656/91.

[20] Population figures are from "Economic and Financial Conditions." An estimate in "Letter from L. B. Grafftey-Smith to Forbes Adam," 31 January 1922 (in "Jeddah Report," 1–31 October 1922, PRO, FO, E 12994/656/91), claims that the population of Medina declined from 70,000 before the war to only 7,000 in 1922.

[21] "Jeddah Report," 1–31 October 1922, PRO, FO, E 12994/656/91.

ticularly in Medina, where a highly organized pro-Turkish party had gained almost unanimous support.[22] They dreamed of Istanbul. They got Riyadh.

An identical set of exogenous changes had led to very different outcomes in the Nejd and the Hijaz. Where the economic equilibrium between Hijazi cities and the tribes broke down, the Al Saud manipulated the same set of circumstances to create an increasingly stable coalition of tribes within an expanding territory. Yet the Kingdom of the Nejd and Its Dependencies, as it was named after the Uqair Conference of 1922, was not a permanently viable economic unit. Anticipating the termination of their British subsidy, the Al Saud turned their army west where they envisioned "riches beyond imagination." The completion of the conquest of the Hijaz in 1925 brought the urban communities of northern Arabia under a single military-political authority.

FROM THREE DOMAINS TO ONE: 1926–50

> Following the old method is not an end in itself. Investigate new sources; and find new people who can pay the *zakat*; and make use of the different tribes as informants to disclose new sources of wealth. These are the instructions of your majesty the King, which you must carry out without any extra expenses.[23]

The territories under the new Saudi king now included the commercial enclaves of the Hijaz, the agricultural regions of Al-Hasa, and the tribal areas of the Nejd and the north. Military control preceded economic and administrative unification. The latter was a truly awesome task. In 1925, when Ibn Saud made the payment of *zakat* (the religious tithe on profits and agriculture) incumbent upon all his subjects in the Nejd and Al-Hasa and banned raiding, he was neither strong enough nor well informed enough to collect taxes directly. In both the agricultural and nomadic communities, tribal and landed elites were critical intermediaries. Rates of taxation were determined through bargaining between the king's functionaries and these elites, who cooperated in assessment, storage, and collection. Governors holding formal political authority were responsible for measuring, recording, and transporting taxes to the central treasury, but a parallel central extractive structure was emerging. By the turn of the decade the yearly visit of the king's own tax collectors was a predictable and established event that intruded into all four regional economies.[24]

[22] "Jeddah Despatch," no. 33 (10 May 1922), PRO.

[23] *Khitab* (no number), "Letter from the Directorate of Finance to the Newly Appointed Financial Secretary of Bisha: Special Instructions," 1352/3/25 (1933–34).

[24] To save on resources used for collection of the *zakat*, the tribes were often assessed biannually or retroactively for several past years. See "The Collection of Taxes," "The Zakah:

Centralized information-collecting and policing mechanisms were in place by the onset of the 1930s, but the extractive apparatus of the nascent Saudi state was hardly uniform. Rather, it reflected the diversity of the provinces: taxes varied according to the natural endowments and social organization of the conquered territories. In each region the king's functionaries set up administrative and extractive bureaucracies in cooperation with new or established local elites. In the agricultural areas of Qasim (in the Nejd province) and Asir, tax farming was employed, based on tributary relationships that often involved the supply of army recruits as well. In Al-Hasa, particularly its rich oasis of Huffuf, the concentration of agriculture in a small landed elite facilitated individual bargains. The nomadic tribes of the Hijaz, Asir, and the Nejd were taxed directly and at great expense.[25]

There was some direct taxation in Jeddah, Tayf, and several other districts, but in Mecca and Medina, as before, the guilds continued to tax and administer the urban economy. Indeed, the guilds became a remarkable facility for the new government, undertaking a variety of state functions with great alacrity and at little expense. The largest revenue generator in the whole kingdom was the *ʿayn al-zubaydah,* a water carriers' guild that collected the head tax on pilgrims, the religious trusts and buildings tax, and the charitable donations that merchants were assessed. In 1935 the *ʿayn al-zubaydah* had dozens of permanent employees, a training program, and the largest independent police force in the Hijaz.[26] Other guilds, besides collecting fees from the pilgrims, performed functions as diverse as gathering gasoline and kerosene fees from Mecca and Jeddah, counting and recording the number of houses in different municipalities and estimating their rents, and collecting and remitting the animal tax charged for camel transport into Jeddah, Mecca, and Medina.[27] The king had neither the information nor the human and financial resources to penetrate the urban economy directly in the early years of his rule. The state budget for Mecca and Medina consisted of the auction figures

---

An Opinion by Shaikh Muhammad Ahmad Abu Zahrah (Professor of Islamic Law, University of Cairo)," and "Tax Collecting in Saudi Arabia," in *Memorial of the Kingdom of Saudi Arabia: Arbitration for the Settlement of the Territorial Dispute between Muscat and Abu Dhabi on One Side and Saudi Arabia on the Other,* Government Document, (31 July 1955) ARAMCO Library: Dahran, 495–518; App. B, pt. 1, 2:291–315; and App. B, pt. 2, 2:316–30.

[25] *Qarar Majlis al-Wukala'* 123, 1357/4/8 (1936), contains orders to a band of tax collectors in the tribal areas of Asir, telling them which routes to take and how to avoid losing their targeted populations. In another document, a telegram from the mission sent to Lith is appended: ". . . when the tax collectors returned to collect taxes they did not find anyone there but the farmers and none of the businessmen or the bedouin were to be found." The instructions of the *Majlis* were to pursue the recalcitrant tribes and, after collecting taxes, to punish them (*Qarar Majlis al-Wukala'* 127, 1357/4/11 [1938–39]).

[26] *Idarah wa-mayzaniyat ʿAyn al-Zubaydah* [The administration of ʿAyn al-Zubaydah], 1355 (1936–67).

[27] *Khitab min al-Maktab al-Khass* [Letter from His Royal Highness Prince Feisal, governor of the Hijaz to the president of *'Ayn al-Zubaydah*] 4, 1350/2/19 (1931–32).

agreed upon by each guild in bargains struck with the Saudi king's treasurers.[28]

Thus, the guilds were great labor savers for the government. For example, in 1935 there were 120 tax collectors and assessors in the port city of Jeddah, whereas Mecca, which had a much larger population and more numerous taxes, had only four state employees, who essentially served as accountants for the guild masters.[29] The guilds administered their own justice—as did the shippers, wholesalers, retailers, and importers of Jeddah—through an arbitration system codified in the Trade Council (*Majlis al-Tijari*). The *wukala'*, a transportation and insurance guild, linked importers and retailers in the different cities, provided guides from among the surrounding tribes, and distributed the tribal subsidy. Local charitable organizations dispensed relief to the needy, and other institutions funded schools and training centers.

Using Hijazi revenues, the Al Saud further centralized the tax system in the kingdom's other regions in 1933, securing urban control over the hinterland.[30] Rates, collection methods, and remittance instructions were placed under the control of the Legislative Council and the Public Treasury in Mecca, which received over 50 percent of all tax yields.[31] In es-

[28] As a last resort, the government might request prominent merchants to extend large loans to the state, which were sometimes paid back in customs exemptions. See "Jeddah Report," 31 July 1926, PRO, FO vol. 1142. In 1929, when the Saudi forces were embroiled in trying to quell the Ikhwan rebellion and a similar request met with no success, the government resorted to collecting customs dues in advance, increasing tariffs, and commandeering cash remitted by merchants in return for drafts on customs payments; see "Jeddah Report," 22 September 1929, PRO, FO vol. 13738.

[29] *Al-Waridah wa-al-Idarah li-Baladiyat Jiddah* [The Revenues and Administration of the Jeddah Municipality], 1354 (1935–36). Taxes in place in Jeddah in 1935 were sales tax, additional sales tax, slaughter tax, medicine tax, commission on auction of animals, tax on gas and petrol, tax for lighting and cleaning, tax on squatters and vendors, tax on restoration and projects, tax on camels entering the cities, fees for inspection of goods, validation tax for diplomas and documents, fee for carpenter's license, fees for stamping and verifying weights, tax on jewelry sales, fee for government land grants, fee on land sales, rent tax, tax on electric machinery, tax on advertising boards, tax for water trucks, bicycle tax, head tax on arriving pilgrims, verification of car purchase tax, licenses for grave-digging, property tax (*Mayzaniyat Baladiyat Jiddah,* 1354 [1935]). But in 1934, when Jeddah had twenty-five different kinds of direct and indirect taxes in place, Mecca had thirty-four. This budget and others of the period show that *jiziyah* taxes—the Islamic tax on non-Muslims, and counterpart of the *zakat*—were collected. Documentation of the existence of *jiziyah* taxes is a remarkable finding, as non-Muslims were legally barred from living within a wide radius of the Mecca and Medina municipalities. See *Mayzaniyat al-ʿAsimah li ʿAm 1355–1356* [The Budget of the Capital for the Year 1936–37].

[30] *Amr Malaki* 836/1156, "From the Acting Head of the King's Office (Prince Feisal) to all Princes and Sheikhs in all regions of the Kingdom," 1353/4/5 (1934–35).

[31] See, e.g., in *Qarar* 114, "Letter from the Legislative Council to the Directorate of Finance in the Capital," and the reply of the Directorate of Finance, 1355 (1936–37). That the central treasury possessed a plethora of information about minute aspects of the administration of outlying areas is demonstrated in the following quote from the above document: "The Council notes that 400 French Riyals [Maria Theresa thalers] and 1400 handfuls of dates and 800 handfuls of wheat are being given to the judge. The Council objects because the same judge was given less salary when he was working at Ta'if. This provision has been

sence, the 1933 reforms wrested fiscal control from the principalities and the provincial governors, consolidating both taxing and spending.[32] Tax farming all but ceased except in the Hijazi cities; uniform salaries for the irregular tax collectors and collaborators provided by the emirates and the extra bonuses received by permanent employees of the emirates, such as police, were rescinded. Taxes on livestock, dates, grains, and trade and the *jihad* tax (military tax) were raised and unified.[33] Taxes in kind, which mainly affected the livestock of the nomadic tribes, were abolished, enlarging the cash economy and relieving the treasury of the burden of transportation costs across inhospitable expanses of desert. A date was fixed for the collection of agricultural taxes, and where taxpayers had no cash, the central government took steps to sell produce at "moderate" prices to offset the effects of on-site sales of large quantities of produce and livestock collected in kind.[34] Most important, the reforms linked the *zakat* rate to the changing budgetary needs of the state. This act contradicted Islamic law and broke with the established pattern of generating new revenues through levies falling outside the scriptural proscription. Although guilds continued to participate in tax collection, in the urban enclaves between 1926 and 1930 the bureaucracy grew in all the municipalities of the Hijaz. In Jeddah, Mecca, Yanbu, Medina, Amlaj, Wajh, Zabdah, Rabigh, Lith, Tul, and Qadimah, civil servants paid by the central government collected "fees and taxes" under the Directorate of Fees (*Mudiriyat Rusum*). Other government agencies at the time included the Ministry of Interior, with only one central office, and a separate directorate for police—but tax collectors in each district had their own police.[35]

---

changed according to the previous salary of the judge," 2. See also, *Qarar Majlis al-Wukala'* 403, 1357/10/6 (1938–39) which includes a series of documents on corruption and embezzlement by Umar Hilmi, treasurer at Abha, a major agricultural region of Asir province, where the Council and the Ministry of Finance determined to the last fraction of a piaster the difference between the reserves and the accounts of the office.

[32] "The emirate has no right to make any claims from the Treasury funds or ask it to spend anything other than the amount designated for its use. If there is an emergency, some money may be spent, but in return the representative of the Treasury must be given a pledge of land or property as a guarantee that the funds will be reimbursed. . . . Any *amir* [prince] who takes the treasury's money or who asks the representative to pay extra amounts other than those hereby prescribed, or who does not maintain the interests of the central government will be subject to severe penalties. . . . Princes in remote areas should enforce these instructions very strictly, as they will bear the consequences for any shortcoming or ignorance in the application of these rules and will be accountable to the government" (*Amr Malaki* 836/1156, "From the Acting Head of the King's Office [Prince Feisal] to all Princes and Sheikhs in all regions of the Kingdom," 1353/4/5 [1934–35]).

[33] *Amr Malaki* (no number), 1353/3/1 (1934–35); *Qarar Majlis al-Wukala'* 23, 1355/4/18 (1936–37).

[34] The responsibility of transporting the goods was delegated downward to the emirates, which were promised compensation for the transport costs of remitting bulky grain taxes to the treasury.

[35] The central police force of the Hijaz in 1930 comprised 703 policemen distributed over only six of the districts. Much of the government bureaucracy was made up of the coast guard and a court system that reached into all areas of the hinterland.

The necessary functionaries of the central state—taxmen, jurists, and police—had established a presence in the cities and throughout the hinterland by the mid-1930s. The vast majority were tax collectors (see Table 2.1). By the end of the 1930s, an extractive bureaucracy had been born. Registers of state employees right through the mid-1950s show that most of the civil service was employed in tax and other revenue collection, assessment, and information-gathering. The courts and police were the only other two sections of the bureaucracy that evolved in a centralized fashion over this period. Indirect taxes such as customs, pilgrim head taxes, and *zakat* from government employees increased.[36] Customs duties were no longer collected in kind.[37] In addition, new direct and indirect taxes were introduced, including, notably, a tax on real estate.[38]

In 1944 a second cluster of major reforms codified the relationship between local municipal employees and the central government, creating unified tax and customs agencies for the entire country.[39] The central government separated its taxes from local fees, and governors of the various provinces were prevented from using the bureaucracy to extract illegal taxes. Checks on arbitrary abuses by local elites were clearly the aim; that the laws were not promulgated by fiat, however, reflected the continuing dependence of the nascent bureaucracy on local elites.[40] Efforts to stem corruption in the emerging extractive bureaucracy were motivated primarily by the need to maximize revenue; in the process, however, these laws generated conceptual links between the king's legitimacy and the state bureaucracy's treatment of his subjects.[41] The government encouraged merchants, tribesmen, and farmers to register their complaints against its taxmen. Most important, in 1943 government officials, princes,

[36] Even foreign ministry employees posted abroad were not exempt from personal taxes. In the late 1930s the *Majlis al-Wukala'* (Higher Council of State) rejected their request of exemption (based on their low salaries), on the grounds that they were not diplomats but low-ranking employees (*Qarar Majlis al-Wukala'* 465, 1357/11/4 [1938–39]).

[37] This decree met with resistance from the merchants because it gave the government the power to determine the value of imported goods rather than allowing the importers simply to turn over a certain portion of the wares to the customs officials. No doubt it also cut down on profiteering by public officials, since receipts began to be issued and deposited in several different offices (*Khitab Wizarat al-Maliyah* 1091, "From the Minister of Finance to the Deputy Prime Minister regarding the preference of the merchants to pay customs in commodity and not cash," 1351/9/27 [1932–33]).

[38] *Sawt al-Hijaz* (23 March 1936), as quoted in "Jeddah Legation Report," 28 March 1936, PRO, FO vol. 20063, E 2102/1041/25, announced a 5 percent tax to be collected by the Ministry of Finance on all properties in the Kingdom that were not owner-occupied. The decree also provided that lists of rented properties be compiled.

[39] Based on my survey of the records of budget and administrative reforms in the National Archives, Institute for Public Administration, Riyadh.

[40] *Qarar Majlis al-Wukala'* 23, 1355/4/18 (1936–37).

[41] Corruption was severely punished in all recorded instances: e.g., *Qarar Majlis al-Wukala'* 403, 1357/10/6 (1938–39), regarding the embezzlement and fraud of the treasurer at Abha.

Table 2.1. Growth in number of Saudi tax officials, 1930–1944

Emirate	Ministry of Finance		Employed in Emirates (nonmilitary)	
	Taxation 1944	Customs 1944	Others 1944	State Employees 1930[a]
Main office	133			
Riyadh	172	1		
Qariat (& areas)	21	2	205	
Buraydah	2		50	
Dammam	96		68	
Qatif	4	12	30	
Mecca	58	5	25	
Hasa oasis	38	33	188	
Medina	24	2	65	
Jeddah	90	106	101	88
Khubar	2	17		
Taif	30		43	
Zafeer	23		50	
Rabegh	8	2		5
Yanbo	22	10	34	24
Amlaj	11	2	16	5
Wajeh	11	6	26	9
Zubah	11	3	26	9
Al Ula	12	3	32	
Al Lith	16		37	4
Tabuk	49	2	36	
Bisha	16			
Qunfadah	57	7	63	
Jauf	7	2	40	
Quriah	7	2	64	
Jaizan	103	18	426[b]	
Sabaiya	4			
Qahmah	4	1	39	
Farsan	2	1		
Jabri & Khubah	5	2		
Mosum		1		
Aardha		1		
Towaal		1		3
Savritha	5			
Mathayyal	13			
Abha	77		232[c]	
Dahran	13	12		
Al Hajra		2		
Hail		1		
Northern areas		45		
Haqf market		2		
Alqaan market		2		
Mughairah market		2		
Hadeethah market		1		
Uqair		12		
Ras al Tanurah		31	20	
Dareen		2		
Jubail		8	15	

Table 2.1. Continued

	Ministry of Finance		Employed in Emirates (nonmilitary)	
Emirate	Taxation 1944	Customs 1944	Others 1944	State Employees 1930[a]
Southern border areas		3		
Quriyah and surrounding areas		16		
Safaniyyah		2		
Hafr		9	57	
Um Radhma		3	31	
Luqa		4	30	
Lina		2	56	
Doweed		2	22	
Munfuhah		1		
Najran		2	65	
Barq		1		
Alb		2		
Hijaz (customs & cigarettes)				35
Mahd			10	
Taubah			19	
Al Kharj (Sullaimaniyyah)			12	
Ab al Qaiq			72	
Doadami			32	
Raniyah			16	
Afeef			33	
Qauwiyyah			19	
Mouwiyyah			33	
TOTAL	1,146	409	2,438	182

Source: Compiled from reports and budgets in the IPA archive.

Note: For the cities for which figures were available for both 1930 and 1944, the increase in the number of tax officials was 118, a 65 percent growth.

[a]Available for the Hijaz only.

[b]Jaizan's own administration consisted of 62 people, but it also administered 14 small emirates with this collective total.

[c]Abha administered eight smaller emirates, which employed 144 of this total.

and administrators were prohibited from participating in trade or other commercial ventures.[42]

The reforms, however incremental, were effective. Throughout the 1930s and 1940s, revenues from direct and indirect taxes and fees increased, despite adverse international conditions that affected both trade and the pilgrimage. Records from Jeddah, Mecca, Medina, and Al-Hasa

[42] *Balagh Rasmi* 83 [Royal Proclamation], in *Umm al-Qura* (31 December 1943).

show a dramatic escalation in the total tax collected over this period.[43] In the municipality of Jeddah, directly collected revenues, not including those channeled through the guilds, rose from 530,000 Qursh Amiri in 1933 to 1 million in 1937. In Mecca, municipal revenues more than doubled between 1932–33 and 1935–36. In Medina, tax revenues rose from 317,000 Qursh Amiri in 1933 to 1.4 million in 1938. Similarly, in the province of Al-Hasa, which included the rich agricultural area of Huffuf, directly collected taxes rose from 29.4 million Qursh Amiri in 1936 to 37.58 million in 1937—a remarkable yield, since administrative costs for tax collection and police were cut by more than half between those two years. Direct taxes continued to generate the largest returns until 1955, when oil revenues suddenly became the primary source of state income. When the first national budget was issued in 1949–50, direct taxes (in the form of *zakat*) made up a full 37 percent of state revenues—a much higher percentage than in most LDCs. Customs and various sales taxes made up an additional 30 percent.

Money Makes Markets: The Unification of Currency

The early history of the Saudi state reveals the links between the creation of a central extractive and regulatory bureaucracy and the emergence of a national market. The creation of a uniform medium of exchange was critical to the birth of a national economy. Metallic currencies were used throughout Saudi Arabia, but each region particularly valued the preferred currency of its trading partners. In the Hijazi entrepot the British gold sovereign, Indian silver rupee, Maria Theresa thaler, Turkish majidi, and several denominations of Ottoman currency circulated simultaneously. In the Nejd and Asir the silver Maria Theresa thaler held sway; in Al-Hasa, the eastern province's longstanding direct trade with India made the Indian rupee the preferred currency. Regional variations in value interacted in unpredictable ways with the international prices of precious metals. When Britain went off the gold standard in September 1931, for example it precipitated a major monetary crisis in the Hijaz, where the exchange system had been precariously based on the sovereign and on strong financial ties to the British colonies of India and Aden.

Multiple currencies embodied and reinforced the multiple economies of the new Saudi Kingdom. Multiple economies, in turn, were a barrier to the emergence of a single political-legal authority, for the long-entrenched forms of social organization and economic exchange under-

[43] All figures are derived from the annual budgets for different municipalities, which provide very detailed information on the various taxes—unlike subsequent "national" budgets, which merge categories and are less useful in analysis (National Archives, Institute for Public Administration, Riyadh).

pinning them did not automatically yield to the new state's authority. Any account of early attempts to unify the currency make a mockery of the conventional wisdom that Ibn Saud was a despot who ruled by decree. The powerful money-changers of the Hijaz defeated the Saudi attempt in 1927 to narrow the number of currencies by eliminating the use of the Turkish majidi, vividly demonstrating the regime's inability to enforce the ban.[44] In 1932, Nejdis refused to accept payment of salaries and subsidies in gold sovereigns, signaling the government's inability to redeploy taxes collected in the Hijaz in a region with a preference for silver thalers.[45] Multiple currencies with varying "real" and "socially constituted" values erected, in very short order, barriers to the expansion of central authority: they undercut the ability of the government to protect consumers through the crisis years of the interwar period, prevented the uniform valuation of property, and blocked the use in one currency region of tax revenues collected in another. The lack of a uniform measure of value, in short, forestalled the government's ability to exercise political power through economic means and to shape the rules that governed the economy. It both reflected and reinforced the disjuncture between military and economic control.

The Al Saud wanted a unified currency for both political and practical reasons; they met opposition from diverse groups of citizens on the same

[44] "Letter from the Citizens of Jeddah to the Kaimahkam of Jeddah, regarding the Restriction of the Majidi riyal," 1346 (1927), notes: "It is known to you that the Majidi riyal has become a heavy burden on the country, and we are afraid that it will bring poverty upon us unless some action is taken to correct the situation with regard to its value. And since the government has annulled this riyal in all circles as is the case for other currencies, we hereby petition you to reinstate the value of the Majidi riyal" (signed by twelve leading merchants and retailers).

The *kaimahkam*, himself a merchant, responded: "To the Crown Prince Regarding the Pricing of the Majidi riyal, From the Kaimahkam of Jeddah," Emirate of Mecca [in this period, as earlier, Jeddah came under the administration of Mecca], letter 982, 1346/4/3 (1927–28): "Because when the *Hajjis* (pilgrims) depart from the Kingdom they leave large amounts of Majidi riyals in Mecca and Jeddah, the price of the Majidi riyal has been 10 Qursh Amiri. But we think that the price should be 9 Qursh Amiri, which would be the equivalent of 18 Qursh Daarij, which would make the proper price of the British pound 12 Majidi riyals and 4 piasters. The new price controls imposed by the government are not acceptable to the money-changers, who are unwilling to change at even the present rate. The merchants are therefore hoarding their Majidi riyals and creating shortages of currency. The alternative, which would solve this problem, would be to fix the price higher."

In another letter, written after Ibn Saud banned the use of the Majidi riyal, the *kaimahkam* wrote: "The Majidi riyal has been stopped from circulation, but this was against the interest of many people. First, the value of this riyal was decreased and no longer accepted as legal tender. When its price dropped to the minimum it caused great damage to many people. Therefore I, the Kaimahkam of Jeddah, ask the Crown Prince to allow the public to circulate the Majidi riyal for a temporary period of 25 days because I have received a written petition signed by many merchants and citizens to discontinue the present policy. I suggest that it is better to allow the currency to circulate so as to decrease its use by encouraging merchants to send this riyal out to markets in Aden and India" ("Letter from the Kaimahkam of Jeddah to the Crown Prince," *Khitab* 2653, 1346/8/14 [1927–28]).

[45] "Letter from Sir A. Ryan to Sir John Simon," 11 January 1932, PRO, FO vol. 77625, E 371/16018.

grounds. In stark opposition to the commonplace notion that groups vie to capture the state, or make demands on it, the initial expansion of institutions governing the market took place despite social opposition. Groups do not make demands on central authorities until those authorities have something to offer. There was virtually no social base of support for policies that would dislodge local barriers to a national market; support had to be created through the legislative acts of the state. Later, these initiatives would yield social support for the national market among the Hijazi commercial elite. In the absence of such support, taxes were not just a necessity but a tool of economic statecraft.[46] By demanding taxes in increasingly restricted currencies, the monarch not only forced a cash economy on his subjects but also, with each successive juncture in the centralization of taxation, took a step toward the unification of currency. A progressively uniform or at least calculable measure of value, in turn, promoted administrative uniformity and generated the institutional preconditions for universal notions of citizenship. In the process, the relationship between the state and key social groups underwent major changes.

Two early allies in forging a centralized market were the Islamic jurists and the commercial elites of the Hijaz. The former would replace guild, local, and tribal law with a uniform legal code, forming the cadres of a legal bureaucracy; the latter would be the first to recognize their economic stake in the expansion of the national market and the institutions that undergirded it. Before the national market could be created, however, the Hijazi guilds and the money-changers (with their restrictive organization and their local monopolies) and the tribes, including large segments of the king's tribal army (with their fundamental antipathy to stable authority) had to be crushed. Only after this had been largely achieved did the Hijazi commercial elite acquiesce to a partnership with the state. The creation and centralization of the Saudi extractive and regulatory bureaucracy and the expansion of the national market were heavily contested. Each juncture in the process was marked by wrenching social struggles in which the economic lifeblood and social organization of local communities were at stake. In the early years of state-building, taxation was the source of all major and most minor conflicts between the state and society. Before the political authority had anything to offer in the way of resources or services, it engaged in destroying internal barriers to exchange and forcibly extracting increasingly large surpluses. At this stage, violence hardly resulted from the demands of social groups on unresponsive state institutions but, rather, from the expansion of the state in the economic, political, and legal realms.

It was in the Nejd, Asir, and Al-Hasa that the direct relationship between violence and taxation gained its full expression. Taxation spawned vio-

[46] This is one of many important points in Joseph A. Schumpeter, "The Crisis of the Tax State," in Alan T. Peacock et al., eds., *International Economic Papers No. 4* (London: Macmillan, 1954).

lence when the enthusiasm of state functionaries and tax farmers tested the narrow limits of state legitimacy. Saudi Arabia has a robust history of tax revolts. Pursued by the taxman, the bedouin simply disappeared. In the settled agricultural areas of Asir and Al-Hasa, however, where exit was impossible, tax rebellions were common. It was not unusual for farmers to take up arms against the tax collectors and to loot the government's treasuries, sometimes in alliance with surrounding bedouin tribes and sometimes against them.[47] The coercive power of the state was visited on tax evaders with impunity: recalcitrant tribes were often pursued and taxed, paying heavily in lives and livestock;[48] settled agricultural areas were the victims of raids and fines when they avoided the taxman.

Thus although the Party for the Liberation of the Hijaz (*hizb ahrar al-Hijaz*) was the longest-lasting and best organized opposition movement, the most severe threat to the early Saudi regime came from the Ikhwan, the bedouin tribes that Ibn Saud had settled on agricultural lands and that constituted both his revenue base and the core of his conquering army in the wars of unification. Tax revolts among the bedouin began early on. In 1916, when Ibn Saud issued his famous demand that all the bedouin of the Nejd and Its Dependent Territories should be required to settle, join the Ikhwan movement, and pay him *zakat* as their recognized leader, many sections of the major tribal confederations and the entire Ajman confederation took up arms against him. The first great tax revolt occurred in 1929, when the king's tribal army was disbanded, sent back to the Nejd and prohibited from raiding. The Ikhwan Revolt was a veritable civil war disputing the basic right of the monarch to collect taxes. Similarly, the 1933 unification of *zakat*, livestock and sales taxes, and fees precipitated a series of revolts among the Hijazi and Nejdi tribes.[49] As

[47] See "Memorandum from Sir Reilly regarding the Dabbagh clan" (Aden, 27 July 1932), which deals with armed resistance to taxes in Asir; for Al-Hasa province, which includes the oases of Huffuf and Qatif, see 23 April 1936, PRO, FO vol. 20064, which gives an account of taxpayers' looting and their recovering £70,000 of the tax collected that year. See also "Jeddah Report," 2 June 1936, PRO, FO vol. 20062.

[48] The most exhaustive discussion of taxation of nonsedentary tribes, with registers showing increases in the amount extracted, is for the southern part of the Al-Hasa region. See "Collection of Taxes," "Zakah," and "Tax Collecting" in *Memorial of the Government of Saudi Arabia* (31 July 1955).

[49] *Amr Malaki* 7079, "Letter from the Deputy of the Prime Minister Prince Feisal to the Minister of Interior on informing the Municipalities of Jeddah and the Capital on the unification of fees," 1351/11/10 (1932–33); *Amr Malaki* 5915, "Letter from Prince Feisal to the Minister of Interior regarding the query of the Wajh Municipality regarding the animal tax and *zakat* and authority over its collection and assessment," 1351/8/15 (1932–33); *Khitab* 1221, Directorate of Finance, "Letter to the Director General of the Finance Office from the Jeddah Municipality" and "Reply of the Director General," 1351/11/4 (1932–33), in which the Jeddah Municipality agrees to the increase and unification of all fees on the condition that these laws be implemented the next year; *Amr Malaki* 5904, "Letter to the Minister of Interior from the Deputy of the Prime Minister asking him to inform the Yanbo Emirate that the taxes on the sale of animals have been raised and unified in all areas of the Kingdom and that the municipality is responsible for collecting these fees in accordance with the instructions of the treasury's assessors," 1351/8/13 (1932–33).

rebellion spread south, the Idrisi tribes of Asir joined forces with the Billi; in response, the Al Saud undertook the conquest of Asir, which was immediately put under the centralizing tax administration.[50]

The early secessionist movements in the north, south, east, and west were responses to the extractive efforts of the state. They were the attempts of local elites to thwart the king's taxmen and to stem the dismantling of existing patterns of local authority, including the local power to adjudicate disputes and to redeploy surplus locally through existing civil institutions. Only after the state had established its regulatory apparatus did these same groups begin to make demands on the state.

Each successive cluster of reforms in the fiscal and administrative system coincided with a reconstruction of the social basis of the emerging Saudi state. The sequence belies a strict Marxist analysis: a stable constituency for the state did not even exist until the 1940s. Before political authority, through administrative and legislative acts, created its social base in the Hijazi commercial elite, three successive conflicts occurred; in each one, the social base of the state changed. By the end of the military conquests in 1932, the first decisive conflict—the destruction of the nomadic economy—had already occurred in the Nejd. The ban on raiding, the drawing of borders, and the termination of cross-border migrations destroyed the nomadic economy and made the urban enclaves of the Nejd permanently secure. The same process of destroying the nomadic economy generated a reliable army, drawn from the disenfranchised Nejdi tribes, which conquered and pacified the Hijaz. Enlisting Hijazi consent on Hijazi taxes and recruiting Hijazi administrators, however, also required the elimination of this same tribal army, which by all accounts was wreaking havoc in the *haj* economy. In 1928 Ibn Saud disbanded his troops and ejected them from the Hijaz, precipitating a massive revolt that was put down only with the help of British military hardware.[51] The tribal army's demands were couched in the language of religion, but as expressed at the Riyadh Conference in 1928, they were clearly a reaction to what had become of nomadic life during their few years of service in the Saudi army.[52]

[50] Instructions from the Directorate of Finance reflect the aim of the central treasurer to gain firsthand knowledge of the resources and expenditures available in the newly conquered Asiri areas and their main treasury in Bisha. The use of a bureaucrat to perform a complete survey indicates that there were extensive information-gathering efforts at this early date. *Khitab* (no number), "Letter from the Directorate of Finance to the newly appointed Financial Secretary of Bisha: Special Instructions," 1352/3/25 (1933–34).

[51] See the detailed notes in "Major Dickson's Report," 17 March 1920, PRO, FO vol. 5062, E 6289/9/44.

[52] At the Riyadh Conference of 1928, Ibn Saud tried to negotiate with the Nejdi rebels that had once made up his army; their demands were summarized by a representative of the British Legation who was present: "Notes on the Riyadh Conference," November 1928, PRO, FO vol. 13713, E 113/E114/3/91. For a detailed account, see Helms, *Cohesion of Saudi Arabia.*

CHANGING BUSINESS-GOVERNMENT RELATIONS

The story of Saudi state-building became a steady narrative only after the conquest of the Hijaz. The conquest made possible for the first time in the history of northern Arabia the establishment of a permanent national administrative and extractive bureaucracy, with a cadre of bureaucrats to identify and collect surpluses systematically. Between 1926 and 1952 the Hijaz provided the bulk of state revenues. The state's fiscal dependence on guilds was the key to the first bargain between the commercial classes and the government. Mediating the extractive efforts of the king gave the Hijazi commercial communities a significant measure of bargaining power through the formal, autonomous institutions they dominated. In contrast, no such institutions were permitted in the agricultural and tribal regions of the kingdom, where local elites were less effective as tax farmers; there, the direct coercive and extractive agencies of the state were responsible for tax collection.

Taxation was the subject of most communication between the Council, the king, and his subjects,[53] and in many instances opposition to taxes was successful.[54] At the apex of the merchant community, composed of Jeddawi importers, informal bankers, and shippers, the king permitted the

[53] The more colorful examples include a petition signed by some seventy-five gravediggers and landowners, asking the king to cut their taxes because "they are making us poor": *Min Sukaan wa-Ahaali Qafrynj ila Malik al-Hijaz wa-al-Najd wa-Mulhaqatiha al-Malik al-Muhabbab* [From the Inhabitants and Families of Qafrynj (a designated area for graveyards in Mecca) to the Revered and Respected King of the Hijaz and the Nejd and its Dependencies], 1348/7/1 (1929–30). The shopkeepers of Fakhariyayn, a Hijazi village, wrote asking for a decrease in the shop tax: *Qarar Majlis al-Shura* 76, 1346/7/11 (1927–28). Traders complained that high export taxes made goods uncompetitive, raising their price by half: *Qarar Majlis al-Shura* 94, "'An Shikayat al-Tujjar min Thamn al-Jumrak" [On the Complaints of the Merchants about the rates of Customs (the Arabic term includes export and import taxes)], 1347/4/17 (1928–29). Importers lamented that customs duties were often collected on orders in advance, though goods were not due for months, creating a volatile secondary market in government chits: "Jeddah Report," 22 September 1923, PRO, FO vol. 13738, E 5410/2322/91. Merchants complained when, in the crisis year of 1931, the government began to collect customs in cash, abolishing the practice of paying in kind. *Khitab min Majlis al-Shura li-Jallalat al-Malik al-Amir Sa'ud* 235 [Letter from the Consultative Council to the Crown Prince Saud], 1351/7/25 (1932–33) agrees to the law. See *Khitab Wizarat al-Maliyah* 1091 [Letter from the Minister of the Treasury to the Deputy Prime Minister, Prince Feisal], 1351/9/27 (1932).

[54] That the king's own minister of finance tried to dissuade him from imposing the commercial tax demonstrates the effectiveness of the merchants of the small port town of Yanbo in making their demands heard: "The request of the merchants of Yanbo is that [although] the scale of first, second, third, and fourth class of taxpayers among the Jeddah merchants accords with their size and the number of branches under them, the Yanbo merchants do not possess such variety, and none of them would come into the first grade of taxpayers if they were to be measured by the [wealth of] the first grade in Jeddah. Your servant does not see the meaning of [these categories] when applied to the warehouse traders of the second or third category, as they are mostly transient stores. As for the standing and stable shops, they are absolutely liable for the yearly tax" (*Khitab min Wizarat al-Maliyah ila Malik al-Hijaz* 933 [Letter from the Ministry of Finance to the King of the Hijaz], 1355/8/29 [1936–37]).

creation of the Trade Council in 1925. Its laws and regulations were drafted by the merchants themselves in an obvious attempt to formalize their existing independence from the religious courts and to protect themselves from the Wahabbi juridical tradition of commercial law offered by the Al Saud. The charter of the Trade Council was quite inclusive; its jurisdiction encompassed the Commercial Law System, the Commercial Court System, and the Commercial Court Fees Law, each of which preserved the independence of the merchants from their Nejdi king.[55]

Ibn Saud began his reign in the Hijaz by issuing a constitution and the *nizam al-intikhabat al-ʿAmmah,* or electoral laws, which legally sanctioned the electoral traditions of all service guild masters, municipalities, and other public officials. The new rules formalized the relationship between the guilds and the government and, far from undercutting their independence, legitimized existing forms of authority and hierarchy. Later, information gathered for the elections was used to tax and regulate the guilds directly. The merchants won formal representation in the government through the Consultative Council (*Majlis al-Shura*), which was composed of prominent Hijazis drawn from major merchant families. In the early years of state-building efforts, this council provided a direct link between the merchant class of the Hijaz and the king.

The scope of activities overseen by the council in this period is broad enough for us to question the conventional wisdom that Ibn Saud was an absolute monarch who ruled alone, without the help of an administrative apparatus.[56] Indeed, though not suggesting that this statement is generalizable outside the Hijaz, evidence indicates that he was just one of the actors and institutions that governed. Indeed, in budgetary and commercial matters the king's decrees were often disputed and overturned. Court records and documents indicate that the Consultative Council, the Trade Council, and the guild masters were powerful organizations that controlled the day-to-day administration of the Hijazi province.[57] Legislation

[55] This long, handwritten document was passed by the Consultative Council the same year the Commercial Council drew up the laws: *Qarar Majlis al-Shura* 137, "Itifaqiyah 'ala Qanun al-Majlis al-Tijari," 1345/11/13 (1926–27). After it was approved, Prince Feisal, then governor of the Hijaz, commented: "The council has been given wide authority without limits and it is the opinion of the authorities that this authority would be limited and confined to the relations between the merchants themselves and trade": *Nizam al-Majlis al-Tijari fi al-Hijaz,* 1345 (1926–27), 1.

[56] Even the British Foreign Office reports for the period take this perspective for granted. See e.g., "Letters from Sir R. Bullard in Jeddah to Mr. Baxter," 16 June 1938, PRO, FO vol. 21903, E 4059/196/25. Subsequent scholarship, relying on the PRO archive, has restated the same conclusion: Helms, *Cohesion of Saudi Arabia*; Helen Lackner, *A House Built on Sand* (London: Ithaca Press, 1978); Nadav Safran, *Saudi Arabia* (Cambridge, Mass.: Belknap Press, 1985). This perspective focuses too heavily on purely political power and does not address the extent of access to legal and administrative matters that different groups enjoyed in the early period of the kingdom's consolidation.

[57] Texts based on sources other than Saudi government documents uniformly portray the Consultative Council as unimportant and ineffectual: e.g., David Holden and Richard Johns,

passed by the Consultative Council in 1926, for example, shows that it not only dealt with dispute resolution but was also involved in structuring the fundamental institutions of the Hijaz, including courts, the treasury, police, and the municipal system of the province and surrounding areas.[58] The king relied heavily on its members' expertise in this early period—perhaps because with neither the staff nor the personal experience to administer a large urban population, he had no alternative. Most important, the budget for the urban areas was entirely in the hands of the council, and though the absolute amount of the budget was small, the allocations were well thought out and specifically documented.[59]

The Consultative Council, representing the merchants and the guilds, often blocked the king's attempts to increase fees and unify taxes.[60] Initially, it forestalled the monarch's attempts to create a national market by breaking down the informal monopolistic rules of the guilds and merchants of the Hijaz. As conflict between the king and his Hijazi subjects grew during the 1930s, the Consultative Council became the forum through which business interests were articulated at the highest level. Sometimes these disagreements involved regional loyalties. In an important case in 1932, a Nejdi merchant with strong ties to the regime, ʿAbdallah al-Jaffali, attempted to break agreements between importers and retailers and those between auctioneers and suppliers of local produce by appealing to the king on the basis of unfair competition. The king justified his position in al-Jaffali's favor as an attempt to protect consumers and pilgrims by enlarging the number of merchants and promoting competition. The Hijazi guilds and merchants viewed these policies as Nejdi

---

The House of Saud (London: Sidgwick & Jackson, 1981), 86–87; Alexander Bligh, *From Prince to King* (New York: New York University Press, 1984), 23–24, 27–28, 43.

[58] *Qarar Majlis al Shura* (Consultative Council Decrees) 375, 1346/6/17 (1927–28), on the court system; 89, 1346 (1927–28), on the system of assigning and monitoring treasury representatives in outlying areas; 52, 1346/6/18 (1927–28), on the First Summary Court; 50, 1346/2/18 (1927–28), on the system of central police in the outlying districts; and 66, 1346/7/4 (1927–28), on the establishment of buildings and salaries for mayors in city districts.

[59] There was considerable correspondence between the appointed mayors of the outlying areas and the Legislative Council; the archive is full of requests from the mayors for payment of various chits and for authorization from the Consultative Council to pay out various sums (e.g., "Document 505," 1346/7/7 [1927–28]). In addition, the Legislative Council kept close tabs on the amount of money owed the treasury by the various Hijazi provinces (e.g., "Council Orders" nos. 70, 71, 209, all passed in 1346 [1927–28]). Such clarifications, orders, and so on went either directly from the council, or from the king or governor through the council, which then transmitted orders to the provinces.

[60] For example, in the debate on the unification of the *takhrijiyyah* fees levied on goods entering or leaving the Hijaz for areas within the kingdom *Qarar Majlis al-Shura* 127, 1352/6/4 (1933–34) shows that the merchants of Al-Wajh, a port town in the Hijaz, successfully opposed the unification of this commodity tax as well as the raising of its rate. This decree ends: ". . . for all these reasons the [Consultative] Council supports the merchants and the previous decision on the rates to be charged and adds that when considering the *takhrijiyyah* fee or other taxes, consideration should be given to the public interest."

attempts to infiltrate their markets. After a series of meetings and debates between the king, representatives of the Legislative Council, the Trade Council, and key Jeddah and Mecca merchants, the Trade Council overturned the king's decision, arguing that market-sharing agreements between the merchants predated the new political authority and were legally upheld in a document signed by the merchants in 1878. The king's subsequent efforts to override the council were rejected because, as the Council argued, its earlier decision "stated the rights of the purchaser and the rights of the seller so as to avoid future conflict and disorder *and to avoid involving the rulers in conflicts which are not their concern.*"[61] Tensions in this initial period centered on the state's attempts to destroy local monopolies and monopsonies, to monitor commerce, and to impose higher taxes.[62] The unified opposition of the Hijazis reflected an initial unity of interest between the guilds and the merchants—which was soon to erode.

The rapidly obsolescing bargain between the king and the unified front of merchants and guilds was reflected in the three institutions that embodied the formal concessions granted in the first pact between business and government: the Trade Council, the Consultative Council, and the statutes of the Hijazi guilds. The coalition between the Hijazi commercial communities and the Al Saud was unstable because the Saudi economy was still exceedingly fragmented, lacking a legal, financial, and administrative system that could support the commercial expansion of the Hijazi elite. One group that stood in the way was the guilds of the Hijaz. Initially, they had been indispensable to the Al Saud, bridging a gap in the fiscal capacities of the government, performing the tasks of an extractive and administrative bureaucracy while the weak regime initiated a systematic drive to collect information on the Hijazi economy. In the late 1920s and early 1930s the government registered and categorized all economic groups and property, defraying costs through registration fees.[63] Detailed tax records of tribes and agricultural areas were completed. Offices were set up to monitor imports and customs and to gather information on the origin and destinations of imports and the sources of trade finance.[64] By the mid-1930s, this expansion of state capacity made the guilds a barrier

[61] Quoted from Legislative Council Decree 193, 1351/10/23 (1932–33).

[62] Prince Feisal's attempt to move the vendors of Mecca into central fixed shops was opposed by the Consultative Council, showing that even the smaller retailers had access to the council: *Qarar Majlis al-Shura* 394, 1349/8/77 (1930–31). Sometimes, after great debate, the treasury had its way despite the council, but only in minor issues: e.g., in *Qarar Wizarat al-Maliyah* 315, 1350/5/14 (1931–32), the council and the Taif merchants failed to convince the government that tobacco should be packaged in different grades and taxed accordingly.

[63] See *Qa'imah wa-Kashaf Mawdu'i bi-al-Anzimah al-Sa'udiyah al-Mawjudah bi-Markaz al-Watha'iq* (Riyadh: Institute for Public Administration, updated until 1986).

[64] In 1945, after its centralization and reorganization into a national institution, the Ministry of Finance made all importers register themselves and their importing activities. See *Umm al-Qura*, 23 March 1945; and "Announcement to Traders," *Um al-Qura*, 24 March 1944.

to economic statecraft. The guild system embodied restrictions to entry, price-fixing, monopolies, and monopsonies that prevented the expansion of the national market over the larger territories now effectively administered by the state. The Hijazi commercial elite, based in the great import houses of Jeddah, were key partners in an emerging state effort to destroy the guilds. As the strength of the state's institutions grew and slowly whittled away the independence of all three representative Hijazi bodies, only the merchant elite was reincorporated in an alternative organization—the *Majlis al-Shura* (Consultative Council). Thus, although the initial concessions won by the traditional merchant classes and guilds had been eclipsed by the 1960s, a partnership between the merchant elite and the state was created in its stead. It was a measure of the financial weakness of the regime and the power of the guilds that the tide did not turn decisively in favor of the Al Saud until the early 1950s, when oil royalties and a greater ability to borrow abroad eased the state's dependence on the revenues and administrative expertise of the Hijazis.

This growing cleft between the merchant elite and the guilds marked the lines along which the second pact would be built. By the 1940s, structural changes in the economy and the expanding administration of the government combined to unify a governmental-commercial coalition against the guilds. The state's efforts to guarantee supplies through the economic crises of the 1930s and 1940s meant that the continued functioning of the Hijaz as an enclave directly conflicted with the state's regulatory efforts and with its ability to stem shortages and fix domestic prices. The effects of restrictive market-sharing agreements became evident, however, before there was an administration strong enough to offer access to national markets. This stalemate continued until the entry of new technologies into the kingdom independently broke the bond between the guilds and the merchants and undercut the legal arrangements that had historically governed relations among the various service guilds. A key event was the spreading use of automobiles, which disrupted agreements between the insurance and transport guilds, affecting everything from their schedule of transfer payments to profit-sharing practices.[65] Technological changes generated disputes that fell outside the purview of guild law and increasingly led both guilds and merchants to seek mediation in

[65] The breakdown of the guild system under the strain of changes introduced by new technologies is detailed in the court records. Conflicts came to a head in 1953 and again in 1955. The long and complicated negotiations between the insurance and transportation guilds—those that cleaned camel refuse from the cities—and the Jeddah merchants who wished to cease using their services are recorded in *Qarar Majlis al-Shura* 110, 1374/10/27 (1954–55), and appended documents. Earlier, in 1931 the Turkish monopoly on the holy *Zamazamah* well and the *Zamazamah* guild was abolished. In this case changes in the government's schedule of fees to be collected by the *Zamazamah*, created disputes between that guild and the well-cleaner and water-bearer guild connected to the *Zamazamah*. Documents appended to *Qarar Majlis al-Shura* 196, 1351/10/26 (1932–33).

the king's courts. The weakening links between Hijazi commercial and guild law increasingly drew the king into the role of arbiter of disputes that had previously been settled outside state courts.

By the late 1930s the rift between guild and merchant elite interests was widely evident in the court records of the Hijaz.[66] Unlike the guilds, whose economic interests were based on the service economy of the *haj*, the merchants had much to gain from the formation of an integrated national market. The expansion of the state's administrative reach made this distinction ever more obvious. It was of little account that the merchants and the guilds were united in opposing regulations that opened up their enclave to competitors from the Nejd, or that they shared an interest in forestalling regulation to protect consumers. The balance of power shifted decisively with the emergence of a coalition of the Jeddawi importers and large commercial houses, which culminated in the elimination of the juridical, organizational, and economic independence of the guilds.

The resolution of the conflict found institutional expression in the transformation of the Consultative Council. Staffed by prominent Hijazis from both the guilds and the importers, the council had initially tried to preserve traditional price-fixing and profit-sharing arrangements against the king's edicts. In the 1920s and 1930s it had wide-ranging authority and took an active part in protecting the interests of both guilds and merchants, even when this meant opposing the king's decrees. In 1938, however, the growing unity of interests between the government and the merchant elite was embodied in the creation of a separate Council of Deputies (*Majlis al-Wukala'*), set up to review and sanction the decisions of the Consultative Council and, in particular, to consider "public affairs

[66] *Qarar Majlis al-Shura* 38, 1353/3/7 (1934–35) resolved a dispute between the transporters' guild, the insurers' guild, and the merchants of Mecca involving the *hamilin* guild (coolies). *Qarar Majlis al-Shura* 136, 1353/8/22 (1934–35), denies the application for a fifty-year exclusive contract from two merchants who thus tried to circumvent existing arrangements for exporting hides and animal products after the ritual Islamic sacrifice at Muna, "because it is difficult to separate fat from meat and violates existing agreements between the exporters and the slaughterers' guild." "Letter from the Merchants of Jeddah to the Governor of Mecca regarding the sale of the hides of animals" (no date) is summarized in *Qarar Imanat al-ʿAsimah* 1424, 1348/12/5 (1929–30), which mediates a conflict between the butchers and the merchants wishing to export the hides. Some disputes were between consumers and the providers of various services, such as one involving a laundryman and his customer: *Qarar Majlis al-Shura* 197, 1351/10/27 (1932–33). Interestingly, women, unprotected by existing guild and trade laws, often appealed to state authority to protect their rights as guild members' dependents. In all such cases found in the archives the government upheld the women's rights on the basis of Islamic law and paternalistic concern for the welfare of this least-represented segment of Hijazi society. Some cases involved relying on documents drafted by the government of King Hussein, as in a dispute between a widow and a merchant entrusted to handle her husband's estate: *Qarar Majlis al-Shura* 247, 1351/12/27 (1932–33). *Qarar Wizarat al-Maliyah* 872, 1355 (1936–37), supports the right of two daughters of a pilgrim guide to a share of his earnings until their sons reach maturity and can take over part of the business from the women's brothers.

touching the state and its preservation."[67] The two councils came into conflict often, mostly in matters relating to the collection and allocation of revenues and the regulation of the activities of the guilds and smaller merchants.[68] Eventually, the Council of Deputies replaced the Consultative Council altogether and, later, would be used by the government to achieve far wider corporative purposes.

OIL AND TAXATION IN THE 1950S AND 1960S

Twenty years of expansion and centralization culminated in 1950, when Ibn Saud issued the first comprehensive unified income tax legislation, exempting only the royal family, the various branches of the military and security forces, ambassadors, livestock taxed through *zakat*, official religious appointees, and those with annual incomes less than SR (Saudi riyals) 20,000. In the same year a Royal Decree reiterating the obligation of citizens to pay *zakat* was issued, and the Department of *Zakat* and Income Tax (DZIT) was created to assess and collect both taxes.[69]

The influx of substantial oil revenues in 1958 did not precipitate the complete withdrawal of taxation, but it did change the target, strengthening the extractive efforts of the Saudi state in some ways while allowing it to withdraw from particularly costly and destabilizing forms of taxation. Growing oil revenues in the late 1950s and 1960s led to a fundamental shift in taxation policies targeting commercial enterprises, contractors, foreign companies, and imports as primary sources of state revenue.[70] Collection of *zakat* and fees from nomads, farmers, and small traders and businessmen was pursued less aggressively. As imports rose, customs receipts became a more important source of revenue and grew at a swift

[67] The formation of the *Majlis al-Wukala'* was announced in June 1938. See "Letter from Sir R. Bullard to Viscount Halifax," 28 June 1938, PRO, FO vol. 21903, E 4187/196/25. Examples of the council's agendas can be found in *Qarar Majlis al-Wukala'* 19, 1356/4/8, and 32, 1356/6/9 (1937–38). A review of many such agendas shows that the *Majlis al-Wukala'* was not a deliberative body in the same sense as the *Majlis al-Shura*. Policy designed in the latter was either amended or rejected by the former. The long debates, including statements and letters from citizens and civil associations, which characterize almost all of the meetings of the *Shura* are altogether missing from the deliberations of the *Wukala'*.

[68] An example in *Qarar Majlis al-Wukala'* 88, 1355/11/28 (1936–37), concerns the registration of the trade activities, addresses, and names of all seaport traders for the purpose of collecting customs as well as "knowing their whereabouts."

[69] Income tax: *Marsum Malaki* 17/2/28/3321, "Nizam Daribat al-Dakhl," 1370/1/21 (October 1950). The DZIT, created by Ministry of Finance Decree 394, dated 1370/8/7 (1950), was located in Jeddah; it was moved to Riyadh in 1970. See also *Marsum Malaki* 17/2/28/8634, "Nizam Faridat al-Zakah," 1370/6/29 (1950).

[70] Decree of the President of the Council of Ministers 161, 1374/11/15 (1954–55), divided foreign contractors into three classes with taxes ranging from SR 800 to 6,000 per year and added fees to be paid for licenses from the Office of Labor and Workers, income tax for foreign and Saudi employees, registration fees, and municipality taxes.

rate. Other indirect taxes included road fees, municipal fees, poll taxes, stamp fees, and various charges for government services.

The changes were not linear but punctuated by reversals due to political exigencies and institutional constraints. The late 1950s and early 1960s were a turbulent time for the Al Saud as a succession battle coincided with the rise of Pan-Arabism and secular socialism in the region. Pan-Arabism bifurcated the Al Saud and eventually drew them into a proxy war with Egypt's Gamal Abdel Nasser on Yemeni soil. Ibn Saud himself became an idiosyncratic factor in fiscal policy in his final years: in 1950, to please his subjects in the age-old tradition of tribal rulers, having just issued the Regulations Governing *Zakat* three months earlier, he cut the Islamic tithe payments in half.[71] In 1952, the last year of his life, he made a special concession to the politically prominent region of Qasim in the Nejd, authorizing its governor, Prince ʿAbdallah, to collect and allot the agricultural tithe locally and exempting him from remitting any revenues to the national treasury.[72] And in the same year he canceled the pilgrimage fees that had formed the backbone of state finance since the conquest of the Hijaz.[73]

Fiscal policy and spending were to become central in the power struggle between the technocrat Prince Feisal and the populist King Saud: from Ibn Saud's death in 1952 until Saud was deposed in 1964, the Saudi bureaucracy became an arena for competition between the two camps. The result was a series of reversals in the patterns of centralization described above.[74] Conflicting regulations were issued by the president of the Council of Ministers (Feisal) and the king (Saud) on several occa-

[71] This tax was collected regularly until 1948, the year the first substantial influx of oil revenues flowed into the Saudi treasury. In the economic recession of the early 1950s, the *zakat* was resumed by royal decree.

[72] Letter from King ʿAbd al-ʿAziz to Prince ʿAbd Allah ibn ʿAbd al-ʿAziz, "al-Samah li-Ahl al-Qasim bi-Jabayah wa-Tawzih Zakat al-Aradh bi-Unfusihim" [Permission to the Qasimis to Collect and Allocate the Land *Zakat* by Themselves], 12 Ramadan 1371 (January 1952), in *Majmuʿat Anzimah: Daribat al-Dakhl wa-Daribat al-Turk wa-Faridat al-Zakah* [Ministry of Finance and National Economy, Department of Zakat and Income Tax] (Riyadh: Government Printing Press, 1977), 559.

[73] On the reduction of dues from pilgrims in 1952 D. M. Riches wrote: "It has also pointed clearly to the shift in the economic center of gravity of the country in recent years. The Wahhabbi conquest of the Hijaz brought them wealth beyond their dreams and the pilgrimage revenue subsidized Najd and the rest of the country. . . . Now the Hejaz and the rest of the country are parasitic on the oil fields of the Hassa and the very pilgrimage revenues can be removed as a gesture or an old King's whim": "Letter from D.M.H. Riches," May 1952, PRO, FO vol. 98847. The Royal Decree published on 23 May 1952 canceled all centrally collected pilgrimage dues and proclaimed that all remaining dues were to be collected in Jeddah. The British legation estimated that this resulted in an annual loss of £2–3 million.

[74] For the succession conflict, see, e.g., Holden and Johns, *House of Saud,* 118–287; Lackner, *House Built on Sand*; and Bligh, *From Prince to King.* Despite what its name suggests, Ibrahim Al Rashid's collection of correspondence from the American Embassy in the 1950s—*The Struggle between the Two Princes* (Chapel Hill, N.C.: Documentary Publications, 1985)—has no bearing on the politics of the Saud-Feisal conflict.

sions. Divisions within the royal family during this turbulent period augmented the power of the religious elite as arbiters of the conflict and reintroduced religious doctrine into fiscal policy debates.[75] In 1955, as part of an overall effort to gain popular support in his fight to keep the throne, King Saud abolished the income tax for all Saudis, stating clearly that citizens, as Muslims in an Islamic state, were not liable to any taxes but the *zakat*. In the same year, a conflicting law originating from Feisal, as the head of the Council of Ministers, announced the continuation of all the taxes Saud had canceled.[76]

In 1955, Feisal issued a proclamation reinstating the tax laws of 1950 and abolished all subsequent amendments; he then managed to have King Saud sign an implementation law.[77] In 1963, as crown prince, Feisal issued a Royal Decree ordering all Saudis participating in joint ventures, limited partnerships, and other business affairs involving foreigners to pay *zakat*, regardless of the taxes paid by their foreign partners. The 1963 *zakat* rules specifically earmarked the religious tithe for the newly created General Organization for Social Insurance (GOSI), a fund for retired, disabled, and needy citizens which was later expanded to include a pension program for foreign workers.[78]

Pilgrimage fees were twice reinstated by Feisal, in 1959 and in 1967, both times in response to King Saud's cancellation of the dues. The second reinstatement begins by addressing the "present misunderstanding about the entry fees for people and goods coming into the kingdom for the *haj*, or trade, or work, or visits" and ends with the following statement: "As for the misunderstanding, it came from the announcement that the fees were excused for the *hajis* [pilgrims]. However, this tax must continue in light of the many expenditures made by the government for the *hajis*. The only exemptions to any taxes are those granted by the Council

[75]This was a dangerous precedent: religious objections to taxes other than *zakat* were regularly invoked by the commercial class in the recession of the 1980s. In practical terms, the introduction of religious doctrine into fiscal policy debates placed constraints on tax policy even in the 1960s. During Feisal's reign (1964–75) new central taxes were called "fees," since under a strict interpretation of Islamic legal principles, an Islamic government cannot tax income and profits directly in any other way than the religiously sanctioned *zakat*.

[76] *Marsum Malaki* 17/2/28/576, 1376/3/14 (1956–57); *Qarar Ri'asat Majlis al-Wuzara'* 26, 1376/2/8 (1956–57).

[77] "Building upon what the financial situation requires regarding the needed increase in revenues for the state and the problem of changing the Shari'a *zakat* from its prescribed amount, . . . it is necessary to create an income tax that conforms with the development of the quality of life and economy of the country and builds upon the current practices of taxation in the rest of the world": *Qarar Ri'asat Majlis al-Wuzara'* 31, 1376/2/2 (1956–57). Feisal initiated the resumption of complete tax collection in *Qarar* 645, which preceded *Marsum Malaki* 17/2/28/577, 1376/3/14 (November 1956). His decree instructs the office of the president to draft a Royal Decree to carry out the reinstatement of the *zakat* tax; see *M'ajmuat Anzimah*, 567.

[78] *Marsum Malaki* 1/5/61, 1383/1/5 (1963).

of Ministers and *no one else had the authority or right to grant exemptions*" (emphasis added).[79] A similar pattern characterized other tax regimes[80] including the road fees.[81]

In short, taxes on wealth, income, and profits escalated during the 1950s and 1960s, even though sharp but temporary reversals of policy hampered efficient collection. More important, the central place of the fisc in the struggle suggested that the comparatively moderate flows of oil revenues did not automatically lead to the rentier syndrome that typified the 1970s. To be sure, without oil revenues, Saud's use of tax policy in the power struggle over the throne would have been impossible. But more than anything, Saud's personal style of governance, heavily influenced by his long tenure as governor of Riyadh and the surrounding provinces, played a crucial role in his use of populist policies to gain support.[82] Taxation was a political issue of substantial import, not least because in 1958,

[79] The first law of reinstatement is *Khitab Wizarat al-Maliyah* 13/1/4/1213, 1380/6/16 (1960–61). The second reinstatement asserts the continuation of the law that pilgrims pay a head tax to the transportation companies, taxes on incoming passengers collected in the kingdom, and levies on all their goods: *Qarar Ri'asat Majlis al-Wuzara'* 803, 1389/10/15 (1969–70).

[80] Two other conflicts between Saud and Feisal concerned whether the stamp fees must be paid by army personnel, and whether the government would collect customs and road taxes. As usual, Saud had issued orders that soldiers were exempt, causing confusion. Feisal wrote to the minister of interior: "In accordance with the set procedures, the most recent law applies and soldiers are to pay the stamp tax. The bill that I mention is valid because it is drafted by the Ministerial Council": *Amr Sami* 1/8175, "Letter from Prince Feisal to the Minister of Interior," 1375/12/28 (1955–56). Again, with the issue of *Amr Sami* (Diwan Ri'asat Majlis al-Wuzara') 20816, 1384/9/2 (1964–65) (later in *Khitab Wizarat al-Maliyah wa-al-Iqtisad al-Watani* [Letter from the Ministry of Finance and National Economy] 3/4/1482, 1385/2/3 [1965]), all army and National Guard personnel were exempted from paying the road tax. Hence, in 1966 Feisal was forced to dispel rumors by restating that the existing customs duties and the road tax were still the law: "The import and tax of goods is governed by the known customs duties and taxes and by special arrangements between countries. Only the Council of Ministers, at the request of the Minister of Finance and the Minister of Trade and Industry, can change these and, even in these cases, only for the purpose of encouraging national industry and agricultural products": *Marsum Maliki* (al-Diwan al-Malikiyah) M/5, 1388/2/28 (1968–69).

[81] The road tax was promulgated in 1954 by a Council of Ministers Decree signed by Feisal and pronounced law in 1958. The same year Feisal sent an announcement to all government agencies noting that no capitalists or even members of the royal family were to be exempt: *Ta'mim Diwan Ri'asat Majlis al-Wuzara'* 1/5278, 1378/8/13 (1958). It was almost repealed in 1959 by King Saud, but preserved by Feisal, and in 1964 made incumbent even on day workers: *Amr Sami* 7487, 1379/4/23 (1959), signed by Feisal as president of the Council of Ministers. *Ministry of Finance Circular* 1/4/8283, 1383/7/4 (1963–64), noted that many government departments had stopped collecting the 2 percent road tax from daily workers, ". . . due to a misinterpretation of a Royal Decree, which is thought to excuse these workers," and reasserted that every government employee must pay the tax, including previously exempt day laborers whose salaries exceeded 500 qirsh per month. The road fees were thus essentially a direct 2 percent payroll tax, the revenues used to build infrastructure.

[82] Feisal, who had served as governor of Hijaz and as foreign minister, was less influenced by Nejdi traditions, which—in theory if not often in practice—associate leadership with the flow of wealth from the top of the social hierarchy to the lower levels.

when Feisal was given full powers to manage the finances of the kingdom, the government was deeply in debt, despite the dramatic increase in oil revenues that year.

Once in charge, Feisal unrelentingly pursued the centralization of the bureaucracy. The 1960s were marked by a burst of administrative reform and a rationalization of extractive and administrative agencies showing continuity with earlier patterns. New institutions, ranging from the General Organization for Social Security (GOSI) to the Central Planning Organization and the National Airlines, were created.[83] The 1960s were Saudi Arabia's modern moment: the creation of new departments and ministries, the increasing predictability of procedures and outcomes, the preciseness of the stated principles that underlay action, the formal coherence of administrative rules, the explicit articulation of a means-end rationality, and a clear differentiation of the functions and authority within and between departments and ministries matched the ideal-type process of Weberian "rationalization."

The administrative reforms of the 1960s and the resulting growth in the Saudi bureaucracy rested on renewed governmental efforts to refine the quality of information available to the state, as the role of government departments in regulating the national economy was itself growing. The drive to implement unified national taxation on personal and corporate incomes coincided with unified budgets and procedures developed for and enforced in all municipalities, ministries, and departments. Administrative autonomy in reallocating tax revenues was eliminated, and mechanisms were devised to centralize budgeting and spending.[84]

These changes were clearly reflected in the organization of extractive and regulatory institutions. Integral to these changes was the penetration of the Ministry of Finance and National Economy into various other ministries to supervise accounts in an effort to ensure adherence to uniform reporting and contracting rules. The escalation of regulatory and extractive efforts resulted in the development of a sense of mission in the DZIT and Ministry of Finance which mirrored the emergence of an overall means-end calculus between revenues extracted from society and the services provided by state.

Not surprisingly, these changes began with and were made possible by more efficient collection of accurate information. In 1955 serious efforts were made to update the Commercial Register—for purposes of taxing employees (through road taxes) and profits—and to collect municipality

[83] These developments are detailed in Ibrahim al-Awaji, "Bureaucracy and Society in Saudi Arabia" (Ph.D diss., University of Virginia, 1971), and Lackner, *House Built on Sand.*

[84] E.g., Ministry of Finance and National Economy Announcement 1382/21, 1382/4/11 (1962) and Ministry of Finance and National Economy Announcement 1/4/4166, 1384/4/3 (1964) both set up new procedures for the accounting, budgetary, revenue-gathering, and remitting procedures to be used by all government departments.

fees.[85] In 1963 these efforts were redoubled when the DZIT specifically targeted Saudi merchants and industrialists in an effort to assess their income, holdings, profits, partnership structure, and the number of employees. Procedures were designed whereby the Commercial Registry, DZIT, Customs Department, and Ministry of Commerce and Industry cooperated to gather information. Specific forms of documentation and certification for each tax to which both foreigners and Saudis were subject began to be required and enforced by law. As with income tax, DZIT officials utilized local contacts to locate and inspect the commercial, agricultural, or personal property of the taxpayer and to assess the *zakat.* Extensive regulations were issued to close loopholes in commercial tax laws.[86]

In 1950 the DZIT had already become a distinct office within the Ministry of Finance. In 1959 the Saudi Arabian Monetary Agency (SAMA), previously subservient to the dictates of the Minister of Finance, was given additional responsibility, including a wide mandate to ensure closer adherence to the national budgets, the power to supervise ministerial accounts, and the right to redeploy deposits. In the 1950s and 1960s the various offices within the Ministry of Finance—Petroleum, Industry and Commerce, Labor and Social Affairs, and Planning—were spun off, first into separate agencies and then into autonomous ministries, showing an increasing pattern of diversification and specialization within and among the economic ministries. The most extreme case of this pattern was the separation of the Ministry of Petroleum, an agency that cooperated closely with the Ministry of Finance to monitor the activities of ARAMCO, the biggest taxpayer in the kingdom. In 1960 the Institute for Public Administration (IPA) was established to train bureaucrats, planners, and technocrats for the growing bureaucracy.

At the same time that diversification and specialization were taking place, the financial departments of the newly created ministries were centralized by staffing them with employees of the Ministry of Finance and National Economy (MFNE) itself. This centralization would prove invaluable in controlling and monitoring government spending during the financial crisis of 1955–58, as all checks issued by any government agency had to be cosigned by the in-house representative of MFNE. All financial

[85] Within one year the Commercial Registry was able to gather complete information on 25 percent of the merchants and 60 percent of the companies in the kingdom. The period of registration was extended for retailers ("Because most of the merchants are illiterate and cannot read . . . and if the fines are applied, about 5,000 shops will be closed in Jeddah alone"), but wholesale merchants and companies faced stringent fines that year for failing to register: *Qarar Ri'asat Majlis al-Wuzara'* 70, 1377/3/12 (1957–58).

[86] See Department of *Zakat* and Income Tax Circulars A/1/2/7213/2/1, 1383/8/7 (1963); D/1/19/7123/10/1, 1383/8/5 (1963); and D/1/16/6819/2/1, 1383/7/28 (1963). For schedules and collection methods for taxes on cars, the road tax, and commercial taxes, see *Qarar Majlis al-Shura* 80, 1346/7/23 (1927–28); and *Marsum Malaki* 6381, 1372/7/21 (1952–53).

matters, however trivial, were the province of these representatives, who maintained direct links with MFNE and SAMA.[87] This system streamlined the collection of taxes from foreign employees and from Saudis by withholding taxes from salaries (and for Saudis, *zakat* and road taxes) on a monthly basis within the relevant government department.[88] The collection of road tax and *zakat* revenues from the government departments was also made more efficient: previously, departments had added these revenues to their annual budgets, but starting in 1969 they were required to remit all collections to SAMA, which then distributed the yearly funds budgeted for each department. A special office was formed to calculate all personal income taxes and customs under a committee whose responsibility it was to set up communications systems among all government agencies and offices and to ensure that unified fees were collected in all parts of the kingdom.[89] Finally, to centralize the revenues from *zakat*, the road tax, and income tax—three taxes that the Ministry of Commerce thought it should be collecting—a system of stamps was instituted to ensure that revenues made their way back to the DZIT.[90] Consistent with its new role, DZIT developed a sense of mission, which was expressed in numerous letters to the Minister of Finance and the Council of Ministers and announcements to all departments of the bureaucracy complaining of their lack of cooperation. At base, the problem was that bureaucratic agencies did not report detailed information on their own employees, nor

[87] Al-Awaji, "Bureaucracy and Society."

[88] Department of *Zakat* and Income Tax Circular D1/16/6819/2/1, 1383/7/28 (1963).

[89] Council of Ministers Decree 238, dated 1383/4/2 (1963).

[90] The confusion arose because, earlier, four different government offices—the *Majlis al-Shura*, the Ministry of Trade, the Ministry of Interior, and the municipal governments—were responsible for collecting different fees and taxes from contractors and other commercial enterprises. The old system was inefficient. For the old law and collection methods, see *Qarar Ri'asat Majlis al-Wuzara'* 161, 1374/11/15 (1954–55). The mandate of DZIT to collect directly all but the municipality taxes is outlined in "Letter from the Representative of the Minister of Finance to the General Director of the *Zakat* and Income Tax Department," no. 3/4105 (1963): "With respect to letter 1/5/8178/45/1/D from the Department of *Zakat*, it is necessary that the current expenses office express its concern that the validation stamps which are given for employment wages in companies and agencies are the responsibility of DZIT and its branches, and that this responsibility is disputed by the Commerce Ministry and other agencies. There is no doubt that DZIT is responsible for collecting road tax of 2 percent from the salary of employees and workers in factories, companies, and agencies and also for collecting income tax. Collecting these two taxes is not possible unless there is a centralization of the operations between the branches and the central office of DZIT. For this it is necessary to issue stamps that are uniformly used by all the offices and all employees must send lists of the monthly wages of their employees to branches of DZIT. If this is not done at this time, DZIT should issue an announcement in the local newspapers asking all factories, companies, and establishments to present it with two copies of their employee lists. We await a receipt of the copy of the newspaper announcement to be issued." Ministry of Finance Circular 2/4/7684, "From the Minister of Finance and the Monetary Agency to the Department of *Zakat* and Income Tax," 1383/6/20 (1963–64), outlines the use of validation stamps. Using the stamps as a verification of tax payments is detailed in Department of *Zakat* and Income Tax Letter 2/5/294, 1389/1/12 (1969–70).

did they cooperate in gathering information on the contractors they used for various projects. These failures to comply resulted in new rules, mandated at the highest level, which decreed that no individual or company, Saudi or foreign, be awarded any government contracts without positive proof that it was registered with the DZIT and had paid its previous year's tax and *zakat*.[91]

In concrete terms, the changes introduced under Feisal were successful: both direct and indirect taxes doubled between 1961 and 1968. As in most developing countries, indirect taxes averaged 76 percent of domestic revenue in those years. The efforts of the bureaucracy continued apace, despite the fact that total domestic tax revenues never rose above 7 percent of all state revenues, which consisted, in the main, of oil rents extracted from ARAMCO, Getty, and the Japanese Oil Company.

Oil revenues did have some effects. In the late 1950s, while taxes on the modern business sector expanded, those that were politically disruptive and difficult to collect were slowly abandoned. Direct and intrusive taxes had formed the basis for initial demands for representation at the local level and constituted the basis for bargaining between social groups. To the extent that these taxes had been the source of healthy conflict between the government and the citizens, their demise would have implications for politics and for political activism. In fact, some of the institutional responses that typified the boom years can be traced to the decade of the 1960s. Most important among these was the government's reliance on indirect forms of information collection for tax purposes. As imports grew, for example, data gathered at the customs offices became a supplementary method of assessing corporate and individual taxes. In addition, with the growth of the state's role as a purchaser of goods and services, state agencies began to mediate the collection of information on foreign and domestic contractors and importers. The extractive agencies had begun to replace direct assessments with information from other branches of the bureaucracy. In the 1970s this became the only source of information, with the result that key aspects of economic statecraft shifted from

[91] Ministry of Finance and National Economy Letter 1/4/5624, 1387/5/11 (1967–68), notes that the workers of DZIT get no cooperation in assessing the correct number of contracts being undertaken by foreign and local companies because "it is in the interest of the ministries to allow the companies to go without paying tax . . . From now on it is ordered that all ministries report the contracts with companies to DZIT so that the treasury is able to collect its due." Ministry of Finance Announcement 13/1/4/6006, "To All Ministries and Departments" (19 October 1960), asks them to help DZIT assess and collect taxes from employees and contractors. Finally, Department of *Zakat* and Income Tax Letter 8853, 1391/4/20 (1971–72) resulted in the rule that all government contractors produce a certificate of payment of *zakat* and income tax before being awarded further contracts: President of the Council of Ministers Letter 8853, "To the Minister of Interior," art. 2 of the appended Council of Ministers Decree, 1391/4/20 (1971–72). Documentation of these bureaucratic struggles is found in *Majmu'at Anzimah,* 245–505.

the realm of direct bargaining between social groups and the state into the realm of bureaucratic politics.[92]

Oil revenues allowed the government to withdraw particularly disruptive forms of taxation, but the account of Saudi Arabia in the 1960s suggests that moderate inflows of such revenues, no matter how significant to state finance, can be used in the service of creating a modern extractive and regulatory bureaucracy and stabilizing exchange. Thus, even though some taxes were repealed (those on citizens with lower incomes and those that were too expensive or labor-intensive), they were replaced with others that were more appropriate to the expanding modern sector.[93] The burst of administrative growth and rationalization of bureaucratic agencies that accompanied new taxes on commerce and wage earners in the 1960s was coupled with a decline in *zakat* taxes levied on nomads and those Saudis living in outlying areas. Taxing remote areas and nomadic communities was expensive, impractical (the DZIT, like other parts of the bureaucracy, faced a severe labor shortage in the 1960s), and politically unpalatable.[94] In 1962, estimates of the cost of sending representatives to collect *zakat* from the region of Hail, for example, were more than twice the estimated *zakat* receipts.[95] The 1962 delegation of tax collectors was the last one to be sent to the nomads and farmers of the northern and eastern provinces, and it was sent only because the arrangements had already been made. And so, the accounts of pursuing the bedouin, of reassessing the farmers, of goose chases in the desert came to an end.

[92] Another pattern that began in the 1960s and was carried to its extreme in the boom years was the devolution of responsibilities for basic regulatory policies to the chambers of commerce, and, ultimately, the merchants and contractors themselves. Key issues were information about market prices and subsidies, and the enforcement of fixed prices for subsidized basic goods. Thus, the overall independent position of the extractive institutions was weakening at the very time that new drives for revenue-gathering were being initiated and increased responsibility laid on customs, chambers of commerce, and nonextractive branches of the bureaucracy.

[93] Among the taxes and fees withdrawn were taxes on cars going to Kuwait (*Amr Sami* 11035, 1373/11/14 [1953–54]); port fees for small vessels (6 April 1939, PRO, FO vol. 23267, E 3190/98/25); fishing licenses and taxes on fish (previously an important source of revenue and concern, as reflected in Deputy Prime Minister Letter 5887, "To the Ministry of Interior," 1351/8/13 [1932–33], and *Qarar Majlis al-Shura* 141, 1353/8/25 [1934–35]). The fishing fee was lifted in the mid-1960s with *Marsum Malaki* 2, 1385/3/12 (1965–66).

[94] It is possible to judge the severity of the DZIT labor shortage by noting that in 1955, plans to tax transit goods were shelved for lack of collectors, treasurers, workers, and a warehouse where goods might be stored while being evaluated: *Qarar Ri'asat Majlis al-Wuzara'* 83, 1376/9/13 (1956–67).

[95] Estimated expenditures needed to collect *zakat* from remote areas of Hail, the northern province, and the southern province of Asir were SR 56,720 and 26,510, respectively, but the total revenue expected from Hail was only SR21,585 for 1962. These figures are recorded in a Council of Ministers' Decree, which recognizes that the collection is not cost-effective but authorizes it anyway, since local personnel were expecting the delegation, and car rental arrangements for travel had already been made: *Qarar Ri' asat Majlis al-Wuzara'* 244, 1382/4/17 (1962–63).

Business and State on the Eve of the Boom

The struggle between Saud and Feisal linked up with underlying divisions in Saudi society in complex ways. To be sure, the former's tenure as governor of Riyadh and the latter's as governor of the Hijaz and as foreign minister had shaped their personal styles. Yet the divide between the two princes was not just between "traditional" and "cosmopolitan" forms of governance but also between their divergent social bases of support. These latent conflicts came to a head in 1953 when Saud, in his first act as king, reorganized the administration of the Hijaz on the Nejdi model, installing his own supporters and strengthening the religious Shariʿa courts at the expense of the secular Hijazi ones. Having gone through many iterations, the coalition between Feisal and the top tier of Hijazi merchants was being consolidated at the time. Feisal's reforms and, indeed, the entire prior process of institutional expansion and centralization had won the support of the Hijazi merchant elite, which had willfully participated in the elimination of the guilds and bargained away much of its own autonomy in return for a voice in national economic policy. By the 1960s the business class had been transformed from an independent force struggling to preserve its control over the rules governing private enterprise to a corporate group with strong institutional links to the government, based on mutually recognized interests. The expanding national economy, government infrastructure, and increasingly stable legal environment and the state's summary treatment of both labor and Pan-Arabist republicans had created an ideal environment for investors. Having struggled and failed to preserve their almost complete control over the market during the period when the state had little to offer, by the 1960s the business elite had developed a close consultative relationship with the new regulatory state. Saud's constituency among the tribal elites of the Nejd and his later resort to Pan-Arabism were anathema to the Hijazi commercial elites. Whatever their qualms about Feisal's national tax reforms, they had strong incentives to join their fortunes to the prince and his economic program.

The new partnership between the Hijazi commercial elite and the "modernist" Prince Feisal was based on a construction of business-government relations that excluded the Hijazi guilds. Three linked structural changes fostered the simultaneous narrowing and strengthening of the developmentalist coalition: the growth of regulatory institutions, the expanding role of the state in the economy, and the consolidation of the traditional business class itself.

The centralization of national regulatory institutions had, as I argued earlier, been a prerequisite for winning the enduring support of the Hijazi merchant elite. Regulation of the private sector occurred in tandem with policies designed to expand the scope of national commerce and industry. It included a systematic program, implemented through the newly created Ministries of Commerce and Finance and National Economy, to monitor prices, consult with the Chambers of Commerce, study and recommend protective tariffs, and collect information on all issues relating to commerce and trade—including the distribution of subsidies, registration of companies, and enforcement of the boycott on Israeli products.[96] Regulation involved the encroachment of the state into a variety of areas, including the control of foreign currency expenditures,[97] taxation, information gathering, law,[98] and the selective protection of local industries. The realm of commercial and labor law expanded,[99] and regulations governing labor, complete with a court to hear disputes between business and labor, were instituted in 1969.[100] An increasing number of disputes between government agencies and private contractors led, in 1955, to the creation of the Board of Grievances, which heard cases against state agencies.[101]

The growth of infrastructure and construction projects financed by the government in the 1960s enhanced the regulatory capacities of the state and generated the tools for creating corporatist associations. Private-sector companies were required to register with the government and to join the chambers of commerce as a prerequisite for bidding on government contracts.[102] The new registration laws naturally favored established busi-

[96] *Qarar Ri'asat Majlis al-Wuzara'* 66, "Laws and Regulations of the Ministry of Commerce," 1374/4/6 (1954).

[97] Foreign Currency Control Committees were created in Jeddah, Riyadh, and Dammam to review applications for import and export permits. Each committee was to serve as a repository for all information regarding the use of foreign currency, imports, and exports: *Amr Malaki* 2393/3/3/3, 1376/11/24 (1956–57). This regulation supplemented previous attempts to stop the smuggling of goods and currency by forcing traders in the rural hinterland to register their names with the Customs Office and provide complete accounts of imported goods: *Qarar Ri'asat Majlis al-Wuzara'* 76, 1373/10/7 (1953–54).

[98] *Royal Decree* 21/1/4470, "Regulations of the Commercial Register and Implementing Rules," and *Qarar Ri'asat Majlis al-Wuzara'* 54, 1375/4/29 (1956), were published in *Umm al-Qura* 1640, 18 June 1956. In 1965 the term "trader" was broadened to include many merchants, contractors, and professionals not previously included who had therefore avoided the payment of dues and responsibilities that registration entailed: *Qarar Ri'asat Majlis al-Wuzara'* 155, 1387/3/15 (1967–68). Stringent sanctions were carried out for those who did not comply. *Qarar Diwan Ri'asat Majlis al-Wuzara'* 862, 1386/12/25 (1966–67), concerns a particular trader, Abu Bakr ba Sa'bah, whose registration was four months late; the decree states that his case ". . . should be a lesson to others."

[99] See *Marsum Malaki* 2932/4/12, 1378/11/30 (1958–59), which corrects Royal Decree 1008/5/2/35, 1374/7/17 (1954–55). In the early 1970s these rules were given extra substance by setting up standard procedures whereby either private individuals or state agencies were to report business fraud and abuses: Ministry of Commerce Circular 7/3/7/12/1701, 1393/12/29 (1973–74).

[100] In Royal Decree M/21, "Labor and Workmen Regulations" (1969), art. 179 sanctions the creation of a Committee for Labor Disputes.

[101] Royal Decree 2/138759, "Board of Grievances Regulations" (1955), was repealed in 1982.

[102] *Qarar Ri'asat Majlis al-Wuzara'* 155, 1385/3/15 (1965–66); Ministry of Commerce Circular 3/3511, 1382/2/26 (1962–63). Earlier, to encourage traders to register, and in re-

nesses in the Hijaz over less experienced entrants from the other provinces.

In designing and implementing these policies, the government increasingly sought the advice and practical assistance of the private sector. The chambers of commerce registered commercial and contracting firms, monitored the allocation of state subsidies, prevented private-sector fraud, and advised the government on a host of economic issues.[103] When, to cite one critical example, the government began to allocate foreign currency through the Foreign Currency Committee in 1959, it actively sought the advice of the chambers.[104] The expansion of the state's regulatory capacities created the means to implement protective legislation against foreign competitors, and the growing corporatist relationship between the chambers and the government provided the channels of communication through which private-sector preferences became policy. The entry of non-Saudis into small commercial ventures was prohibited, and pilgrims, some of whom had routinely stayed in the kingdom to participate in trade, were prevented from starting up enterprises.[105] Most important, the

---

sponse to complaints of the high registration fees, the Council of Ministers had canceled the dues for Saudi companies but kept the requirement to register yearly: *Qarar Ri'asat Majlis al-Wuzara'* 310, "Algha Rusum al-Sajl al-Tijari," 1380/7/21 (1960–61).

[103] E.g., *Qarar Ri'asat Majlis al-Wuzara'* 22, 1383/1/7 (1963–64), outlines the role of the chamber and the Ministry of Commerce in distributing and monitoring the government subsidy for sugar and monitoring scarcities of basic goods in the local markets.

[104] Examples of such in-depth analysis of local needs and of balancing protection of local industry with consumers' interests are in *Marsum Malaki* 21 (cement), 1379/11/20 (1959–60); Council of Ministers Decree 222 (pasta), 1379/11/18 (1959–60); Council of Ministers Decree 211 (cement), 1379/11/14 (1959–60); Council of Ministers Decree 512 (clothes), 1386/6/24 (1966–67); Customs Department Letter 1/7197, 1377/6/2 (1957–58); Council of Ministers Decree 254 (Arab Oil Co.), 1387/2/12 (1967–68). Decisions were made on the basis of factory and product-level calculations, which take into account local protection from competition, preferential rates on raw materials, etc. As a more general example, all customs duties on iron used for industrial purposes were removed in 1959: Council of Ministers Decree 21, 1380/1/4 (1960–61), and *Marsum Malaki* 7, 1380/1/4 (1960–61). Semifinished goods for local factories were exempted in the same year: Council of Ministers Decree 259, 1379/12/28 (1959–60). Industrial machinery had been exempted from customs in 1951 (Council of Ministers Decree 89, [February 1951]), and tariffs on some goods were later raised to protect domestic industry (Council of Ministers Decree 1961, 1396/11/15 [1976]). Luxury goods such as cars and electronics were heavily taxed (15 percent and 40 percent, respectively), as they were not considered priorities.

[105] *Amr Sami* 14191, 1386/3/19 (1966), and *Qarar Ri'asat Majlis al-Wuzara'* 324, 1386/5/19 (1966), prohibited non-Saudis from conducting trade in the northern areas and denied all non-Saudis new shops for trading. On the protection of Saudi citizens from Sudanese and Hadrami merchants who had previously been free to enter into trade, see *Qarar Ri'asat Majlis al-Wuzara'* 609, 1387/7/15 (1967). The decision to grant business permits to Hadramis already engaged in trade was postponed in 1966 until the Ministers' Council made a decision regarding the status of non-Saudis engaged in retail and wholesale trade. This was a particularly thorny problem in the Hijaz, where a large part of the merchant community was composed of migrants from Hadramaut. In the mid-1960s, during Saudi Arabia's war with Egyptian troops in the Yemen Arab Republic and the Adeni revolution, the status of the Hadrami merchants was further complicated: *Amr Sami* 26577, 1386/11/20 (1966). These directives abolished King Saud's earlier decree allowing all Arab traders mar-

merchants were protected against the flagrant conversion of political power to profit (which would occur in the 1970s with the open entry of government officials and princes into commercial ventures): the 1956 law prohibiting the participation of civil servants and princes in private business was strengthened and stringently enforced beginning in 1959, when several ministers were reprimanded for engaging in private business ventures.[106]

The second structural change that favored the emergence of the developmentalist coalition was the expanding role of the state in the economy. As the government began to regulate imports directly and to initiate construction projects and tax, the private sector, still dominated by the old commercial classes of the Hijaz, increasingly assumed the role of partner. The chambers of commerce began to receive significant subsidies from the government, and their charters clearly reflect the new partnership, emphasizing the importance of actively advising the government on a wide range of economic issues.[107] Some members of the Jeddah Chamber of Commerce resigned in protest against increasing government intervention in the affairs of the private sector, but the cooperative trend was clearly dominant. In 1961 the Jeddah Chamber laid out a specific set of policies formalizing its role in the formulation of economic policy.[108]

---

ket access if they registered with the Company Registration Office but (with obvious political motivation) ordered all non-Arabs to leave the kingdom immediately: *Marsum Malaki* 2860/12/12, 1378/11/22 (1958). *Amr Malaki ila Diwan Ri'asat Majlis al-Wuzara'* 1155, 1380/1/17 (1960), brings to the attention of the council the complaint of several Saudi merchants against the continuing stay of some foreign pilgrims and their participation in trade.

[106] The 1956 law, issued by Feisal, imposed a large fine and ten years' imprisonment on any government employee who participated in any economic activity apart from his government job. State employees who accepted gifts, favors, or promises of future favors (monetary or not) were also to be punished, as were those who resolved personal problems by means of government influence, used the administrative apparatus for any personal ends, or abused power in any other way: *Amr Sami, min Diwan Ri'asat Majlis al-Wuzara'* 150, 1377/11/25 (1957–58). *Amr Sami* 5316, "To the Ministry of Foreign Affairs," 1380/3/9 (1960–61), notes three instances of government employees who directly or indirectly owned parts of companies; Ahmad Zaki Yamani and Tahir al-Rafi'i are mentioned as having already been reprimanded.

[107] The subsidies began in 1961, with SR 24,531 for the newly formed Riyadh Chamber of Commerce: *Qarar Ri'asat Majlis al-Wuzara'* 587, 1382/11/20 (1962–63). By 1964 all the existing chambers (in Jeddah, Mecca, Riyadh, and Dammam) got a yearly subsidy of SR 100,000 each: *Qarar Ri'asat Majlis al-Wuzara'* 135, 1384/2/29 (1964–65). By 1969 the Chambers of Jeddah, Riyadh, and Dammam were getting a subsidy of SR 750,000 each to build new offices, on the condition that they raise a matching amount. The maximum subsidy for other chambers (at the time, only Mecca's) was set at SR 500,000: *Qarar Ri'asat Majlis al-Wuzara'* 587, 1391/7/6 (1971–72).

[108] Among these were recommendations for customs tariffs on different goods, problems relating to the port and tenders, the import of foodstuffs, articles of association, draft laws covering all chambers of commerce in the Kingdom, and commercial arbitration committees. The session of the Jeddah chamber that began in 1963 was even more focused in its aims and more successful in promoting its recommendations on the cement shortage, direct foreign purchases by the state, customs dues, tendering regulations, protection against un-

By the 1960s the Jeddah, Riyadh and Dammam chambers (in decreasing order of importance) were wielding institutionalized influence over state policy. While the earlier merchant organizations had sought to forestall the entry of the government into regulation and commercial law, the new charter of the Jeddah Chamber of Commerce, for example, specifically noted that its primary aims were to advise the government and keep businessmen informed of government policies, and to implement and, when called upon, to enforce those policies. In part, the influence of the chambers of commerce stemmed from their increasing assistance to the government in gathering information about the private sector. For example, in the mid-1950s, before appropriate government institutions existed to control the prices of basic goods in local markets, the Jeddah, Mecca, and Dammam chambers were commissioned to perform this task; they ensured that retailers made no more than a 5 percent profit on foodstuffs and no more than 10 percent on other merchandise. Similarly, when the state failed in its attempts to regulate the money-changers, the Jeddah and Mecca chambers were enlisted to assist in implementing controls on exchange rates in the currency market.[109] By 1966 the chambers were more important than the Ministry of Commerce in gathering information on imports and foreign currency movements.[110]

The third key factor in the emergence of the developmentalist coalition was structural change in the size and composition of the traditional business class itself. The guilds had already been eliminated as a political force.[111] In 1964, they were eliminated as an organizational entity as well: a comprehensive and restrictive law placed them under the control of the Ministry for Pilgrimage and Religious Endowments (MPRE), an institution that had come to be dominated by the most conservative of the Nejdi *ulema* (religious jurists/scholars). The 1964 regulations abolished the in-

---

fair competition from foreign manufacturers and agencies, and increased subsidies to the chamber of commerce. The 1967 session made recommendations regarding non-Saudis who "are unwarrantly [*sic*] dealing in commerce and import." Summaries of these deliberations are found in *Jeddah Chamber of Commerce and Industry: Adventure and History*, n.d. Jeddah Chamber of Commerce and Industry, Jeddah.

[109] *Amr Malaki* 1281/4/12, 1377/4/12 (1957–58); *Qarar Majlis al-Shura* 204, 1373/11/25 (1953–54).

[110] For example, permission to import goods was needed from the chamber even by traders in the remote areas where SAMA had no formal branches. See *Amr Sami min Diwan Ri'asat Majlis al-Wuzara'* 6176, 1386/3/15 (1966–67), regarding traders in the border territories of the eastern province.

[111] The election laws of 1924 had given the guilds wide-ranging authority, which rested on their ability to serve as tax farmers and administrators for the government. In 1953, however, the guilds lost the right to collect head taxes when SAMA took over the collection of entrance fees for the pilgrims. Prince Feisal and the president of the Council of Ministers clashed with the Legislative Council on this point, and the latter won; a year earlier the Consultative Council had decreed that the *mutawwifin* would continue to collect the taxes. Feisal's decree: *Qarar Ri'asat Majlis al-Wuzara'* 34, 1374/2/22 (1954–55); cf. *Qarar Majlis al-Shura* 5/817, 1373/11/4 (1953–54).

ternal guild courts and completely revised the election of guild masters, registration, and fee schedules. Guild masters were turned into civil servants to perform specific tasks for a salary, and the MPRE took over administrative and coordinating functions that had been the exclusive province of the guilds.[112]

The consolidation of the Hijazi business class in the 1960s was, in fact, directly related to the elimination of barriers to markets upheld by the guilds. The burst of economic growth in the 1960s, including the increase in state projects, overwhelmingly favored a very small number of old, established Hijazi merchant houses, largely from the Jeddawi community. Not only did this group have the expertise necessary to undertake state contracts and to fill the increasing demand for imported goods, but in some cases its members had strong personal ties to King Feisal, who had long served as governor of the Hijaz.[113] Consequently, the top layer of the Hijazi commercial elite expanded its activities, while the traditional private sector shrank in numbers between 1925 and the 1960s. The increase in the volume of imports and maritime transport benefited the few large firms and business families that enjoyed the overseas contacts and financial backing necessary to import large amounts of foodstuffs and consumer goods, while smaller wholesalers who had specialized in overland trade with Yemen, Iraq, Syria, and Jordan went into decline.

The Hijazi elite were the most credible claimants to the role of national bourgeoisie, but they were not alone. On the eve of the boom period the business class of Saudi Arabia was bifurcated, with two commercial centers stretching inland from east and west. As imports and small industrial plants concentrated in the Hijaz, large-scale industry and contracting related to oil exploration and extraction was growing rapidly in the eastern province.[114] By the early 1960s, the growth center of the Saudi economy

[112] The 1964 law cut at the root of the guild system by announcing that anyone could provide the services regardless of their family affiliation or guild membership. The guild president was still elected but was paid a salary by the MPRE, and most important, dispute resolution was placed under MPRE. Guild members too became salaried: the government collected most of the fees due them and at the end of the pilgrimage redistributed the funds through what was termed a subsidy. The *'Ayn 'Aziziyah* and *'Ayn Zubaydah* guilds which were previously large revenue generators for the government were also given a subsidy. *Qarar Majlis al-Wuzara'* 19622, 1383/7/29 (1963–64), lists the payment to the *mutawwifin* for the year 1382/83 from the Ministry of Haj and *Awqaf* (religious endowments) as SR 3,310,800. See *Qarar Majlis al-Wuzara'* 394, 1380/8/19 (1960–61), for the subsidy to the water distribution guilds; on the courts, *Qarar Ri'asat Majlis al-Wuzara'* 347, 1385 (1965–66); on salaries, Ministry of Haj and National Economy Announcement 19622, 1383/7/29 (1963–64).

[113] For the close relationship between the Ali Reza family and King Feisal, see Marianne Alireza, *At the Drop of a Veil* (Boston: Houghton Mifflin, 1971).

[114] In 1960 only 77 factories in the kingdom employed more than 10 people; by the late 1960s there were 294. The Hijaz had 25 percent of total invested capital and half (149) of all industries, and employed over half of the total industrial labor force. The eastern province, where ARAMCO is located, had 70 percent of total industrial capital invested in the kingdom, concentrated in only 55 industries, which employed only a fifth of the work force. The central province at that time had 85 industries, one-eighth of industrial capital, and

had moved east from the Hijaz to Al-Hasa, where ARAMCO was building the oil extraction infrastructure. As a result of this shift in contracting activity, and related imports of heavy machinery and construction materials, an entirely new group of entrepreneurs emerged to service the needs of the company. The two groups did not, in reality, compete. The Jeddah merchant houses continued to specialize in commodity imports, viewing the infiltration of Qasimi merchants as their main competition in the Hijaz. The new eastern group was much more oriented toward contracting and construction projects.

ARAMCO's involvement in promoting, training, and funding the new businessmen in Al-Hasa was virtually complete. Education and training institutes were set up, ranging from elementary schools to advanced courses in management and business. ARAMCO sent Saudis abroad to study. ARAMCO's Local Industries Development Department (LIDD) included an Agricultural Assistance Division and an in-house consulting team that evaluated and funded new projects and supported a variety of ancillary businesses, including manufacturing, agriculture, processing, and service industries.[115] Loans were made for everything from private electrical companies to celery production, and ARAMCO contracts were awarded to local businessmen trained and established with company assistance. Unlike the traditional business community, the new business group was small and divided. Individual businessmen had strong ties to the oil company, but as a group they could not have been more different from the Hijazis. Some were migrants from Nejd; none belonged to the established merchant families of the central province; and very few of the Hijazi commercial elites moved into the construction sector in the eastern province; hence, the oil company's clients faced little competition from the established houses of Jeddah and Mecca.[116]

---

one-fifth of the industrial labor force. The northern and southern provinces together had only 5 factories. See Industrial Studies and Development Center, "Technological, Economic, Industrial Structure and Growth Prospects in Saudi Arabia: Report and Recommendations," 3 vols. (mimeo), Riyadh, 1973.

[115] For the profound involvement of CASOC, later renamed ARAMCO, in the promotion of local education, agriculture, training, and business, see Joy Winkie Viola, *Human Resources Development in Saudi Arabia* (Boston: International Human Resources Development Corporation, 1986), esp. 1–69.

[116] Some who started with ARAMCO training and funding, and later sold their products and services to the oil company, went on to establish contacts with high-level government officials and major business elites. "Many of the new tycoons of Arabia came from ordinary, sometimes desperately poor, families. Starting as ARAMCO employees at the bottom of the wage scale, they were trained, advised, and often financed by ARAMCO in setting up their own contracting businesses to do ARAMCO's work. Beginning with one truck on contract haulage or a dozen men doing pick-and-shovel work, they have built up organizations employing hundreds, and in some cases thousands, of men. It was startling to discover that several men I saw daily, Arabs who looked like ordinary white-robed storekeepers or khaki-clad welders, were in fact millionaires" (Michael Cheney, *Big Oil Man from Arabia*, quoted in Viola, *Human Resources Development*, 19). Sulaiman Olayan, most prominent among these, was luckier than many, since he came from Anizah, in the Qasim, where his family had held prominent political positions under both the Al Rashid and the Al Saud from the 1800s to

To the extent that commercial elites had abrogated their independence, links between business and the state had changed radically since the 1920s. The numerically smaller but more diversified business elite of the 1960s had both formal and informal links to political decision-makers and state institutions. At the top level, interaction between key merchants and the government was not uncommon. Three prominent merchants served on the board of directors of SAMA,[117] and two presidents of the Jeddah Chamber of Commerce, Sheikh 'Abdallah 'Ali Reza and Sheikh Muhammed al-'Awadi, were named ministers of commerce and industry.[118] In addition to the institutionalized influence on state policy enjoyed by the commercial class through the chambers of commerce and industry, during the late 1950s and early 1960s the press provided a forum where subsets of the private sector could voice their opinions and air their grievances on economic issues, from the protection of domestic industry to the regulation of banks and companies.[119]

In economic terms, the points at which Hijazi commercial interests conflicted with both the tribes and the restrictive Hijazi guilds are easy to understand. Even easier to explain is their willingness to forgo formal participation in return for a consultative role and monopoly profits in the emerging industrial sector, particularly when the frightening prospect of Nasserism or Ba'thist Pan-Arabism emerged as a genuine threat. Less obvious, however, is the extent to which these political concessions, made for economic interest, set the stage for the Al Saud's abandonment of the Hijazi elite in the 1970s. By the time the boom happened, not only had

---

the early twentieth century. Olayan managed many foreign investment portfolios for King Fahad, for which he was awarded the presidency of the Riyadh Chamber of Commerce even after he lost the election in 1984. For a suspiciously sanitized, almost breathless version of the man and the fortune, see "Sulaiman Olayan," in Michael Field, *The Merchants* (Woodstock, N.Y.: Overlook, 1985), 311–31.

[117] In 1956 these members were Ahmad al-Jaffali, Fahad al-Qusaybi, and Ahmad Jamjum (the third being the only Jeddah merchant on the board): Royal Decree 27, 27 Jamadi Awwal 1377 (1957–58). By 1970 all the merchants on SAMA's board were Nejdis—Sheikhs Abd Allah ibn 'Awdan, Muhammad al-'Ulafi, and Ahmad al-Jaffali: Royal Decree M/6, 1389/6/11 (1969–70).

[118] *Jeddah Chamber of Commerce and Industry,* 31, 44.

[119] See, e.g., a request for government protection of local cement and soft-drink industries in *Al-Nadwah* 59 (21 August 1958); *al-Nadwah* magazine's conference on the monopolization of foodstuffs by big importers was reported in *Al-Nadwah* 106 (9 December 1958). Merchants complained of government red tape and bureaucratic hurdles in *Al-Bilad al-Sa'udiyah* 2853 (21 September 1958); small shareholders of several companies complained of the abuses of larger partners and asked the Ministry of Commerce to protect their rights in *al-Bilad* 17 (13 February 1959); the small shareholders of Riyadh Bank accused Rashad al-Dabbagh of favoring the interests of Sharbatli (another major merchant) in *Al-Bilad* 17 (13 February 1959). An editorial in *Hirah* 126 (18 August 1959) encouraged the *mutawwifin* to form a union, as "the only way to protect their rights," and noted that journalists too were demanding their right to a union; a letter signed by ten *mutawwifin,* however, considered "the formation of a union for them a waste of money." Requests not specifically from merchants also made their way into the press: e.g., in *Hirah* 131 (24 August 1958) the people of Bani Shahr asked the government to build a school and clinic closer to them than Taif, which was a seven-day automobile ride from their dwellings.

the revenue needs of the state shifted, but the dense network of ties that had made the Hijazi elite politically indispensable to the Al Saud had eroded. The time was ripe for a new coalitional shift that left the Hijaz out altogether.

Two factors that were critical to this shift in business-government relations during the 1970s were firmly in place by the 1960s. First, as the role of the government in regulating the economy and purchasing services from the private sector grew, so too did the ability of political elites to favor members of the private sector through the administrative and legal apparatus of the state.[120] Second, on the eve of the oil boom, although commerce and domestic industry in Saudi Arabia remained in the control of segments of the traditional Hijazi merchant elite, the bureaucracy and the military were dominated by Nejdis. Aside from the handful of Hijazis who had long tenure in the Council of Ministers, Nejdi dominance of the bureaucracy, which would singlehandedly dictate economic programs in the 1970s, was complete by the 1960s.

In the process of claiming their place as a national commercial class, the Hijazi elite were well aware of Nejdi dominance in the institutions that governed the market. Indeed, the issue of recruitment into the bureaucracy—particularly into strategic posts in the Ministries of Haj, Finance, and Education—had been a point of contention between the Hijazis and the Nejdis as early as 1926, when police appointments were at issue; similar fears were voiced in 1929, when civil servant transfers and appointments were centralized in the hands of the king and his viceroy, then Prince Feisal.[121] Early complaints of the Nejdi domination of the bureaucracy and the police force were connected to the broader Hijazi agenda of preserving their control over commercial law and administration and the guilds. With time, the Hijazis who had staffed the technically demanding civil service posts were slowly replaced, starting with the police force[122] and the religious elite.[123] In 1961, when the central government

[120] The handful of beneficiaries of initial government contracts and gifts include some of the most colorful Saudi businessmen—Adnan Khashoggi, Ghayth Pharoun, Ahmad al-Qusaybi, Sulaiman Olayan, and the Jaffali brothers—and old and respected Hijazi families such as the Ali Rizas. Apart from these isolated instances of favoritism, the government had not engaged in the widespread informal distributive measures that were to characterize the boom years. Abuses were prevented by prohibiting the participation of princes and civil servants in business ventures.

[121] "Jeddah Report," 31 July 1926, PRO, FO vol. 11442; *Nizam al-Mamuriyin al-'Amm* [Regulations concerning Civil Servants], 1350 (1930–31), summarized in "Jeddah Report," 1 February 1929, PRO, FO vol. 13728, E 1028/94/91.

[122] In 1927 the chiefs of police in Jeddah and Mecca were replaced by Nejdis, precipitating broad-based Hijazi protest. As the British vice-consul wrote: "A significant cause of the unrest is to be found in the gradual insinuation [*sic*] of Najdians into executive positions in the Hijaz. Najdians have now been appointed chiefs of police in Mecca and Jeddah and are credited with the intention of replacing the existing forces by recruits from their own country" ("Jeddah Report," 1927, PRO, FO vol. 12250, E 5083/644/91). Before this the police had been commanded by a Syrian officer of the late Turkish army; see "Jeddah Report," 1927, PRO, FO vol. 11442, E 5283/155/91.

[123] The king began by making a drastic reduction in the number of imams of each of the

moved from Jeddah to Riyadh, Hijazi civil servants were dismissed en masse and replaced with Nejdis.[124] Thus, the domination of the middle ranks of the bureaucracy by Nejdis began in earnest in the 1960s, even though important posts in the Ministries of Planning, Commerce and Industry, and Oil, plus the directorship of SAMA, remained in the hands of Hijazis.

At the time, state employment was not a particularly lucrative or otherwise attractive option. Moreover, state spending patterns were such that the disproportionate representation of Nejdis in the bureaucracy had little impact on contracts and the distribution of wealth in the private sector during the 1960s.[125] Yet the contemporaneous growth and centralization

---

four *Sunni* sects that had previously led prayers at Mecca; next, he decreed that only one imam per sect would be allowed in the Holy City; and in July 1929 he dismissed all religious scholars and functionaries except those belonging to the Wahhabi sect. In addition, he abolished the sectioning of mosques according to sect, thereby at once placing the control of Hijazi religious institutions in the hands of Nejdis and forcing pilgrims and Hijazis to attend Wahhabi mosques. See "Jeddah Reports," 20 July 1929 and August 1929, PRO, FO vol. 13740, E 3947/91 and E 4208/3947/91, and a telegram of 20 August 1929, E 4586/3947/91, which report that the regular imams at Medina had also been replaced by two Nejdis and one negro [*sic*] from Timbuktoo. The religious elite were the first to have a weekly meeting with the king on the model of the tribal *majlis* common in Nejd; see *Um al-Qura* (19 December 1924). On the changing role of the ulama and the Al Shaykh (the founding family of the Wahhabi sect), see Alexander Bligh, "The Saudi Religious Elite (Ulama) as Participants in the Political System of the Kingdom," *International Journal of Middle East Studies* 17 (February 1985): 37–50.

[124] Ministry of Finance and National Economy Letter, 1/1/812, 1381/1/20 (1961).

[125] Rare instances of favoritism are illustrated in these examples: the king awarded entry to Bahraini merchants if they chose the Qusaybi family as their sole agents in Saudi Arabia. *Qarar Ri'asat Majlis al-Wuzara'* 69, 1381/2/7 (1961–62), notes that the request of Yusuf Khalil al-Mu'id and Sons to sell British "Blackstone" agricultural machinery in Saudi Arabia is granted "with the understanding that Muhammad al-Qusaybi and 'Abd al-'Aziz al-Nasr and Muhammad al-Aqili will be the sole agents for Blackstone in the kingdom." Muhammad al-Qusaybi, Ibn Saud's banker after the conquest of the eastern province, had remained a close associate and adviser on monetary and financial matters. Examples of the cancellation of import fees for defense contractors and specific industrialists, at a time when materials imported for state projects were not exempt from customs duties, may be found in *Qarar Ri'asat Majlis al-Wuzara'* 467, 1381/5/29 (1961–62)—'Abd al-Qadir Jazzar was paid the sum he owed in customs on defense procurement—and *Qarar Ri'asat Majlis al-Wuzara'* 762, "To the Ministry of Communications," 1391/9/13 (1971–72).

A larger "favor" involved the switch of government accounts from the National Commercial Bank (NCB), owned by two Jeddawi money-changers of Hadrami extraction, to the Riyadh Bank, a smaller and less successful concern owned mainly by four tribal notables from the Qasim area in the Nejd. In 1961 the informal relationship between NCB and the government, which had existed since the founding of the bank in 1948 (and involved NCB performing all banking transactions for the government), was formalized in *Amr Sami, Diwan Ri'asat Majlis al-Wuzara'* 15948, 1382/8/26 (1962–63). But the main shareholder of NCB was Sheikh Bin Mahfuz, originally a Yemeni from Hadramaut who had several times offended Ibn Saud and Saud by refusing them loans. In 1967, Riyadh Bank took over the distribution of government checks and the collection of revenues from areas where no branch of SAMA had yet been built. The state's business was lucrative. Riyadh Bank got 34 halalah for every SR 100 it transferred or transacted, and SR 5 for every telegram it sent in performance of its varied duties: Ministry of Finance Circular 2/12/5020, 1389/4/9 (1969–70).

of the bureaucracy accompanied recruitment patterns that would become critical to economic policy and accumulation during the boom of the 1970s. The growing confluence of regional and occupational cleavages had a profound influence on subsequent developments in Saudi Arabia.

The transformed structure of the private sector was itself critical to setting the stage for the coming boom years. The Saudi commercial middle class, entirely uninterested in democracy, literally prepared the way for its own destruction. The traditional commercial class was narrower than it had been in the first three decades of the kingdom's existence, but the activities of the remaining elites were much more diversified. In establishing the corporatist contract, the merchants had participated in the destruction of the guilds and other civil institutions in the Hijaz. This same contract also limited the scope of permissible debate, with the result that no independent national civil institutions or political parties arose in tandem with the establishment of the national market. Thus, although the Hijazis made use of the press to express their discontent on specific economic issues, they rarely strayed from the topic at hand.[126] The narrow contours of these debates placed strict limits on the extent to which social groups could organize to influence government policy in subsequent years. The egalitarianism of the Pan-Arab republicans in the underground and broader political currents in the Middle East were as threatening to the Hijazi elite as to national bourgeoisies in Egypt, Iraq, Syria, and Lebanon. The unity of state and commercial interests in the 1950s and

[126] In 1958–59 the Hijazi press published many articles critical of the government and its policies: *Hirah* 134 (27 August 1958) criticized the Nejdi merchant Sheikh Ibrahim al-Jaffali, a close associate of the king, for embezzling municipal funds through his control of the electric generators of the three cities of the Hijaz; *Hirah* 135 (28 August 1958) printed a demand by merchants for a codification of their legal rights and commercial regulations; *Al-Nadwah* 96 (23 May 1959) criticized big capitalists and government officials for investing abroad rather than at home; *Al-Bilad* 143 (23 July 1959) condemned the artificially inflated exchange rate and the level of customs duties; *Al-Bilad al-Saʿudiyah* 2846 (12 September 1958) criticized the recently opened Riyadh Bank for not keeping its initial promise to participate in projects for national development. To this the bank replied that it had plans for building a cement company in the Nejd and a gas company in Riyadh in *al-Bilad al-Sa'udiyah* 2837, (14 October 1958); in an article published in *Hirah* 119 (10 August 1958) a reader took exception to an advertisement by ʿAbd al-Rahman al-Qusaybi (a Najdi merchant and onetime banker for the Al Saud) that he was building a cold storage plant in "the capital," when he meant Riyadh (the writer maintained that moving the ministries to Riyadh did not make it the capital, and that Riyadh was properly called the "Governorate of Riyadh," while Mecca remained the "Governorate of the Capital"); both *Hirah* 122 (13 August 1958) and *Al-Bilad al-Saʿudiyah* 2819 and 2821 (12 and 14 August 1958) openly discussed women's issues and criticized the regulations for full veiling—an issue that would never appear in the boomtime Arabian press; *Al-Bilad al-Sa'udiyah* 2825 (19 August 1958) harshly criticized the government for favoring bids made by "certain merchants" (the article was signed "The Bespectacled One"); two editorials detailed the religious basis of government taxation and *zakat* in *Al-Nadwah* 100 and 127 (27 May and 5 July 1959); editorials in *Al-Bilad al-Saʿudiyah* 2840–42 (6–8 September 1958) criticized the budget, customs procedures, and economic projects of the government.

1960s held together against the tide of protest in the 1960s, when the Free Prince Movement, Arab nationalism, and socialism emerged as genuine alternatives supported by segments of the armed forces and by labor. In the 1970s, with Nasserism laid to rest, the government was already well positioned to reshape the private sector at will.

Summary: State and Market Building as Symbiosis

Unlike that of the Mandate territories, whose borders were drawn by Britain and France at the conclusion of World War I, state-building in Saudi Arabia was relatively free from external influences. Yet the drawing of the contiguous borders of surrounding states had a profound effect on the patterns of political and military authority in the Nejd, whence the first military force capable of conquest and of maintaining order emerged. The new ability to disrupt prior patterns of redistribution by enforcing national borders permitted the formation of a permanent tribal army, which signaled the ascent of the urban communities over the nomadic and provided the military force for the conquest of the Hijaz. Thereafter, a unity of interests that had developed between Nejdi urban groups extended to the Hijazi merchant classes, eventually merging the interests of Hijazi commercial and Nejdi military-political elites. This unity of interests did not precede but rather followed the stabilization of a rudimentary state structure. Military and political unification preceded the formation of a central bureaucracy and a national market, and economic elites formed a stable coalition with the military-political elite only after local legal, tax, and police institutions had stabilized and the promise of a national market under a single, uniform governance became credible.

The stabilization of this coalition transformed business-government relations from secession to support. The origins of the national bureaucracy and the national market are found, then, not in the purposive acts of individual rulers, or in the teleological evolution of "efficient" institutions, but in shifting and ever narrowing coalitions among political-military elites and various social groups. Each coalition, moreover, was forged through intense conflicts in which there were more losers than winners. Only the creation of a uniform legal-military order made it possible to unite the actions of different groups into a mutually comprehensible language of uniform "economic interest" and "rational choice."

The central proposition of this discussion, that the fiscal basis of the state determines its structure, is not in itself remarkable. Indeed, it is central to both Rudolf Goldscheid's and Joseph Schumpeter's classic discussions of the political economy of taxation. The claim here is somewhat more specific. The emergence of central extractive and regulatory bureaucracies cannot be explained as the simple extension of the state's coercive and administrative reach. Rather, there is a symbiotic relationship between economic and social organization on the one hand and the expansion of an extractive bureaucracy on the other. Capacities generated by relying on existing organizations in society are later deployed in shaping a host of new institutional, political, and legal relationships. As the organizational capacities of state structures change, relationships critical to one rendition of the tax state obsolesce, reshuffling the political fortunes of groups. The manner in which these relationships are mediated and the ways they change are reflected in shifting business-government relations; revealing quite clearly the impermanent social basis of the extractive and regulatory state.

In Saudi Arabia, where no colonial state existed and no national commercial class had taken form before the 1950s, a business-state coalition stabilized only after the rudiments of a national legal, financial, and regulatory system were in place. Only then was sufficient social support for a unified national economy generated among business elites with national aspirations. The control of territory, a uniform legal code, the destruction of internal barriers to exchange, and the creation of a national currency preceded the construction of a powerful alliance between the Hijazi commercial elites and the Al Saud.

Nejdi-Hijazi relations changed three times between 1925 and 1960. In the earliest period, the state depended heavily on the Hijazi guilds and merchants for tax collection, exchanging autonomy and representation for revenue and administrative assistance. In the crisis of the interwar period, an alliance between political elites and consumers enabled the bureaucracy to eliminate incrementally the restrictive Hijazi guilds. The numerically smaller but wealthier commercial elite that survived subsequently formed a national developmentalist alliance with the government. In this transition, commercial elites exchanged political participation and legal autonomy for access to an expanding national market and protection against imports; only at this point did the coalition for a national market stabilize. The terms of this alliance had profound implications for subsequent patterns of business-government relations in the 1970s. The corporatist relationship that linked business and government on the eve of the boom embodied regional fissures between the Nejdi political elite and the Hijazi economic elite. The Hijazi merchant elite that entered the boom period was not just numerically small and isolated; it had systematically bargained away its legal and economic independence for the support of a regulatory bureaucracy that soon stopped needing allies.

The creation of the central bureaucracy and establishment of the national market were mutually reinforcing, linked processes, which went through three distinct transitions in Saudi Arabia. Each of the three transitions was marked by the destruction of the social groups that had supported the previous rendition of the tax state: in eliminating their immediate rivals—the tribal confederations, the guilds and the smaller merchants—the business elite laid the grounds for their own obsolescence in the longer term.

Thus, the creation of the national economy was at once a destructive act and a process that opened up the possibility of a completely new form of economic and social organization. As the administrative reach of the nascent state grew, precapitalist institutions that had been highly instrumental in stabilizing public finance at an earlier juncture became constraining forces against the unification of the market. The elimination of the money-changers and the service guilds was both a political and an economic process in which technological change, the stability of legal institutions controlled by the state, and class conflict all played a part. The groups that stood in opposition to this process changed over time, but it was only after the rudiments of a central administration and a national market were in place that social groups began to make positive demands on the state. Before that moment, politics had been a struggle between local groups and the state in which the former attempted to preserve their existing forms of organization against the intrusions of the latter.

The story of Saudi state-building, I have argued, matches the broadest sequencing patterns of state-making in early modern Europe. There are, of course, numerous and important differences; one in particular bears mention. The fact that Saudi Arabia was a partially nomadic society meant that military and economic power were delinked, a situation completely unlike the union of military, economic, and political power that typified the late feudal period. European towns and cities were connected to the process of expansion and centralization through public finance, but the formation of standing armies ultimately depended on agricultural labor, not tribal levies. This difference meant that even after the Al Saud brokered an urban-tribal coalition, the two realms remained sociologically distinct, embodying different social constructions of rationality. Moreover, the crucial event that propelled the Nejd out of its steady-state urban-tribal balance was an exogenous one: its agents were the British colonial powers, not local changes in demography, technology, or economy.

Having empirically demonstrated the symbiosis between the origins of state and market institutions, it is possible to revisit the question of the social base of the state, which was raised at the beginning of this chapter. In Saudi Arabia the rudiments of a national market predated the incorporation of the merchant elite into a stable national coalition. The class basis of the Al Saud and their tribal military is even more problematic for Marxist notions of the social basis of the state, since the Nejdi tribal confederations that functionally united the territorial state were simultaneously destroying the basis of the tribal economy and setting the stage for a new conception of social order, based on a new set of economic imperatives, in which they themselves had no place.

Not least for the tribes and eventually also for the guilds and the small local merchants, the process by which the institutions that governed the national market were forged was brutal. Between 1925 and 1973 the Saudi state underwent several transmutations in which forces antithetical to the formation of a national market and a centralized administration were (in most cases quite literally) eliminated. The protagonists in these conflicts changed over time, but each successive consolidation signaled a narrowing of the social basis of the state. In sequence, the material foundations, institutional constructs, and ideational systems of the autonomous nomadic tribes, the Al Saud's tribal armies, the guilds, and the smaller merchants were destroyed. In each case, they were destroyed after having been directly instrumental in the creation of the new national order and having come into conflict with the next rung of social groupings whose co-optation was necessary for the centralization and expansion of national institutions. In each successive reformulation of state-society relations, then, social groups indirectly participated in their own destruction—albeit unwittingly—until only a highly vulnerable and very narrow group remained. By the 1960s the aspiring commercial-industrial elites of the Hijaz had formed the social basis of the newly created national market; previously independent business communities were utterly transformed into a dependent corporate group with strong institutional ties to the economic ministries.

Access and representation did not go together. Initially, the Hijazi commercial elites and guilds had been able to extract significant concessions from the government, including the independence of their system of commercial dispute resolution, political representation, and many specific policy concessions of particular importance to the business elite. The weak state exchanged representation and autonomy for the administrative and extractive skills of the Hijazi communities. Later, the Hijazi commercial elites bargained away their independence and abandoned their allies in return for the destruction of barriers to national exchange. The much smaller but more affluent group that remained on the eve of the boom was highly dependent on government economic policies for protection, adjudication, and access. This dependence would have profound implications for their efficacy following the oil boom of 1973, when another major administrative and political transformation occurred.

Taxation had motivated both the expansion of the Saudi state and the construction of its bureaucracy in the 1950s and 1960s. Taxes were also the means of achieving a central feature of the national economy: a unified currency. But the state's independence from domestic sources of revenue during the oil boom allowed it to craft a completely new constituency in the 1970s. The structure and functions of the new bureaucracy and the coalition created to support it were entirely different from the one that preceded it. Politically suspended above the vibrant economic networks of the Hijazi past, and dependent on the new regulatory state of the 1960s, the new national business classes of Saudi Arabia could hardly have been less prepared for the 1970s.

Chapter Three

Taxation and Economic Fragmentation

In Saudi Arabia the construction of a centralized bureaucratic-legal order made possible a stable business-government coalition with a shared interest in a unified national market. In Yemen, efforts to build the same set of institutions at the same moment in history produced the opposite outcome: state centralization produced three distinct regional economies dominated by three different commercial elite groups, none of whom had an interest in supporting the creation of a national market. The fragmentation of the economy under the leadership of the Yemeni imams followed their escalating efforts to tax *without* the assistance of a regular standing army. The result was the migration of the largest segment of the Yemeni commercial classes to the free port of Aden and the subsequent division of the Yemeni market into three institutionalized zones. The largest commercial faction, composed of *Sunni* merchants from the south, took shape outside the Yemeni border, in the British colony of Aden. Thus a stable and viable coalition for a national market governed by a single set of legal and monetary institutions failed to emerge in Yemen until the late 1940s. By then, a complex set of exogenous events had simultaneously undermined the economic niche controlled by the *Sunni* absentee bourgeoisie in Aden and created an economic boom for those parts of the Yemeni economy controlled by the San'a-based *Shi'ia* private sector. This confluence of events sparked renewed efforts by the Aden-based elite to depose Imam Ahmad (1948–62), this time in collusion with Yemeni labor unionists in Aden. The ensuing struggle among rival commercial groups for the definition and control of a national market culminated in the toppling of the traditional leadership in 1962 and a protracted civil war that lasted from 1962 to 1971.

The process through which market and state institutions were forestalled, constructed, and reconstructed in Yemen prior to the oil boom differs from the pattern of symbiosis between state- and market-building processes which typified the Saudi experience. In response to the same set of exogenous events that produced the same pressures on political leaders to expand their revenue base, interim results in Yemen and Saudi Arabia could not have been more different. Political leaders in both cases attempted to change the rules that governed the economy and to establish a central bureaucracy, and eventually a set of national institutions emerged in both cases. In both, the support of commercial elites was critical to the stabilization of national state and market institutions; moreover, in both, the forces that drove institutional creation and change in the pre-boom period were qualitatively different from those that developed in the 1970s. Yet the divergence of the Yemeni pattern between 1918 and 1948 is more than a historical curiosity, for it demonstrates the conditions under which efforts to build a central state can produce, sustain, and institutionalize fissures in economic exchange: it offers a way of explaining both historical and contemporary failures to construct viable centralized states and national markets.[1]

Periods of centralization tend to create tensions between business and political elites, often producing some of the most radical instances of state intervention on record.[2] The Yemeni case is hardly unique in this regard. It does show, however, that the emergence of elite interest in supporting a unified national economy with a single currency and legal system is contingent on the prior establishment of a military and administrative infrastructure. The absence of a military infrastructure (order) precludes the creation of an administrative one; both are necessary to attract business support. The Yemeni experience of aborted state-building underscores the importance of stable business-government coalitions in generating mutually enforcing mechanisms between building a state and forging a national market. In contrast to Saudi Arabia, where the coalition between the Hijazi merchant elite and the Nejdi government initiated a period in which the two processes came to reinforce each other, two important factors prevented a similar outcome in Yemen. First, the strength and cohesion of the Yemeni tribal confederations resulted in the inability of the imam to raise a standing army and therefore his failure to control the financial drain

[1] For a contemporary case of efforts to tax resulting in regionalization and the demonetization of the economy, see David Woodruff, "The Barter of the Bankrupt" (paper presented at the annual meeting of the American Political Science Association, Chicago, 1995).

[2] Kiren Aziz Chaudhry, "The Myths of the Market and the Common History of Late Developers," *Politics and Society* 21 (September 1993): 245–74.

created by the tribal mercenaries in his employ. Second, the existence of a viable retreat, the British colony of Aden, made the "exit" option possible for the over-taxed southern *Sunnis*. The Yemeni case illustrates the contingent nature of elite preferences for economic fragmentation and economic centralization in periods of fundamental institutional change; economic elites do not automatically support a national market.

"Domestic" social formations in this case prove notoriously difficult to define. Yemen shows the importance of geo-political location in shaping domestic outcomes by the opening or closing of exit as a strategy for domestic groups. For the Hijazi commercial elite there was no viable substitute for the robust *haj* economy, and Yemen's location between two vibrant enclave economies, Aden to the south and the Hijaz to the north, made the construction of national institutions particularly difficult. Twice in Yemeni history the migration of entire social classes changed the course of domestic institutional change, exposing the problematic nature of a nation-based view of class. The flight and gestation of Yemen's dominant commercial and financial classes in Aden from 1890 to 1962, and their return after the coup of 1962, constituted a dramatic example of a process that has occurred in different ways in almost all Middle Eastern and North African countries. Similarly, the migration of three-fourths of Yemen's active labor force in the 1970s, and the immigrants' return in the 1980s and 1990s, marked a radical disjuncture in the basis of social support for standing institutional arrangements. If fundamental legal, bureaucratic, and economic institutions reflect the outcome of social struggles, the exit or return of entire social classes at particular junctures can be expected to put enormous pressure on institutions. Again, the pattern is hardly unique to Yemen. Virtually every country that has had a serious episode of economic nationalism or revolution—Russia, China, Cuba, the Eastern European states, Algeria, Iraq, Iran, Syria, the People's Democratic Republic of Yemen, and countless African states—has produced an exodus of economic elites who often return once private capital is in favor again. Location can shape domestic institutional outcomes by making exit easy or difficult. Classes formed and organized outside the national borders need not coincide with broader episodes of economic internationalization of the structural sort that occurred in the 1970s.

This chapter begins with an account of the external and internal constraints that shaped the process of Yemeni state-building before the 1940s. Next, I discuss the formation of the absentee bourgeoisie in Aden and the emergence of a successful anti-imam business-labor coalition outside the national borders. Finally, I outline the way that the civil war of 1962–71, by solidifying regional and sectarian cleavages in public and private sectors, set the domestic political-economic context as Yemen entered the boom period of the 1970s.

STATE, TRIBE AND ACCUMULATION IN IMAMIC YEMEN

The departure of the Turkish garrison from San'a and Hudaydah just before World War I and the formal withdrawal of the Turks in 1918 ended an oscillating pattern of collaboration and contestation between the Ottoman Porte and the *Zaydi* imam. The imam's role as a mediator between his *Shi'a* sect and the dominant *Sunni* Ottoman hierarchy had endured in some form since the seventeenth century, changing with the ebb and flow of Ottoman interest in Yemen and the Red Sea. Occasional Ottoman efforts to establish direct rule in Yemen had been largely unsuccessful. When, in response to the Turkish withdrawal in 1918 Imam Yahya (1904–48) attempted to construct an independent theocratic absolutist state, he had neither a standing army nor an effective administrative apparatus. Like the Al Saud and Sherif Hussein of Mecca, Yemen's imams were urban-based political brokers with very small permanent constituencies. For the Al Saud, World War I opened the way to permanent territorial control, a steady source of revenue, and the formation of a standing army. For the Yemeni imam, the war undid prior mechanisms of control but foreclosed effective responses to the challenges of state-building and economic unification.

Two constraints critically circumscribed the scope of state authority. First, Yemen was more or less equally divided into *Shi'a* and *Sunni* communities located, respectively, in the northern and southern parts of the country. Social divisions in Yemen overlapped with regional, economic, sectarian, and cultural fissures. The *Sunni* south had long been a settled agricultural region with a relatively stringent social hierarchy underpinned by a highly unequal distribution of land. Landless tenants were not uncommon, and landed elites in the more remote regions of Taiz and Ibb had direct control over policing, law, punishment, sustenance. These hierarchies had long since replaced ties of kinship in the main tribal confederation of the south, the *Madhaj*, through inmigration and plunder from the north. In the early twentieth century the southern regions of Taiz and Ibb, once the producers of substantial coffee exports, were critical to supplying the internal market. The *Shi'a* north, in contrast, was largely arid, with a predominantly tribal population organized into confederations that comprised social, military, and economic units. In analytical terms, the eastern regions bordering on the Empty Quarter are properly included in the "north." The Tihamah Plains and western highlands formed sociologically and economically distinct but politically weaker regions that assumed temporary importance in political events but are not central to this discussion (see Map 3.1).

The sectarian cleavage between north and south generated two separate religious hierarchies. This structure, in the absence of a monopoly on violence, erected insurmountable barriers to the imam's religious author-

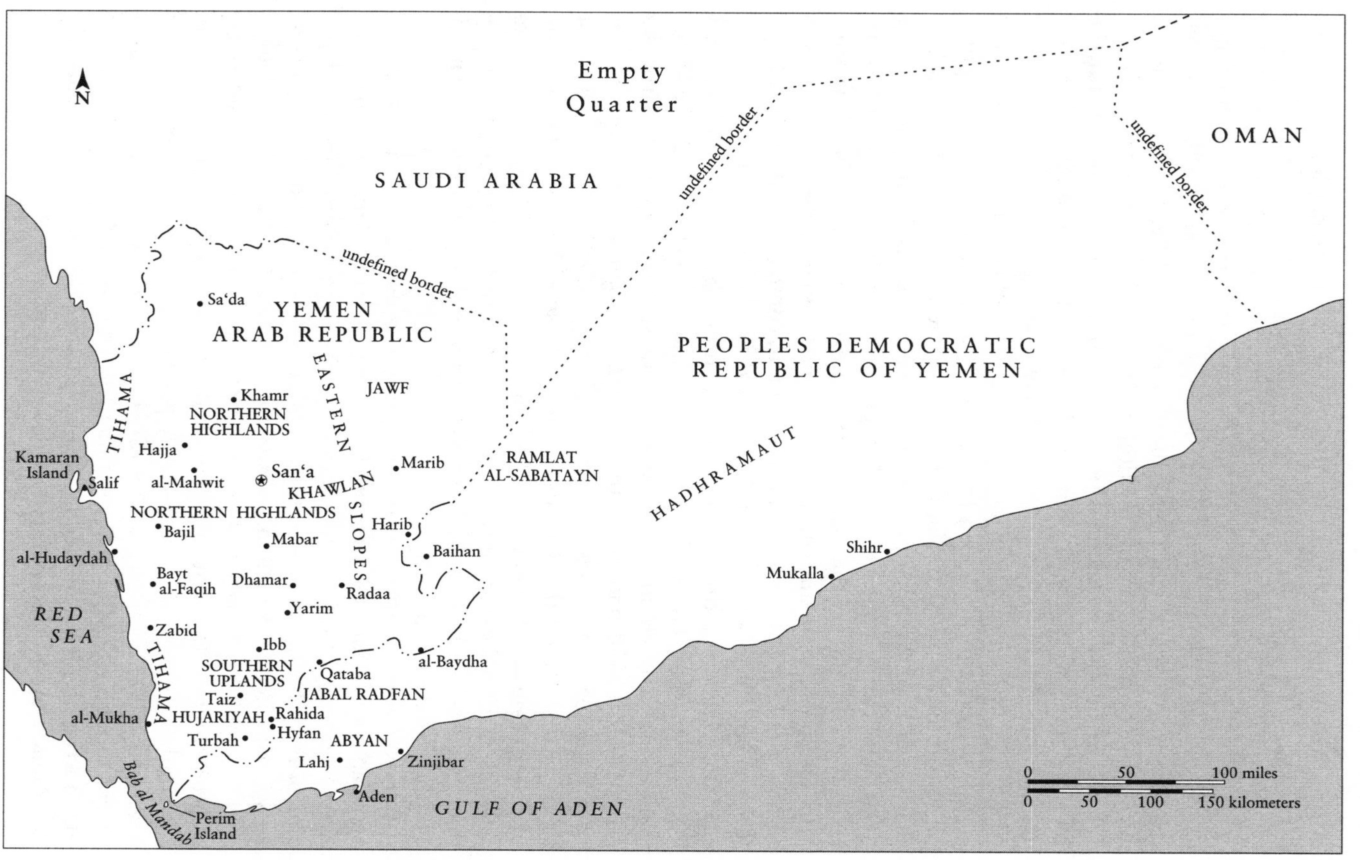

Map 3.1 Yemen Arab Republic, 1990

ity over his southern subjects. Further, at least three major legal traditions existed simultaneously in Yemen, each with an entrenched hierarchy. The northern *Shariʿa* courts practiced *Zaydi* jurisprudence; in the south, a class of *Sunni sayyids* (descendants of the Prophet Muhammed) dispensed justice based on *Sunni* doctrine with the tacit consent but not the financial support of the imam; and in the hinterland, *ʿurf* (customary law) was administered by tribal sheikhs functioning independently of both *shariʿa* traditions. In his best moments the imam guaranteed security but not the law, for there was no agreement on which law should prevail and no permanent way of imposing a uniform system by force.

Second, and more important, the Yemeni tribal confederations were highly centralized, organized hierarchically and efficiently as both political and military units. In stark contrast to the shifting tribal allegiances characteristic of the northern Arabian confederations from which the nascent Saudi army emerged, the Yemeni tribes were invulnerable to the kind of manipulation that served Ibn Saud so well in the Nejd. Despite what one prominent student of the northern Yemeni tribes observed concerning the lack of cohesion in tribal Yemen, compared with the northern Arabian confederations the Hashid and even the Bakil were pictures of efficient collective action.[3] A centralized, "ultimate" leader who had absolute sway over an entire confederation made its less noble lineages unavailable for co-optation. Unable to co-opt subbranches of a particular group, as Ibn Saud had done, the *Zaydi* imams had access to tribal levies only at the sufferance of confederation chiefs, and then only in return for subsidies distributed through the tribal leadership. By supplying this flow of resources from the paramount tribal sheikh to his people, the imams were in many ways responsible for strengthening the corporate groups that would later prevent the last imam from building a militarily centralized bureaucratic state.

Between the powerful tribal chiefs on the one hand and the southern agrarian populations that formed his tax base on the other, the imam had virtually no way of establishing a monopoly on the production of violence and order. The imams maintained power not by eliminating rival claimants but rather by balancing northern demands for subsidies and their own financial needs against southern resistance to taxes. The Yemeni state as it emerged in the first two decades of the twentieth century was, from the southern perspective, thoroughly predatory, geared exclusively to the goal of taxation. Contrary to the widely accepted view that imamic absolutism functioned without a bureaucracy,[4] the extractive agencies of the imam were highly developed, and functionaries responsible for collecting taxes made up over 60 percent of the state's employees.[5]

[3] See Paul Dresch, *Tribes, Government, and History in Yemen* (New York: Oxford University Press, 1989), 83–106.

[4] See, e.g., ibid., 228.

[5] It is estimated that the imam employed about 2,000 nonmilitary personnel, of which

Like Saudi Arabia's before the boom, Yemen's tax system was comprehensive.[6] Direct taxation of southern agriculture and livestock was central to state finance and made up by far the most important source of revenue.[7] Despite their marginal contribution to state revenues, both import and export duties were high, and customs houses were used to collect a variety of other taxes, including a "social tax" for charities, an entry tax, a health tax, and a storage and transportation tax.[8] In addition, municipal authorities taxed sales in seasonal and permanent markets; treasury employees collected fishing, salt, and real estate taxes.[9] Transportation fees on trucks and caravans were collected by the "director of cars" in each sub-province. The Rahida checkpoint, through which the Aden-Yemen traders passed, remitted the most revenue. In the urban areas of San'a, Taiz, Ibb, and Zabid, craft and trade guilds collected and remitted taxes for the imam's treasury and shouldered the expense of supplying security in urban marketplaces.[10] In the harvest season, temporary employees were recruited to form teams of mobile tax collectors under the supervision of permanent *Zakat* Department employees. This was a lucrative enterprise, and both permanent and seasonal tax collectors were most often chosen

---

some 1,400 were involved in extractive activities: Muhammad 'Ali Al-'Ubaydi (executive board, San'a Chamber of Commerce and Industry), interview with author, San'a, 5 May 1987; and Haj Muhammad Amir al-Badawi (tax collector for Imams Ahmad and Yahya and employee in the Department of *Zakat*, Ministry of Finance), interview with author, San'a, 17 March 1987.

[6] For parallels in the collection and assessment methods of Saudi Arabia and Yemen during the 1950s and 1960s, see "Report on Yemen by Muhammad I. Massoud" (11 November 1946) and "Memorandum of Conversations with Sir Bernard Reilly and others at the Department of State" (3 November 1947), in Ibrahim Al Rashid, ed., *Yemen Enters the Modern World* (Chapel Hill, N.C.: Documentary Publications, 1984), 4–5, 125. See also Mohammed Yahya al-Aadhy, "Growth of Revenues in the Yemen Arab Republic" (manuscript, Faculty of Commerce and Economics, San'a University, 1982); Mohammed Anam Ghalib, *Government Organizations as a Barrier to Economic Development in Yemen* (San'a: National Institute for Public Administration Press, 1979); and Mohammad Sayed al Attar, *The Social and Economic Backwardness of Yemen* (Algiers: Algerian National Press, 1965).

[7] In 1943–44, agricultural taxes collected in cash were 6 million Maria Theresa thalers (a much larger amount was collected in kind); customs receipts were less than 2 million thalers (Ghalib, *Government Organizations,* 105).

[8] Information on customs rates varies. Ghalib states that export duties on coffee were 15 percent of value, those for other goods 7.5 percent, and import duties a uniform 12 percent, excluding additional charges for weighing, storage, and other taxes (*Government Organizations,* 102–5). According to a document published in *Majallah al-Maliyah* 3 (1977): 7–9, however, the import duty rates were 10 percent on clothes and 20 percent on luxury goods; export duties on coffee and raisins were one thaler per 10k bag, or about 10 percent. Health, charity, entry, and storage taxes were collected in addition.

[9] See al-Aadhy, "Growth of Revenues."

[10] In organization and functions both the Hijazi and the Yemeni guilds resemble the Turkish guilds in Gabriel Baer, "The Administrative, Economic, and Social Functions of Turkish Guilds," *International Journal of Middle East Studies* 1 (January 1970): 28–50. Of comparative interest is Baer's "Decline and Disappearance of the Guilds," in his *Studies in the Social History of Modern Egypt* (Chicago: University of Chicago Press, 1969), 149–60. On the Yemeni guilds, see R. B. Serjeant and Ronald Lewcock's masterful *San'a, an Arabian Islamic City* (London: World of Islam Festival Trust, 1983).

from among the class of *sayyids* and *qadis* (jurists) that comprised the court elite.[11]

The relationship between taxation and the funding of a standing army was complex and multifaceted: most of the imam's army was made up of temporary tribal levies lent to the ruler on a contract basis. Imam Yahya maintained civil security by exploiting economic scarcity, most often quartering troops in the homes of troublemakers until their poverty made them humble.[12] Similar tactics were used to collect taxes, cutting collection costs to virtually nothing.[13]

Since the northern region was a net drain on the fisc and could not be subdued militarily, taxes were most heavily visited upon the agriculturally rich south. Major trade routes through the south from Aden to the northern provinces also made it a natural center for customs collections. Northern tribes paid tribute irregularly, depending on their shifting acceptance or rejection of the imam's authority.[14] Not surprisingly, southern reactions to taxation were deeply enmeshed in ongoing sectarian-regional conflicts. Northern tribes friendly with the imam bartered their services as collectors in lieu of taxes; being the imam's taxman was a way of entering the monetized economy without leaving the tribe. The tribal collectors who performed these functions were, by all accounts, ruthless and did not hesitate to force peasants off the land in the name of the imam's treasury.[15]

Regional-sectarian cleavages in Yemen and the distinctive organization of the Yemeni tribal confederations forestalled the creation of a national army that had a monopoly on violence. Simply put, maintaining incumbency required of the imam an escalating level of tribal subsidies, which could be collected only with the cooperation of northern tribal levies. Paradoxically, this reverse flow of revenue from ruler to ruled was the linchpin of continued tribal cohesion. In a very real sense, the imam's bureaucracy was a legitimizing conduit through which the northern tribes extracted surplus from the southern agricultural areas. His military dependence on the tribes inscribed regional-ascriptive differences in the imam's relationship with the south.

Given these fundamental constraints, escalating efforts to tax generated perverse outcomes, linked not just to the ruler's military powerlessness

[11] Al-Aadhy, "Growth of Revenues."

[12] "Conversations with Sir Bernard Reilly," in Al Rashid, *Yemen Enters the Modern World,* 125.

[13] Ghalib, *Government Organization,* 102–5.

[14] In the tribal areas where tributary payments were not already established, assessors estimated the yield and collected livestock taxes through the tribal sheikhs. If they refused, as was often the case, the imam sent soldiers to stay indefinitely as guests until the tribes paid up. According to officials who had been tax collectors with the imam's government, the tribal regions of Jawf, Marib, Sa'dah, and Al-Baydah presented the most trouble: Muhammed 'Abdallah Al-Hadrami (Department of *Zakat,* Ministry of Finance, and tax official for Imam Ahmad), interview with author, San'a, 12 April 1987.

[15] Robert Stookey, *Yemen* (Boulder, Colo.: Westview Press, 1978), 195.

but also to opportunities for exit to the rich enclaves of Aden and the Hijaz. The imam was quite literally engaged in pauperizing his southern subjects on behalf of his northern mercenaries; agricultural taxation in the region of Ibb was so high that production of winter crops and livestock declined on a yearly basis.[16] Ibb, Taiz and Hujariyah were bordered on the south by the tribes of the Adeni hinterland, who, along with the British in Aden and the imam, competed for tax revenues from the overland trade between the Yemeni hinterland and the port of Aden. The southern trade was thus subjected to multiple taxation by a variety of authorities. Coffee exports from Hujariyah were taxed in sequence by the Yemeni imam, by the Mansuri, Makhdumi, and Rijaʿi branches of the nomad Subayhi, by the Arqabi sheikh, and finally by the sultan of Lahj.[17] Taxes on exports and imports of raw materials precipitated the decline of artisan communities in all regions, but especially in Zabid and the southern cities of Ibb and Taiz. Excessive taxation and the imam's frequent use of corvée labor for large projects fed into southern discontent.[18]

The process of redistributing surplus between the *Shiʿa* north and the *Sunni* south had changed many times since the establishment of the Zaydi imamate in Sanʿa in the ninth century. In this context, Aden, a British colony (since 1839) at the tip of the Arabian Peninsula became increasingly important to the struggle between southern Yemen and the imam. Whereas in the past the British free port had made Yemen the site of competition between Britain and the Ottoman Porte—generating alternative authority structures in what would become the Yemen Arab Republic (1962) and the People's Democratic Republic of Yemen (1967)—under the imam it became a destination for overtaxed southerners.

Fixed assets, it is correctly argued, are easier to tax than mobile ones.[19] As taxes on agriculture grew and production declined, *Sunni* southerners "voted" by migrating to Aden and beyond, undercutting the imam's tax base. More important, migration spawned a distinctly southern *Sunni* commercial and financial elite located outside Yemen's borders, in Aden. Until the early 1940s this group profited from and eventually developed a strong interest in maintaining the monetary and economic fragmentation of their own country.

Migration to Aden was a well-established pattern even before World

[16] Ibid., 194–95, esp. n. 52.

[17] In the 1870s the imam's protests against the British, and his negotiations with a French company to build a port at Shaykh Saʿid to bypass both the Turkish-controlled Mocha port and Aden, brought British military action against him. See R. J. Gavin, *Aden under British Rule* (London: C. Hurst, 1975), 126, 119.

[18] On forced labor, see Sheila Carapico and Richard Tutwiler, *Yemeni Agriculture and Economic Change* (Sanʿa: American Institute for Yemeni Studies, 1981), 17.

[19] Contrast Albert Hirschman, *Exit, Voice, and Loyalty* (Cambridge: Harvard University Press, 1970) with Robert Bates and Da-Hsiang Donald Lien, "A Note on Taxation, Development, and Representative Government," *Politics and Society* 14, no. 1 (1985): 53–70.

War I, but in the interwar period it became a major constraint on the imam's efforts to centralize authority, and structural economic changes in Aden itself combined with the imam's growing appetite for taxes to polarize the Yemenis in Aden and the court in San῾a. In the 1930s the collapse of commodity prices of Yemen's substantial exports in raw materials coincided with a sudden boost in the imam's demands for southern surpluses to meet the costs of conducting war with Ibn Saud over control of Asir. Formally a Yemeni province, though long under the de facto control of Idrisi chieftains, Asir was annexed by Ibn Saud in 1934. A year later Yemen's southern borders were fixed by the British. Neither event expanded the imam's administrative and military control over Yemeni territory, but both spurred his ultimately unsuccessful efforts to establish a permanent military force. The result was an escalation in tribal subsidies and increasingly arbitrary taxation, which continued long after the conflicts had ended.[20] It was during this period that southerners began migrating to Aden en masse.

In the face of outmigration, declining agricultural yields, and plummeting trade taxes, the imam identified state monopolies and monopsonies as an alternative source of revenue—with far-reaching results. Starting in the 1930s, economic policy was geared to achieving enough closure in the economy to ensure the success of the monopoly strategy of revenue extraction. It was out of this strategy, which coincided globally with economic autarky and protectionism, that Yemen's fabled isolation from the world began to be pursued consciously and methodically. Lacking the means to regulate the overland trade, migration, and production, the imam deployed a state policy of systematic and complete economic, cultural, and political seclusion through which he sought to monopolize maritime trade and thereby gain a steady source of state income. The dimensions of this closure are legendary. Until the late 1940s, Yemen was arguably the most autarkic country in existence. Private imports and exports were banned; no foreign embassies or missions were permitted; and foreigners could not enter the country except by the personal invitation of the imam.[21]

Imam Yahya's pursuit of national isolation as a strategy for maintaining

[20] This pattern is of course historically the norm, as Charles Tilly has argued. Others have tried to generalize this finding to all taxes; see Edward Ames and Richard T. Rapp, "The Birth and Death of Taxes" (with comments by James Millar), *Journal of Economic History* 37 (March 1977): 161–78.

[21] According to one eyewitness, writing in 1946, "No means of communications exist and the only means are an old wireless station and the new radio station presented to them by the American government. There is not even one telephone in Yemen. No roads worth the names exist, particularly on your way to the south. No dams, no irrigation systems, no development, no construction at all" (quoted from "Report on Yemen by Muhammad I. Massoud," in Al Rashid, *Yemen Enters the Modern World,* 5). See also J. E. Peterson, *Yemen* (London: Croom Helm, 1982), 10–68; Manfred W. Wenner, *Modern Yemen* (Baltimore: Johns Hopkins University Press, 1967); and Stookey, *Yemen,* 167–212.

incumbency in the absence of stable bureaucratic-military power had important implications for business organization. Yemen's mountainous topography meant that the country's economy was already prone to fragmentation. The imam's policies institutionalized the existing fissures by promoting permanent flows of goods and money designed explicitly to take advantage of or to circumvent these policies. The imam's fiscal desperation and the policies to which it gave form resulted in the creation of the three Yemeni commercial classes that laid more or less permanent claim to distinct niches in the economy.

The first—properly characterized as the only stable social base of imamic authority—grew directly out of the organizational imperatives of trade restrictions. The state monopolies in imports, staples, utilities, and services gave rise in the north to a small but powerful merchant class—drawn largely from the *sayyid* strata of society in the capital—which managed and profited from state monopolies. The house of al-Jabali acted as an overseer of the "companies" set up by the imam. The San'ani commercial houses of Aslan, Withari, Thawr, Zubayri, Adhban, Sunaydar, Ghamdan, Amiri, and Thulayah, specializing in wholesale, distribution and retailing, made up the rest of the core group.[22] The second cluster emerged as a result of the prohibition against the direct docking of foreign vessels at the Hudaydah port. Here a class of importers of Hadrami and Indian origin linked foreign firms in Aden with the San'ani merchants, shipping goods from Aden up the Red Sea by dhow for distribution inland through the state companies.[23] The third group, which would become economically ascendant after 1962, was made up exclusively of the southern *Sunni* commercial and financial elites based in Aden (henceforth referred to as the absentee bourgeoisie), who specialized in the overland trade between Aden and the southern regions of Yemen.

These three commercial classes were born of policies designed to overcome the fiscal crisis of the imamic state. Those policies, in turn, were undergirded by the militarily dominant northern tribal confederations, whose social codes prevented them from participating in trade and commerce. The mercenary army, which became a major drain on the treasury as the 1930s wore on, was essentially a rentier group separate from the world of commerce and entrusted with maintaining restrictions on private business.[24] A monopoly on coercion and economic ascendancy were neatly

[22] Ghalib, *Government Organizations,* 36.

[23] From 1987 interviews with merchants in Hudayah, I discovered that the Indian merchants specialized in exporting tobacco and importing spices; Arabs specialized in sugar, rice, textile, and foodstuff imports and acted as agents for foreign companies interested in Yemen's exports of coffee, resins, and hides for overseas markets and raisins, barley, and produce for the Adeni market.

[24] In this period, tribal elites considered it dishonorable even to enter the marketplace; they employed merchants to deliver goods and act as intermediaries. See Carapico and Tutwiler, *Yemeni Agriculture.*

divided among the regional groups of Yemen; the ruler belonged to none of these groups.

The fragmentation of the internal market and the control of niches within the economy by segments of the commercial class both reflected and enforced the difficulties of state-building that would confront Yemen both before and after its 1962 "revolution". Each merchant cluster was formed by a geographically and culturally distinct confessional group; for the largely Indian Hudaydah merchants, ethnicity was a factor as well. All these groups were formed and influenced, in one way or another, by the absolute prohibition against the entry of foreign companies into Yemen and the myriad restrictions on economic activity. Relying explicitly on the fragmented domestic market, the three merchant groups constructed workable, if not stable, mechanisms to circumvent or take advantage of the state's prohibitions. Until the late 1940s, all three groups shared an interest in maintaining the niche economy; none had an interest in creating a unified national market.

Thus, in Yemen as in Saudi Arabia, the end of the Ottoman Empire generated a new drive for state revenue. In neither case were political elites initally allied with economically dominant groups. In Yemen, the tribal structure of the northern confederations prevented the imam from pursuing a policy of conscription and co-optation, leading him to pursue, instead, the Sherifian strategy of building a tax state without a permanent army. The existence of Aden, however, circumscribed the extent to which the tax strategy could proceed, and eventually the imam had to change his tack and turn to monopolies as a substitute for taxation. In the process, his policies institutionalized and strengthened the rifts between the three regionally based commercial classes of Yemen, pushing well into the future the possibility of generating a coalition in favor or a national market but also forestalling a struggle among the commercial elites to expand control beyond their own niches.

In the 1940s, however, a confluence of external and internal changes disrupted the equilibrium of the niche economy, raised the possibility of a national economy, and precipitated a protracted struggle among the three commercial groups for the dominant role in defining the institutions that would govern that economy. Structural changes in both Aden and Yemen shattered the common interest of the three merchant groups in the divided market and initiated a struggle for the dominance of a single national market. These antagonisms came to the fore after 1948 and continued well after the deposition of the imam in 1962.

LABOR, BUSINESS, AND COLONIALISM IN ADEN

The events that precipitated the intra-elite struggle in 1948 occurred as much in Aden as in Yemen itself. There were, to simplify, three relevant economic groupings in the free port of Aden: the absentee bourgeoisie, a Yemeni migrant labor force, and the Adeni commercial and service classes. During the interwar period the Adeni economy had undergone a major structural change that transformed it from an entrepot to a booming port servicing oil tankers from the Gulf and Iran. This change not only transformed the size, role, and organization of the Yemeni migrant labor force in Aden but also disrupted the economic and financial ties between the laborers and the Aden-based Yemeni commercial class. New lines of conflict and competition emerged between the Adeni merchants—who were citizens of the colony—and the absentee bourgeoisie, who were not British subjects. This conflict arose in the context of an increasingly radicalized labor movement in Aden, led by Yemeni migrant laborers, which led to Adeni demands for protection from the unionists and their co-sectarians in the commercial and banking sector.

The legal frame of colonialism transformed a class conflict into an ethnic polarization that cut across class lines. Throughout the 1950s, politics in Aden became increasingly polarized between the Adeni elite and their British protectors on one hand, and a coalition of Yemeni commercial elites and Yemeni migrant labor on the other. The Aden-based Yemeni coalition of business and labor was ultimately responsible for the successful campaign to topple the imam.

Aden had been a key link between Red Sea and Indian Ocean trade networks since the fourteenth century.[25] It assumed a special importance for Yemen in the mid-eighteenth century, when dwindling coffee production led to the decline of the ancient port of Mocha.[26] The ascent of Aden as a port reestablished parts of the ancient overland trade route from Aden to San'a, the Hijaz, Qasim, and beyond. Aden had long been a point of departure for migration to East Africa, Europe, and the United States, but only after British occupation in 1839 did the port city itself became a major market for Yemeni labor.[27] The growth of the British bureaucracy in Aden during the nineteenth century created a substantial demand for workers to fill military, construction, and civil service jobs; and successive years of drought, instability, overtaxation, and landlessness pushed thousands of Yemenis south. They soon formed the bulk of the increase in Aden's permanent population, growing from 34,860 in 1881 to 44,079 in 1891. Temporary migrations, which did not merit entry in the British administration's reports, were even larger. By the turn of the

[25] For a sketch of the Indian Ocean trade, see K. N. Chaudhuri, *Trade and Civilization in the Indian Ocean* (Cambridge: Cambridge University Press, 1985), esp. 99–117.

[26] By the late eighteenth century, coffee from European colonies was flooding even the Arab markets. As European purchases of Yemeni coffee had been compensated in specie, Mocha joined the many victims that littered the path of European maritime trade. By 1835, when the inflow of specie had dried up, the once robust population of Mocha had declined to less than 1,000 inhabitants. See Gavin, *Aden under British Rule,* 19–20.

[27] Jon Swanson, *Emigration and Economic Development* (Boulder, Colo.: Westview Press, 1979).

century these Yemeni migrations had changed the ethnic and cultural composition of the colony. "In the 1890s almost half Aden's population was Arab—a striking change from the position at the middle of the century when Arabs formed less than a quarter of the community and were greatly outnumbered by the Indians. The bulk of the migrant laborers, who formed a large part of the 'new' Arab population, came in from the Hajariya [Hujariyah], Baydha and other parts of the Yemen highlands."[28]

The top layer of Aden's business community was a mixture of Parsi, Sindhi, Gujerati, and Hyderabadi minorities, London agents, British second sons, and opportunists—a combination not atypical of British free ports elsewhere—which directly controlled international trade links with India. Yemenis started out in the lower reaches of the colony's community, specializing in dock work, transport, and salaried employment. These were the sectors in which the trade unionist movements of Aden took form. The migrant population was temporary, with laborers staying little more than three to four months at a time and shopkeepers moving back and forth every six or eight months.[29]

As the entrepot trade grew, the Yemeni migrants diversified into inland commerce and finance. The British promoted the overland trade between Aden and the Yemeni highlands by creating a stable market for inland products, by facilitating the steady inflow of foreign merchants, companies, and bankers, and by partially quelling the longstanding tribal wars that had plagued the immediate hinterland of Aden. By the turn of the century a powerful and organized business class composed almost exclusively of Yemeni migrants had emerged in Aden to manage the hinterland trade and related transportation services. The absentee bourgeoisie made its place in informal banking, trade, labor contracting, and remittance transport, its members inserting themselves into a heterogeneous financial community.[30]

Further, the southern merchants became the almost exclusive mediators between international companies, the hinterland, and the colony through their management of Yemeni migrant labor and its inland remittances. In contrast to earlier waves of Yemeni migration to Britain, the United States, and Europe, where remittances were controlled by the Adeni banks, labor migration to Aden itself opened new opportunities for

[28] Gavin, *Aden under British Rule*, 189; see also 227–76 on British dealings with the tribal confederations of South Yemen.

[29] Ibid., 190.

[30] Using *suftaja* (bills of exchange) and *musharika* (a form of financing similar to the commenda, a cooperative method of financing long-distance trade that began in medieval Europe) Yemeni merchants expanded long-distance trade to the hinterland. See Robert Lopez, *The Commercial Revolution of the Middle Ages, 950–1350* (Cambridge: Cambridge University Press, 1976), and 'Abd al-'Aziz Ahmad Sa'id Haydarah al-Muqtari, *Al-Nuqud wa-al Siyasah al Naqdiyah fil Iqtisad al-Yemani al-Hadith* [Money and monetary policy in the contemporary economy of Yemen] (Beirut: Dar al Hidathah, 1985), 38.

Yemeni merchants to gain direct access to labor remittances for trade finance. For the absentee bourgeoisie, labor contracting became a lucrative and growing field as they supplied the port and territories beyond that could be reached only through Aden, including Djibouti, Somalia, and South Africa.

Labor recruiters linked migrants' savings with the inland merchants through the *muqaddam* (labor-brokering) system[31] of mutually binding rights and obligations between migrant laborers and remittance agents. These multifaceted informal contracts were often built on kinship networks or common domicile in Yemeni villages. Informal bankers, migrant agents, and labor recruiters linked expatriate communities and the Yemeni work force in Aden with the domestic subsistence economy. Remittances were the absentee bourgeoisie's source of commercial finance; the merchants, somewhat differently from those elsewhere, built their fortunes on the backs of the migrant laborers.

The dependence of the absentee bourgeoisie on migrant workers meant that the former's fortunes were intimately connected to the individual decisions of the latter. Changing migration patterns—such as the growing attraction of East Africa and Asir[32]—and the innovations they spawned resulted in a massive injection of capital into trade finance, which broadened the southern merchant classes and permitted them to expand their activities. During the interwar period, migration to Aden swelled, especially as the domestic economy constricted under the imam's monopolies and taxes. By the 1930s, Yemeni commercial finance was benefiting from larger infusions of capital, closer links with the Indian and Parsi communities, and, most of all, exchange differentials between the price of the Maria Theresa thaler in Aden and its value in the hinterland. Whereas in the 1920s the four trading concerns of Basalamah, Thalib, al-Mansub, and Hufrayn had dominated all trade with the hinterland, by the 1930s more than fifteen major merchant houses were plying the overland trade routes from the town of Ibb alone.[33]

In a very real sense, the disunity of the Yemeni market—the absence of infrastructure and communications, the multiplicity of currencies, and the disequilibria of supply and demand—resulted in the second foundation of capital accumulation for the absentee bourgeoisie: money-changing. The commercial elite shaped their activities in economic niches created by the imam's restrictive policies, turning the thriving informal

[31] Gavin, *Aden under British Rule*, 326–27.

[32] Sizable groups of Yemeni merchants were also concentrated in Ethiopia. According to the American legation in Addis Ababa in 1946, "There are in Ethiopia about 10,000 to 14,000 Yemenis, mostly minor or medium traders, which constitutes about 90% of the active and non-tribal Muslim population of Ethiopia . . ." (quoted in Gavin, *Aden under British Rule*, 326–27).

[33] Qasim al-Mansub (Director, Sholaq Foreign Exchange operations in Ibb and Taiz), interviews with author, Ibb, December 1986.

banking system into profit. Monetary instability, the principal prerequisite for informal banking and exchange, was a permanent feature of the Yemeni economy.[34] Saudi coins, the Maria Theresa thaler, the Indian rupee, East African shillings, and various denominations of Ottoman currency circulated simultaneously well into the 1960s.[35] Yet unlike Europe, where money exchanging was big business in centers of international trade, Yemen developed an exchange system that resisted change, precisely because the country was a residual economy, bordered by the vibrant entrepots of the Hijaz in the north and Aden in the south.[36]

The use of remittances in financing trade, exchanging currencies, and later in letters of credit with specially designed maturity periods helped conceal both commissions and interest, which were strictly prohibited by the imam.[37] Whereas in Europe by the mid-sixteenth century the amount of interest considered to be usurious varied with local economic conditions and the balance of secular and religious authority, the Islamic prohibition is absolute, and the imam's dedication to enforcing it was reflected in the near monopoly of Jewish and Indian Banyan traders in the lending and exchanging professions in the *Zaydi* north.[38] The imam's inability to create a unified currency and his restrictions on trade directly generated the environment in which the remittance-trade link was forged. Import restrictions created shortages that yielded profits high enough to make the overland trade attractive.

The sudden and dramatic changes in the Adeni economy introduced by World War II disrupted evolving relationships between the different segments of the commercial classes in Aden and undid the economic basis of the *muqaddam* system. From the onset of the war, the entrepot trade declined, and servicing the expanding traffic from the oil fields of the Gulf assumed primary importance. By the early 1950s Aden was, in

[34] A silver Yemeni riyal was not minted until July 1963 by Bank Misr, the financial appendage of the Egyptian forces then in Yemen. The silver Republican riyal was minted in Egypt; by July 1964 an estimated 8,375,000 had been introduced: "Economic Survey for Yemen, 1963 with July 30, 1964 Balance Sheet of the Yemen Currency Board" (Joint State/Aid Despatch from American Embassy in Taiz, Yemen Arab Republic, 1963), 75 (hereafter cited as "Economic Survey for Yemen, 1963").

[35] See Charles P. Kindleberger, *A Financial History of Western Europe* (Boston: Allen & Unwin, 1984), 15–152. Specifically on banking and currency problems in imamic Yemen, see "Conversation of U.S. Representative to the Special Diplomatic Mission with Merchant Ahmed Tahir Bajab, Representing the Views of the Imam of Yemen" (San'a 12 May 1946), in Al Rashid, *Yemen Enters the Modern World,* 33.

[36] Kindleberger, *Financial History,* 42, describes the role of money-changers in extending credit, remitting funds, and banking deposits. On economic relations between Aden and Yemen, see "Memorandum of Conversation with Prince Abdallah of Yemen" (U.S. Department of State, 29 July 1947), in Al Rashid, *Yemen Enters the Modern World,* 114–18.

[37] Informal banking practices, however, were supported by religious doctrine. See Abraham Utrovitch, "Bankers without Banks," in *The Dawn of Modern Banking* (New Haven: Yale University Press, 1979), 225–74; Serjeant and Lewcock, "Coins and Mints," in *San'a.*

[38] Kindleberger, *Financial History,* 35; cf. Utrovitch, "Bankers without Banks," and Jacques le Goff, "The Usurer and Purgatory," both in *Dawn of Modern Banking,* 225–74, 25–52.

the account of one of her most devoted students, the busiest port in the world after New York, boasting massive investment in infrastructure, construction, and services. The dramatic growth of the British bureaucracy and accelerated recruitment into the British army, all supplied with Yemeni labor, fundamentally transformed the structure of the Adeni economy, including the organization of labor and intra-elite relationships.[39] The trade unionist movements of Aden emerged as a result of that shift from an entrepot managed by a skeleton bureaucracy and police force to a service economy dominated by foreign companies engaged in transporting oil.[40] In the entrepot, no single organization had employed large groups of laborers. The entry of large foreign companies shifted employment patterns radically, consolidating the work force in opposition to a few employers.

The British bureaucracy and army, which grew rapidly from the 1930s and 1940s on, themselves became major employers. In these two realms, trade and labor union organizers found eager converts among both Yemeni migrants and workers from the immediate Adeni hinterland. Neither group had the privileges awarded to citizens of Aden, yet they outnumbered them several fold. The large wave of migrants that entered Aden in 1943 in the wake of a major harvest failure marked the beginning of serious and sustained opposition to both the British and the imam. The rise of the unions simultaneously transformed the economic links between the Yemeni merchant elite and Yemeni labor in Aden. By 1948 these changes had rendered parts of the *muqaddam* system obsolete and eclipsed the more fragmented and diverse private sector of the previous century. Labor unions increasingly engaged in collective bargaining in an economy dominated by large shipping corporations, oil companies, and the British bureaucracy and army.[41]

The southern labor-business coalition in Aden grew out of the dual pressures that the absentee bourgeoisie experienced in adjusting to these structural changes. The two groups were united, however, only in their opposition to the British, the Adeni British citizens, and the imam. At first glance, it appears paradoxical that the obsolescence of the *muqaddam* system and the rise of highly organized labor unions would create a coalition between the Yemeni absentee bourgeoisie and the unions against the British and the Adeni elite, but closer examination reveals a strong confluence of interests. Under the colonial political system, "proper" Adenis—citizens of the British colony—had many rights and entitlements that were shared neither by the subjects of the sultanates in the immediate

[39] Gavin, *Aden under British Rule,* esp. 318–19.

[40] On the labor unions, see Helen Lackner, *The People's Democratic Republic of Yemen* (London: Ithaca Press, 1985); and D. C. Watt, "Labor Relations and Trades Unionism in Aden, 1952–60," *Middle East Journal* 16 (Fall 1962): 443–56.

[41] Gavin, *Aden under British Rule,* 310, 326–27.

Adeni hinterland nor by the Yemeni merchants and laborers resident in Aden. They were also largely of Indian extraction. Thus, not only was the growing militancy of the unionists threatening in class terms, but as the 1950s wore on, their anticolonial political agenda was increasingly couched in Pan-Arab rhetoric, which was anathema to the protected Adeni citizenry.

Not unlike other sectarian, ethnic, or religious minorities, the Adenis viewed Pan-Arabism as a direct political and economic threat, kept at bay only by the colonial administration.[42] The rise of Aden as a shipping center, in increasing the independence of Yemeni labor from the absentee bourgeoisie and their associated labor contractors, also enhanced the position of the Adeni segment of the colony's merchant group. The decline of the entrepot trade had precipitated growing competition between Adeni and Yemeni merchants in which the former increasingly brought their privileges to bear, gaining preferential access to opportunities created by the growth of state spending in the 1940–60 period, when government services and foreign transactions eclipsed the local private sector. As the independence movement in Aden gained strength in the late 1950s and early 1960s, direct confrontation arose between the commercial classes, pitting the Yemeni absentee bourgeoisie against the colony's local commercial and service elite. Meanwhile, the trade unionist movement, composed of Yemeni labor, increasingly adopted the language of Pan-Arabism and antiimperialism to match their already robust vocabulary of class opposition to the Adeni elite. British policy, under the dual tensions of labor unrest and pressure from the Adeni commercial elites, turned generally discriminatory against all Yemenis in Aden.

Discrimination and social polarization in Aden was a "push" factor for the absentee bourgeoisie and even the labor unionists. It revealed in stark relief the benefits of a protected national market, and contemporaneous developments in Yemen fueled the impulse toward a national market. Demands on the Yemeni treasury grew rapidly in the late 1940s, largely as a result of Imam Ahmad's efforts to balance the growing ranks of "free Yemenis" in Aden with stronger ties to the courtly elite and the northern tribes. Threat of defection had always been the centerpiece of the northern tribal elite's political strategy, and the anti-imam movement in Aden was credible enough to rationalize tribal demands for higher subsidies. Ahmad's abandonment of his father's time-tested strategy of holding hostages to control the tribes expanded his fiscal needs at a moment when agricultural taxes were already past their limit.

Overland trade and state monopolies were the obvious alternative revenue sources, and Ahmad pursued both. Customs duties were increased,

[42] The attitude of the Adenis toward Pan-Arabism was shared by such groups as the Maronite Christians in Lebanon and the *Shi'a* in Syria.

and between 1945 and 1948 all trade in the northern areas was declared to be the monopoly of the Yemen Company for Industry, Agriculture, and Transport.[43]

Imam Ahmad soon reached the limit of these sources and, in desperation, initiated another strategy for increasing revenues: in a general opening of the Yemeni economy in the late 1950s and early 1960s, he finally agreed to allow the entry of foreign aid. The Chinese, Americans, and Russians quickly initiated infrastructure projects, particularly in roads, construction, and communications.[44] The new projects eased transportation constraints on trade, and the growing foreign community created a new market for local goods. Better communications enhanced the ability of the imam to tax and control the merchandise flowing across the southern border, thus substantially undercutting profits from the overland trade, especially as merchandise began to move directly from the newly reopened port of Hudaydah.

The opening of Yemen to foreigners jostled the fortunes of Yemen's three economic groups, to the detriment of the absentee bourgeoisie: the entry of foreign donors naturally tipped the balance of domestic economic activity in favor of the San'a- and Hudaydah-based merchants; and American, Soviet, and Chinese projects, particularly in road construction, gave the imam the power to handpick local interlocutors from among the court-based elite.[45] To preserve their exclusive control over these lucrative sub-contracts, the Hudaydah merchants successfully lobbied the imam to ban the entry of the Aden-based overland merchants into the port of Hudaydah, through which much of the development aid passed. Then, in 1961, the Hudaydah merchants formed a chamber of commerce that explicitly excluded the merchants from Taiz, Hujariyah, and Aden. As a result, the southern overland merchants were forced to make the small and not easily accessible town of Bayt al-Faqih the central distribution point for the Tihamah market.[46]

Economic policy changes initiated by Imam Ahmad thus at once increased the attractiveness of the Yemeni market and spawned attempts by the courtly elite to exclude the Aden-based absentee bourgeoisie from sharing in the benefits of trade liberalization. Together, the growing costs of exclusion from the Yemeni market and the escalating levels of discrimination in Aden generated a strong anti-imam reform movement in the Yemeni communities in Aden. For the absentee bourgeoisie, the costs of

[43] The company was short-lived because direct control over trade proved more lucrative for the government, and the imam soon reverted to the time-tested agent system whereby the government sold grain to individual merchants in return for commissions. The name of the company was retained, however. See Carapico and Tutwiler, *Yemeni Agriculture,* 19–21.

[44] See Stookey, *Yemen,* 208–10; and "Economic Survey for Yemen, 1963."

[45] Stookey, *Yemen,* 201–4.

[46] Hudaydah merchants, interviews with author, January 1987; and review of founding documents of the Hudaydah Chamber of Commerce.

continued imamic rule increased at the same time that the potential economic benefits of unfettered access to the Yemeni market multiplied.

A third entirely exogenous event, the independence of India, jolted the system in 1947, simultaneously squeezing the absentee bourgeoisie involved in the overland trade and laying the groundwork for their eventual domination of finance. Indian independence scrambled the precarious balance of currencies in the Arabian Peninsula. Two years after Independence, the legal tender of British Aden was changed from the Indian rupee to the East African shilling, and international merchants who relied on Adeni banks switched their holdings. Preference for the thaler endured in the hinterland of Aden and north Yemen, however, and the thaler also continued to dominate the basket of currencies used in the haj economy of the Hijaz.

When the major Adeni banks and their corporate clients stopped using the rupee, they upset India-Aden-Hijaz trade patterns and, more important for this story, severely disrupted Yemeni remittances between the Hijaz, Aden, and interior Yemen. In contrast to the rupee, which had been widely used by merchants trading with India, the African shilling was scarce and not generally accepted as a means of exchange inside Yemen. As a result of this exogenous shock, the remittance system underwent a radical change involving nothing less than its transformation into a service and its disconnection from the overland trade, thus accelerating the decay of the *muqaddam* system. The remarkable entrepreneur who took advantage of the situation and continued to restructure the money-changing business in Yemen into the 1980s was ʿAbduh Ahmad Sholaq, a Hujariyan merchant who had traded on the Aden-Taiz axis as a small wholesaler and retailer.[47]

Sholaq simultaneously revolutionized and centralized trade finance and the transmission of labor remittances. Before 1947 the remittance business had been used almost exclusively to meet the financial needs of the overland merchants.[48] Sholaq severed this connection. The old system of

[47] The material on Sholaq and his foreign exchange business is drawn from my 1986–87 interviews with his closest associates, including Husayn al-Saqqaf, his general manager in Yemen, and Qasim al-Mansub, his first associate in Ibb. In 1936 Sholaq opened shops in Aden to retail his own exports from Taiz. By the onset of World War II he had built a substantial enough business to buy sugar and tobacco from the Bess Company for wholesale in Hudaydah. Leaving the Aden and Taiz retail shops to employees, he moved to Jeddah in 1952 to open exchange offices there and in Mecca. Like other Hijazi exchangers, his trade was tied to the annual Mecca pilgrimage; he monopolized the substantial business of Yemeni pilgrims, who reportedly preferred him to the Hadrami exchanger Bamatraf.

[48] This pattern is also found in early merchant banking and exchange businesses in Europe's maritime trade centers; see Stanley Chapman, *The Rise of Merchant Banking* (London: Allen & Unwin, 1984). Unlike their European counterparts, however, exchangers did not regularly extend loans to merchants who were not closely affiliated with them. Deposit-taking was rare as well. The reluctance of money-changers in Aden to make loans was in marked contrast to the practice of money changers elsewhere in the Middle East: e.g., cf. al-Muqtari, *al-Nuqud,* 32, and Saʿid Humadeh, *The Monetary and Banking System of Syria* (Beirut: American Press, 1935), 173–219.

transporting remittances through trade cycles ended, and a new remittance service, in which profit margins were based not on trade but on the different currency values between Jeddah, Yemen, and Aden, began.[49] As the new method of remitting migrant earnings spread, merchants became increasingly reliant on Sholaq and affiliated money-changing houses for finance. The centralization of financial capital occurred essentially in response to an external event, but it signaled the onset of a growing rift between the majority of the southern overland merchants and a much smaller group of financiers.

This complex confluence of events—intra-elite conflict in Aden, the opening of the Yemeni market, and the centralization of credit and finance—fueled the absentee impulse to gain control of the Yemeni market. The coalition the absentee bourgeoisie formed to achieve this goal included migrant labor in Aden and segments of the Sanʿani court elite. Until the 1940s, the Sanʿa, Hudaydah, and southern elites had had a mutual interest in the closed Yemeni market and restrictions on trade, for it was in the gaps of this remarkably autarkic system that they had inserted themselves, whether through monopoly, links with labor, or illegal trade. In 1960 this union of interests collapsed. The economic opening undid the de facto market-sharing arrangements of the past and raised the question of who would control the domestic market and under what terms. In this context, the absentee business-labor coalition stood in opposition to the *Zaydi* and Hudaydah-based commercial classes. The coalition's efforts to depose the imam intensified in the context of historically constructed fissures that divided the Yemeni commercial and military elite. The conflicting and mutually exclusive interests of the merchant groups, the tribes, and the old political elite shaped the struggle against Imam Ahmad.

The Civil War and the Return of the Absentee Bourgeoisie

The absentee bourgeoisie and the migrant laborers in Aden and East Africa had long been the most sustained source of anti-imam activity. In the early 1940s, for example, the two political parties, the *Hayat al-Nidal* and the *Jamʿiyat al-Islah,* were both formed in Aden, as was the "Free Yemeni" movement that inspired an unsuccessful 1948 coup led by Zubayr, Wazir, and other *sayyids.* With the failures of that coup and another in 1955, Yemeni political movements in Aden became increasingly radicalized. The reformist efforts of the 1940s and 1950s were replaced by a

[49] Sholaq's personal profits had little to do with the commissions. These were farmed out to local agents depending on their efforts and the level of risk they assumed. Thus, the Taiz and Ibb correspondents received a 1.5 percent commission, whereas the Hudaydah correspondent, Khadim al-Wajih, got 5 percent.

revolutionary agenda that sought not just to replace one set of religious elites with a more progressive group but to rearrange the entire social and political system. One aspect of the reorientation of political opposition to the imam was clear: with the failure of the San'a-based reformist group, the Aden-based merchants and trade union leaders became the uncontested leaders of the anti-Imam movement.

As in Saudi Arabia, political debate in Yemen during the 1960s was temporarily thrust into a discursive realm originating in Syria, Egypt, and Iraq. Yemeni society itself remained divided along ascriptive lives, but a small group of army officers and the million-strong migrant and merchant population catapulted domestic debate into the Pan-Arab fray. Ultimately, the emotionally charged, liberating abstractions of Ba'thism, Pan-Arabism, socialism, Nasserism modified the way segments of the population perceived their struggle.[50]

In the context of this regional debate, the language of the migrant labor movement in Aden was drawn not from the Yemeni political scene but rather from the wider ideological currents of anticolonialism and Arab nationalism which dominated political debate in the Arab Middle East during the 1950s and 1960s.[51] The intermingling of anti-British and Yemeni nationalist movements generated exceedingly complex symbiotic relationships between the politics of northern and southern Yemen, which outlasted the violent overthrow of both the imam and the British. The Yemeni revolution of 1962 that gave birth to the Yemen Arab Republic (YAR) was led and sponsored by Yemenis in Aden through organizations that combined a variety of ideologies and forms of organization. Similarly, the National Liberation Front (NLF), which was to defeat the more moderate Egyptian-backed Front for the Liberation of South Yemen (FLOSY) after the British departed in 1967, was actually created in San'a in 1963. The combination of local economic demands and regional ideologies not only splintered the Yemeni agitators in Aden but also created political ties—and political rifts—so intense that armed conflict continued to erupt between the newly formed Yemen Arab Republic in the north and the People's Democratic Republic of Yemen (PDRY).[52] Most important, the labor movement and anticolonial mobilization gave rise to the belief, held by large segments of the *Sunni* south and the hinterland populations surrounding the British colony, that South Yemen (Aden) and North Yemen (San'a) were, in fact, one nation.

The antigovernment activities of Yemeni merchants and trade unionists

[50] The standard text is Fouad Ajami, *The Arab Predicament* (Cambridge: Cambridge University Press, 1981), see esp. 16–21. See also Ajami, "The End of Pan-Arabism," *Foreign Affairs* 57 (Winter 1978): 355–73.

[51] On the history, organization, and beliefs of these groups, see Lackner, *People's Democratic Republic of Yemen,* 27–80.

[52] See Robin Bidwell, *The Two Yemens* (Boulder, Colo.: Westview Press, 1983); and Lackner, *People's Democratic Republic of Yemen,* 35–61.

in Aden went through several incarnations, each of which generated clusters of supporters within Yemen itself. And although the coup that finally toppled the imam was carried out by a handful of army officers of *Zaydi* origin who had trained in Egypt, the absentee bourgeoisie played a decisive role in fomenting anti-imam sentiment by providing financial backing and armaments, working through the press, and molding the platforms of labor unions whose members constituted the bulk of Yemen's Republican population.[53] Initially, the radicals took over in both the People's Democratic Republic of Yemen (established in 1967) and the Yemen Arab Republic (1962), but whereas the former veered further left in 1968, the latter took a decisive turn to the right. Between 1962 and 1968, in the context of an ongoing civil war, control over the political agenda was wrested from the labor union organizers by a newly forged coalition between the absentee bourgeoisie who had returned from Aden and East Africa, the military, and segments of the court-based *Shiʿa* political elite in Sanʿa.

The real struggle to define the institutions that would govern the economy of the Yemen Arab Republic began after 1962. The revolution opened up conflicts that were multifaceted and ambiguous: one among the three branches of the commercial elite, another between all the Republican forces (which included large segments of the *Zaydi* court elite) and the tribal north. Almost immediately after the imam was deposed, the unifying force of Pan-Arabism dissipated, revealing the fundamental divisions that plagued Yemeni society. In the brief interim between the declaration of the republic and the emergence of the full force of the civil war, sectarian divisions appeared. The Republicans among the army officers were a small faction in the overwhelmingly *Zaydi* army, which itself was considerably weaker than the tribes. The southerners were hardly represented at all in the army and the bureaucracy, but they still dominated private-sector commerce and the skilled labor force, composed largely of returnees from Aden.

The struggling government's attempts to grapple with these divisions were amply demonstrated in the early attempts to form a government. In September 1962 southerners were equally represented with northerners in the first cabinet; by January 1963 they were a one-third minority and held less sensitive positions than the *Zaydis*. Their incremental exclusion from positions of power generated attempts by southern elites to reverse the trend, including the creation of a national guard staffed by *Shafiʿis* and overtures to the British for a confederation with Aden.[54]

While *Zaydi* and *Shafiʿi* Republicans struggled over the distribution of

[53] Although most historical texts on Yemen get hopelessly sidetracked by the byzantine politics of the Republican period, both Stookey and Lackner recognize the decisive role of Adeni-based merchants and labor organizers in fomenting anti-imam sentiment.

[54] Stookey, *Yemen,* 233; Carapico and Tutwiler, *Yemeni Agriculture,* 18.

state power, a major new claimant to political power emerged in the form of *Zaydi* tribal confederations of the Hashid and segments of the Bakil. Funded by Saudi Arabia, the confederations armed themselves to reinstall the imam. Overt Saudi involvement prompted Nasser to send Egyptian troops to shore up the Republicans. Efforts to resolve sectarian and regional tensions between *Shafiʿis* and *Zaydis* of the Republican camp erupted in a protracted civil war during which Yemen became the arena for a regionwide contest between Arab monarchs led by Saudi Arabia's King Feisal and Republicans led by Egypt's Gamal Abdel Nasser.[55] During the eight-year civil war the Egyptians controlled virtually all aspects of the Republican side, providing not only arms and troops but also substantial amounts of aid. The southerners and most segments of the largely northern formal army cooperated, under Egyptian leadership, to prevent the return of the imam.[56]

The intense involvement of Saudi Arabia and Egypt in supporting Royalists and Republicans, respectively, linked up to deep divisions within the northern and southern elites, preventing the relative political and economic stature of the two groups from coming to bear on either the conflict or its resolution. High levels of external support meant that the Yemenis ended the civil war without generating political institutions that reflected the strength of the social factions that fought it. As opposed to the pattern that theorists of consociational democracy might have expected, neither the will nor the resources of domestic participants were tested.[57] Instead of a postwar period in which the conflicting groups' mutual "exhaustion" could generate a consociational settlement, the hostilities ended in an elaborate stalemate, which nevertheless gave currency to the notion that two separate realms could exist side by side in mutual noninterference. This agreement took the form of the republican pact when, following the Arab-Israeli war of 1967, Egypt and Saudi Arabia made peace and withdrew their troops from Yemen.

REPUBLICAN ADMINISTRATION

During the civil war that followed the 1962 coup, taxation was sporadic, despite the imposition of a plethora of new direct and indirect taxes. Immediate attempts were made to establish a national budget, but tax collection was erratic, and in 1963 the government registered a deficit of 14 million Maria Theresa thalers. The deficit was made up by loans from

[55] On inter-Arab regional tension, see Malcolm Kerr, *The Arab Cold War*, 3d ed. (New York: Oxford University Press, 1971), 106–17.

[56] The most detailed, if journalistic, discussion is Edgar O'Ballance, *The War in the Yemen* (Hamden, Conn.: Archon Books, 1971), 65–202.

[57] For the predicted sequence leading to stable consociational democratic outcomes, see Arend Lijphart, *Democracy in Plural Societies* (New Haven: Yale University Press, 1977).

the Yemen Bank for Reconstruction and Development (YBRD), and assistance from the United Arab Republic (the temporary—three-year—union between Syria and Egypt), Iraq, Kuwait, Yugoslavia, China, and the Soviet Union. Some foreign assistance took the form of commodity grants, which the government sold to Yemeni merchants.[58] Supported by Saudi Arabia and Egypt, respectively, both royalists and republicans depended on external military assistance and the private donations of businessmen and tribal sheikhs.

The rift between the north and the south in the YAR grew precipitously during the boom period of the 1970s and early 1980s, but the origins of the division were firmly rooted in imamic Yemen and the effects of Saudi and Egyptian intervention in the civil war. Saudi support for the nominally royalist tribes of the north contributed to their intransigence both during and after the war.[59] Indeed, Saudi patronage and the resources it bought the tribes from a Yemeni government trying to buy cooperation offered an alternative to entering the work force which lasted long after the end of the civil war.[60]

The republican pact, as it emerged after the civil war, set the stage for northern domination of the bureaucracy and the army and southern control of commerce, finance, and industry. A handful of southerners were employed in technical positions, but political power was firmly in the hands of the *Zaydi* military, which, after the 1970 Jeddah conference, secured domination of the 1971 Consultative Council—the national legislative body—and upheld the northern tribes' demands for regional autonomy. Both economic policy and business-government relations in the boom period were influenced by the fact that on the eve of the oil boom of 1973, which was to send both remittances and aid skyrocketing, the population of Yemen was already divided along occupational and regional lines that conformed to sectarian divisions. Conflicts between the various segments of the Yemeni elite were amply reflected in government institutions. Though administrative reforms set the main institutions in place soon after 1962, they were not to begin operations until 1971. The Republican government began by registering Yemeni companies. To buttress its failing finances, it tried, on the recommendation of Egyptian advisers, to encourage members of the private sector to invest in "mixed-sector" projects with the state. The new companies often had monopoly privileges for certain imports and exports, and private investors were encouraged to invest in the YBRD and the Yemen Foreign Trade Company. But since the civil war was funded by resources unconnected to the local economy, at-

[58] "Economic Survey for Yemen, 1963," 72.

[59] See Stookey, *Yemen,* 213–50; M. S. al Azhary, "Aspects of North Yemen's Relations with Saudi Arabia," in B. R. Pridham, ed., *Contemporary Yemen* (London: Croom Helm, 1984).

[60] Stookey (*Yemen,* 262) lists the 1971–72 subsidies from the regime of Sallal to the northern tribes at YR 39,852,000. In that year *zakat* collection yielded only YR 10,756,000.

tempts to centralize taxation on fishing and trade and to register private companies for the purpose of taxing corporate and personal profits were postponed until the onset of the 1970s.[61]

Well after the civil war ended, Saudi subsidies both military and financial, enhanced the autonomy of the tribes and substantially increased their military strength. The central government lacked the military power and perhaps even the political will to challenge the trend. Thus, the pact of noninterference more or less solidified the military autonomy of the northern tribes and allowed them to manipulate the terms of the pact.

The ʿAbdul Karim Iryani government, which forged the 1970 agreement to end the civil war and issued the "Permanent Constitution of the Yemen Arab Republic," vacillated wildly between north and south.[62] Between 1970 and 1974 five different cabinets were appointed, each in an effort to balance the objections of northern or southern elites. The marginal role of the central government became clear when responsibility for public order in the north was formally placed in the hands of the tribal sheikhs in 1973. Finally, in 1974, Iryani appointed his fifth and last cabinet, headed by the southern economist and merchant Hassan Makki. ʿAbdallah al-Ahmar, paramount chief of the Hashid confederation, responded by rallying troops to occupy the capital. It was in this context that al-Hamdi, third-ranking military officer in the country, became a national hero, Ataturk style, by stalling the Hashid army and appointing Muhsin al-ʿAyni, a southern union organizer and head of the Iraqi Baʿth in Yemen, to form a government. Subsequently, al-Hamdi abolished constitutional rule, dismissed al-ʿAyni, and put the country under the seven-man Military Command Council.[63]

At the onset of the oil boom of 1973, the struggle for Shafiʿi representation in the armed forces and the bureaucracy was still in full force. In contrast to Iryani, who had tried to straddle the diverse ideological, social, political, and sectarian cleavages in Yemeni society, al-Hamdi (1974–78) made the first and final attempt to establish the central state as an independent force in the Yemen Arab Republic: he disbanded the Consultative Council, removed tribal elites from the Military Command Council, and suspended tribal subsidies in 1975. In 1977 he staged a showdown with the Hashid tribal leadership by promoting *Shafiʿis* to important posts, banning automatic weapons, and tacitly supporting NLF fighters in Hujariyah. ʿAbdallah al-Ahmar responded by attacking Khamir and Sadaʿa

[61] This paragraph is based on my review of tax institution and withdrawal documents, Ministry of Finance, Sanʿa, 1986–87.

[62] The text of this inappropriately named document is reproduced in "The Permanent Constitution of the Yemen Arab Republic," *Middle East Journal* 25 (Autumn 1971).

[63] The best discussion of these events is in Stookey, *Yemen*, 252–62; see also Peterson, *Yemen*, 113–29.

with 40,000 tribal fighters, thus regaining tribal representation and subsidies in July 1977.[64]

Although the oil boom of the 1970s did not change ongoing struggles between the Republican military and the tribal confederation, it did strip al-Hamdi of his main constituency: labor. Al-Hamdi was a populist who had little elite support in his confrontation with the Hashid; as the oil boom began, he would soon lose his main constituents among the southern labor groups as well. The southern merchants, who had already extracted concessions from Iryani, subsequently abrogated their leadership of the labor unionist elements in particular and the southern population in general. At the end of the civil war, their split from the radical elements that had been their close allies in the Adeni labor movement reflected the merchants' singular interest in guarantees of free trade and the unfettered opportunity to pursue commercial and industrial investments. Since at no time in the entire period of war and reconstruction was the sanctity of free trade an issue in political struggles, the southern business elite did not see relinquishing power over the bureaucracy and the army as a concession. For the merchants, the 1975 appointment of the *Shafiʿi* ʿAbd al-ʿAziz ʿAbd al-Ghani—former chairman of the Central Bank and a returnee from Aden—as prime minister guaranteed that their interest in free trade would be represented at the highest reaches of Republican Yemen's government.[65] The merchants, in short, were more interested in trade and industry than in the byzantine politics of the capital in which their poorer co-sectarians were, of necessity, enmeshed.[66]

It was at this moment that the oil boom opened lucrative opportunities for Yemeni laborers in Saudi Arabia and al-Hamdi's primary domestic constituency in the south—the only social group large enough to balance the northern tribes—disappeared. Like the British tenure in Aden, the oil boom made migration an attractive alternative to interminable political contests at home. This time, the migrant group was composed exclusively of labor; the southern bourgeoisie stayed home.

The Absentee Bourgeoisie Consolidates

The absentee bourgeoisie of Yemen had returned in several waves. In 1962 the major capitalists, including the leading industrial families of

[64] See Bidwell, *Two Yemens,* 274; Colin Legum et al., eds., *Middle East Contemporary Survey,* vol. 2 (New York: Holmes & Meier, 1977–78), 652–53. Itamar Rabinovich and Haim Shaked, eds., *Middle East Contemporary Survey,* vol. 9 (Tel Aviv: Westview Press, 1984–85), 656.

[65] ʿAbd al-Ghani has held high posts, either prime minister or minister of trade and economy, ever since. Until 1986, according to almost all the merchants I interviewed in Yemen in 1986–87, he was viewed by members of the private sector as an effective guarantor of their interests.

[66] See Stookey, *Yemen,* 226–27.

Hail Said, Thabit, Hazzah, and Shaybani, moved their main offices from Aden to Hudaydah and initiated fixed capital investments in industry, storage, and transportation. The middle tier of Yemeni merchants in Aden established branches in Hudaydah but also expanded their control of overland trade between Aden and Yemen. In 1967, when the Adeni revolution and the departure of the British initiated military clashes between the NLF and the Egyptian-backed FLOSY, the middle-tier merchants returned to the YAR permanently, fearing nationalization in the event of an NLF victory. In 1969, in the wake of NLF-led nationalization of all industry, property, and commercial capital in Aden, the last of the Yemeni merchants there returned home. Then, between 1970 and 1972, the Yemeni merchant communities in Djibouti and Addis Ababa came home, driven out by political unrest in Somalia and Ethiopia. Most of this last wave came back to Hudaydah, where the port was being expanded.

For the San'ani merchants and their collaborators in Hudaydah, the return of the southern absentee bourgeoisie was nothing short of disastrous. The community of Indian merchants based in Hudaydah fled to Aden and East Africa in 1962, and the old Hadrami merchant houses of Hudaydah were displaced into minor retailing and wholesale activities. The Hudaydah Chamber of Commerce, which had successfully excluded the southerners from the Red Sea coast, was taken over, to a man, by returnees from Aden.

The absentee bourgeoisie had several natural advantages in their new Yemeni environment. Unlike the San'ani merchants, who were accustomed to dealing with foreign companies only through their intermediaries in Hudaydah, the southerners had built longstanding commercial relations with Indian, African, British, and European companies. The founders of all the major Yemeni merchant houses, and even those of the second tier of wholesalers, had at some point served as purchasing agents for one or more foreign companies.[67] The returnees also controlled emerging national financial institutions such as the Yemen Bank for Reconstruction and Development; the San'ani and Hudaydah merchant communities lacked both the capital and the international contacts to compete. The return of the *Shafi'i* merchants thus precipitated intense competition and led to bankruptcies at all levels of the locally based business classes. It is estimated that between 1971 and 1978 as many as 500 wholesalers, retailers, and service providers from San'a were driven out of the market and forced to seek employment in the army and the civil service.[68]

[67] In the top tier, the Adban brothers, Hail Said, Sholaq, Muhammed Kaid Saif, Radman, and the Thabit brothers were agents for Bess Company and others.

[68] Interviews conducted by the author with the following merchants: Muhammad al-Withari, San'a, 18 January 1987; Jassim al-Thawr, San'a, 21 January 1987; Abu Bakr Shammakh (president, Hudaydah Chamber of Commerce), Hudayah, 1 February 1987; Yahya Ba Qirsh, Hudayah, 1 February 1987; and Muhammad al-'Ubaydi.

The San'ani merchant group, particularly the imam's collaborators, were virtually bankrupted.

Unlike the *Shafi'i* merchants, who entered immediately into industrial investments and were able to capture the markets in real estate and building created by aid donors, the San'ani merchants held back. Anticipating the return of the imam, the houses of Thawr and Withari, for example, did not re-enter the market until the late 1970s.[69] Initially, even the southerners' investments in industry were small. In 1971, on the eve of the boom, there were 351 industrial firms employing five or more workers and encompassing a total work force of 6,706.[70] All industrialists had previously been based in Aden and, although there was no explicit import substitution policy at the time, many had invested, with the assistance of foreign companies, in the production of commodities that they had previously imported. Unlike the Hadrami businessmen, who preferred low-risk investments in real estate and trade, the southern merchants made sizable investments in food processing, household wares, and light consumables. Given their greater experience, it is not surprising that apart from two industrial plants set up in the early 1980s, all of Yemen's industries through the 1980s have been owned by families from the arid southern region of Hujariyah.[71] When the San'ani elite did begin to invest, almost a

[69] Muhammad al-Withari, the *shaykh al-mushayyikh* (paramount leader) of the San'ani traders and subsequently head of the San'a Chamber of Commerce, so firmly believed in a royalist victory that he bought the imam's *jambiyah* (ornamental dagger) to present to him when he returned: Muhammad al-'Ubaydi, interview.

[70] Richard Gable, "Government and Administration in the Yemen Arab Republic," (USAID paper, Washington D.C., 1979), 17.

[71] The family histories of the largest industrial houses illustrate the trajectories followed by Yemeni industrialists after the revolution. By far the largest, the Hail Said group, began in the 1940s in Aden (they had walked from Hujariyah and worked on French ships to accumulate seed money) and traded in Mocha and Taiz via overland routes until 1962. After the revolution the family started the first shipping company founded in Hudaydah. Until 1969, when they moved out of Aden completely, they bartered coffee, hides, and skins for petroleum products. They also held the agency for Shell Company. In 1970 they began their first industrial venture in biscuits and sweets; a complex of three industrial plants has a combined capacity of 42,000 tons per year. In 1974 they invested in five factories for domestic and industrial products, pipes and fittings. In 1975 the group established an edible-oil plant and a soap and detergent plant; in 1979 they set up a bottling plant for soft drinks and a mineral water plant. Because of domestic labor shortages created by the outflow of workers in the 1970s, all their industrial plants were highly capital-intensive, employing the most sophisticated technology available. The industrial concerns of Hail Said alone employed 5,800 workers in 1987, 1,500 of whom were women. They exported their products to Aden, Djibouti, and Saudi Arabia. In addition they held several exclusive dealerships for heavy machinery and automobiles, a shipping company, two insurance companies (set up in 1968), travel agencies, a company specializing in prefabricated construction, and a construction firm.

Yemen's second largest industrial family, the Thabit brothers, also came from Hujariyah and started in Aden as shippers and importers. In 1968 they invested in a shipping, clearing, and forwarding company based in Hudaydah, set up agencies for heavy machinery, and formed a contracting company. In 1980 they invested in a large dairy and juice plant; in 1986 an edible-oil factory.

The founder of the Shaybani industrial family of Hujariyah began in Aden as a dock-

decade after the revolution, they had little success. By pooling their resources in the San'a Company for Trade, Industry, Construction, and Hotels, the houses of al-Thor, Withari, al-Yemeni, Ghamdan, and others, hoped to compete. But the company failed in 1976 when the management split over a decision to expand into industry, the stronghold of the Hujariyah branch of the *Shafi'i* elite.[72]

By the onset of the 1970s the agenda and politics of the returned merchant groups had changed dramatically since they spearheaded the independence and anti-imam campaigns in Aden. Soon after the onset of the civil war the southern business-labor coalition had come apart; the sectarian alliance realigned into class divisions. It started to weaken early on, in May 1963, when the first trade union was organized in Taiz (mainly at the United States Mission, Yemen Airlines, and the Taiz Electric Company); soon thereafter the *Shafi'i* business elite were openly opposing organized labor. Famous labor organizers and activists who had forged the business-labor coalition in Aden, such as Amin al-Aswadi and Muhammad al-'Ayni, became major importers in Hudaydah.[73] Cut off from the economy that had given birth to collective bargaining, the labor movement weakened for structural reasons as well. The influx of returning migrants immediately after 1962 had created serious unemployment and even more widespread underemployment, neither of which helped the cause of organized labor. Thus, although the Taiz union maintained ties until 1969 with its parent organization in Aden, the ATUC (Aden Trade Union Congress), first oversupply and then migration to Saudi Arabia considerably eroded labor's power.[74]

The postrevolution business class was from the onset dominated by a small group of capitalists who had diverse holdings in a variety of commercial, service, and industrial enterprises. As the need for investment capital grew, the largest and most stable business families began to sell junk bonds to select merchants from the *Shafi'i* business group in order to finance machinery, demonstrating both a reluctance to use banks and the high level of domestic liquidity in the 1970s. Although the upper echelon

---

worker, then set up small cafes, and eventually moved into the distribution of soft drinks; he also started to construct and rent buildings and became an agent for local manufacturers in South Yemen. The family left Aden in 1969 and set up a soft drink plant and a paint plant in Taiz. After 1980 they expanded into various food products, aerosol insecticides, cosmetics, and perfumes. In 1983 they too established a mineral water bottling plant and later a food industries complex. The other major industrial families, including those of Radman, Hazzah, Qaid, and al-Wadud have similar histories.

[72] Jassim al-Thawr, interview with author, San'a, 21 January 1987.

[73] Amin al-Aswadi had been the assistant secretary general of the Aden Trade Union Congress and editor-in-chief of the influential newspaper *Al-'Amal*; he left Aden in 1967 and arrived in Hudaydah in 1968 to begin his career as a major importer of building materials and real estate speculator: interview with author, Hudaydah, 5 February 1987. See also Lackner, *People's Democratic Republic of Yemen,* 27–30, 32–33.

[74] On the Yemen General Trade Union, see "Economic Survey for Yemen, 1963," 49–51.

comprised exclusively of returnees from Aden, there was little change in the retailing and wholesale sectors before the late 1970s. Between 1962 and 1972, traditional industries in weaving, housewares, and construction declined in the face of competition from imported goods and disappeared almost completely during the boom.

On the eve of the oil boom, the rift between north and south along sectarian, regional, and occupational lines was complete. The army of 39,850 and the paramilitary force of 20,000 tribal levies were *Zaydi* almost to a man; the powerful Permanent Council was securely in the control of the northerners as well. Al-Hamdi's successors and alleged assassins, Ghashmi and ʿAli ʿAbdallah Saleh, were both Hashids, and they proceeded to formalize *Zaydi* domination of the government and the armed forces. Their success was signaled by the resignation of Ahmad Dahmash, a representative of the National Democratic Front, as minister of social affairs and by the final purge of remaining *Shafiʿi* officers from the army in March 1978.[75] Delegates to the People's Assembly, formed in 1978, were chosen from various corporate groups, but executive power remained in the hands of the tribal elite and their military collaborators.

Summary: Institutions and Society on the Eve of the Boom

The dissolution of the Ottoman Empire generated similar processes of state-building and market unification in Yemen and Saudi Arabia. In response to new fiscal pressures, political entrepreneurs in both countries intensified domestic taxation. Initially, the extractive efforts of Imam Yahya and the Al Saud produced broadly similar local responses: nascent tax states met resistance from society either individually (exit) or collectively (secession). Well before social groups thought of making demands on state institutions, they tried by all means possible to hold the state at bay, to dislodge its authority before it became permanent.[76]

By the mid-1930s, however, significant differences emerged in the two cases: in Saudi Arabia, military and administrative consolidation occurred in tandem with the strengthening of the urban corporate groups in the Hijaz; in Yemen, where the imam failed to achieve a monopoly on the production of violence, large segments of the heavily taxed southern population migrated to the neighboring free port of Aden. As the 1960s came to a close, these differences intensified. In Saudi Arabia, the de-

[75] Legum et al., *Middle East Contemporary Survey*, Vol. II (1978–79): 2:800.

[76] The pattern of social demands on the state is Huntington's overarching framework in *Political Order in Changing Societies* (New Haven: Yale University Press, 1968), esp. chap. 1. Yousef Cohen et al., "The Paradoxical Nature of State Making," *American Political Science Review* 75 (December 1981): 901–10, describes the phase of opposition to state expansion and centralization as the "primitive accumulation of power" that precedes the permanent establishment of state power at a "higher level."

struction of the guilds and the tribal economy, coupled with the unification of financial and commodity markets, set the stage for a stable business-government coalition between the Hijazi commercial elite and the Nejdi political-military elite. In Yemen, the division into three segments of the commercial elite and their respective military supporters, both local and regional, plunged the country into an almost decade-long civil war.

The two countries in the pre-boom period are fertile ground for examining the social origins of a central bureaucracy and a unified national market. Initial similarities are a useful starting point against which to measure different outcomes. First, both countries experienced fiscal and military pressures following the territorial reorganization of the Middle East after the collapse of the Ottoman Empire. Second, no "overdeveloped" colonial bureaucracy existed in either country, and these nascent states' respective intrusions into the myriad legal, political, and economic institutions of their divided societies were particularly disruptive, involving direct confrontations between the agents of the government, taxpayers, and regional elites. Third, both Yemen and Saudi Arabia were heterogeneous societies whose populations cleaved along three axes: an urban-agricultural-tribal divide; a regional-economic divide that linked people from different locations in long-distance trade networks; and cultural-ascriptive divisions centered on sectarian differences in Yemen, and in Saudi Arabia a cultural-religious (and to some extent ethnic: the Hijazis were substantially of non-Arab and even more of nontribal origin) divide. Finally, military-political elites were of a different regional, cultural, and ascriptive group than economic elites. In both cases, military power was monopolized, in the main, by tribal groups mobilized by urban-based political families with claims to religious authority. Economic elites, by contrast, were largely commercial-urban groups, which in the Yemeni case had strong ties to the southern agricultural regions.

Starting with these similar characteristics, the two cases had diverged considerably by the 1960s. A point supported by both is that the construction of extractive and regulative bureaucracies and the creation of unified national markets are distinct but related processes. The latter requires the former, but there is no guarantee that the former will result in the latter. Economic actors and, in particular, commercial elites functioning in existing systems of local and long-distance exchange cannot be assumed to have an interest in the expansion of the uniform institutions of a national market. Political-military elites produce collective goods in pursuit of revenue, but these goods—security, uniform weights and measures and monetarization—are not necessarily perceived as "goods" by commercial elites. Segments of the economic elite may come to view these developments, once established, as beneficial, but much larger groups of local economic actors are marginalized by transaction-cost cutting. In countries where military-political elites are entirely separate from economically ascendant commercial groups, this initial lack of support raises important questions about the class basis of the state in its origins. Neither Marxist conceptions, which correlate political and economic power, nor transaction-cost/deductive-rational-choice theories, which use the language of individual choice to describe aggregate-level outcomes, find support. Aggregate conceptions of economic efficiency, in particular, are deeply problematic when the boundaries of the economy are in formation and the rules that govern the economy are in dispute.

The differences between the Saudi and Yemeni experiences illustrate the tensions and synergies between state-building and the unification of national markets. Four points are worth emphasizing. First, the divergence of the two was the result of the inability of the Yemeni imam to create a standing army; and the availability of economic alternatives for southern agriculturalists through migration to Aden. The imam inadvertently strengthened tribal cohesion by channeling subsidies through the tribal leadership. Efforts to establish a standing permanent army failed, but military expenditures continued to rise. As taxation of southern agriculture reached its limits, precipitating large-scale migration, the imam turned to state monopolies for fiscal solvency, tightly constraining private trade to achieve market dominance. Revenue constraints, brought on by location and social organization, produced an extreme form of rent-seeking. In Saudi Arabia, by contrast, where the Al Saud were able to acquire and maintain a monopoly on the production of violence, gains in security eventually won the cooperation and support of the Hijazi guilds and merchant elites.

Initial responses to fiscal pressures in the two cases set in motion a secondary set of changes, which, compared, reveal the tensions between processes of state-centralization and market-building. In Yemen, restrictive state policies worked against the future formation of a national market, generating three separate commercial elites that thrived on and shared an interest in maintaining fragmented economic and monetary enclaves. In the late 1950s and early 1960s, when the liberalization of trade coincided with the decline of the absentee bourgeoisie's fortunes in Aden, the ensuing all-out struggle among the three commercial groups precipitated the civil war. This pattern contrasts starkly with that found in Saudi Arabia, where, as the government's capacity to provide security, law, administration, and a uniform medium of exchange increased, loyal opposition replaced secessionism. The Saudi monopoly on violence, in the form of a standing army, undergirded this transformation.[77] As the government's ad-

[77] The sequence fits a well-recognized pattern of state-building. See Charles Tilly, "War Making and State Making as Organized Crime," in Peter Evans, Dietrich Rueschemeyer, and Theda Skocpol, eds., *Bringing the State Back In* (Cambridge: Cambridge University Press, 1985), 169–91; and Tilly's "Introduction" in Tilly, ed., *The Formation of National States in Western Europe* (Princeton: Princeton University Press, 1975), 3–83.

ministrative capacities grew, the ruling coalition narrowed; the independent tribes and the guilds were smashed, and even stronger ties were established between the political leadership and the upper echelons of the Hijazi commercial elite. In short, the Yemeni imam's responses to fiscal pressures generated economic fissures that came to be dominated by three distinct commercial elites, whereas the Al Saud's systematic destruction of internal barriers to exchange and of the social groups that profited from them generated a unified national market that underpinned a strong business-government relationship.

A second point illustrated by these two cases is that taxation procedures and contexts, as well as differences in the military base of the leadership, produce very different private-sector attitudes toward the emergence of a unified national economy. Differences in the tax base of the state, as Robert Bates and Da-Hsiang Donald Lien have argued, lead to different political outcomes. Yet location can undo the relationships posited by social scientists between taxation and fixed and mobile assets. The Saudi government was primarily taxing trade in the Hijaz. The Yemeni government was primarily taxing agriculture in the south. Albert Hirschman's account would lead us to expect the Hijazis to exercise the "exit" option and the Yemeni southerners to exercise "voice." Yet, in support of Bates and Lien's argument, the contrary outcome ensued: holders of mobile assets in the Hijaz—commercial elites—exercised "voice"; the guilds, tied directly to the service economy of the haj, however, suffered a quiet decline. Labor, usually viewed as a fixed asset, migrated en masse from Yemen, largely in response to high agricultural taxes—an outcome not predicted in either rendition of asset mobility theory.

Third, the Saudi and Yemeni cases hint at the relationship between state-building efforts and the impact on domestic politics of redistributive movements and ideologies. Divisions among commercial elites had important implications for their ability to withstand the challenges of Pan-Arabism. Unlike Saudi Arabia, where elite unity forestalled the spread of Pan-Arab ideologies, Yemen experienced divisions within the private sector and between tribal and Republican elites which led to a civil war in which the two main rivals for regional dominance, Saudi Arabia and Egypt, became directly involved. In Saudi Arabia, elite cohesion meant that only small segments of the military and professional groups found Pan-Arab ideologies attractive; the strength of the corporatist relationship between the Hijazi commercial elite and the Al Saud balanced even the defection of important segments of the royal family. Divisions in the Yemeni elite, in contrast, merged with the broader regional conflict between Pan-Arabists and old elite classes, precipitating a proxy war. Efforts to reinstate the imam failed, but the war institutionalized the military power of the northern tribes and precluded the creation of a strong central government.

These social, political, and administrative developments made up the domestic context into which oil revenues entered in the 1970s. For very different reasons, Pan-Arabism in both countries meant nothing less than the political neutralization of what Barrington Moore called the "bourgeois impulse" in politics.[78] The political activism of the traditional business classes in both Yemen and Saudi Arabia was, from the start, narrowly instrumental. The Hijazi merchant elite opposed the Al Saud until the moment when the possibility of economic domination of an already unified national market emerged. Then, in return for a fair share in commerce, industry, and state projects, it slowly bargained away the independence of the civil institutions that had been its key means of aggregating interests and resolving commercial disputes. As a result, few independent civil institutions remained in the 1970s to counter government policies that precipitated the full-scale decline of the Hijazi elite. The weaknesses of the society that confronted the newly wealthy Nejdi government in the boom period were located in this obsolescing bargain between business and government. The corporate bargain between the government and the commercial classes never transformed into demands for participation, for the threat of Pan-Arabism in Saudi Arabia strictly circumscribed the role that the bourgeoisie would play in national politics.

Similarly, Yemen's absentee bourgeoisie had been deeply politicized prior to 1963, when it organized and funded the revolt against the imam in collusion with organized labor in Aden. The ouster of the imam and the defeat of the San'a and Hudaydah merchant groups marked the southerners' withdrawal from politics and the end of their coalition with labor. In Yemen, Pan-Arabism appealed to the much larger group of professionals in the bureaucracy and the army who, under different conditions, might have created a more interventionist, redistributive economic regime after the civil war. At the same moment that this set of conflicts came to the fore during al-Hamdi's tenure, however, the oil boom created a set of opportunities that directly undercut his constituency in labor because labor left.

A fourth point, raised in particular by the Yemeni case, concerns the interaction between the formation of classes and a national market when the "exit" option is viable. As this chapter has illustrated, the process of class formation in Yemen was deeply influenced by the massive migrations of the pre-boom period. Indeed, Yemen presents clear empirical material on the emergence of national classes outside national borders. If Pan-Arabism undercut the bourgeois impulse in Saudi Arabia and Yemen, the migration of Yemeni labor, first to Aden and then to Saudi Arabia, deeply influenced the construction of the rules that governed the Yemeni economy both before and after the boom. Yemeni labor was, in fact, never

[78] See Barrington Moore, *Social Origins of Dictatorship and Democracy* (Boston: Beacon Press, 1966), chaps. 1, 9, and Epilogue.

incorporated into the political system. Had Al-Hamdi's efforts at building a strong state in coalition with labor succeeded, the institutional structure of Yemen might have been quite different. The national market that emerged in Yemen on the basis of the republican pact was constructed precisely on the exit of Yemen's labor force from the domestic political economy in the early 1970s. Labor's absence from the scene for almost two decades after 1973 thus had profound implications for the political economy of Yemen.

The pre-boom histories of Saudi Arabia and Yemen set the stage for what happened in the 1970s. In both, the domestic context into which flows of international capital entered was politically and economically loaded. In both, the state and business were controlled by different groups, divided by sect, region, and historical experience: northern *Shiʿa* tribes and southern *Sunni* returnees in Yemen; Nejdi tribal elites and the Hijazi merchant elite in Saudi Arabia.

Whereas in Saudi Arabia the relationship between the traditional merchant class was repeatedly renegotiated over four decades, in Yemen the first stable accommodation between business and government followed a protracted civil war that began with the overthrow of the imam, funded by the absentee bourgeoisie in Aden. External involvement in the war fed deep fissures in the three Yemeni elite groups, generating a resolution that excluded labor and hardened sectarian and regional divisions within the north-dominated military and bureaucracy and the south-dominated business class. It was under a pact of mutual exclusion and noninterference between business and government that Yemen entered the boom period of the 1970s. Although the republican pact that ended the Yemeni civil war was the political outcome of a military stalemate, it proved remarkably resilient throughout the boom period. Not until the recession of the 1980s, when fiscal pressures on the Yemeni government intensified, did its terms come under renewed renegotiation. In contrast, what appeared in the 1960s to be an inviolable corporate relationship between business and government in Saudi Arabia turned out to be extremely fragile once the oil boom hit.

Part II

THE BOOM

Chapter Four

The Business of the Bureaucracy

By the onset of the oil boom of the 1970s, a unified national market had emerged in Saudi Arabia, governed by an encompassing and increasingly stable set of interlocking public and private institutions. Implausible as it may seem in light of subsequent events, these institutions conformed to the evolutionary rationalist trajectories of modernization theory. The Saudi bureaucracy possessed extractive, regulatory, and information-gathering capacities that had adapted successfully to the dramatic economic transformations of the 1950s and 1960s. The centralization of state and market institutions had occurred in symbiosis with substantial social changes. A centralized bureaucracy had replaced the complex system of subcontracting through which the nascent state had ruled in collaboration with the guilds, trading houses, tribes, and local notables. Bureaus and ministries had become specialized, differentiated, and organizationally linked in defined hierarchical structures. Financial institutions, both public and private, became formalized and were increasingly operating under a set of uniform legal and administrative norms. Business, once a staggeringly diverse collection of guilds, merchant associations, and independent traders, had been transformed into a much smaller, nationally organized corporate group with strong formal ties to the bureaucracy. These institutional and social outcomes cannot be described as "efficient" or "inefficient" in absolute terms, for the same bureaucracy that unified the national market and created central administrative and legal institutions destroyed other forms of organization. If the new institutional ar-

[1] Neoinstitutionalist economists make a binary distinction between efficient and ineffi-

rangements were a good match for the new national business elite and the political centralizers, they were just as clearly constructed from the debris of the social and economic worlds of the tribes and the guilds.

When the oil boom ended ten years later, hardly a vestige of this preboom institutional construct remained. In a mere decade the regulatory and extractive capabilities of the Saudi state had all but vanished. Taxing and regulating agencies, so painstakingly constructed in the previous five decades, had been replaced by a larger but functionally narrower distributive bureaucracy that governed the economy solely through the domestic deployment of oil revenues. The boom had also transformed Saudi society: in place of the Hijazi commercial elite a substantially larger, richer, and entirely new class of Nejdi business elites dominated the economy. The mushrooming state sector became the biggest employer, creating a new class of salaried employees from both the traditional farming sector and the sedentarized tribes. New ties of ascription, kinship, tribe—historical enemies of the universalizing state in Arabia—not only blossomed during this period of unprecedented economic growth but did so, ironically, through the ostensibly neutral actions of a formal distributive bureaucracy pursuing a single universalistic goal: growth. The coalitional base of the oil state thus represented a fourth change: this rendition united Nejdi political and bureaucratic elites with a private sector of their own making, their own kin.

Incrementalist accounts of institutional and social change cannot explain the pace and depth of these changes. The almost instantaneous institutional transformation of the Saudi state in the early 1970s negates the fundamental neoinstitutionalist tenet of limited institutional malleability.[2] Just as clearly, it fails to confirm Marxist conceptions of the relationship between social forces and political institutions, for the new distributive state had no clear domestic constituency until one was created through state spending. It was a measure of the oil-based independence of the Saudi government that it did away with the old Hijazi elite, but state autonomy cannot explain why the bureaucracy then created a new business elite and why that elite took the form that it did. The role of the Saudi state in rapidly creating and destroying large social groups in the 1970s likewise belies the key assumption of both Marxist and liberal theo-

---

cient outcomes without specifying either the content of transaction-cost cutting institutional arrangements or the characteristics of efficient property rights. Economic performance becomes the only measure for institutional "efficiency," with the result that efficiency cannot be judged separately from economic performance. The NIEs do not, moreover, limit themselves to national economic indicators; much of their "evidence" is drawn from premodern or local examples. Thus the unit to which growth (and therefore efficient institutions) are being ascribed is typically difficult to identify.

[2] Douglass North, "Institutions and Credible Commitment," *Journal of Institutional and Theoretical Economics* 149, no. 1 (1993): 17.

rists that class formation is a slow process resulting from broad-based economic and technological change.

The sources and processes through which institutional changes occurred in boomtime Arabia were radically different from those in the pre-boom period. In the pre-boom era, institutions were born of social conflicts that produced a series of narrowing coalitions; during the boom, institutional changes occurred largely *within* the organizations of the state itself without social conflict. As such, they are best analyzed and explained through resource-dependence theory, which focuses on how organizations respond to changes in resources. The oil revenues of the 1970s created new channels through which resources circulated within the bureaucracy, rendering extractive and regulatory agencies obsolete and reorienting bureaus toward the distributive branches of government. Exogenous resources changed the institutional shape, organization, and capacities of the Saudi bureaucracy, severing the earlier link between taxation and organizational change. The extractive and regulatory branches of the bureaucracy were replaced with dozens of distributive agencies that managed the economy through the deployment of oil revenues.

Where taxpayers had struggled hard and long against the fiscal demands of the extractive state, the distributive state shaped society without evincing protest. The Hijazi business elite, severed from other commercial and service groups of the Hijaz by its own earlier actions, confronted the new power of the distributive state without allies and without an ideational framework for demanding entitlements: the state's intervention in the economy came now in the form of contracts, commissions, and loans disbursed by a bureaucracy with which they had no links and on which they could make no special claims. Unimpeded by domestic commercial classes, multinational corporations, or the now obsolete branches of the old bureaucracy, the new distributive organs of the Saudi bureaucracy became the exclusive motor of the economy in the 1970s. The financial autonomy of the distributive state in the domestic arena depended heavily on the international market—but only in the most abstract sense, for the international oil market was not an identifiable agent acting on behalf of particular interests in the domestic economic arena.

From a purely economic perspective, one might argue that the withdrawal of previous human and material investments in regulation and taxation represented an appropriate and efficiency-maximizing response to new economic conditions. And undoubtedly, in the prosperous years of the oil boom the relative returns from taxing Huffuf dates hardly warranted the resources the old tax state had invested in that enterprise. The decline of the tax bureaucracy, however, had hidden effects: the atrophy of extractive and regulatory agencies eliminated the primary mechanisms through which the state acquired information about the economy that it now so thoroughly controlled. The distributive bureaucracy's lack of information not only precluded the emergence of a technocratic planning model but also meant that other goals would arise within the distributive bureaucracy to fill the gap.

In trying to explain the social outcomes of the boom years, we find that the Saudi case presents the classic problem of reconciling the existence of formal organizational structures with empirical findings that suggest their functional irrelevance.[3] The puzzle can be stated as follows: how can the social and distributional outcomes of the boom period be reconciled with the ostensibly rational and universalistic goals of the institutional vehicles through which they were carried out? My argument is that the wholesale reconfiguration of Saudi society between 1973 and 1983 occurred through the workings of a formal distributive bureaucracy that applied, at one level, the "letter of the law." The parameters of the transformation may well have been set through a confluence of exigency, accident, and political agency; but the transformation occurred, in the main, not in the king's *majlis* or even the ministers' private offices but in the day-to-day choices of middle-level bureaucrats and functionaries. Explaining the rise of a Nejdi private sector with strong kinship links to the bureaucracy, in short, requires an explanation of the social origins, goals, and institutional constraints under which middle-level bureaucrats functioned. The bulk of revenue allocation during the boom occurred through newly created formal state institutions operating under universalistic norms. Yet in Saudi Arabia—unlike Iraq and Algeria, where the demands of organized urban labor and attendant struggles over resources and rules generated economic policies explicitly designed to redistribute wealth—no vision of the collective future attended the growth-based model. Although the state maintained strict limits on social and political freedoms, the acts of the bureaucracy had no ideological or even developmentalist rudder. In the pursuit of growth, the powerful agencies of the formal bureaucracy generated secondary goals, and it was here, at the level of the middle bureaucracy, that the social structure of Saudi Arabia was rebuilt. The deliberate neutrality of the growth goal and the ideological commitment to the free market—not prebendalism, sultanism, or sheer corruption—produced the economic and social outcomes of the 1970s.

With the country's limited population, Saudi economic policy in the oil boom was not by any means predetermined. Indeed, like those of Libya, Saudi decision-makers might have chosen to use the resources of the oil boom to destroy rather than build formal state institutions.[4] Alternatively, as in Kuwait, a foreign investment strategy coupled with slower domestic

[3] See John W. Meyer and Brian Rowan, "Institutionalized Organizations," in Walter Powell and Paul J. DiMaggio, eds., *The New Institutionalism in Organizational Analysis* (Chicago: University of Chicago Press, 1991), 41–62.

[4] Kiren Aziz Chaudhry, "Business and Labor in the Making of the Rentier State" (manuscript, Berkeley, Calif., 1992).

investment might have been pursued. Retrospectively, it is possible to define three fundamental components of Saudi economic policy that led to the outcomes of the boom period: a domestic development strategy designed to involve the local population in national development through various channels of access; a sectoral emphasis on infrastructure, fashioned to consolidate the domestic market, ensure state control over territory, and set the stage for the expansion of a national bourgeoisie; and a capitalist economic philosophy that valorized growth as a supreme objective and explicitly delegitimized linking economic policy to distributional issues. Together, these policies meant that the formal institutions of the distributive state had aims that were utterly open to individual interpretation. At the same time, the decline of the information-gathering capacities associated with the regulatory and tax bureaucracy gave bureaucrats freedom to define economic reality at will.

New revenue sources generated an unexpected set of organizational outcomes that, in turn, formed the mechanisms through which the distributive bureaucracy reshaped domestic classes in its own image. Both the scope of these changes and the fact that they occurred through the formal-legal bureaucracy belie the interpretation that traditional patrimonialism or corruption alone were responsible. Although nepotism and corruption are clearly an important part of the Saudi story, perhaps even central to explaining patterns of capital accumulation for the wealthiest, these factors alone are inadequate explanations of the social outcomes of the boom. The comprehensive restructuring of classes cannot be accounted for by ad hoc corruption and rent-seeking. Rather, it was the very absence of distributive conflicts and goals, combined with the massive flow of resources through the formal bureaucracy, that generated boom-time outcomes. The Saudi case, in this regard, negates many of the alleged characteristics of the rentier state.

This chapter begins by presenting evidence of the decline of the extractive and regulatory bureaucracy, analyzes the diverse methods through which the distributive bureaucracy shaped the economy, outlines the effects of distribution on regional and absolute inequality, and traces the origins of the new Nejdi business elite in a particular sub-set of distributive policies. An explanation of institutional change is then presented using the insights of organization theory. A case study of sectoral development in agriculture illustrates the full host of mechanisms at work in the boom.

The Decline of the Extractive Bureaucracy

To say that the oil boom was responsible for the atrophy of regulatory, distributive, and extractive agencies is not to suggest that this transformation was a planned event. Rather, the oil boom created resource flows that made taxation unnecessary: the decline of the extractive apparatus followed. The rapidity with which the tax relationship and the tax bureaucracy changed belie an incrementalist interpretation; the dismantling of the extractive bureaucracy began almost immediately after the 1973 oil embargo. Most of the taxes on Saudis and fees on resident foreigners were withdrawn; foreign companies were given five-year tax holidays (and extensions granted thereafter); and personal income taxes on foreign workers were eliminated. The government canceled private-sector social security payments and began funding the General Organization for Social Insurance (GOSI) directly from the current budget. Unable to abolish the religious tithe outright, the government simply stopped collecting *zakat* in 1976.[5]

Virtually all indirect taxes were eliminated as well. The mainstays of the old treasury, pilgrim fees and taxes on services in the holy cities of Mecca and Medina, were rescinded. Special fees on imported tobacco, overland tickets, the head tax, fishing taxes, and a variety of others were canceled in 1974, and the road tax—King Feisal's hard-won direct tax on salaried workers—abolished the same year.[6] The carefully calibrated indirect taxes that had been the backbone of the import substitution regime met a similar fate. The elimination of most import tariffs not only terminated the substitution strategy of the 1960s but signaled the destruction of the single most important economic tool at the government's disposal, for import permits and allocations of foreign exchange had been its primary means of shaping investment strategies and consumption patterns.[7]

The end of taxation, in turn, precipitated the rapid dismantling of the extractive bureaucracy. Department of *Zakat* and Income Tax (DZIT) offices closed across the kingdom. Whereas almost every village had had a DZIT representative (see Table 2.1), only seven offices were left by the mid-1970s.[8] In the 1960s the extractive bureaucracy was the fastest-grow-

[5] Royal Decree M/16, "Tax Exemptions for Foreign Companies," 1393/6/9 (1973–74); Sheikh Husayn 'Abd al-Latif (director, DZIT), interview with author, Riyadh, 7 January 1986; Royal Decree M/37, "Withdrawal of All Income Taxes on Foreign Workers," 1395/5/4 (1975–76); Council of Ministers Decree 529, "Implementing Rules," 1395/5/3 (1975–76); Council of Ministers Decree 529, "The Withdrawal of *Zakat* from Joint Stock and Limited Liability and Other Companies and Commercial Agencies," 1396/11/15 (1976).

[6] Council of Ministers Decree 1402, 1394/9/21 (1974–75); Royal Decree M/67, 1394/12/5 (1974–75); Council of Ministers Decree 961, 1394/9/23 (1974–75); Council of Ministers Decree (no number), "Telegraph Fees," 1396/6/3 (1976); Council of Ministers Decree 573, "Airport Entry and Transfer Fees," 1396/4/5 (1976); direct tax on salaries: Royal Decree M/45, 1394/7/23 (1974–75).

[7] In 1974, customs duties, which had furnished an average of 80 percent of non-oil domestic tax revenue before the boom, were lowered from highs of 50 percent for luxury goods to 2–10 percent. All imports remotely associated with industrial projects, basic goods, agriculture, education, building, and health were exempted from duties altogether: Royal Decree M/44, 1394/7/24 (1974–75).

[8] SAMA's twenty-three branches across the kingdom in the 1970s handled disbursements

ing government agency, employing more Saudis than all other administrative departments combined.[9] In the 1970s, while the rest of the bureaucracy mushroomed and other bureaus in the Ministry of Finance became ascendant, employment in DZIT stagnated.[10] Its functions shrank rapidly; for example, its role in taxing foreign companies, including ARAMCO, was assumed by the Saudi Arabian Monetary Agency (SAMA) in 1974. Perhaps the most telling sign of the diminished importance of the Department of General Revenues, in which the DZIT was housed, was the fact that Minister of Finance Muhammad Abu al-Khayl did not bother to appoint a director of revenues between 1974 and 1978.[11]

Trends in the Customs Department were similar, with a few minor differences. The number of people employed by the department grew during the boom period but only in the security division, which was turned into a formal subdivision in 1978. In the 1960s, the nonsecurity branch of customs had grown faster, since Saudi Arabia, like most LDCs, had relied heavily on import duties as a major source of revenue. In the 1970s, however, the Customs Department ceased to be a revenue generator. Indeed, its own expenditures exceeded its receipts as it became a key part of the rapidly expanding national security services, geared to intercepting a growing list of banned goods such as alcohol, pornography, and political texts. Despite its growing importance to national security, its branch offices decreased from 77 in 1970 to 29 in 1985, reflecting the irrelevance of customs as a revenue source.[12]

Organizational obsolescence and decline is generally explained in terms of exogenous shocks, systemic entropy, and changes in the power exercised by interested coalitions.[13] More specifically, resource dependence theory suggests that as the Ministry of Finance and National Economy gained alternative sources of revenue, its dependence on and interest in

---

and government transfers but were not involved in tax assessment and collection: Hamdi Ahmad Sa'd al-Sarani, "Nizam al-Raqabah al-Dakhiliyah fi Masihat al-Zakat wa-al-Dakhl [The internal organization of DZIT]" (M.A. thesis, Institute for Public Administration, Riyadh, 1984), 48–49. The Institute for Public Administration at Riyadh is hereafter cited as IPA.

[9] By 1957 the Ministry of Finance employed 2,381 civil servants, of which 1,256 were in the Customs Department and the DZIT, plus 1,662 seasonal tax collectors. The next year, Customs and DZIT had grown by 23 people and seasonal employees by 70: IPA archives, internal documents of the Ministry of Finance, presented in budgets for 1378–79 and 1379–80.

[10] Al-Sarani, "Nizam al-Raqabah," 50–51; Joy Winkie Viola, *Human Resources Development in Saudi Arabia* (Boston: International Human Resources Development Corporation, 1986), 247. DZIT employees in Riyadh increased only from 404 to 562 in the same period (Riyadh, DZIT Reports).

[11] Salih al-Shuaybi (consultant to the Ministry of Finance on administrative organization), interview with author, Riyadh, 18 January 1986.

[12] See Kiren Aziz Chaudhry, "The Price of Wealth" (Ph.D diss., Harvard University, 1990), 208, table 5.3.

[13] Lynne G. Zucker, "Where Do Institutional Patterns Come From?" in Zucker, ed., *Institutional Patterns and Organizations* (Cambridge, Mass.: Ballinger, 1988).

maintaining the DZIT evaporated.[14] When DZIT no longer mediated relationships between taxpayers and the state in political terms, it ceased to be a significant arena of conflict and competition.[15] The experience of the Saudi tax bureaucracy supports the unorthodox view that organizations, even extremely important ones, can emerge and disappear quickly in response to what one scholar has called "social dilemmas."[16] Changes in funding were crucial sources of institutional innovation for both the extractive and the distributive branches of the Saudi bureaucracy, but on a much larger scale than theorists of organizations have thus far suggested.[17]

Rulers do not, apparently, tax as much as possible[18] for as long as possible.[19] When they can, they borrow—that is, they tax future generations and thereby avoid political resistance—or, in exceptional circumstances such as those of major oil states, they stop taxing altogether. Changes in technology, asset mobility, and financial integration may change the technical abilities and political calculus of states in search of revenue, but these were not the forces at work in Saudi Arabia.[20] Especially in light of the large role of government contracts in boomtime Saudi Arabia, the origins of extractive regression lay not in administrative difficulties but in altered priority structures made possible by plenty. The decision to stop taxing, made out of expediency, had important unintended administrative consequences.

Oil rents rearranged the relative importance of extractive, distributive, and regulatory bureaucracies in Saudi Arabia. That the bureaucracy expanded rapidly at the same time that its extractive functions atrophied suggests the importance of revenue dependence to the shape, structure, and functions of the state. At first glance, these developments conform to economic lines of explanation, which would suggest that the decline of the tax bureaucracy represented an efficient response to changed economic circumstances. But the demise of taxes also meant the demise

[14] See Jeffery Pfeffer and Gerald R. Salancik, *The External Control of Organizations* (New York: Harper & Row, 1978), esp. chap. 3.

[15] Paul DiMaggio, "Interest and Agency in Institutional Theory," in Zucker, *Institutional Patterns,* 13.

[16] Zucker, "Where do Institutional Patterns Come From?"

[17] Pamela S. Tolbert, "Institutional Environments and Resource Dependence," *Administrative Science Quarterly* 30 (1985): 1–13.

[18] This assumption is common to all rational-choice treatments of state institutions and is even found in Tilly's later work. See his "War Making and State Making as Organized Crime" in Peter B. Evans, Dietrich Reuschemeyer, and Theda Skocpol, eds., *Bringing the State Back In* (Cambridge: Cambridge University Press, 1985), 169–91; see also Margaret Levi, *Of Rule and Revenue* (Berkeley: University of California Press, 1988).

[19] Edward Ames and Richard T. Rapp, "The Birth and Death of Taxes" (with comments by James Millar), *Journal of Economic History* 37 (March 1977): 161–78.

[20] For the difficulties of taxing in contexts of international financial integration and easy capital mobility, see Hugh Ault and David Bradford, "Taxing International Income," in Assaf Razin and Joel Slemrod, eds., *Taxation in the Global Economy* (Chicago: University of Chicago Press, 1990), 16, 19, 38.

of the state's most important source of economic information, an unintended consequence that would profoundly influence a panoply of institutional and social relationships. As a result of the decline in taxation, the massive distributive bureaucracy that reshaped Saudi society between 1973 and 1983 functioned in a veritable information void.

Patterns of Distribution

The tax bureaucracy atrophied during a period of administrative genesis and expansion for Saudi Arabia, for employment in the rest of the bureaucracy tripled—from 96,000 in 1972 to 298,000 in 1983.[21] This new bureaucracy was geared exclusively to the goal of allocating oil revenues in the domestic economy. Dozens of distributive agencies, prominent among them five development banks (see Chapter 6), were set up to allocate revenues through subsidies, loans, gifts, and state contracts.

Like many tribal societies, Arabia before the al-Saud had a robust tradition of distribution and reciprocal exchange involving redistributive institutions quite different from those found in early agricultural societies. Key among them was the practice of raiding and the distribution of booty through tribal leadership patterns where resources flowed from the powerful to the lowly. Like other instances of moral economic activity, *ghazu* (raiding) was governed by complex tribal customs and laws that had little relationship to, and often contradicted, the orthodox Islamic legal traditions that sanctify private property. Raiding had an urban analogue in ritualized almsgiving, managed, especially among the established communities of the Hijaz, by the guilds. This fact has prompted observers of the modern Saudi state to impute cultural continuity to boomtime patterns of economic policy.[22] But the cultural view is indefensible: not only were the socially embedded redistributive systems of the first four decades of the century entirely different from the re-distributive policies initiated by the Saudi state in the 1960s, but these in turn differed fundamentally from the distributive patterns and mechanisms of the 1970s.

These differences were not simply of volume. In contrast to raiding and tribal redistribution, a subsistence-maintaining mechanism that flourished in the absence of effective central power, the central bureaucracy in the 1960s created two distinct flows of state redistribution: one designed to cement state ties with corporate groups, and one to fund national-level social welfare programs. The former organized potentially troublesome groups (the Ulema and the Society for the Preservation of Good and the

[21] Viola, *Human Resources.*

[22] Sumner Scott Huyette, *Political Adaptation in Saudi Arabia* (Boulder, Colo.: Westview Press, 1985).

Prevention of Evil,[23] the chambers of commerce,[24] journalists and newspapers, the guild masters of the Hijaz, craftsmen, and students) under the Ministries of Commerce, Information, Religion, and Education.[25] The latter erected a subsidy program for national social insurance, basic goods,[26] and utilities[27] which formed a safety net for the poor.[28]

The distributive policies of the 1960s consolidated recipients into formal, universal categories and used subsidy scales to achieve specific goals.[29] Even slaveowners were compensated for freeing their slaves at abolition in 1962,[30] and tribal subsidies for the sedentarized confederations were stan-

[23] This society is commonly referred to as "the religious police" in texts on Saudi Arabia. They do not have the formal religious training of the ulama, although they sometimes lead prayers.

[24] The Jeddah and Mecca Chambers of Commerce predate the Riyadh one by almost eighteen years yet got no subsidy until 1964.

[25] *Qarar Ri'asat Majlis al-Wuzara'* 92, 1390/4/4 (1970–71).

[26] Under the basic goods program, imported sugar, rice, grains, vegetables, and flour were subsidized beginning in fiscal year 1961–62, when the basic commodities subsidy was SR 39 million; in 1962–63 it was raised to SR 50 million; and in 1963–64 the SR 30 million budgeted was later raised to SR 50 million: *Qarar Ri'asat Majlis al-Wuzara'* 127, 1384/3/3 (1964–65). In 1965, basic commodities were subsidized by SR 40 million: *Qarar Ri'asat Majlis al-Wuzara'* 530, 1385/10/25 (1965–66). Finally, in 1978, the government adopted the general policy of providing enough to reduce the prices of basic goods by 25 percent of their cost each year: (*Qarar Ri'asat Majlis al-Wuzara'* 928, 1399/6/15 (1978–79).

[27] In 1951 total revenues generated by state-controlled public utilities were SR 1.4 million. By the early 1960s the government subsidy for the production of electricity was SR 3.4 million: *Qarar Ri'asat Majlis al-Wuzara'* 521, "Assistance to Electrical Companies," 1383/7/10 (1963–64). In 1966 the fuel used by electrical companies also began to be subsidized: *Qarar Ri'asat Majlis al-Wuzara'* 63, 1386/1/18 (1966–67). Not till 1971, however, did the government set a definite scale of consumption tariffs for electricity: *Qarar Ri'asat Majlis al-Wuzara'* 1089, 1391/11/23 (1971–72). In the 1960s, consumption tariffs for industries were lower than those for ordinary household consumers. Electrical companies were eligible for subsidies only if their profits were at least 7 percent of the capital invested in the previous year; if so, each company, regardless of size, got SR 15 million: *Qarar Ri'asat Majlis al-Wuzara'* 1099, 1391/11/30 (1971–72). The 1971 law, biased toward large profitable enterprises, replaced the previous requirement that profits not exceed 10 percent of the total investment: *Qarar Ri'asat Majlis al-Wuzara'* 746, 1386/10/12 (1966–67). In the 1970s the electrical companies were turned into privately owned joint stock companies. *Then, in the 1970s, profits of privatized electrical companies were subsidized at 15 percent, and consumer subsidies were kept in place.*

[28] GOSI was created in 1962, along with the Ministry for Labor and Social Affairs, to address the immediate needs of the poor and to find employment for Saudi nationals. In 1973–83 that ministry was drastically restructured to focus on arbitration of labor disputes and agreements with labor-exporting countries.

[29] Like other economic policies, the distributional efforts of the 1960s evince a detailed ends-means reasoning behind the subsidy rates. In education, for example, teachers salaries differed between remote and central areas, as did subsidies for schools that charged fees and those that did not: *Qarar Ri'asat Majlis al-Wuzara'* 375, 1391/5/19 (1971–72). On student stipends for higher education, also initiated in the 1960s, see *Qarar Ri'asat Majlis al-Wuzara'* 690, 1390/6/22 (1970–71).

[30] Earlier, the king had frequently purchased the freedom of a particular slave in response to petitions, but the "Agreement to donate SR 160 million for compensating the masters of slaves and gifts for the basic necessities required by the freed slaves" in *Qarar Ri'asat Majlis al-Wuzara'* 106, 1383/2/3 (1963–64), distributed a general stipend to owners and freed slaves alike when slavery was abolished.

dardized in the form of monthly salaries.[31] These revenue flows were dutifully recorded in the national budget as governorate-level administrative costs; they were public and transparent. Ad hoc grants were rare in this period.[32]

In small ways, the 1970s represented an expansion of the subsidies and welfare programs initiated in the 1960s: the corporatist strategy of using direct subsidies to preempt demands and organize relations with the press, the chambers of commerce and students continued at a higher level.[33] As before, the state chose its friends; although subsidies to the Jeddah, Mecca, Medina, Dammam, and especially Riyadh Chambers of Commerce were increased, stipends for the head of the *mutawwifin* (pilgram guide) guild, instituted in an earlier phase when guild cooperation was an administrative necessity, were actually reduced.[34]

The massive social welfare program that the Saudi government set up in 1973 was again enlarged after the second oil boom of 1981. Welfare programs defined citizenship: they were universalist for Saudi nationals, but unavailable to imported labor. As such, they carved a growing gap between domestic and imported labor. Pensions and social security benefits for Saudi workers were increased, and new programs were begun for the handicapped, abandoned women, and illegitimate children.[35] Monthly stipends and living allowance were supplemented with one-time gifts

[31] Tribal-sheikhs, associated with the administration of particular areas, were given funds in their capacity as administrators rather than tribal chiefs in the 1960s. The stipends of minor tribal leaders in such positions were raised in 1972 in response to a request by the *umara* (an ambiguous term that means governor or prince, or both): *Qarar Ri'asat Majlis al-Wuzara'* 161, 1392/1/12 (1972–73). Sedentarization programs for bedouin were also funded by the state, although the use to which such grants were to be put was unclear. See, e.g., *Qarar Ri'asat Majlis al-Wuzara'* 694, 1380/11/25 (1960–61) on the subsidy for the northern tribes.

[32] See Chaudhry, "Price of Wealth" (1990), chap. 3.

[33] In 1975 the press subsidies distributed by the Ministry of Finance totaled SR 4.377 million: Council of Ministers Decree 724, 1395/6/9 (1975–76). These were increased in 1976: *Qarar Ri'asat Majlis al-Wuzara'* 226, 1396/1/1 (1976). The main increases were for *Al-Yamamah,* whose subsidy was retroactively raised to SR 300,000 a year; for all English newspapers (SR 500,000 a year each); and for monthly magazines (SR 75,000/year). Starting in 1975, publishers with large or expanding readerships were entitled to larger subsidies covering 10 to 20 percent of yearly costs: *Qarar Ri'asat Majlis al-Wuzara'* 225, 1397/3/4 (1976–77); and Council of Ministers Decree 724, 1395/6/9 (1975–76).

[34] *Qarar Ri'asat Majlis al-Wuzara'* 274, 1394/2/23 (1974–75). The subsidy to the *mutawwifin* guild for 1962 from the Ministry of Haj and *Awqaf* was SR 3.3 million: *Qarar Ri'asat Majlis al-Wuzara'* 19622, 1383/7/29 (1963–64). In 1974 the government gave the "grand representative of the *mutawwifin*" a monthly payment of only SR 200/month and denied the applications of other guild members: *Qarar Ri'asat Majlis al-Wuzara'* 302, 1394/2/26 (1974–75).

[35] In 1974 such children under the age of six began to receive a stipend of SR 520 per year; in 1981 this was raised to SR 1,000 per month: Council of Ministers Decree 610, 1395/5/13 (1975–76). The stipend for those over six was raised from SR 650 to SR 1,200 per month in 1981. Stipends for the handicapped were doubled to SR 400–800, and handicapped children were given monthly pocket money of SR 100–120: *Qarar Ri'asat Majlis al-Wuzara'* 157, 1401/9/12 (1980–81).

Table 4.1. Production and consumption subsidies and social security in Saudi Arabia (in million SR)

	Subsidies				
Year	Food	Agriculture	Social Security	Electrical	Total Subsidies
1969–70					
1970–71			39	1	40
1971–72			45	1	46
1972–73		4	55	15	74
1973–74	300	20	76	14	410
1974–75	750	69	358	13	1190
1975–76	700	333	500	25	1558
1976–77	600	603	653	175	2031
1977–78	700	772	864	312	2648
1978–79	800	829	971	563	3163
1979–80	1450	586	1005	749	3790
1980–81	3000	766	986	1234	5986
1981–82	5000	1129	1391	2586	10106
1982–83	4150	1472	1586	2816	10024
1983–84	1600	1173	1540	3548	7861
1984–85	2633	1478	1485	2750	8346
1985–86	1950	994	1461	1750	6155
1986–87	1864	480	1280	1433	5057
1987–88	2687	335	1064	92	4178
1988–89	693	404	1001	—	2098

SOURCE: Kingdom of Saudi Arabia, Ministry of Planning, *Achievements of the Five Year Plans.*
NOTE: These figures do not include subsidies to corporate groups such as the press.

earmarked, for example, for "various handicapped people so that they can either enter family businesses or begin small trading concerns."[36] Health services were expanded and made available free of charge to Saudi nationals. New entitlement groups were created: in the heady years of the 1970s, women students at home and abroad were given handsome scholarships to pursue secondary, undergraduate, and postgraduate degrees.[37]

The magnitude of this category of state spending notwithstanding, fortunes were not made on basic goods subsidies, free health care, and social security. Capital accumulation occurred, rather, through the direct and indirect sectoral development programs of the 1970s, which marked a genuine departure from the policies of the 1960s. Direct sectoral develop-

[36] *Qarar Ri'asat Majlis al-Wuzara'* 219, 1400/11/27 (1979–80).

[37] Women students studying to be teachers in secondary and elementary schools were given special economic incentives (*Qarar Ri'asat Majlis al-Wuzara'* 1283, 1393/10/23 [1973–74]), and *Qarar Ri'asat Majlis al-Wuzara'* 620, 1392/6/21 (1972–73), gave the children of teachers extra scholarship money. Those studying in religious institutes or Arab universities received extra stipends: *Qarar Ri'asat Majlis al-Wuzara'* 951, 1391/9/21 (1971–72); 1072, 1393/9/15 (1973–74); and 496, 1393/4/17 (1973–74).

ment programs channeled loans and production subsidies through the Real Estate, Industrial, Agricultural, Contracting, and Saudi Development Funds. With the exception of the Agricultural Development Bank, formed in 1963, all the state banks and funds were created after 1973, for the specific purpose of granting interest-free loans. Together with ancillary production and consumption subsidy agencies, the massive sectoral development programs managed by the state banks fixed prices through and for the benefit of the private sector.[38]

Formal, institutionalized sectoral development programs using price incentives to supplement so-called "market mechanisms"—for the kingdom was decidedly capitalist—were undoubtedly the primary source of capital accumulation in each sector. In industry, subsidies were given for machinery, raw materials, employee training, production costs, and finished goods.[39] Interest-free loans were provided for starting up new plants. Contractors received subsidies and interest-free loans from the Saudi Credit Fund for Contractors to make them competitive with foreign companies. The Real Estate Development Fund made interest-free loans for the purchase and development, residential and commercial, of urban land. In agriculture, production subsidies covered all outputs and the full costs of machinery, salaries, and inputs.[40] Everything from date production to fishing was subsidized, making new ventures risk-free and highly profitable.[41] These subsidies were different from conventional import substitution policies, for they were not accompanied by quotas or tariffs on imported products that competed with domestically subsidized goods. Table 4.2 summarizes trends in interest-free loans made by the Saudi Industrial Development Fund (SIDF), the Real Estate Development Fund (REDF), the Saudi Agricultural Bank (SAB), the Saudi Credit Bank (SCB), and the Saudi Credit Fund for Contractors (SCF). It shows the rapid growth of state lending and subsidies between 1973 and 1984,

[38] Ministry of Trade Announcement 7/3/16/3/2768, "The Reduction of the Market Price for Flour," 1395/11/27 (1975–76); the price of imported flour was lowered again in 1976 by Ministry of Trade Decree 1129, 1396/3/6 (1976).

[39] Industrial training subsidies were started in 1976: *Qarar Ri'asat Majlis al-Wuzara'* 1697, 1396/11/2 (1976).

[40] The agricultural tools subsidy was created in 1973 by Council of Ministers Decree 52, 1393/1/19 (1973–74).

[41] Starting in 1976, dates were subsidized by the kilogram; farmers in the largest production category received SR 50 per date palm for maintenance, and were reimbursed in cash for 50 percent of their processing cost: Council of Ministers Decree 553, "Date Cultivation," 1396/3/30 (1976), which also dealt with fishing. The production of sheep and camels was subsidized twice for those with flocks of more than forty. The government gave SR 15 per sheep and promised to buy them back at 5 percent above average market price; the estimated annual expense for the sheep production subsidy was SR 37.5 million. The subsidy for camels was similar at an estimated annual cost of SR 31.24 million: Council of Ministers Decree (no number), "Subsidies for bedouin and Settled Sheep Farmers," 1394/11/20 (1974–75). Poultry had a production and a consumption subsidy; the latter covered 50 percent of the price of imported poultry: *Qarar Ri'asat Majlis al-Wuzara'* 924, 1394/6/20 (1974–75).

Table 4.2. Lending by specialized interest-free banks and state subsidies in Saudi Arabia (in million SR)

Year	Loans					Total Loans	Total Subsidies	Loans and Subsidies
	SIDF	REDF	SAB	SCB	SCF			
1969–70			16			16		16
1970–71			17			17	40	57
1971–72			17			17	46	63
1972–73			20			20	74	94
1973–74			36	9		45	410	455
1974–75	35		146	40		221	1190	1411
1975–76	1699	2159	269	81	118	4326	1558	5884
1976–77	2273	8901	490	158	33	11855	2031	13886
1977–78	4341	7534	586	103	22	12586	2648	15234
1978–79	7657	5766	709	55	21	14208	3163	15371
1979–80	6477	8575	1219	32		16303	3790	20093
1980–81	7654	7598	2531	357		18140	5986	24126
1981–82	5425	7141	2933	330		15829	10106	25935
1982–83	5908	8307	4166	243		18624	10024	28648
1983–84	5218	8909	3496	233		17856	7861	23017
1984–85	2416	8598	2322	251		13587	8346	21933
1985–86	926	6795	1551	275		9547	6155	15702
1986–87	355	4114	1019	240		5728	5057	10785
1987–88	543	3972	841	267		5623	4178	9801
1988–89	439	3312	755	276		4782	2098	6880

SOURCE: SIDF figures from Annual Reports of the Saudi Industrial Development Fund. All other figures from *Achievements of the Second Five Year Plan,* pp. 171–72. Saudi Industrial Development Fund (SIDF); Real Estate Development Fund (REDF); Saudi Agricultural Bank (SAB); Saudi Credit Bank (SCB); Saudi Contractors Fund (SCF).

a period in which about $59 billion was distributed through these mechanisms alone.

Social welfare programs and production subsidies were, in a fundamental way, mutually reinforcing, for they represented the state's intimate involvement in creating both supply and demand. Producer and consumer subsidies applied simultaneously to all basic goods, with the state fisc at once ensuring profits for importers and domestic producers, and holding down prices for consumers.[42] For example, the government subsidized imported sugar under the "basic commodities" program, *and* gave domestic sugar a 15 percent subsidy to cover the difference between Saudi process-

[42] The consumer subsidy for agricultural products was introduced in 1974 to lower consumer prices to 50 percent of the official prices already set by the Ministry of Agriculture and Water: *Qarar Ri'asat Majlis al-Wuzara'* 515, 1394/4/7 (1974–75). The production subsidy for milk, begun in 1974, coexisted with a price subsidy on imported milk. All basic goods were exempt from import duties: *Qarar Ri'asat Majlis al-Wuzara'* 731, "Production Subsidy and Price Support for Milk," 1394/5/29 (1974–75).

ing costs and the subsidized price of imported sugar.[43] Similarly, when the money-losing state electrical companies were consolidated into four large joint stock companies in 1975 and sold to the private sector, they were guaranteed annual returns of 15 percent at the same time that the consumption of electricity was heavily subsidized.[44]

In addition to direct loan and subsidy programs, *indirect* distributive policies—designed to involve local businesses in economic activities that were, in the main, the preserve of foreign companies—were an equally important source of private accumulation. Immediately following the oil price hike of October 1973, new projects and increased demand for goods and services generated the sudden influx of thousands of foreign companies. The most sustained foreign presence came in construction, where scores of American, Japanese, Korean, and European firms competed for massive state infrastructure contracts. It was by rewriting the rules governing foreign entry into the Saudi market that the government most radically reshaped domestic business. In stark contrast to other LDCs, where international integration took the form of linkages between multinationals and local industry, in Saudi Arabia it was possible for *any* Saudi to mediate foreign access to the Saudi market. Incorporation into the world economy thus took a very specific and unusually direct form in the kingdom; it produced not one class of interlocutors, but a whole society of commission entrepreneurs.

At the onset of the boom the government issued three key sets of legal requirements for foreign firms planning to function in Saudi Arabia. First, they had to hire local sponsors for everything from selling goods and services to submitting bids for government projects, to performing contracts in construction, maintenance, and consulting, to opening agencies. The result was to insert Saudi middlemen into all economic transactions. With foreign access to and competition in the Saudi market necessarily mediated by Saudi nationals, there was room in the sponsorship and commission hierarchy for Saudi entrepreneurs ranging from small-time influence peddlers (those who sold their names to Yemeni or Egyptian retailers for a fixed sum) to sponsors of foreign bids for multimillion dollar infrastructure projects.

Second, the 30 Percent Rule, passed in 1977, required foreign contractors who won state projects to subcontract 30 percent of their projects to

[43] The production subsidy for domestically produced sugar began in 1977: *Qarar Ri'asat Majlis al-Wuzara'* 351, 1397/3/18 (1976–77).

[44] On the electrical companies, see Council of Ministers Decree (no number), 1395/5/7 (1975–76), and note 27 above. The 15 percent guaranteed profit on electrical company shares is outlined in *Qarar Ri'asat Majlis al-Wuzara'* 452, 1396/3/16 (1976). In 1973 the subsidy to producers in rural areas was raised to 50 percent of all operating costs, to encourage rural electrification: *Qarar Ri'asat Majlis al-Wuzara'* 1115, 1393/9/21 (1973–74).

Saudi companies.[45] Legally, priority for government contracts was reserved for 100 percent Saudi firms, second priority for 75 percent Saudi-owned firms. Too small to participate in the infrastructure projects initiated by the government in the 1970s, Saudi contractors instead assumed the role of commission entrepreneurs. As interlocutors and local agents, their sole purpose was to mediate between foreign firms and the state, acquiring contracts, permits, and labor import licenses. The 30 Percent Rule offered enormous opportunities for arbitrage in state contracts, for once the formality of the rule was fulfilled, Saudi firms were free to negotiate their share with other foreign firms through a lively secondary market in sub-contracting. Although the rule fulfilled the goal of involving Saudi firms in the economic boom, it failed to generate a group of competitive local firms, for until 1986 no legislation prevented the common practice of selling 30 Percent Rule documents for lump sums.[46]

Third, the Service Agency Regulations of 1978 decreed that foreign firms employ a Saudi agent through whom all bids for government service contracts (sanitation, management, and so on) were channeled. Successful service agents were entitled to a commission of up to 5 percent (but more typically 2 percent) of the contract total.[47] The 1977 Tender Law set a limit on commissions, signaling the government's dissatisfaction with high costs, but was widely reported as ineffective.[48] According to one study, Korean service contractors regularly paid up to 40 percent of the contract amount as local commission.[49] Similar rules applied to commercial agents for exporters to the kingdom's markets, dealerships, and agencies.[50] With the expansion of domestic consumption in the boom, the implications of this last set of rules were far from trivial: distributorships in automobiles and heavy machinery, for example, created some of the biggest fortunes in the kingdom.[51]

Labor sponsorship was another lucrative source of profits, since no foreign individual or firm could enter the kingdom without a Saudi "sponsor." In addition to some 1.8 million Yemenis, by the mid-1970s Saudi Arabia was host to at least 1.4 million other foreign laborers, clerical

[45] Ministry of Finance and National Economy Resolution 2131/17, "Tender Regulations" and "Tender Regulations Implementing Rules," 5/5/1397 (1976–77).

[46] Qaiser Javed Mian (attorney at Saud Shawaaf Law Firm and coauthor with Alison Lerrick of *Saudi Business and Labor Law* [London: Graham & Trotman, 1982]), interview with author, Riyadh, 15 November 1985.

[47] Royal Decree M/2, "Service Agents Regulations" (1978). A number of these rules are explained in Lerrick and Mian, *Saudi Business and Labor Law.*

[48] See Lerrick and Mian, *Saudi Business and Labor Law,* 111, 135.

[49] Chung-In Moon, "Korean Contractors in Saudi Arabia," *Middle East Journal* 40 (Autumn 1986): 620.

[50] This stipulation was included in Royal Decree 11, "Commercial Agencies Regulations" (1962) but was not implemented until 1981 in "The Implementing Rules for Commercial Agencies."

[51] The most dramatic case is al-Jaffali's exclusive agency for Mercedes Benz; see Michael Field, *The Merchants* (London: Overlook Press, 1985).

workers, and consultants. Well-connected individuals were able to import thousands of laborers at a time without specifying the projects for which they would be employed. Sources of profit included up-front fees from hopeful migrants in the country of origin and similar fees at each stage of the employment process: extensions of visas, papers for official transfer of contracts, and so on. The exploitation of migrant workers was often extreme, involving grotesque abuses of human rights and financial arrangements resembling debt peonage.

Thus, the three branches of the distributive state that emerged in Saudi Arabia in the 1970s—general welfare and subsidy programs, direct distribution, and indirect market-based mechanisms—had distinct mandates and spheres of operation. Some direct measures, especially consumer subsidies and social welfare programs, were universalistic in design and in fact. Others, such as the state lending and sectoral development programs, were potential sources of large-scale capital accumulation but had elements of universalist access, particularly in housing and real estate. In contrast, market-driven indirect distributive measures, largely in the form of legal requirements for foreign companies, contractors, and workers, opened up arenas for capital accumulation that were almost completely dependent on political contacts and ties to the bureaucracy.

Credible gossip suggests that informal gifts made a substantial comeback in the boom years.[52] It is demonstrably clear, however, that *formal* institutions were the main distributive channels and that these functioned on the basis of universalistic categories to which, in theory, there was equal access. In conception, they were hierarchical organizations with a mandate to evaluate applicants on the basis of transparent qualifications. Moreover, the bureaucracy and the government had no stated distributive aims. Throughout the boom the government valorized capitalism as the true embodiment of orthodox Islamic principles, and government policy had no other legitimizing goal than growth itself. The fact that this formal distributive bureaucracy spawned a new business class that mirrored its ascriptive character, generated dramatic levels of economic inequality,  and presided over the decline of the traditional commercial classes who were presumably best placed to achieve the growth goal must therefore be explained in terms that account for a substantial disjuncture between form and content. Such an explanation, however, cannot precede a description of the social outcomes of the boom decade.

[52] Among the few such cases that made it into the archive in the boom years were a gift of SR 30,000 to a widow and her daughters (*Qarar Ri'asat Majlis al-Wuzara'* 108, 1394/2/9 [1974–75]); a gift of SR 10,000 to the amir of Southern Dahran for his help in the Yemeni war (*Qarar Ri'asat Majlis al-Wuzara'* 288, 1394/2/26 [1974–75]); a monthly living stipend to a royal retainer, Saud bin Jalud, and his household of SR 700 per month (*Qarar Ri'asat Majlis al-Wuzara'* 1066, 1394/8/17 [1974–5]); and two gifts of SR 10,000 and SR 15,000 to two privates in the army for their "bravery in the Yemeni war and their faithfulness to the cause of the Saudi army" (*Qarar Ri'asat Majlis al-Wuzara'* 373, 1396/3/1 [1976]).

Wealth, Poverty, and the Nejdi Ascent

Available information on income distribution at the end of the 1970s tells a story of unequal access to oil wealth. The rise of income inequality in Saudi Arabia during the 1970s is widely recognized but has not been documented. Data from an internal government report reveal that in 1980, 42 percent of Saudi households (which are generally extended families) lived on less than $5,000 a year.[53] Income distribution had a striking urban-rural division (see Table 4.3). Average annual income varied from SR 80,000 in the very large cities to SR 20,700 in the rural farming communities and only SR 14,200 in the bedouin community.[54] Absolute poverty was heavily concentrated in non-urban populations: 80 percent of nomadic and 67 percent of rural populations fell in the lowest income bracket.

Even more telling were the regional dimensions of income distribution. By the end of the 1970s the oil boom had transformed the Nejd, once the poorest province, into a rich enclave.[55] With only 26 percent of the total urban population, it was home to 44 percent of those in the highest income bracket (Table 4.4). The Nejd had three times more residents in the highest income bracket than did the much more populous Asir province. More than 72 percent of the Saudi population had incomes under the mean value for the Nejd. Poverty thus had a regional profile: low-income groups were concentrated in the southern and eastern regions (see Table 4.5).[56]

Important changes in income distribution occurred directly through public-sector employment: the majority of the Saudi middle-income groups were civil servants or military personnel.[57] But the principal bene-

[53] This section draws heavily on findings presented in *Changes in Urban, Rural, and Bedouin Communities,* a report of a survey conducted by the Société d'Etudes pour le Développement Economique et Social for the Ministry of Labor and Social Affairs in 1981. Its representative sample spanned all the regions of Saudi Arabia and covered nomadic, rural, and urban populations. Having compared the data in this report with the figures available in official publications, I have chosen to use the former to the exclusion of other sources. Its four volumes, titled *Social Change in the Bedouin Community, Social Change in the Rural Community, Social Change in the Urban Community,* and *Synthesis Report,* are hereafter cited as *Bedouin Report, Rural Report, Urban Report,* and *Synthesis Report.* For a cursory analysis of similar issues using official information, see Riza S. Islami and Rostam Mehraban Kavoussi, *The Political Economy of Saudi Arabia* (Seattle: University of Washington Press, 1984), 44–56.

[54] *Urban Report,* 58; *Synthesis Report,* 19.

[55] The report that provided the most reliable figures by region deals only with the urban population. Since the majority population in the south and east is located in rural communities, the data presented here underrepresent the true dimensions of income disparity between the Nejd and the other provinces.

[56] *Synthesis Report,* 94.

[57] In large cities the government employed close to 50 percent of the total work force except in the southern province, where total salaried urban employment was only 37 percent. Almost 60 percent of lower-middle income groups worked in the civil service or the military. See *Synthesis Report,* 42.

Table 4.3. Income distribution in Saudi Arabia, 1981

	Total annual income of households (in SR)						
	1–10,000	11–20,000	21–30,000	31–40,000	41–50,000	51–100,000	>100,000
National	19%	23%	18%	13%	8%	13%	6%
All urban	8	18	20	16	11	17	10
small cities	16	26	22	13	8	12	3
large cities	9	19	22	18	12	15	5
very large cities	4	14	18	15	11	22	16
Rural	37	30	15	8	4	5	1
Bedouin	48%	32%	13%	4%	1%	2%	—

SOURCE: Ministry of Labor and Social Affairs, *Changes in Urban, Rural, and Bedouin Communities*, Vol. 4, *Synthesis Report*, 1981.

Table 4.4. Income brackets in urban areas of Saudi Arabia by province, 1981

	Total annual income of households (in SR)				
	<20,000	21–50,000	51–100,000	>100,000	TOTAL
Center (Nejd)	22%	24%	31%	44%	26%
South (Asir)	19	16	15	9	16
East (Hasa)	14	12	10	12	12
West (Hijaz)	36	39	36	30	37
North	9	9	8	5	9
TOTAL	100%	100%	100%	100%	100%

SOURCE: Ministry of Labor and Social Affairs, *Changes in Urban, Rural, and Bedouin Communities*, Vol. 3, *Social Change in Urban Communities*, 1981.

ficiaries of the boom, as Table 4.6 shows, were high-ranking civil servants and businessmen—categories that were not, as we shall see, strictly separate.[58] A full 84 percent of the highest-income group was made up of civil servants and independent businessmen, and 44 percent of this group were Nejdis. The wealthy constituted a predominantly literate group, but 20 percent were illiterates or "traditionally educated" elites, suggesting a recent rural-tribal background.

The most striking social development of the 1970s was the rise of a large new Nejdi private sector to institutional and political prominence over the old commercial elites of the Hijaz. The business classes in all regions of the kingdom experienced growth in the boom. The magnitude of these changes is illustrated in Table 4.7, which shows available compar-

Table 4.5. Mean urban income values and concentration of income by Saudi province, 1981 (in SR)

Region	Mean Value of Total Income	Concentration of total income: 25% less than	50% less than	75% less than	% Total Income under Mean Value
Center	82,000	22,000	36,000	70,000	80
South	44,000	18,000	32,000	47,000	73
West	56,400	20,000	31,000	50,000	81
North	45,200	18,000	32,000	47,000	73
East	55,150	17,000	30,500	49,000	79
National	60,100	19,500	32,000	52,500	59

SOURCE: Ministry of Labor and Social Affairs, *Changes in Urban, Rural, and Bedouin Communities*, Vol. 3, *Social Change in the Urban Community*, 1981.

[58] The data presented in the survey explicitly exclude the royal family: "Among the 'rich' elements, members and direct relations of the Royal Family occupy a special position, outside the scope of this study" (*Urban Report*, 308 n. 1).

Table 4.6. Percentage of occupational categories in income brackets, 1981

	Total Annual Income of Saudi Households (in SR)				
	<20,000	21–50,000	51–100,000	>100,000	TOTAL
Businessmen	31	22	33	51	29
Civil servants	23	46	46	33	39
Armed forces	5	13	8	6	10
Public Service Employees	15	11	6	3	10
Unstable/temporary	13	5	4	4	7
Pension, etc.	13	3	3	3	5
TOTAL	100	100	100	100	100

SOURCE: Ministry of Labor and Social Affairs, *Changes in Urban, Rural, and Bedouin Communities,* Vol. 4, *Synthesis Report,* 1981.

ative data on the number of people holding registrations in Saudi chambers of commerce and industry.[59] The most unusual private-sector growth, however, occurred in the Nejd, where the business class (measured by membership in chambers of commerce and therefore not including retailers and most wholesalers) increased ninety-five-fold between 1962 and 1985. The Qasim chamber's membership, mostly residents of Buraydah (a small town in the middle of the Nejdi desert which had been critical to the al-Saud's success in a major war during unification), increased from only 240 at the end of the 1970s to almost 6,000 in 1986.

Individuals and firms could register with more than one chamber, so these data are not entirely reflective of the regional distribution of the commercial class. A supplementary measure of the exceptional growth of the Nejdi business class can be found in the percentages of Saudis engaged in "independent activities" such as business and contracting: the national average was 23 percent in 1981; the figure for the Nejd was 30 percent, compared with only 15 percent in the south.[60]

State spending and allocation precipitated the relative and absolute decline of the traditional merchant class. Many old Hijazi merchant families simply disappeared into the ranks of retailers. Others concentrated on foreign investments. The holdings and activities of even such families as the Ali Reza, from whence Hijaz drew many of its governors in imamic

[59] In 1980 the estimated number of Saudis engaged in some sort of private business was close to 15 percent of the work force, but the figure includes "independent professions" such as taxi driving. According to 'Abd Allah al-Dabbagh, president of the Council of Saudi Chambers of Commerce (interview with author, Riyadh, 18 November 1985), the number of Saudis registered in trade, contracting, commission solicitation, etc., was about 100,000—the combined membership of all chambers of commerce. Of these, about 60 percent were involved in collaboration with some sort of foreign partners.

[60] For the northern, western, and eastern provinces, the proportion of independent activities remained constant at about 20 percent. See *Synthesis Report,* 44.

times, shrank in the boom period.[61] The decline in the importance of the Jeddah Chamber of Commerce and the rise of the Riyadh chamber reflected the dissolution of the 1960s pact between the state and the traditional commercial elite. In 1981, when the state created chambers of commerce in outlying areas such as like Majamʿa and Qasim and put all the chambers under the umbrella of the Riyadh-based Saudi Confederation of Chambers of Commerce, Industry, and Agriculture, the ascendance of the new merchant elite over the traditional commercial classes was given institutional form. The confederation had the exclusive right to bargain with the government on issues relating to economic policy, and beginning in the early 1980s the confederation's decisions formally reflected the dominant position of the new Nejdi entrepreneurial classes. Since the vast majority of the new chambers were created in the Nejd and each chamber held a single vote in the confederation, ascendancy of the Nejdi group was virtually guaranteed.[62]

The loss of position suffered by the Hijazis in the 1970s can also be at least partially explained by a combination of caution and political ineffectiveness. Those I interviewed among the Jeddah and Mecca merchant communities noted that the hesitation of the old merchant classes to expand into the construction and service areas was partially due to their past specialization in trade. The prohibition against the entry of non-Muslims and the terrain of the cities excluded Mecca and Medina from the consumption and construction boom. There was thus a sectoral dimension to the decline of the Hijazi elite, but the relatively more robust impact of state contracts is nevertheless clear in producing this outcome.

Table 4.7. Number of members in Saudi chambers of commerce

Chamber	Reference Year/#		Latest Year Available/#	
Riyadh	(1962)	193	(1986)	21,000
Taif	(1979)	881	(1985)	520
Majma'a (Nejd)	(1981)	30	(1986)	1,512
Abha	(1982)	700	(1985)	2,000
Qasim (Nejd)	(1979)	240	(1986)	5,877
Dammam & Jubail	(1981)	5,837	(1985)	8,297
Medina	(1966)	36	(1986)	1,297
Hail	(1981)	180	(1985)	321
Hasa	(1981)	700	(1985)	3,200
Jeddah	(1977)	2,500	(1984)	20,073

SOURCE: Author's survey questionnaire distributed through the Riyadh Chamber to all chambers of the Saudi confederation, 1987.

[61] On the Ali Reza family, see Field, *The Merchants,* chap. 1.

[62] In "Political Power and the Saudi State," *MERIP Report,* no. 91 (October 1980): 5–22, Ghassan Salameh, a leading authority on Saudi Arabia, argued that the old commercial elite continued to dominate all aspects of Saudi business. My research shows this claim to be plainly inaccurate.

The origins of the new Nejdi business class are quite specific. Rather than "big government" in general, their rise occurred largely through the sectoral development programs. If direct distributive policies such as subsidies, loans, and grants were responsible for the growth of absolute and regional inequality, the true rekindling of tribal and kinship links was precipitated by indirect but formal distributive policies such as exclusive agencies, contracting, sponsorship rules, and government purchasing. These mechanisms transformed the composition of the business community in the 1970s and recast business-government relations from the consultative model of the 1960s into kinship-based partnerships between the state-created business class and the bureaucracy. By the mid-1980s this largely Nejdi group had displaced the old merchant classes of the Hijaz at the apex of the business community.

It is widely believed that princes and politically important persons were the main beneficiaries of the sectoral development programs, and the most colorful examples of instant riches in Saudi Arabia do suggest the importance of personal contacts with the royal family.[63] Yet the size and breadth of the new middle and upper classes bespeaks a much broader involvement of the bureaucracy. Soon after the first oil boom, mechanisms to stem the excessive concentration of private-sector opportunities were put in place. In 1977 the new Tender Law placed a limit of ten agencies per individual to prevent excessive concentration in a handful of influential princes and tribal notables. Moreover, as their experience grew, foreign companies developed a strong prejudice against royal family members precisely because they could manipulate local laws and regulations, often to the detriment of their foreign partners. Chung-In Moon's unusual study of Korean contractors in the kingdom puts the percentage of agencies held by traditional families in 1983 at only 13.6 percent of the total and those of tribal leaders in the outlying Nejdi provinces at 12.7 percent. In contrast, a full 50 percent of Korean agencies were held by "new middle class merchants." As Moon correctly points out, this finding debunks the widely held misconceptions, first, that ". . . Saudi wealth is monopolized by royal family members, and second, that the highly personalized business style in the Kingdom leaves no room for business maneuvering by the new middle class."[64] Moon fails to note, however, the extent to which "technocrats," "new middle class merchants," and "local-tribal leaders" were overlapping categories comprised of individuals with identical ascriptive characteristics.

The expanding role of the new entrepreneurial class rested on links

[63] The kingdom's largest dairy farm was owned by Prince ʿAbd Allah al-Feisal, son of King Feisal. Prince Sultan bin Muhammad bin Saud al-Kabir owned Masstock Saudia, huge agricultural joint venture with an Irish firm; see *Quarterly Economic Review of Saudi Arabia*, no. 4 (1984): 18. Prince Talal bin ʿAbd al-ʿAziz owned the Consolidated Contractors Company, which was very active in the 1970s; see *Country Report: Saudi Arabia*, no. 2 (1987): 23.

[64] See Moon, "Korean Contractors," 628 and n. 28; 625.

with the middle and upper echelons of the bureaucracy rather than with the royal family proper. Family, tribal, and kinship connections with bureaucrats were utilized by aspiring Nejdi businessmen not only to get permits, register agencies, and so on, but also to gather and peddle supposedly confidential information about upcoming government tenders and projects. Such practices are common in many countries. In Saudi Arabia, however, they were unique, not just because of the amounts of money involved and the proportion of economic activity covered but also because the distribution system was deliberately constructed to facilitate the entry of nationals into intermediary positions between the government and foreign companies. Thus, although the government had no stated position of helping Nejdis enter the business world (as, for example, the Malaysian government deliberately encouraged the *bumiputra*), the regulations governing the economy were clearly designed to generate a domestic entrepreneurial group.

Links between bureaucrats and new businessmen became both legal and formal in 1975, when partnerships involving civil servants were decriminalized.[65] An earlier law had sanctioned agencies functioning in state procurement even in the sensitive area of armaments.[66] Such partnerships extended through all levels of the bureaucracy; civil servants at minister and deputy minister levels were frequently involved—although as a gesture to popular sensibilities, both at home and abroad, bureaucrats often used close blood relatives as go-betweens.[67] And certainly, examples of direct involvement of members of the royal family, including the king himself, are not difficult to find.[68]

[65] *Qarar Ri'asat Majlis al-Wuzara'* 448, 1396/3/14 (1976), overturned *Qarar Ri'asat Majlis al-Wuzara'* 150, 1377/11/25 (1956–57), which had introduced stringent punishments for any government employee who participated in trade or economic activity, such as accepting favors or gifts (monetary or other), while in the civil service. A maximum ten-year prison term and a fine of no more than SR 20,000 was prescribed for any government employee convicted of "(a) Resolving a personal problem by using government influence; (b) abuse of power of any kind over subordinates or other members of the public; (c) accepting money to perform a task; or (d) using the administrative power or apparatus for personal ends of any sort." A 1960 letter from King Feisal to the Ministry of Foreign Affairs, shows that these rules were used to reprimand some of the highest-ranking officials (*Amr Sami, Ri'asat Majlis al-Wuzara'* 5317, 1380/3/9 [1960–61]), including Ahmad Zaki Yamani and Tahir al-Rafaʿi.

[66] For the lifting of prohibitions against intermediaries in military purchases, cf. Council of Ministers Resolution 1275 (15 September 1975), which prohibited Saudi intermediaries, sales agents, representatives, or brokers from mediating arms sales to the kingdom, with the following retraction by Crown Prince Fahd, president of the Council of Ministers: ". . . even in the situation involving armament sales where the commission to local representatives is apparently banned, we have no objection to the fact that companies manufacturing arms appoint Saudi agents who would be compensated for their services to these companies in the fields of maintenance, services, and construction" (interview with Crown Prince Fahd in *Al-Anwar,* 28 November 1975). For both the decree and the Fahd quotation, see Lerrick and Mian, *Saudi Business and Labor Law,* 102–103 and n. 30.

[67] See Moon, "Korean Contractors," 624.

[68] King Fahd himself was an owner of the Makkah Construction and Development Com-

Professional and social alliances also played a role in facilitating access. Links between business and the state were strengthened by the large-scale exodus of top-level bureaucrats from the civil service to the private sector starting in the mid-1970s, when private-sector opportunities began to exceed public-sector salaries. According to the secretary general of the Riyadh Chamber of Commerce, more than 80 percent of the new Nejdi business class was composed of former government officials. Given their knowledge of the inner workings of government offices and their contacts, former senior government officials were also preferred agents and facilitators for foreign firms.[69] Linking business and government, these new entrants to private business were easily able to assume the leadership of the Riyadh Chamber of Commerce, Industry, and Agriculture.

Administrative Frailty in the Distributive State

The rise of the Nejdi business elite in the boom period, I have argued, occurred through a subset of the state's distributive policies that manipulated prices and enforced laws designed to deliver the fruits of the economic boom to Saudi nationals. The transformation of Saudi society occurred not through sheer corruption or "sultanistic" informal gift-giving but rather through formal, legal mechanisms. Thus, at one level, the parameters of boomtime changes were set in the early decision to pursue domestic development rather than a foreign investment strategy. The peculiar character of the domestic development program was that despite the overarching importance of the state's role in the economy, ideologically the acts of the omnipotent state were couched in the language of capitalism and laissez-faire. The political goal of avoiding distributional issues and the government's reluctance to join debates on questions of equity in the broader Arab arena meant that the domestic development programs had no goal except growth. Universalistic, formal agencies functioning under this growth mandate sparked ascriptive identities of kinship and produced wide regional disequilibria in access to oil wealth. The workings of a formal bureaucracy dedicated to the apparently universalistic goal of growth produced an extreme form of clan organization, sanctioned in this case, by the rhetoric of the free market. At one level, this can be explained by the professional and kinship networks that linked

pany, which in 1987 "won" the contract for a mosque expansion in Mecca and Medina worth SR 20 billion (*Country Report: Saudi Arabia,* no. 3 [1987]: 5).

[69] Saleh al-Toaimi (secretary general, Riyadh Chamber of Commerce, Industry, and Agriculture), interview with author, Riyadh, 5 November 1985. Abdelrahman al-Hegelan and Monte Palmer discuss this phenomenon in "Bureaucracy and Development in Saudi Arabia," *Middle East Journal* 39 (Winter 1985): 48–68. See also Moon, "Korean Contractors," 627; *Urban Report,* 71, 276, 286–87.

bureaucrats and new Nejdi entrepreneurs. Yet as powerful as this explanation is, such links do not adequately explain the dimensions of regional bias in the bureaucracy. A full explanation must also account for the frequent inability of the state's distributive agencies to achieve their stated goals. While some unanticipated outcomes had to do with the institutional logic of the distributive bureaucracy, others were a direct result of the social composition of those that staffed the bureaucracy; of *who* the state *was*. The institutional changes wrought by the boom and the ways these changes shaped staff decisions are key components of a comprehensive explanation.

A paucity of domestic resources and planning skills was important in foreclosing the possibility of a technocratic, highly efficient, developmentalist strategy. More important yet in producing the outcomes of the boom years, however, were the unintended consequences of the decline of the extractive and regulatory bureaucracy. That decline had some striking effects on statecraft, which appear at first glance to be quite mundane. The obsolescence of extractive institutions itself illustrates the interdependence of extractive and regulatory institutions and the crucial role that taxation plays in the collection of information needed by decision-makers in both public and private sectors. Indeed, the Saudi case reveals justifications and motives for taxation that are not related to revenue at all, since by the early 1970s domestic taxation was already insignificant: the contribution of all domestic revenues to total government revenues was never more than 1 percent throughout the boom years.

If domestic taxes were such a small percentage of revenues, why was the end of the extractive bureaucracy significant? Most important was the consequent elimination of the government's main source of information about the economy. Direct taxes had supported the incipient bureaucracy and generated the information and the institutions necessary for the emergence of a national economy where economic transactions occurred with some measure of predictability. The direct taxes that the government had so painstakingly put in place in the four decades prior to the boom were not just economic tools or the source of government funding; they were also an important source of information without which distributive policies themselves could not be effectively (let alone equitably) carried out.

Unlike direct exchange, national market economies cannot function without a basic information reservoir maintained by the state. Scarcity of or unequal access to information not only prevents competition but makes informed investment decisions impossible. Taxation has historically been a critical source of economic information, particularly in nonindustrial settings. Moreover, paying taxes modifies the behavior of private business by encouraging uniform accounting and project designs; apart from generating a record of income distribution and property holdings, taxation is a tool for enforcing uniform standards of information across a variety of activities. While reserving judgment about their political consequences, distributional effects, and liberatory possibilities, one can argue that once these institutions are in place they have the potential to cut transaction costs and generate shared perceptions of the economic community. Investors are unlikely to make accurate decisions if, as in Saudi Arabia, the size of the domestic population is unknown; and not paying for ones' government undermines base-line ideas about citizenship.

With the decline of the tax bureaucracy the Saudi state lost not only a fundamental set of economic tools to govern the economy but also its main source of economic information. The massive interventions of the distributive bureaucracy occurred, as a result, in a vacuum. The sequence of the unraveling is fascinating: the initial hiatus in taxes undercut the state's ability to perform regulatory functions. The first bit of recorded evidence that the withdrawal of taxes had affected DZIT's ability to monitor the activities of companies came in 1978, when some tax-exempt companies again became liable for corporate taxes. The five-year tax holiday beginning in 1973 had meant that DZIT had been without the legal mandate to collect independent information during a period of dizzying economic change and had begun to rely on government contracts as its sole source of information. Although enormous government spending should have made it possible to substitute information from distributive state agencies for DZIT's own efforts at information gathering, for a variety of reasons it did not. For one thing, government contracting agencies had clear incentives to resist cooperation, for in the boom years the institutional goals of DZIT were in direct conflict with those of the state contracting agencies. Taxes ate into the resources available for new projects, and the government's interest in low bids conflicted with the goal of taxing profits.

Reports drafted by the Ministry of Finance and DZIT suggest that this dilemma did not go unappreciated. Indeed, there were even some attempts to reverse the trend: parts of the bureaucracy tried, unsuccessfully, to preserve their *legal* right to collect information on private-sector activities. In 1978, for example, the Council of Ministers issued a decree urging DZIT to continue to estimate personal *zakat* taxes, even though the taxes themselves were null; and the Ministry of Finance asserted its right to manipulate tariff rates to protect domestic industry, although duties were lowered again in 1980.[70] By the late 1970s the government was literally unable to collect any taxes at all, for DZIT simply lacked the institutional, organizational, and informational requisites. An excerpt from a Council of Ministers communication to the minister of finance illustrates the point:

[70] Council of Ministers Decrees 237, 1398/2/21 (1977–78); and 547, 1398/9/7 (1977–78).

> In reference to letter # 96/5220 of the Minister of Finance, dated 1396/9/16, regarding Royal Decree M/20 issued in 1390/7/1 (1970) on the collection of the jihad tax on (1) revenue resulting from the expenditures of the public treasury and (2) personal and corporate profits of Saudi individuals, agencies and companies resulting from commercial and real estate transactions. . . . The acquisition of the jihad tax in the first category is possible through withholding from income and the second is the Muslim duty of all citizens. However, the collection of this tax has been a problem, especially in the case of investments and profits from rent and real estate. This is the result of the large number of land and real estate owners and our lack of knowledge of their holdings and the constant transfer and exchange of the deeds from one owner to another. The lack of contact between these landowners and the centers and projects of the government, and their refusal to cooperate in paying the tax, has led to much evasion.[71]

The document closes with the Council of Ministers' decision to abolish the jihad tax because it could not be assessed.

The point here is simple but powerful: the voluntary removal of some taxes, for reasons of economic statecraft or politics, created gaps in the state's information reservoir that made collection of the remaining taxes administratively impossible. Even collecting *zakat* on imports, the easiest and least labor-intensive of all, was postponed repeatedly because of administrative difficulties.[72] The only direct tax that remained in place during the boom years was the *zakat* on Saudi businesses, at the rate of 1.5 percent of net profits. Yet because there was no way to determine profits directly, using import documents as the sole measure of profit assessment meant that large segments of the business community—including local wholesalers, retailers, and contractors—completely escaped paying taxes.[73] Moreover, regulatory goals unrelated to taxation could not be achieved. For example, as thousands of foreign companies entered the kingdom, it became impossible to separate them from local Saudi sponsors. Initially, this was not a significant problem, as all companies were granted a five-year tax holiday; however, many reregistered under the names of their Saudi sponsors, thereby concealing their identities. Foreign companies thus joined the ranks of tax-exempt local firms and enjoyed permanent tax holidays. Commissions to Saudi sponsors of foreign companies were difficult to monitor and so were alternately treated as salaries (on which the company would not owe taxes) or profits (which were liable to taxation). The means chosen to

[71] From Council of Ministers Decree 1243, 1397/1/25 (1976–77).

[72] Council of Ministers Decree 853, 1397/6/25 (1976–77), grants the request of the minister of interior that the new plans for collection of *zakat* on imports be held off until the next fiscal year, as ". . . there is no time to implement the collection of this tax for the 1397 fiscal year."

[73] Husayn 'Abd al-Latif (Director General, Department of *Zakat* and Income Tax), interview with author, Riyadh, 7 January 1986.

pursue the growth goal, in short, directly undercut the possibility of gathering information and of monitoring the private sector's activities. In the absence of a revenue-collecting motive, institutional devolution occurred. After the registration of companies moved to the chambers of commerce in 1974, no government agency had comprehensive data on the composition of the private sector. By 1976, DZIT and the Customs Department resorted to estimating the *zakat* dues of companies on the basis of import figures from 1970—a method that not only underestimated incomes but left out the vast majority of companies, which, after all, had formed *after* 1970.[74]

The absence of information naturally affected planning as well. Without detailed economic data, the budgetary process became opaque and abstract, and the allocation of revenues by the government was increasingly connected to particularized goals that were the outcome of bureaucratic struggles. Government statistics were literally manufactured in the Ministries of Finance and Planning. All but the first of the various Five-Year Plans begin with fictitious parameters based on unsupported assumptions and proceed to build even more fantastic projections. In 1981 the budget format was "reformed" to make already opaque figures even more impossible to interpret. Coordination among government agencies, if it existed at all, was unsuccessful, with the result that huge differences in the national budgets were reported by different ministries and even bureaus within the same ministry.[75] Then, starting in 1982, virtually all data ceased to be published.

Taxation (or its absence) determined not just what the government knew but what it could do: for distribution required knowledge, and the distributive state no longer knew much about the society it ruled. In some cases, this became clear relatively early. For example, the difficulty of distributing subsidies to livestock producers without accurate information on individual and tribal holdings was recognized in 1976. A committee of representatives from the Ministries of Finance, Interior, and Agriculture recommended re-instituting the yearly tax assessment simply to gather information on agricultural and livestock holdings. The problem, as the committee identified it, was to verify the applications of livestock producers, and the solution was to adapt the old mobile tax units (*hamilah*) to record the livestock holdings of both settled and nomadic herdsmen.[76]

[74] See Ministry of Finance Decree 2622/27, 1395/5/11 (1975–76).

[75] For divergent state budget figures see Chaudhry, "Price of Wealth" (1990), 212.

[76] The personnel for this proposed operation were not to be connected with DZIT in any way; rather, an internal police group called the *mujahhidin*, affiliated with the Royal Guard, were to record the livestock holdings of all regions. Groups of assessors were organized exactly in the manner of the old *hamilah*, with some responsible for the nomadic tribes of the center and others for the settled communities of the eastern, southern, and western regions. Whether this plan was implemented is unclear. The plan itself is outlined in Office of the President of the Ministers Council Circular 3/S/19409, 1396/8/13 (1976).

There were similar problems regarding private companies that received government subsidies in the form of working or start-up capital.[77]

Despite the decline of regulatory and extractive mechanisms and the proliferation of distributive agencies with undefined and overlapping jurisdictions, the government's pivotal role in the economy during the boom years should have given it the ability to collect information. Laws passed in the 1960s, such as the requirement that providers of goods and services to the government obtain certificates from DZIT, had been designed precisely for that purpose; with the rise of distributive programs that subsidized virtually all industrial, contracting, and agricultural projects, the potential for this kind of regulation grew enormously. Yet even though they existed on paper, no laws of this sort were applied in the boom years, and some mechanisms for control were directly eliminated, such as the law requiring certificates of *zakat* and tax payments as prerequisites for bidding on government projects.[78]

Moreover, changes in funding sources produced innovative if not wholesale redesign of bureaucratic organizations and agencies.[79] Many established ministries and agencies underwent radical transformation as their regulatory functions diminished. While its extractive role eroded, the size and functions of distributive agencies within the Ministry of Finance and National Economy (MFNE) expanded rapidly to supervise new subsidy programs, specialized lending institutions, infrastructure, gifts, and contracts. The Planning Commission was turned into a full-fledged ministry, responsible for charting the long-term allocation of resources. Both the General Organization for Social Insurance and the Ministry of Labor and Social Affairs grew enormously as well.

Organizationally, these changes delinked regulatory and distributive functions within particular bureaus and ministries: the distributive agencies grouped under MFNE outstripped the regulatory agencies still located under the old ministerial structure. Distribution had no required levels of interdependence and coordination, precisely because allocation, unlike regulation and taxation, did not necessitate consultation with other ministries or even bureaus within the same ministry.[80] Resource de-

[77] The Implementing Rules of the Livestock Subsidy were not issued until 1978 (Council of Ministers Decree 237, 1398/2/21 [1977–78]), and the criteria for private companies to qualify for government assistance not until 1979. Such was the lack of information on distributions that the Office of General Accounts was in the position of having to ask private companies to report voluntarily the amounts of subsidies they received—six full years after the subsidy had been started. See Office of General Accounts Letter 3/909, "Rules for the Private Companies Receiving Help from the Government in the Form of Working or Initial Capital," 1398/6/23 (1977–78).

[78] ʿAbd al-Latif, interview with author, Riyadh, 7 January 1986.

[79] For a discussion of this point in a very different set of institutions, see Tolbert, "Institutional Environments."

[80] On the relationship between interdependence and coordination, see Donald Chisholm, *Coordination without Hierarchy* (Berkeley: University of California Press, 1989).

pendence on the MFNE meant that other government agencies actively sought links with that ministry.[81] At the extreme, this tendency was reflected in the formal grafting of MFNE "branch" offices onto other ministries, where they assumed political and organizational prominence.[82] The MFNE had control even over distributive agencies that would logically have been connected to other ministries. For example, the Agricultural, Real Estate, Saudi, and Industrial Development Funds were not, as one might expect, supervised by the Ministries of Agriculture, Housing, Social Affairs, and Industry, respectively, but grouped under MFNE, leaving the other ministries with little power to coordinate sectoral development priorities. Overlapping jurisdictions were common as well: some education subsidies were distributed by the Ministry of Labor and Social Affairs; others, such as stipends to students studying in Saudi Arabia, were given through the Ministry of Information; still others were directly allocated by the Ministry of Finance.[83] In short, bureaucratic responsibilities became blurred, and serious gaps emerged in the information available to any one organization about a particular sector.

New organizations spun off to implement distributive programs further complicated the exchange of information. The independence of GOSI from the Ministry of Labor and Social Affairs, and of the General Grain Silos Organization (GGSO) from the Ministry of Agriculture and Water are but two examples. At the same time, key economic ministries increasingly combined conflicting regulatory and distributive aims: in the mid-1970s the Ministry of Water, which had a strictly regulatory mandate, merged with the Ministry of Agriculture, which had a distributive function.

Markets and Kinship

On its face, the progression of distributive trends from purely patrimonial to institutionalized and market-linked mechanisms suggests a pattern of development reminiscent of modernization theory. How, then, did market-linked distributive mechanisms encourage monopoly and economic inequality and reinvigorate ascriptive ties? Why did not the

[81] This point is stressed in Osama ʿAbdul-Rahman, *Petroleum Bureaucracies and the Dilemma of Development* (in Arabic) (Kuwait, 1982); and Ibrahim al-Awaji, "Bureaucracy and Society in Saudi Arabia" (Ph.D. diss., University of Virginia, 1971). Al-Awaji notes that the expansion of the bureaucracy and the extreme centralization of decisions was coupled with vague delineation of authority both within and among government organizations: "This practice has become so common-place that one may wonder if overlapping authority and vagueness of laws is not a pre-meditated mechanism to allow officials a great deal of flexibility" (218).

[82] Pfeffer and Salancik, *External Control of Organizations,* esp. chap. 3.

[83] *Qarar Ri'asat Majlis al-Wuzara'* 1452, 1395/10/13 (1975–76). *Qarar Ri'asat Majlis al-Wuzara'* 1893, 1394/10/19 (1974–75), gave the teachers of Riyadh a special subsidy of SR 1 million, distributed directly by the Ministry of Finance.

Hijazi elite, already well placed to implement the growth mandate, simply expand their scope of operations to dominate the boomtime economy?

The answer is twofold. First, distribution occurred solely on the basis of the laissez-faire growth dogma that encouraged large projects and favored firms and individuals able to absorb the most funds, by themselves or in association with foreign firms. Given the government's policy of injecting as much of the oil revenue into the domestic economy as possible, it was both in the institutional interest of bureaucrats and administratively simpler for them to conceive of large projects and subsidies.[84] Second, institutionalized distributive programs carried out under the aegis of the market paradigm resulted in patterns of spending that favored Nejdis on a scale that suggests more was at work than simple corruption. Indeed, formal distributive institutions actually widened the scope for systematic discrimination in favor of prominent Nejdis with links to the bureaucracy—partly because the decay of extractive institutions progressively lowered the quality of available economic information, but also because formal structures in the institutions that linked state spending and market forces were far from neutral. The indirect market-led mechanisms and sectoral development plans in real estate, industry, agriculture, and contracting which became the sinews of accumulation in the 1970s delegated the task of allocating funds to middle- and upper-level bureaucrats and functionaries.[85] In the absence of allocative goals, the social composition of the bureaucracy responsible for injecting oil revenues into the domestic economy became an important factor in distributive policy, and the majority of top-level bureaucratic positions were filled by Nejdis.[86] In 1969, according to Ibrahim al-Awaji's survey of Saudi bureaucrats, 61 percent of the top positions were filled by Nejdis, 28 percent by Hijazis, and only 1 percent and 3 percent, respectively, by Asiris and Hasawis. With this distribution at the

[84] The issue of extreme centralization is explored in ʿAbdul-Rahman, *Petroleum Bureaucracies*; for a descriptive-historical account, see ʿAbd al-Muʿti Assaf, *Administrative Development in the Kingdom of Saudi Arabia* (in Arabic) (Riyadh, 1983).

[85] The role of formal institutions in setting and achieving the goals of expanding education, infrastructure, and social welfare increased during the 1960s. In the 1930s the government had donated to existing charities and societies for the handicapped in the Hijaz and tried to provide direct funds only in the case of natural disasters; in 1960 all social services were unified under the Office of Labor and Social Affairs (*Qarar Riʾasat Majlis al-Wuzara*ʾ 487, 1380/9/20 [1960–61]); in the 1970s, the government dismantled existing social welfare organizations such as the cooperative societies, charities, and institutes connected with *waqf* endowments and took over all social welfare functions directly.

[86] In historical terms, the representation of Nejdis in the bureaucracy can be traced to the transfer of the national capital to Riyadh from Jeddah in 1961. That year the existing cadre of civil servants, many of whom were Hijazis, were dismissed with a severance pay of one month: Ministry of Finance and National Economy Letter 1/1/812, 1381/1/20 (1961–62). Some agencies such as SAMA, to take advantage of the technical expertise of the Hijazi population, remained in Jeddah until the mid-1970s—when their transfer to Riyadh also resulted in the dismissal of Hijazi technocrats.

onset of the boom period, the regional representation in the bureaucracy became progressively more skewed toward the Nejdis during the 1970s.[87]

The undergirding coalition of the regime was located in key groups who were integrated into the bureaucracy itself, and in the absence of formal political representation, the composition of different branches of the bureaucracy reproduced itself in the private sector.[88] In the boom years, even the Ministries of Commerce and Industry, which had been the preserve of the established merchant class, were restaffed with Nejdis who had ties to the new business elite. Leadership positions in the Ministries of Defense, Foreign Affairs, and Interior were reserved strictly for prominent members of the royal family. Other top posts were given to representatives of prominent groups or regions: Justice and Education to the Ulema, Agriculture to the al-Shaykh, and Finance to the politically important tribal elite of Qasim.[89] The switch of the bureaucracy from regulatory to distributive functions created clusters of clients in society who were linked in their common efforts to get state funding by lobbying their patron ministry; thus, the composition of the bureaucracy, itself transformed at an earlier juncture, became critical to distributive outcomes. By the bureaucrats' own admission, ascriptive sentiments played a pivotal role in their behavior. According to al-Awaji's survey of the upper echelon of the Saudi bureaucracy, 72 percent of the respondents said that they thought favoring a relative or a clansman was a "social duty," and 26 percent openly admitted seeing employment in the civil service as an opportunity to combine public and private interests.[90] After 1975, when the prohibition on civil servants' participation in private business was lifted, bureaucrats openly engaged in partnerships with the private sector. State contracts, subsidies, and development programs quickly created a business class that mirrored the social background of the upper cadres of the bureaucracy. Merchants, entrepreneurs, and businessmen who maintained strong personal, economic, family, or tribal ties with state functionaries prospered. The Saudi government's distributive policies lacked both specific goals as to their intended social effects on the population and any

[87] The provincial distribution of the Saudi population is perhaps the best-kept secret in the kingdom, but informed sources agree that about 60 percent live in the densely populated southern province of Asir.

[88] Al-Awaji, "Bureaucracy and Society," 234–35.

[89] The connection between top bureaucratic positions and political prominence is a generally recognized fact within Saudi Arabia, and the conflicting positions of individual ministers as representatives of powerful social groups affect the workings of the state agencies. Thus, for example, a businessman might have strong ties to the Ministry of Finance but be completely unwilling and unable to push demands through the Ministry of Justice or the Ministry of Agriculture. The only direct mention of this phenomenon is in al-Awaji, "Bureaucracy and Society," 177–78. His research was completed in 1969, which accounts for his statement that the Minister of Commerce represented the Hijazi business elite, but his description of the Department of Justice as the preserve of the Nejdi ulama and the Ministry of Finance as the province of Qasimis remained accurate into the late 1980s.

[90] Al-Awaji, "Bureaucracy and Society," 181, 191.

ideological commitment to equal distribution. The Five-Year Plans, deliberately stripped of both distributional and developmental goals, were focused simply on meeting sectoral growth quotas through "market mechanisms," and the individual preferences of bureaucrats assumed paramount importance in the allocation of state revenues.

Before the oil boom, what would become Saudi Arabia's distributive institutions had been largely captured by informal organizational networks that favored a select group of Nejdis. Informal channels of influence, cooperation, and information gathering are increasingly recognized as important components of formal organizational behavior, with the potential to affect social stratification and access in significant ways.[91] One might thus interpret the Saudi boom period experience as a case in which the universalistic distributive goals of political leaders were subverted by such informal networks—but such an interpretation would be incorrect. The formal rules that guided organizational decision-making during the boom were in fact designed to further the aims of the informal networks that had *already* captured key components of the bureaucracy. The neat correspondence between the bureaucracy's need to distribute large sums of money and the capacity of key clients to spend those sums was, in organization theory terms, no accident. This isomorphism emerged precisely because formal control of the distributive institutions had already been achieved by an ascriptive group through a confluence of historical serendipity and political entrepreneurship.[92]

In their efforts to enhance their prospects for survival, distributive organizations both orient themselves toward those who control broader decisions about sectoral policy and seek to cultivate clients in society.[93] Given the prior patterns of state-building in the Saudi case, the distributional biases that emerged during the boom should not be surprising. Far from being subverted, the goals of those who crafted the formal rules of the bureaucracy were in fact largely achieved when the universal principles underlying those rules were thoroughly undermined.

First Property Rights and the Creation of a Landed Elite

The transformation of Saudi agriculture from subsistence farming to capital-intensive production for domestic and foreign markets highlights the role of the government in shaping domestic market, class, and institutional relationships, neatly illustrating the way organizations, transformed by oil money, reshaped society at the core. Historically, moreover, agricul-

[91] See Chisholm, *Coordination without Hierarchy,* 29–32.

[92] DiMaggio, "Interest and Agency," 13.

[93] The relationship between centralization of resource supply and isomorphism is explored in Paul DiMaggio and Walter W. Powell, "The Iron Cage Revisited," *American Sociological Review* 48 (April 1983): 147–60.

ture was by far the most important economic activity in the kingdom, supporting a much larger, albeit less affluent, portion of the population than the service enclave of urban Hijaz. In 1953 the majority of the Saudi population was involved in farming or livestock activities. Farmers constituted 12 percent of the total population; breeders and herdsmen, 66 percent.[94] The largest traditional farming communities were concentrated in the rain-fed agricultural areas of Asir, which made up 80 percent of arable land in 1960 and included small pockets of intensive oasis cultivation centered on dates, vegetables, and fodder. The largest oases were the Shi'a areas of Huffuf and Qatif in the eastern province. Smaller enclaves of subsistence farming existed in Riyadh and Qasim in the Nejd and in the hinterland of Medina in the Hijaz.[95]

In the main, traditional agriculture involved small landholdings that utilized family labor. Except in Asir, where branches of a single family specialized in either agriculture or breeding, animal husbandry was the preserve of the nomadic and seminomadic tribes. This division between farming and breeding formed the basis for commercial relations between nomadic tribes and farming communities. Historically, the constraint on the expansion of agriculture was not land but water: the southern farmlands, where maize, millet, wheat, vegetables, and fruits were grown were rain-fed; the al-Hasa oases were watered by natural springs and an extensive irrigation system; and the Nejdi oases fared unevenly, depending on a variety of ecological and social factors.

The stage for boom-time developments in agriculture was set relatively early with the distribution of property rights in land. The abolition of the collective rights of tribes over traditional grazing lands in 1925 marked a significant juncture in the centralization of state power and the erosion of the economic and social base of the old tribal order. This is not to suggest that tribes suddenly became obsolete, but it is clear that the transfer of land-use rights from the tribal confederations to the king changed the power balance in the latter's favor. Moreover, the confiscation of collective lands gave Ibn Saud, as imam and as sheikh of all tribes, the authority to choose tribal leaders by controlling access to grazing rights and by determining migration patterns.[96]

[94] Food and Agricultural Organization of the United Nations, *Expanded Technical Assistance Program: Report to the Government of Saudi Arabia on Agricultural Development,* Report No. 76 (Rome, 1953).

[95] Douglas D. Crary, "Recent Agricultural Developments in Saudi Arabia," *Geographical Review* 41 (July 1951): 381, contrasts patterns of agriculture among al-Kharj and Huffuf farmers. In Qatif and the oases of al-Hasa, date palms are grown in 75 percent and 68 percent of the area, respectively: Sami Labban, "Agriculture in the Main Oases of the Eastern Province of Saudi Arabia," July 1982 (ARAMCO Library Archive, Dahran), 15. Table 4.11 shows the area under cultivation in al-Hasa in 1960 was smaller than that in either Hijaz or the Nejd. Since the al-Hasa oases contained the most fertile land, however, their annual yield was higher than that of the other oases.

[96] Islamic law stipulates that land belongs to God and may be held by individuals if, when,

With the abolition of collective lands, a system was created to register the ownership of urban and cultivated rural land.[97] Following an earlier practice in the Hijaz, the Land Registration Law—which required title documents or proof of continuous land use—was applied in Asir, Nejd and al-Hasa in 1952. If neither qualification could be demonstrated to the satisfaction of the authorities, title in the land at issue reverted to the state. These measures, introduced at the initial stages of Saudi state-building, put large parcels of urban and rural land under the absolute control of the king (or, until 1960, regional emirs). Subsequently, in piecemeal actions grounded in motivations ranging from patronage to settlement schemes for nomads, the distribution of urban and rural land set the stage for the accumulation of wealth in the 1970s.

The earliest land distribution program in Saudi Arabia was undertaken to settle nomadic tribes, from which regular taxes and military recruits could then be drawn. Some 200 *hijrahs* (settlements of nomadic tribes who had adopted the strictest interpretation of Wahhabism) had been founded by 1930 as a backbone for Saudi military conquests west and south.[98] A second sedentarization program was initiated in 1960, when a total of 1,000 hectares was distributed among 644 individuals, along with pumps, seeds, fertilizers, and regular cash payments. Both the first and second programs focused on the Nejdi tribes that formed the rank and file of Ibn Saud's conquering army, plus tribes from the northwest territories of Tabuk, Quriyat, and Jawf.[99] Then, in 1968, true to the administrative style of King Feisal, the Public Lands Distribution Ordinance was proclaimed, outlining the available areas of land according to a cadastral and water resources survey conducted by the newly formed Public Land Management Department in the Ministry of Agriculture.[100]

Land grants became progressively larger over time. The earliest grants

and as long as they cultivate it. Thus, as the religious leader (imam), the king was justified in laying claim to all uncultivated land in the name of his Muslim subjects, and it was his prerogative as paramount (self-proclaimed) leader of the tribal confederations that owed him allegiance to decide matters relating to the collective lands. These doctrinal and customary rationales underpinned the abolition of tribal lands. In practical terms, tribal *dirahs* (homelands) were the source of much conflict. The notion that particular tribal confederations had control over large parcels of land was not only contrary to the theory of a nation-state, in which citizens could move freely within national borders, but also a threat to the control of the central government over its territory. See *Synthesis Report*, 26–28.

[97] The system was not formalized in strictly doctrinal terms under the Shari'a courts until 1952.

[98] See Nadav Safran, *Saudi Arabia* (Cambridge, Mass.: Belknap Press, 1985); John Habib, *Ibn Saud's Warriors of Islam* (Leiden: Brill, 1978); and Christine Moss Helms, *The Cohesion of Saudi Arabia* (London: Croom Helm, 1981).

[99] Howard Bowen-Jones and Roderick Dutton, "Agriculture in the Arabian Peninsula," *Economist Intelligence Unit Report*, no. 145 (April 1983): 24.

[100] Royal Decree M/26, "Regulations for the Distribution of Uncultivated Lands" (September 1968).

had been quite small, ranging from less than 1 to 3 hectares. After 1973, 4,000 new holdings of 5–10 hectares were distributed. By 1980 a total of 123,000 hectares of public land had been distributed to 14,400 individuals and 87 large agricultural corporations. Then, from 1980 to 1984, at the height of the Wheat Program, 36 percent of a much larger area—435,000 hectares—went to 10 joint stock agricultural companies, 40 percent to 1,456 individually owned large agricultural projects, and 24 percent to 18,621 "individual farmers." The attraction of land and the ability of the allottees to turn a profit on land expanded in tandem with the rise of the distributive systems of the boom era. The size of the individual holdings distributed in successive land grant schemes grew between 1971 and 1981.[101] Indeed, as Table 4.8 shows, from a context in which private property was not a recognized institution in much of the country, Saudi Arabia had, by the end of the 1970s, one of the most unequal land distribution ratios in the world. The disparity between the size of traditional farming units in al-Hasa and Asir and that of government land grant farms in the Nejd also grew over the boom years. In 1971 only 15 percent of private land was composed of holdings of 500 hectares or more. By 1981 a full 24 percent was in large individual and company holdings. The rapid rise of large capital-intensive agribusiness in the boom reshaped agriculture in its entirety: in 1974, 4 agribusiness companies held a total of 670 hectares; in 1981, 74 companies controlled 48,680 hectares; and in 1984, 84 companies owned a total of 202,680 hectares.[102]

Significant as they are, these figures represent only a fraction of the total expansion of privately held land from state distribution schemes. Between 1974 and 1981 alone, the number of rural landholdings grew from 180,000 to 211,686—an addition of over 41,000 new holdings. Private lands grew from 1.1 million hectares in 1974 to 2.3 million hectares in 1981 (see Table 4.9). Official figures of the Ministry of Planning, however, account for only 559,693 hectares listed as having been distributed between 1970 and 1984.[103] One reason for this underestimation is that it includes only central government grants, ignoring the fact that until 1960 provincial governors could make land grants independent of the central government. According to a reliable survey based on independent research, by 1980 two of every five farms had been ac-

[101] The bigger-is-better growth dogma is nicely illustrated in how the Ministry of Planning describes this fact in its report on the agricultural sector: "This scale of land distribution exceeded the Third Plan target about fivefold [*sic*]; as a result, the average farm size increased greatly during this period. Large-scale modern agriculture has now become firmly established in the Kingdom" (*Fourth Five-Year Plan: 1985–1990* [Riyadh: Ministry of Planning, 1986], 184).

[102] *Census of Agriculture, 1981–82* (Riyadh: Ministry of Agriculture and Water, 1982), with tables obtained from the ministry. The 1984 figure is from *Fourth Five-Year Plan,* 183.

[103] See *Census of Agriculture 1981–82*; *Fourth Five-Year Plan,* 184.

quired through state distribution of lands for a total of about 84,674 individual holdings acquired through distribution programs since their inception.[104]

As commercial production intensified in newly distributed lands, secondary markets in rural land further consolidated holdings in the hands of the affluent few. In Asir, the Hijaz, and the eastern province, Islamic inheritance laws fragmented landholdings, making traditional farms available for sale to local merchants and notables. By 1981, through state grants and purchase, 82 percent of private land was held by 16.2 percent of the *landowning* population, making Saudi Arabia's one of the most inequitable land tenure systems in the world. By the end of the 1980s the government owned virtually no land. A key property right had been allocated.

Almost all the new farms distributed by the government were located in the northern and central provinces (see table 4.9), and almost none of the state land grants went to traditional farmers. Under the application of the "growth first" mandate of the boom years, traditional farmers failed to obtain government funds not only because they rarely met criteria for eligibility but also because they were not attractive candidates to bolster Ministry of Agriculture budget and production projections.

Table 4.8. Private holdings and land distribution patterns, 1971 and 1981

Size (ha)		# Holdings	% of Total	Area (ha)	% of Total
under 0.5	(1971)	34,208	19.0	9,240	0.8
	(1981)	39,527	18.6	11,201	0.5
0.5–4	(1971)	106,192	58.8	173,444	14.5
	(1981)	113,919	53.8	189,045	9.3
5–9	(1971)	17,714	9.8	117,572	9.8
	(1981)	23,905	11.2	158,094	7.8
10–49	(1971)	18,928	10.4	349,288	29.2
	(1981)	27,863	13.1	525,826	26.0
50–99	(1971)	1,999	1.1	126,489	10.5
	(1981)	3,627	1.7	231,927	11.5
100–199	(1971)	986	0.5	121,355	10.1
	(1981)	1,838	0.8	219,082	10.8
200–499	(1971)	442	0.2	118,111	9.8
	(1981)	731	0.3	199,003	9.8
500 and over	(1971)	153	0.08	179,708	15.0
	(1981)	276	0.1	479,501	24.0

SOURCE: Ministry of Agriculture and Water, Riyadh, mimeos of sections of cadastral surveys of 1971 and 1981–82. Total area of kingdom approximately 2.25 million square kilometers.

[104] *Rural Report*, 70.

Table 4.9. Government land distribution, 1970–1984

Region	Area (ha)	% of Total
Nejd	300,913	53.7
Northern	195,053	34.8
Hasa	45,162	8.0
Hijaz	7,003	1.2
Asir	10,562	1.8
TOTAL	559,693	99.5

SOURCE: *Fourth Five Year Development Plan: 1985–1990,* Ministry of Planning Kingdom of Saudi Arabia, Riyadh, 1986.

The fact that bureaucrats could directly benefit from land grants and subsidies was a third factor working against traditional farmers. Land was distributed mainly in the Nejd and the northern tribal areas, and recipients were increasingly drawn from prominent Nejdi families with close ties to bureaucrats and political elites. Thus, the historical evolution of land distribution matches and illustrates a broader pattern in the allocation of state resources: an overall movement toward institutionalized land distribution based on formally universal legal principles coincided with increasing concentration on a small group of Nejdi entrepreneurs. As one internal government report put it: "It is striking that the main recipients of these allotments are nearly exclusively members of a specific set of socio-professional categories (large merchants, important officials) or otherwise individuals with some local eminence (heads of tribes, members of socially influential families, etc)."[105]

Bureaucratic agencies associated with agriculture exhibited the mixture of ideological, political, and institutional characteristics that typified the transformation of the state in general during the boom years. In line with other sectoral initiatives, agricultural policy was based on planned produc-

Table 4.10. Percentage of land under cultivation, 1960–1986

Province	1960–61	Mid–1970s	1981–82	1982–83	1983–84	1984	1985	1986
Eastern	4	2.5	4.0	3.0	3.0	3.0	3.3	3.9
Central	10	23.0	39.0	39.0	57.0	56.8	64.4	63.1
Northern	—	2.5	6.2	5.0	10.0	10.0	9.6	10.8
Western	6	24.0	16.4	15.0	10.0	9.6	7.3	6.8
Southern	80	48.0	34.2	38.0	20.0	20.6	15.4	15.4
TOTAL	100	100	99.8	100	100	100	100	100

SOURCE: Derived from Table 4.11.

[105] *Rural Report,* 133.

Table 4.11. Hectares under cultivation, 1960–1984

Province	1960–61	Mid–1970s	1981–82	1982–83	1983–84	1984	1985	1986	Change 1960–1986 (in 1,000 ha)
Eastern	6,947	10,059	23,667	24,301	23,276	23,508	31,437	37,052	+30.1
Central	56,110	89,040	230,605	281,499	439,689	439,788	603,390	593,054	+536.9
Northern	597	10,385	36,809	33,574	76,163	76,795	88,674	100,357	+99.7
Western	35,640	96,698	97,428	106,408	74,841	74,855	68,397	63,775	+28.1
Southern	419,763	186,381	202,524	278,243	159,953	159,997	145,089	144,755	−259.9
TOTAL	519,057	392,563	591,033	724,025	773,922	774,943	936,987	938,993	275

SOURCES: Ministry of Agriculture data files, based on 1981 cadastral survey and follow-up reports; Nasir A. Saleh, "Provincial and District Delimitation in the Kingdom of Saudi Arabia," 1981, p. 308; *Second Development Plan*, Ministry of Planning, Riyadh, 1975, p. 119; and *Agricultural Statistics Yearbook*, 1988.

NOTE: Figures converted from Saudi donums (10.1 donums = 1 hectare) and rounded to nearest hectare.

tion targets, uninformed by social and distributional goals; traditional farming, it was thought, could not provide the base for the large-scale horizontal growth ordained by the Ministry of Planning. The Saudi agricultural sector illustrates the real workings of neutral free-market ideologies coexisting with state control of law and finance. The former justified the absence of attempts to create the institutional prerequisites for competition among economic actors; the latter pumped vast resources into a system built for few but available to all. Where agribusiness flourished, traditional farms and farming regions experienced a decline that can only be described as comprehensive: Asir fell from having 80 percent of the cultivated land in Saudi Arabia in 1960 to 20 percent in 1984; the Nejd expanded its share from 10 percent to 57 percent in the same period (Table 4.10). Such was the crisis of traditional farming communities that the area under cultivation in what had been the kingdom's breadbasket, Asir, *fell* by 62 percent between 1960 and 1984 (Table 4.11).

The organizational symptoms and administrative frailties of the agricultural sector illustrate nicely what had occurred in the Saudi bureaucracy at large. The burgeoning distributive functions of the Ministry of Agriculture coincided with its waning regulatory and extractive role. Once the *zakat* was effectively withdrawn, the ministry stopped sending its representatives with the DZIT tax collectors, thus depleting its overall information about the agricultural sector. Agricultural surveys had been carried out on a yearly basis between 1964 and 1970. After 1973, no survey was undertaken until 1982. By the late 1970s the Ministry of Agriculture no longer had the information needed to distribute its production subsides.[106]

The ministry abandoned both the decentralized approach and the specific projects approach that had been the hallmark of agricultural policy in the 1950s and 1960s.[107] In the 1970s and 1980s, unlike the pre-boom period, the fragmentation of state agencies was such that no single organization was responsible for the agricultural sector. New institutions such as the GGSO were given independent status but placed under the ultimate control of the Ministry of Finance; in 1974 the Agricultural Bank too was relocated under the Ministry of Finance, reflecting organizational change wrought by resource dependence. Stripped of its role in supervising the main distribution programs, the Ministry of Agriculture was charged with distributing some but not all of the agricultural production subsidies. This left considerable room for overlap and duplication of loans and subsidies. Funds for machinery, agribusiness projects, subsidies, salaries, and buildings from the Agricultural Bank, the Industrial Development Bank, the Ministry of Agriculture, the Ministry of Labor and Social Affairs, and the Real Estate Fund could all be combined for a single project. Often, a

[106] Ministry of Agriculture Memorandum 19409, 1397/8/13 (1976–77).
[107] Bowen-Jones and Dutton, "Agriculture in the Arabian Peninsula," 31.

commercial bank loan for the total amount of a project already fully funded through other state agencies was simply invested abroad. Organizational logic dictated that the Agricultural Bank, the Ministry of Agriculture, the Ministry of Finance, the General Grain Silos Organization, the Ministry of Labor, and the Industrial and Real Estate Development Funds had an incentive to demand large budgets but no incentives to gather information about or respond to the problems of the agricultural sector as a whole.

Over the boom years, then, the recipients of land grants were able to tap the successive booms in real estate speculation, industrial loans, and agricultural promotion programs. In some cases, fortunes were made simply by selling back to the government some of the land it had distributed earlier.[108] When land was used as collateral for long-term agricultural loans, distributional institutions automatically favored those borrowers with larger landholdings. Once agricultural projects were initiated with government finance, vertically integrated commercial ventures were better able to transport produce to government silos and take advantage of guaranteed purchase programs. Large landowners were also better able to realize profits by simultaneously obtaining industrial, agricultural, and commercial loans and by taking advantage of government purchase guarantees.

In the context of institutional fragmentation and low levels of accurate information, it is not surprising that these programs uniformly favored large commercial farmers. In fact, distributive agencies relied heavily on the new agriculturalists to ensure that yearly quotas in subsidies and loans were injected into the private sector. Such "farmers" were able to provide feasibility studies, prices of imported machinery, operation costs, and guarantees that were simply beyond the reach of smaller traditional farms and family farming units. Decision mechanisms automatically favored those deemed capable of meeting the production targets set by the Ministry of Planning. Practically, this group was restricted to merchants, princes, and bureaucrats with abundant land and assets and the political connections to ensure that labor permits and other necessary conditions would be met. In a word, it was simply easier for the distributive agencies of the agricultural sector to work with the larger claimants.

In contrast, the traditional farming communities were discriminated against by the application of the necessary criteria to receive a land allotment: that is, possession of "the necessary capital and know-how." Bedouin with state land allotments were automatically eligible for state sup-

[108] The government began to buy back urban and rural land quite early—at 20 percent above market value in the 1960s, with the stated rationale of stemming land speculation (*Umm al-Qura,* 28 July 1961). In the boom, when land prices increased by a factor of 5, the sale of land to the state at even higher prices above the market became a key method for well-connected individuals to turn huge, instantaneous profits.

port as part of resettlement schemes, but traditional farmers were required to demonstrate their creditworthiness individually, by the exact letter of the law.[109] Only 24 percent of traditional farmers received government help, whereas 30 percent of former bedouin had received a loan from the Agricultural Development Bank (ADB) by 1980, and 35 percent of this same group had obtained land through state allotments.[110] "Market forces" in agriculture followed and deepened patterns of access already set by the state's prior distribution of land, loans, and subsidies, to specific subgroups.

Favor fed on itself; because the large farms that could meet quotas were in the central provinces, government allocation of financial assistance for the agricultural sector was almost automatically biased in favor of the Nejdi population. A cursory examination of interest-free lending by the ADB, for example, shows that the average size of loans to the central province was far greater than that for other provinces. In 1971, while containing only 11 percent of the kingdom's cultivated land, the central province received 45 percent of all the ADB loans. In 1983, it got 72 percent of loans, by which time "market forces" had increased cultivated land there to 67 percent of the national total. The annual reports of the Agricultural Development Bank show that the majority of large medium- and long-term investment loans went to the central province, while the eastern and southern provinces continued to get small, seasonal short-term loans (see Tables 4.12 and 4.13).[111]

The toe-to-top interventions of the state in the agricultural sector might be described as market-led, because whoever could give guarantees and meet the growth targets was the preferred recipient of state largess. But

Table 4.12. Average value of loans from Agricultural Development Bank, 1971 and 1983

Province	Average 1971 (SR)	Average 1983 (SR)
Nejd	5,000	290,000
Hijaz	3,470	66,400
Northern	3,500	184,000
Hasa	5,500	212,000
Asir	2,400	56,700

SOURCES: Agricultural Development Bank, *Report for 1390–91*; and *Annual Reports*, 1393, 94, 95, 98; Saudi Arabian Monetary Agency, *Annual Report*, 1984.

[109] *Rural Report*, 18, and *Synthesis Report*, 207.

[110] *Rural Report*, 63, 92–93.

[111] Saudi Arabian Agricultural Bank, Ministry of Finance and National Economy, *Annual Reports* (Riyadh, 1970–71, 1973–74, 1977–78, 1978–79, 1980–81, 1981–82, 1982–83).

Table 4.13. Percentage of total agricultural loans, 1970–1983

Province	1970–71	1973–74	1974–75	1977–78	1978–79	1980–81	1981–82	1982–83	1983–84	1984–85	1985–86	1986–87
Nejd	45	60	59	52	57	72	69	72	75	83	84	88
Hijaz	26	19	21	29	27	12	9	8	7	3	3	2
Hasa	10	11	13	9	4.5	5	5	5	6	4	3	4
Asir	19	10	7	10	11.5	11	17	15	12	10	10	6
TOTAL	100	100	100	100	100	100	100	100	100	100	100	100

SOURCE: Agricultural Development Bank, Annual Reports.

the land distribution schemes assured that the benefits of state spending would be enjoyed unequally. Thus, from 1973 to 1974, when interest-free agricultural loans quadrupled from SR 36 to 146 million and agricultural production subsidies jumped from SR 20 to 69 million, formally neutral allocative criteria produced radically unequal results. This was only the beginning; in 1983 agricultural loans worth SR 3.4 billion were distributed. Government purchases of domestic wheat to fill the newly built silos (at the "encouragement price" of $1,050 per ton, compared with the international market price of $120 per ton) rose to SR 5.1 billion. The full swing of the Wheat Program was not coupled with import restrictions of any kind. In three years of the early 1980s the government spent about $2.8 billion just to repurchase wheat that would have cost about $395 million on the international market.[112] According to members of the business community, several large fortunes were made in the late 1970s and early 1980s by purchasing imported wheat in the Saudi market at the subsidized rate of $60 per ton, repackaging it, and selling it back to the government as domestic wheat at $1,050 per ton.[113] That Ronald Rogowski cites Saudi Arabia's turn to agriculture as successful exploitation of factor endowments suggests something of the weaknesses of crude trade theory when applied to real-life economies. For not only was the Wheat Program the most expensive fiasco in late twentieth-century agricultural history, it also created an ecological disaster by depleting aquifers formed in more humid periods 15,000–30,000 years ago. Water, not land, had limited Saudi agricultural production, even in a relative returns analysis. Subsidies made it possible to employ technology without capital constraints, enabling the new farmers to draw water to the surface from depths of 500–1,500 meters. Many areas of the central Nejd previously blessed with the Wheat Program no longer have drinking water.[114] A full 73 percent of all cultivated land in the central and northern provinces was planted with wheat in 1983–84, compared with only a historically stable 5 percent in the southern province.[115]

The sectoral development program in agriculture literally created a new landed elite in Saudi Arabia. Just as the distributive programs and incentives of the early 1970s prompted the return to Riyadh of many

[112] See Chaudhry, "Price of Wealth" (1990), 326, table 7.10.

[113] *Pick's Currency Yearbook:* 1982, 645–60.

[114] Ronald Rogowski, *Commerce and Coalitions* (Princeton: Princeton University Press, 1989); Bowen-Jones and Dutton, "Agriculture in the Arabian Peninsula," 22, 29, 30.

[115] Of 516,449 hectares under cultivation in the central and northern provinces, 377,924 were sown with wheat; in the southern province, whose total cultivated area had shrunk to 159,953 hectares by 1983, only 8,684 were in wheat (data provided by Ministry of Agriculture, Riyadh). According to a 1981 report, of seventeen very large wheat farm projects, nine were located in Al-Kharj (outside Riyadh), four in Riyadh, four in Qasim. These farms range from 200 to over 3,000 hectares each and have average fixed costs of more than SR 30,000 per year. By the end of 1981, forty new applications for similarly large projects had already been filed. See Bowen-Jones and Dutton, "Agriculture in the Arabian Peninsula," 29.

Nejdis who had emigrated to the Hijaz in search of business opportunities, the rise of the agricultural sector in the 1980s brought a second wave of Nejdi emigrés back to Buraydah and Anizah, where large-scale wheat farming was expanding.[116] The rise of a new class of commercial farmers in the kingdom, particularly in the late 1970s and early 1980s, was coupled with the destruction of rural farming communities. Income figures for traditional farmers provide some indication of the magnitude of the crisis. In 1980, 60 percent of farmers had incomes below the threshold of SR 10,000 per year, and family farmers had a lower average income than any other Saudi group: SR 5,660 a year. When bedouin settled in rural areas and abandoned livestock breeding, only 31 percent of them entered farming. More dramatic still was the change in traditional settled rural communities. Whereas 63.9 percent of this population practiced farming in the 1950s, in 1980 only 44 percent continued to do so. Both settled bedouin and traditional farmers were often forced to take other employment. The pressure from commercial agribusiness coupled with the inability of small farmers to get government assistance created large-scale emigration to urban areas. In some provinces the proportion of the population living in very large cities such as Dammam, Riyadh, and Jeddah increased from about one-fifth in 1956 to over two-thirds in 1980.[117]

The Saudi government had initially pursued a deliberate policy of undermining institutions that relied on local initiative and resource mobilization, including the guilds and independent merchant associations of the Hijaz, and the local cooperative societies of the eastern province. The destruction of both local social institutions and the tax state undermined the ability of the government to reach the large segments of the population that were not represented in the bureaucracy itself or that lacked ties with the government. Traditional farmers and nomads were certainly among these groups.[118] The state was not entirely oblivious to the economic utility of local institutions. After failing in the task of directly distributing production subsidies to traditional farmers and herders, for example, the government began to encourage farmers to reestablish cooperatives that the same government had so recently destroyed.[119] The

[116] Muhammad al-Rashudi (sheikh of Buraydah), interviews with author, Buraydah, Al Qasim, January 1986.

[117] *Rural Report,* 61, 51. About half of the rural community did not work in farming at all but in the civil service or the military (see *Rural Report,* 52, 54, tables 2.3 and 2.3c). The percentage of the population involved in herding and farming dropped from 78 percent in 1956 to 19 percent in 1980.

[118] See *Synthesis Report,* 209, 217–19.

[119] The livestock subsidy, intended to help herders meet costs in proportion to size, began by paying out money simply upon verbal declaration of herd size. Eventually, the government sought to collect information about herds by reinstating the animal *zakat* system previously in force (*Qarar, Diwan Ri'asat Majlis al-Wuzara'* 3/S/19409, "Idarat al-Shuʿun al-Maliyah wa al-Anzimah wa al-Mushariyah," 1396/8/12 [1976]). "The reaction of the ministry

new cooperatives, unlike the old, were created through subsidies and for the purpose of monitoring the use and allocation of grants and loans.[120] Also unlike the organizations they replaced, these reconstituted groups were linked solely by their mutual interest in securing state funding.

At the apex of the distributive system, the state-sponsored agriculturalists—like their counterparts in commerce, real estate, contracting, commission, and agency enterprises—found institutional expression of their common interests in the Agriculture Committee added to each chamber of commerce and industry. These committees almost immediately became a powerful lobby representing the interests of large commercial farmers connected by family ties, tribal lineage, and business interests to the Ministries of Agriculture and Water, Rural Development, Municipal Affairs, and Finance. Reflecting the dominance of Nejdis, the Riyadh committee became both spokesman for the national committee and sponsor of a steady stream of memoranda to the Ministry of Agriculture on the needs of the new agricultural elite.[121] Thus, both locally and nationally, the boom years witnessed the replacement of independent groups by organizations born solely of the state's largess. In the recession of the 1980s, these very state-created groups would spearhead opposition to austerity policies to preserve their entitlements.

Summary: What's Bred in the Boom . . .

Major oil exporters have rightly been seen as test cases for theories of economic development.[122] The absence of the capital constraint that is conventionally cited as the source of economic backwardness[123] simul-

---

which was in addition clumsy and partial (checks continued to be distributed while other bedouins were told to wait for payment orders which never arrived) was harshly criticized by those stock breeders who had suffered from the drought . . . [and] lapsed into debt because they counted on money which never arrived" (*Bedouin Report,* 72). In 1979 subsidized animal feeds could be purchased at 50 percent of the normal price. The effect of this policy change was actually an upstream one, benefiting wheat farmers and retailers whose prices were not monitored by the government.

[120] Royal Decree 26, "Regulations for Cooperative Societies," 30 November 1962, repealed in 1974 and reinstituted in 1978. Details on this case and the payment schedule for employees of the cooperative are in *Qarar Ri'asat Majlis al-Wuzara'* 420, 1397/4/1 (1976–77). Other general rules on subsidies for starting capital, buildings, accounting services, etc., are in *Qarar Ri'asat Majlis al-Wuzara'* 419, 1397/2/21 (1976–77).

[121] Adnan Abu al-Husayn (chair, Agriculture Committee, Confederation of the Saudi Chambers of Commerce), interview with author, Riyadh, November 1985.

[122] This point was emphasized in a seminal article, H. Mahdavy, "The Patterns and Problems of Economic Development in Rentier States," in M. A. Cook, ed., *Studies in the Economic History of the Middle East* (London: Oxford University Press, 1970).

[123] The classic statement is Simon Kuznets, *Economic Growth and Structure* (New York: Norton, 1965). See also W. A. Lewis, "Objectives and Prognostications," in Gustav Ranis, ed., *The Gap between Rich and Poor Nations* (London: St. Martin's Press, 1972); Hollis B. Chenery et al., *Structural Change and Development Policy* (New York: World Bank and Oxford University Press,

taneously imbues studies of economic performance in oil exporters with theoretical significance and, given their consistently disappointing economic showing, underscores the institutional foundations of economic achievement. Economists' forays into the study of oil exporters, rare as they are, have largely focused on the "Dutch Disease" as a syndrome.[124] A modification of neoclassical economic theory, the literature on the "Dutch Disease" advocates the analysis of oil exporters in a single framework that emphasizes the propensity of overvalued exchange rates to favor the production of non-tradables. The most consistent finding in this literature is the decline of agriculture in oil-exporting countries as diverse as Iran, Trinidad, Venezuela, Nigeria, Algeria and Iraq.[125] Oil windfalls tend to generate "consumption" economies, even when initial pressures to consume are resisted.[126] Despite net inflows into agriculture, biases in favor of large agribusinesses decimate traditional farming, generating large-scale dislocation.[127] Tradable sectors, empirical research shows, do not shoulder these effects equally: industry is favored over agriculture, whether for structural or political reasons.[128] So powerful are the effects of the "Dutch

---

1979). For a critique of the "two gap models" advocating aid, see P. T. Bauer, "The Vicious Cycle of Poverty and the Widening Gap," in Bauer, ed., *Dissent on Development,* rev. ed. (Cambridge: Harvard University Press, 1976), 31–68.

[124] The best summary and survey is W. M. Corden, "Booming and Dutch Disease Economics," *Oxford Economic Papers* 36, no. 3 (1984): 359–80. See also Manoucher Parvin and Hashem Dezhbakhsh, "Trade, Technology Transfer, and Hyper-Dutch Disease in OPEC," *International Journal of Middle East Studies* 20 (November 1988): 469–77; W. M. Corden and Peter J. Neary, "Booming Sector and Deindustrialization in a Small Open Economy (Dutch Disease)," *Economic Journal* 92 (December 1982): 825–48; and Alan Gelb et al., *Oil Windfalls* (New York: World Bank and Oxford University Press, 1988).

[125] Iran: Mohsen Fardmanesh, "Terms of Trade Shocks and Structural Adjustment in a Small Open Economy," *Journal of Development Economics* 34, nos. 1–2 (1990): 339–53; Homayoun Katouzian, "The Political Economy of Oil Exporting Countries," *Peuples Mediterranéens,* no. 8 (July–September 1979): 3–22; M. A. H. Katouzian, "Oil Versus Agriculture," *Journal of Peasant Studies* 5 (April 1978): 247–69. Trinidad: Richard Auty and Alan Gelb, "Oil Windfalls in a Small Parliamentary Democracy," *World Development* 14 (September 1986): 1161–75. Venezuela: Terry Karl, "The Political Economy of Petro-Dollars" (Ph.D. diss., Stanford University, 1982). Nigeria: Michael J. Watts, "Introduction," and "Agriculture and Oil-Based Accumulation," both in Watts, ed., *State, Oil, and Agriculture in Nigeria* (Berkeley: Institute of International Studies, 1987), 1–33, 58–84. Algeria: Mahfoud Bennounne, *The Making of Contemporary Algeria, 1830–1987* (Cambridge: Cambridge University Press, 1988); Peter Knauss, "Algeria's 'Agrarian Revolution,'" *African Studies Review* 20 (December 1977): 65–78.

[126] H. Katouzian, "Political Economy of Oil Exporting Countries"; Otwin Marenin, "The Nigerian State as Process and Manager," *Comparative Politics* 20 (January 1988): 215–32; Mahdavy, "Patterns and Problems of Economic Development." For a description of this pattern, see Auty and Gelb, "Oil Windfalls"; Patrick Conway and Alan Gelb, "Oil Windfalls in a Controlled Economy," *Journal of Development Economics* 28 (February 1988): 63–81.

[127] Massoud Karshenas, "Oil Income, Industrialization Bias, and the Agricultural Squeeze Hypothesis," *Journal of Peasant Studies* 17 (January 1990): 245–72.

[128] Karl, "Political Economy of Petro-Dollars"; Fardmanesh, "Terms of Trade Shocks," 339; and Nancy Benjamin, S. Devarajan, and R. J. Weiner, "The 'Dutch Disease' in a Developing Country," *Journal of Development Economics* 30 (January 1989): 71–92. The argument for the political nature of discrimination against the peasantry is made in H. Katouzian, "Political Economy of Oil Exporting Countries."

Disease" that sectoral policies to support local agriculture and industry collide with the overvalued exchange rates that result from the dual pressures of real appreciation and state preferences to maximize the local value of foreign currency reserves.[129]

Although it is well accepted that all oil exporters face similar pressures and opportunities,[130] their pursuit of different sectoral and industrial strategies belies the uniform outcomes posited by the "Dutch Disease" framework. In the realm of policy, oil exporters have pursued very different strategies: Iraq, Malaysia, Iran, and especially Algeria, for example, countered the pressures against investment in tradables by initiating industrialization programs.[131] Similarly, while agriculture declined in almost all oil exporters, Saudi Arabia, a country with little comparative advantage in agriculture, initiated a large program of agricultural development in the 1970s.[132]

Beyond the uniform constraints of the international market and relative prices, oil exporters share some fundamental characteristics inevitably expressed by theorists as "outcomes" rather than processes. In this category, theories of the rentier state far outstrip detailed empirical analysis of actual cases. For example, although there is wide agreement that oil states have the capacity to create and destroy social classes, little attention has been devoted to explaining how and why particular patterns of class formation occur or why boomtime spending produces such divergent outcomes in different cases.[133] Efforts to stretch the theory of the rentier state to fit the case often result in contradictory analytical trajectories that originate in the same set of initial observations. For example, despite wide agreement on the rise of regional and other forms of economic inequality during oil booms,[134] the relevance of inequality for collective action is interpreted variously as revolutionary or "unimportant."[135] Oil, judging from

[129] Mahdavy, "Patterns and Problems of Economic Development," 436.

[130] Karl, "Political Economy of Petro-Dollars," 91, 109–10, argues forcefully for the common responses to the oil boom.

[131] A comparative study of Iraqi and Algerian industrialization, analyzed within the "Dutch Disease" paradigm, is Kiren Aziz Chaudhry, "Prices and Politics" (Paper presented at the Annual meeting of the American Political Science Association, New York, 1994).

[132] These developments were not, as Rogowski suggests in *Commerce and Coalitions*, the result of a rational calculation of domestic endowments and comparative advantage.

[133] The broad-based ability of the oil state to create and destroy classes is discussed but not documented in M. Katouzian, "Oil Versus Agriculture"; and H. Katouzian, "Political Economy of Oil Exporting Countries."

[134] Gobind T. Nankani, "Development Problems of Mineral-Exporting Countries," World Bank Staff Working Paper 354 (Washington, D.C.: World Bank, 1979); Richard Auty, "Third World Response to Global Processes," *Professional Geographer* 43 (February 1991): 68–76; Watts, "Introduction"; Hal Hill, "Regional Development in a Boom and Bust Petroleum Economy," *Economic Development and Cultural Change* 40 (January 1992): 351–80; Mahdavi, "Patterns and Problems of Economic Development"; and Hazem Beblawi and Giacomo Luciani, "Introduction," in Beblawi and Luciani, eds., *The Rentier State* (London: Croom Helm, 1987), pp. 1–21.

[135] Giacomo Luciani, "Allocation vs. Production States," in Beblawi and Luciani, *Rentier State,* 74.

the literature, at once forestalls political debate, forming a political "lubricant" for otherwise unstable alliances,[136] and generates substantial social unrest.[137] Similarly, beyond a commonsensical set of defining characteristics, two opposing pictures of the rentier state portray governments in oil exporters as either "strong" and "autonomous"[138] or "weak" and ineffective.[139] Pictures of business-government relations are equally schizophrenic.[140] Despite the obvious problems of employing classical theories of rent on oil exporters,[141] the concept of the rentier state has sometimes been expanded to encompass all forms of "rent seeking."[142]

Clearly, oil exporters vary not only in their levels of dependence on oil revenues but also in the mix of endowments and historical legacies that condition policy and political outcomes. Yet there can be little argument that fiscal and bureaucratic developments are substantially altered during oil booms, with profound implications for a host of domestic relationships. The most important change is the decline in domestic taxation in general, and direct taxation in particular.[143] Two generic types of administrative alternatives have historically replaced the extractive and regulatory

[136] Marenin, "Nigerian State," 222; Mahdavy, "Patterns and Problems of Economic Development"; Hill, "Regional Development," 370–71; Kiren Aziz Chaudhry, "The Price of Wealth," *International Organization* 43, no. 1 (Winter 1989): 101–45; Karl, "Political Economy of Petro-Dollars," 133–36.

[137] See Theda Skocpol, "Rentier State and *Shi'a* Islam in the Iranian Revolution," *Theory and Society* 11 (May 1982): 265–83.

[138] Tawfic Farah, "Political Culture and Development in a Rentier State," *Journal of Asian and African Studies* 24 (January–April 1989): 106–13; Beblawi and Luciani, "Introduction"; Luciani, "Allocation vs. Production States."

[139] According to Mahdavi, the rentier state lacks organization and administrative coherence ("Patterns and Problems of Economic Development," 453, 466–67); Karl, "Political Economy of Petro-Dollars," 138, 142, makes a similar argument. See also Michel Chatelus, "Policies for Development," and Dirk Van de Walle, "Political Aspects of State Building in Rentier Economies," both in Beblawi and Luciani, *Rentier State*, 108–37, 159–71.

[140] In contrast to Mahdavy, who argues that the rentier state creates a rentier class in the public and private sectors ("Patterns and Problems of Economic Development," 467), Karl argues that an already weak bourgeoisie is further debilitated by the oil state ("Political Economy of Petro-Dollars," 132, 142–43).

[141] Cyrus Bina, "The Laws of Economic Rent and Property: Application to the Oil Industry," *American Journal of Economics and Sociology* 51 (April 1992): 187–203.

[142] See, e.g., the two otherwise excellent discussions in Catherine Boone, "The Making of a Rentier Class," *Journal of Development Studies* 26 (April 1990): 425–49; and Barnett R. Rubin, "Political Elites in Afghanistan," *International Journal of Middle Eastern Studies* 24 (February 1992): 77–99.

[143] Chaudhry, "Price of Wealth" (1989); Chaudhry, "The Myths of the Market and the Common History of Late Developers," *Politics and Society* 21 (September 1993): 245–74; Chaudhry, "Economic Liberalization and the Lineages of the Rentier State," *Comparative Politics* 27 (October 1994): 1–27; Chaudhry, "Prices and Politics;" Hazem Beblawi, "The Rentier State in the Arab World," in Giacomo Luciani, ed., *The Arab State* (Berkeley: University of California Press, 1990), 85–99; Mahdavi, "Problems and Patterns of Economic Development"; Auty and Gelb, "Oil Windfalls"; Fathallah Oulalou and Larbi Jaidi, "Fiscal Resources and Budget Financing in the Countries of the Maghreb," and Hesham Garaibeh, "Government Income Sources and the Development of the Taxation System," both in Beblawi and Luciani, *Rentier State*, 172–93, 194–210.

bureaucracy. In the first or "productive" bureaucratic pattern, governments directly take over property, land, and industry. This pattern is characteristic of countries with strong historical legacies of class conflict and nominally egalitarian developmentalist regimes, usually propelled to power in anticolonial struggles. In the Middle East and Africa, production-oriented bureaucracies emerged only in oil exporting countries with a domestic labor force (Algeria, Nigeria, Iraq, Iran) and a powerful, if divided, domestic capitalist class; in these cases, wide-scale nationalizations occurred, and government agencies directly assumed the management of enterprises and industries. In contrast, the second or purely distributive administrative response occurred in countries with no domestic working class to speak of, a very small population, and little history of direct class conflict (Libya, Saudi Arabia, Kuwait, Qatar, the United Arab Emirates). The inclusion of Saudi Arabia and Libya in this group suggests that geographical size and ideology are largely irrelevant to administrative responses to oil booms, at least at the highest level of generality.[144] The centrality of fiscal imperatives in defining patterns of administrative growth, state-building, market formation, and coalition-building (as described in Chapters 2 and 3) suggests the critical importance of a decline in taxation for domestic social and political relationships but does not empower us to deduce these effects. However exciting the theoretical implications of a purely distributive state, the way the decline in taxes affects institutions and politics is ultimately an empirical question. Beyond the observation that allocative and production responses differ fundamentally, the two clusters of cases have very little else in common.

Among oil exporters, Saudi Arabia represents the "pure" distributive pattern. With a population of less than five million at the onset of the boom, oil revenues were more than adequate to fuel the national economy. Yet unlike other purely distributive cases, Saudi Arabia had a large territory, making it strictly comparable only to Libya. The outcomes of the boom in Saudi Arabia, nevertheless, have important implications for social theory and for political economy in general. The new revenue base of the Saudi state profoundly changed both the structure and the functions of the bureaucracy. The rise of the distributive state shows how unique sets of economic opportunities in the international system can generate novel institutional constructs in late developers. Oil revenues freed political elites from reliance on domestic taxes. The withdrawal of taxes, in turn, precipitated the dismantling of the extractive and regulatory bureaucracy and the construction of an alternative set of institutions designed to govern the economy solely through the domestic deployment of

[144] Chaudhry, "Price of Wealth," 1989; Luciani, "Allocation vs. Production States," distinguishes the two types. The ideal pairs for comparison—Iraq and Algeria; Libya and Saudi Arabia—are explored in Chaudhry, "Business and Labor."

oil revenues. Although the outcomes superficially match what Middle East experts call patrimonialism, the distributive state was nothing like the patronage networks in pre-boom Nejd or Hijaz.

The formal organizational structures of the distributive bureaucracy, functioning under universalist rules, were conditioned by three key factors. First, the distributive instruments of the state, however interventionist in fact, functioned in the ideational construct of laissez-faire economics, which deliberately removed issues of economic justice and equality from the agenda. Second, as the decline of the tax bureaucracy deprived the economically powerful oil state of its main source of economic information, alternative criteria shaped the decisions of the bureaucrats responsible for allocating state funds and contracts. Third, these two facts combined with the social composition of the largely Nejdi bureaucracy to create allocative decisions that favored the kin and region of bureaucrats. The organizational logic linking these three factors is vividly demonstrated in the responses of government bureaus and agencies to the new incentive structures of the 1970s. The distributive bureaucracy in Saudi Arabia was neither chaotic nor as centralized as is often believed. Rather, its decisions emerged from a confluence of historically determined institutional parameters that favored large projects over small ones. Lacking other guidelines, and given a distribution of initial property rights that favored the Nejd, bureaucrats pursued individual strategies that had less than optimal results. Market principles, applied in a particular institutional and social construct, yielded neither efficiency nor equality.

The fiscal autonomy of the boom-era Saudi state and the distributive policies it subsequently pursued had a profound impact on domestic social classes. Yet to understand this impact, one must not only distinguish between the different functional characteristics of the state but disaggregate the distributive bureaucracy itself. Not all distributive programs fueled private accumulation; rather, wealth was specifically generated in the market-driven sectoral development programs and the indirect distributive mechanisms set in place during the boom. The workings of this segment of the distributive bureaucracy resulted in the creation of entirely new social classes in Saudi Arabia. As a direct result of distribution, a landed elite was created in less than a decade, and the relative economic fortunes of other groups rose and fell. In particular, the oil boom undid the corporate relationship, stabilized in the 1960s, between the old commercial elites of the Hijaz and the Nejdi state. Through the distributive acts of the formal bureaucracy and a set of laws validated by the rhetoric of laissez-faire, a large class of Nejdi business elites emerged over the boom decade, eclipsing in numbers and in wealth the old Hijazi elite. The transformation of extractive relations created an entirely new private-sector elite with strong kinship and financial links to the bureaucracy.

This analysis contradicts existing portrayals of economic policy in major oil exporters. In exploring the social effects of the domestic deployment of state-controlled oil rents, analysts invoke paternalism, clientelism, patrimonialism, and sheer corruption.[145] The terms in which the distributive imperatives of the rentier state have been described are usually intended to suggest the ambiguous class basis of governments in oil exporters, as reflected in their policies and the social outcomes of distribution. The paternalist and clientelist nature of the oil state is, in short, deduced from the observed rise of ascriptively based wealth accumulation and the ascent of religious, tribal, or regionalist forms of collective mobilization.[146] These formulations raise but fail to answer the critical question of the link between the institutional effects of oil revenues on the extractive and regulatory capacities of the state and the social outcomes that state spending produces. As others have suggested, the strengthening of regional, tribal, and kinship cleavages in society through state spending programs during the oil boom directly challenges widely accepted notions about the relationship between social and economic change as enshrined in the teleological constructs of modernization theory. It is inaccurate, though common, to see the distributive policies of the boom years as established patterns of patronage writ large,[147] or to view the entitlement groups as the top layer of an emerging "modern" class society.[148] My argument is quite different. It stresses the interaction of laissez-faire distributive imperatives undertaken for growth alone, the lack of economic information, and the preexisting composition of the bureaucracy in explaining social outcomes that appear to be the result of sheer corruption. The theoretical claim that emerges from this discussion is straightforward: the extent to which the market undercuts or invigorates the political economy of ascription depends on the organization and composition of the institutions that govern the economy. Formal, organizationally "modern" institutions are just as capable of generating and sustaining the politics of ascription as is the proverbial monarch's purse of gold.

The 1970s in Saudi Arabia illustrate the role of economic resources in undoing historically constituted social and institutional relationships. In-

[145] Karl, "Political Economy of Petro-Dollars," 149, observes the lack of separation between political and private economic activity; for the patrimonial argument, see Marenin, "Nigerian State"; Watts, "Introduction" and "Agriculture," argues for the corruption and rent-seeking paradigm in explaining the Nigerian experience; Auty, "Third-World Response," and Hill, "Regional Development," make similar arguments. On "dormant" networks invigorated through oil rents, see Paul M. Lubeck, "Islamic Protest and Oil-Based Capitalism," in Watts, *State, Oil, and Agriculture,* 268–90.

[146] See esp. Jacques Delacroix, "The Distributive State in the World System," *Studies in Comparative International Development* 15 (Fall 1980): 3–21.

[147] See, e.g., Mordechai Abir, *Saudi Arabia in the Oil Era* (London: Croom Helm, 1988).

[148] See, e.g., Mark Heller and Nadav Safran, "The New Middle Class and Regime Stability in Saudi Arabia," Harvard Middle East Papers (Cambridge, Mass., 1985); and William Rugh, "The Emergence of a New Middle Class in Saudi Arabia," *Middle East Journal* 27 (Winter 1973): 7–20.

stitutional change of this magnitude, in turn, allows us to examine directly the ways that institutions can first alter and then embody changes in social and political relationships. Clearly, the fiscal autonomy of the Saudi state was critical in the reconfiguration of business-government relations. Yet this simple fact does not explain the ease with which the transformation took place. How, then, can the lack of resistance that characterizes responses to the state's actions in Saudia Arabia—as opposed to, say, Iraq or Algeria—be explained?

Although it is not a definitive answer, the source of the Hijazis' acquiescence possibly lay in the way they bargained away not only their political but also their organizational autonomy in the initial period of market unification. In fact, the absence of a politically unified domestic labor force was critical to the ideological abstinence of both the state and the Hijazi business elite. Saudi Arabia had no national moment; as a society, it never confronted the problem of incorporating an industrial urban work force into the political system. During the boom, when substantial industrial investments were made, the labor force was almost exclusively an imported one that was stripped at the outset of aspirations to citizenship, let alone participation. Thus, the laissez-faire economy was built on the explicit exclusion of the foreign working classes. In the absence of a threat from organized labor, neither the state nor the old business classes consolidated politically. The bourgeoisie and political elites unified against Pan-Arabism in the 1950s and 1960s but had little to unite them later.

The Saudi case raises fundamental questions about the influence of international capital flows on domestic class creation and on the institutional development of the state. At the same time, the oil revenues that transformed the Saudi political economy also drew 1.8 million Yemeni workers into the construction projects, retailing businesses, and manual labor force of the kingdom. If Saudi Arabia had no domestic labor force, Yemen managed to export its labor force abroad. In the confines of the regional economy that emerged, international flows of capital and of labor complemented each other. Labor existed at the regional level in the 1970s but not as a national force and not with a national political agenda. The disembodied nature of class and the temporary absence of a politics of confrontation shaped developments in the boom and also affected the reconsolidation of opposition groups in the recession.

CHAPTER FIVE

Migrants and Magnates

As the oil boom of 1973 sent government revenues skyrocketing in Saudi Arabia, neighboring Yemen underwent economic changes of similar magnitude. Although smaller than Saudi oil revenues, labor remittances and development aid made up a substantial proportion of Yemen's economy, more than 120 percent of the country's official GNP in the early 1980s.[1] Developmental aid averaged 43 percent of the overall Yemeni budget, and aid from oil-rich Gulf states covered the Yemeni government's entire current budget for much of the 1970s (see Table 5.1).[2]

The dual flows of foreign currency in the 1970s, one to the government, one to the private sector, simultaneously shaped state institutions and civil organizations. Aid and remittances entered and reconfigured Yemeni economy and society through very different mechanisms and organiza-

[1] This calculation is based on information provided by Husayn al-Saqqaf, managing director of Shalaq Foreign Exchange House, the informal bank that handled 80 percent of Yemeni labor remittances until 1986. Even the conservative figures of USAID indicate that as much as 85–90 percent of GNP growth was directly or indirectly related to remittances; see Donald McClelland, "Some Major Aspects of the Economy of the Yemen Arab Republic," USAID discussion paper (Washington D.C.: United States Agency for International Development, 1980), 5. These estimates merely depict the dimensions of the reliance on remittances. The inaccuracy of government data do not permit definitive judgments.

[2] Percentages and figures in this section are derived from World Bank, USAID, and Ministry of Finance (YAR) sources. Recent reports put direct aid at about $1 billion; see "North Yemen," *Economist,* 16 January 1982, 44–45. See M. S. El Azhary, "Aspects of North Yemen's Relations with Saudi Arabia," in B. R. Pridham, ed., *Contemporary Yemen* (London: Croom Helm, 1984), 198, on foreign aid from other Arab countries; Claus Burghard and Michael Hofmann, "The Importance of the Oil Producing Countries of the GCC for the Development of the Yemen Arab Republic and the Hashemite Kingdom of Jordan" (Berlin: German Development Institute, 1984).

tions, producing complex patterns of change in the public and private sectors. Remittances entered the economy through informal banking networks largely invulnerable to state detection, feeding the Yemeni private sector with ample foreign exchange. Bilateral aid, in contrast, was directly controlled by the government. Labor remittances were by far the larger source, however, outstripping the entire state budget by an average of 500 percent between 1973 and 1976 and reaching a high of about $4.8 billion in 1981.

The very late emergence of a coalition for a national market in Yemen had forestalled the linear progression of administrative centralization characteristic of Saudi Arabia in the pre-boom period. Nevertheless, on the eve of the oil boom Yemen had achieved a degree of administrative and economic stability, including the unification of its currency, the establishment of a central bank, the removal of internal barriers to trade, the creation of a formal bureaucratic corps, a modern military, and modern commercial institutions. Yemen's tortuous path to the unification of the national market and the centralization of key government organizations had included an eight-year-long civil war (1962–70) that had pitted a largely *Shiʿa* royalist courtly and tribal elite against the Republican majority. Dominance of the commercial sector had been won by the absentee commercial classes, who had both funded and organized much of the initial resistance to the imam. However conclusive the economic victory of the *Sunni* merchant classes, important political struggles between *Sunni* southerners and *Shiʿa* northerners for representation in the higher ranks of the military and the bureaucracy were still being waged as the 1970s opened. A series of stalemates eventually culminated in the increasingly confrontational tactics deployed by the populist military officer al-Hamdi in his efforts to centralize power, to strengthen the formal army, and to mobilize workers, peasants, and farmers against the tribal confederations.

As suggested at the end of Chapter 3, al-Hamdi's efforts were aborted almost as they began by the economic boom of 1973–74, when large portions of Yemen's labor force migrated to Saudi Arabia. The first effect of the boom—a dramatic rise in private-sector wages and the stagnation of public-sector wages—substantially undercut support for al-Hamdi's policies. For major labor exporters such as Yemen, the onset of the oil boom belied the central assumption of Arab political thought in the nationalist era: namely, that the state was the sole arena for economic competition. Bred on Nasserism and Ba'thism and a firm believer in the right of the state to shape economic outcomes, al-Hamdi began in 1973 to carve out a place for his constituents in a public sector that had already been surpassed by the burgeoning boomtime private sector. So dramatic was the shift in public and private wages, and so swift the response of the Yemeni work force, that by the mid-1970s large segments of the bureaucracy and the educational system were being run by Sudanese and Egyptian migrants.

Table 5.1. Government revenues in the YAR, 1971–1983 (in million YR, current prices)

	1971	1972	1973	1974	1975	1976	1977	1980	1981	1982	1983
Tax on wages	2	2	3	10	5	8	16	134	170	273	312
Corp. profit tax	—	—	—	6	10	13	22	73	116	147	166
Zakat	7	11	12	16	15	21	33	38	25	101	125
TOTAL DIRECT	9	13	15	32	30	42	71	245	331	521	603
Indirect taxes	10	20	22	28	39	46	38	287	279	270	285
Customs	53	77	113	156	222	394	929	1,795	1,634	1,840	2,213
Non-tax revenues	24	28	41	49	80	66	218	617	715	651	745
Other[a]	0.4	1	4	3	3	3	3	33	34	44	56
Stamp dues	—	—	4	9	9	13	34	74	362	370	522
TOTAL DOMESTIC (WITHOUT CUSTOMS)	43.4	63	86	121	161	170	364	1,256	1,701	1,856	2,211
TOTAL DOMESTIC	96.4	140	199	277	383	564	1,293	3,051	3,335	3,696	4,424
Net external (reported)	119	171	117	239	536	609	786	3,669	2,465	2,955	1,752
GRAND TOTAL[b]	215.4	311	316	516	919	1,173	1,899	6,720	5,800	6,651	6,176

SOURCES: International Monetary Fund, *Recent Economic Developments in the YAR,* 1977 and 1984; and revenue schedules from the Ministry of Finance, San'a, YAR (figures rounded to the nearest million Yemeni riyal).

[a]Consumption taxes and taxes on government services.

[b]"Total" includes foreign aid.

Aid and remittances were crucial to the success with which elites negotiated a stable agreement of mutual coexistence following the civil war. If the economic changes of 1973–74 stalled efforts to establish military and political control over the northern tribes by stripping al-Hamdi of his planned domestic constituency—al-Hamdi had been a leader of the cooperative movement and came to power in 1973—aid and remittances also created separate resource flows that underpinned what is known in Yemeni historiography as the "Republican Pact," essentially an agreement of noninterference between *Sunni* private-sector elites and the *Shiʿa* military-bureaucratic elite. In practical terms, the flow of aid and remittances not only terminated ongoing struggles over who would control the state but also provided two autonomous sources of foreign exchange that enabled each realm to prosper without infringing on the other. The northern tribes retained their autonomous status, including their ability to make claims on resources controlled by the state apparatus; the southern merchants, buoyed by remittances, achieved even more control over the lucrative import, real estate, and informal banking sectors. The migration of substantial portions of Yemeni labor—at any time during the boom over two-thirds of the active labor force—was critical to achieving this accommodation, because it not only eliminated pressures for distributive justice from below but also forestalled movements for government accountability and formal representation. In short, the national political arena and the public sector were eclipsed by the private sector and by local politics very soon after 1973.

As remittances fueled growth in all levels of the private sector, development aid (plus, though to a far lesser extent, customs duties on remittance-funded imports) enabled the government to develop a parallel institutional structure disconnected from the private sector. Downward revisions of import tariffs and general deregulation of all aspects of the economy meant that few arenas of contention remained between the *Sunni* private sector and the *Shiʿa* government. At base, however, the elite pact rested on a *temporary* rearrangement of Yemen's social structure: the departure of labor as a political force. The migrant labor force, through their home remittances, were the economic backbone of a political accommodation that they, as a group, were not party to. Aid, like the Saudi oil revenues, enabled the government to subsist and even expand without enlarging the domestic tax base. In the 1970s, as both the public sector and the economy were growing at an unprecedented rate, Yemen's extractive bureaucracy shrank. In stark contrast to the imam's robust tax bureaucracy, Yemen's boomtime tax base contracted until it was nothing more than a customs house.

Yemen had entered the boom period with a divided society in which occupational, regional, and sectarian cleavages coincided. The prosperity of the 1970s and the unconnected, parallel growth of the public and private sectors depoliticized distributional issues. Yet at the same time the inflow of aid and remittances fed into and accentuated the ascriptive cleavages that separated the northern bureaucratic-military sphere from the southern private sector. Remittances controlled by millions of migrants, mostly from the *Sunni* south, were eventually accumulated and used by the old southern merchant classes of Yemen through complex informal banking networks. The boom thus added a stark economic dimension to existing social divisions, signaling the closer alignment of new occupational and economic cleavages with old regional and sectarian ones. Fueled by labor remittances, virtually all echelons of the private sector came to be dominated by the southern *Sunni* groups, while bureaucracy and the army remained the preserve of the northern *Shiʿas.*

Where oil revenues gave the Saudi state wide powers to manipulate the economy for political ends, the inflow of both state and private resources created distinct political and economic spheres in Yemen. Unlike in Saudi Arabia, Yemeni elites did not replace its declining regulatory and extractive institutions by distributive agencies. Aid was not sufficient to embroil the Yemeni government in the kind of wholesale restructuring of society undertaken by the Saudi state. Instead, government services in many areas were actually scaled back. As the state retreated from the remote regions of Yemen, withdrawing its services, remittances encouraged grassroots developmental associations that replaced receding state tax institutions, generated local infrastructure projects and social services, and fueled private investment through channels that were thoroughly independent of the state. Migrant labor thus established its own institutional infrastructure, at once separate from but ultimately linked to that of the private-sector elite.

Major Labor Exporters as Anomalies

If labor remittances have not generated bodies of theory commensurate with those inspired by oil revenues, it is not because remittances were less important to labor-exporting countries. In fact, the economies of extreme cases such as boomtime Yemen contradict virtually all the attributes typically associated with developing countries. By the late 1970s Yemen was in the anomalous position of being classified simultaneously as a "least developed," "capital abundant," and "labor-scarce" Third World country.[3] That all these adjectives applied indicates the magnitude of disjunctures created between different sectors of the economy. Measured by infant mortality, education, life expectancy, access to safe water, and other quality-of-life indicators, Yemen remained in the lowest tier of developing

[3] John Cohen, "Capital-Surplus, Labor-Short Economies," *American Journal of Agricultural Economics* 61 (August 1979): 523–28; Cohen et al., "Development from Below," *World Development* 9 (November–December 1981): 1039–61.

countries. Yet in constant 1973 prices, remittances raised the per capita GNP from $172 in 1973 to $469 in 1976 and to about $1,500 in the early 1980s.[4] Per capita GNP was far above the $420 ceiling necessary to qualify for multilateral aid—a fact that accounts for the government's wide-scale manipulation of economic information in its efforts to retain the coveted status of a "least developed" country.

Yemen's level of reliance on labor remittances stemmed from its special relationship to its northern neighbor: unlike all other foreign laborers, Yemenis did not require work permits to migrate to Saudi Arabia. As a result, migration was completely unregulated on both sides of the border: at any given time during the oil boom, two-thirds of Yemen's labor force was in Saudi Arabia. At the height of the oil boom, at least 1.8 million Yemenis were regularly remitting money from Saudi Arabia and the Gulf states.

The sheer size of the migratory flows had dramatic effects on key aspects of the economy, starting with the domestic labor market. Wages in the oil-rich states and Yemen were almost equalized in the mid-1970s. In 1973, wages were $0.32 an hour, but by 1977 they had risen to $1.22 (compare the $0.17 wage found in the same period in South Korea).[5] Migration created severe labor shortages in Yemen—a 25 percent shortage was registered in the agricultural sector in 1980.[6] Private-sector wages in the non-agricultural sector increased by 80–100 percent in 1975–76 alone, whereas public-sector salaries rose by only 10–15 percent in the same period, precipitating an exodus from public-sector jobs; as many as 20 percent of government posts were vacant in 1978.[7] By the mid 1970s the severity of these shortages turned Yemen itself into a major importer of foreign labor, mainly from Egypt, India, and Sudan.[8]

Remittances severed the link between imports and domestic economic

[4] The first two figures obtained from USAID, Country Development Strategy Statement, Yemen Arab Republic (San'a, 1978), 1; the third from "North Yemen Has Many Reasons for Playing Down Oil Potential," *Christian Science Monitor*, 12 November 1985.

[5] McClelland, "Major Aspects of the Economy," 38–40.

[6] Ibid., 38. See also USAID Country Development Strategy (1978), 5.

[7] IMF, *Recent Economic Developments in the Yemen Arab Republic* (Washington, D.C.: International Monetary Fund, 1977), 2; McClelland, "Major Aspects of the Economy," 76.

[8] In 1979 the Ministry of Social Affairs and Labor estimated a foreign work force of some 50,000—a fivefold increase in three years. Most imported laborers were skilled and educated, recruited to staff middle-level managerial positions in the public and private sectors or to teach in secondary schools and the university, but some were recruited by the private sector for construction and factory work. The framers of the First Five-Year Plan expected an overall labor deficiency of 38 percent—most likely a gross underestimation, since the Yemeni government does not officially recognize the extent of temporary migration among Yemenis (official estimates of foreign workers in the YAR in 1985 were 45,000, a number that should have been significantly lower—given the general economic downturn—if the 1979 figure was correct). On labor imports, see Nader Fergany, "The Impact of Emigration on National Development in the Arab Region," *International Migration Review* 16 (Winter 1982): 757–80; and International Bank for Reconstruction and Development (IBRD), *Staff Appraisal Report for the Yemen Arab Republic* (Washington, D.C.: World Bank, 1985).

activity: Yemen's trade deficit worsened dramatically at the same time that it showed a large balance-of-payments surplus. Agriculture, previously the mainstay of the economy, was the first victim of the migration boom. Higher wages abroad and in urban areas combined with the rapid growth of completely unregulated food imports to precipitate a dramatic decline in domestic production and to fuel rapid urbanization. In a single year, 1975–76, 26 percent of the total acreage under cultivation was abandoned.[9] National output of cereals and overall production declined by 25 and 15 percent respectively between 1974 and 1978. By the mid-1970s output was considerably lower than it had been during the civil war. The delinking of imports from domestic production, a characteristic of earlier migrations to Aden, was even more striking during the 1970s.[10] In short, despite the decline of the domestic economy, Yemen faced no foreign currency constraint during the boom period, and—unlike the situation in labor-exporting countries where existing exchange and import regimes encouraged governments to behave as if they had shortages—import and exchange rates reflected the real currency surpluses in the economy.[11]

Having failed to create a large developmentalist state prior to the boom, and therefore lacking institutional inertia, Yemen had probably the least regulated economy in the world between 1974 and 1984. The reasons were deeply political. The broad distribution of remittances and the minimal role of the state automatically achieved an equity-related goal that most development plans failed to realize: they put money directly into the hands of the rural poor. Moreover, the informal banking system gave private investors access to ample foreign exchange, thereby undercutting the need for state creation and regulation of formal financial institutions.

Migration, Aid, and Economic Organizations

In different ways and through a variety of mechanisms, both labor remittances and development aid precipitated a contraction of the Yemeni state's post-war nascent extractive agencies: direct taxes in boomtime Yemen declined, despite unusually high levels of economic activity. The modern tax system that had partially functioned since 1966 was shelved. In contrast to those of the imamic period, direct taxes were never a large

[9] McClelland, "Major Aspects of the Economy," 38. The decline of agriculture is illustrated by the cotton crop. In 1970, when the civil war had disrupted agricultural production, the yield was 1,900 tons; in 1974, it rose to 27,200 tons; by 1979–80, however, it had declined dramatically to 2,100 tons. See IBRD, *YAR Manufacturing Industry* (Washington, D.C.: World Bank, 1980), 26.

[10] See USAID Country Development Strategy (1978), 1.

[11] On the policies that result from assuming foreign exchange constraints when they do not exist, see Tariq Banuri, "Macroeconomic Effects of Worker Remittances" (Ph.D. diss., Harvard University, 1986), chap. 1.

portion of the Yemen Arab Republic's fisc. In the boom, rudimentary efforts were undone: *zakat*, for example, fell from 8 percent of domestically collected revenue in 1972 to less than 1 percent in 1980 (see Table 5.2). In real terms, direct taxes on wages and corporate profits declined as well. In the entire boom period, only two new taxes (on real estate transactions and *qat* production) were passed, both motivated by social, not fiscal, concerns.[12] But neither tax was collected systematically until 1986; the absence of property registration in both the urban and rural areas had made the real estate tax impossible to assess.[13]

The Yemeni case thus shows that the argument that governments seek, in some absolute sense, to expand their revenues is clearly subject to a number of important caveats, including political and administrative constraints and the availability of external revenue sources. Table 5.2 summarizes the available data on domestic and foreign revenues. Corrected for inflation, they would demonstrate that, other than customs, all taxes declined or stagnated during the boom period. Lower revenues came at a time of rapid growth in the bureaucracy: the number of civil servants swelled from 4,000 in 1962 to 13,500 in 1970 and 31,300 in 1975, while taxes on public-sector wages, which are exceedingly easy to collect, plummeted from YR (Yemeni riyals) 10 million in 1974 to 5 million in 1975.[14] Similarly, the taxes on corporate profits, almost exclusively from banks, registered a negligible growth even in current prices. *Zakat* taxes were collected and spent by the Local Development Associations between 1977 and 1986, making the figures in Table 5.1 subject to more than the usual suspicion with which Yemeni government data should be viewed. The most significant jump in indirect taxes occurred in 1980 with the institution of a consumption tax on *qat*, which was levied at security checkpoints on the highways.

During the boom, customs duties replaced direct taxes as the primary source of domestic revenue. Yemen's expanding dependence on customs duties in the boom period was directly related to the volume of her remit-

[12] *Qat*, a narcotic leaf cultivated in Yemen and East Africa, has effects similar to cocaine. It is legal in Yemen, and prominent Yemenis including the president have daily gatherings that include its consumption but are also important in aggregating opinion and providing a forum for discussion of political and commercial issues. The recent misuse of chemical insecticides on *qat* crops and their subsequent ingestion by humans has invigorated a debate on the public health effects of the drug. See Thomas Gerlholm, "Market, Mosque and Mafraj" (Ph.D. diss., University of Stockholm, 1977). The *qat* sales tax was announced in July 1975; the real estate tax (January 1977) was designed to stem the land speculation that accompanied the inflow of remittances. See John Cohen, "Review of Literature and Analyses of Rural Development Issues in the Yemen Arab Republic," Working note no. 6 (Ithaca: Center for International Studies, 1981), 38–41; and Richard F. Nyrop, ed., *The Yemens* (Washington, D.C.: American University, Foreign Area Studies, 1986), 106–8.

[13] Serious attempts to collect both taxes in 1986 accompanied a cadastral survey and the complete reorganization of the essentially nonfunctioning Land Registration Department.

[14] World Bank, *The Yemen Arab Republic* (Washington, D.C.: World Bank, 1979), 40.

Table 5.2. Percentage of government revenues derived from internal and external sources

	1971	1972	1973	1974	1975	1976	1977	1980	1981	1982	1983
Zakat as % of domestic	7	8	6	6	4	4	3	1	—	3	3
Direct Tax as % of total	4	4	5	6	3	4	4	4	5	8	10
Direct & indirect Tax as % of total	9	11	12	12	8	8	6	8	10	12	14
Direct Tax as % of domestic	9	9	8	12	8	7	4	4	10	14	14
Customs as % of domestic	55	55	57	56	58	70	72	59	49	50	50
External as % of total	55	55	37	46	58	52	32	55	44	44	28

SOURCE: Derived from Table 5.1.

tance earnings. For, unlike other LDCs, where foreign exchange constraints limit the state's reliance on customs duties by forcing authorities to choose between import quotas and devaluation, Yemen had no such constraints. Remittances provided the private sector with ample foreign exchange, thus allowing imports to remain completely unregulated, so that even though tariffs were lowered repeatedly during the boom, the sheer volume of imports swelled customs duties from YR 53 million in 1971 to 2.2 billion in 1983.[15] Customs had always been a major source of government revenue, averaging 45–50 percent of state revenue in the 1960s; depending on which figures are used, they had skyrocketed to either 72 or 87 percent of all domestically collected revenues by 1977.[16]

Historical studies of taxation in developing countries reveal an inverse correlation between economic development and reliance on customs duties. Direct income taxes and taxes on corporate profits tend to become more significant as economies grow. This empirical observation is accompanied by the argument that ". . . customs constitute an acceptable revenue source, by usual standards, in the earliest years of economic development. But analysis suggests and empirical studies support the thesis that they become progressively less acceptable in terms of development goals

[15] The ratio of import duties to imported goods declined in the late 1970s from 36 to 21 percent. See Ziad A. Zabara, "The Impact of External Financial Resources on the Economic Growth in North Yemen during the Period 1963–1983" (Ph.D diss., Howard University, 1986), 63–64.

[16] Ibid. This figure is substantially higher than the percentage in Table 5.2, which is based on Ministry of Finance statistics.

as the process of development continues and ultimately deteriorate in productivity of revenue [*sic*]."[17]

In general, LDCs rely more heavily on customs revenues than do industrialized countries. While total tax income from customs and stamps varied from 0.7 percent in Sweden and Canada to 5.6 percent in Italy, import taxes in representative LDCs provided an average of 20–25 percent of government revenue (see Table 5.3). Even by the standards prevailing in that sample, Yemen's dependence on customs revenues was very heavy and, rather than diminishing over time, grew in the 1970s despite substantial gains in industrial investment.

Clearly, the main benefit of relying on customs duties was their administrative simplicity and political unobtrusiveness. In the short run, they were an ideal solution for a politically weak government with severe personnel shortages. In the long run, however, they had deleterious effects not just for the regulatory and administrative capacities of the state and its ability to manage the economy but also for the broader goal of national integration. For a variety of reasons, customs duties become a less tenable source of state revenue as economic development progresses. High rates come into conflict with the larger goals of industrial development as the composition of imports changes from finished products to capital, parts, and raw materials for domestic industry. Tariffs initially protect local industries, but taxation of intermediate goods and materials discourages local industry in the medium and long term. Moreover, once domestic industry has gained market share, lower customs duties spur competition and control the quality of domestic production. At higher levels of industrial develop-

Table 5.3. Average distribution of domestic revenue sources in seventeen LDCs (percent of total)

Source	1953–55	1969–71
Income tax	20.64	23.67
Import tax	36.40	26.94
Property tax[a]	6.66	4.08
Internal production	32.90	43.78
Other	3.40	1.53
TOTAL	100.00	100.00

Source: Derived from C. Lowell Harris, "Property Taxation and Development," table 1.4. The sample includes Brazil, Chile, Costa Rica, Ecuador, Egypt, Ghana, Guatemala, Honduras, India, Indonesia, Kenya, Korea, Morocco, Paraguay, the Philippines, Thailand, Tunisia.

[a]Data available for only fifteen cases.

[17] John F. Due, *Indirect Taxation in Developing Economies* (Baltimore: Johns Hopkins University Press, 1970), 53–54.

ment, import taxes create unwanted protection. Heavy reliance on customs distorts business practices and fails to generate the institutional capabilities necessary to pursue progressive taxation or to achieve social welfare goals.[18]

In Yemen's case, the primary drawback was that reliance on import duties, by allowing the government to contract its administrative agencies in the boom, undercut the development of revenue sources that could replace customs and aid in the recession. In practice, the decline of direct taxation meant a wholesale withdrawal of state agencies—police, administrators, courts—from substantial portions of the country, which following the civil war had important political implications for nation-building. The administrative withdrawal was, moreover, based on an impermanent confluence of seemingly fortuitous conditions. Thus, although in the short term local organizations funded by migrant donations filled the organizational gap, providing funds for schools, roads, clinics, and other collective projects, in the long term the retreat of state agencies fed centrifugal forces in Yemeni society, creating fissures that would outlast the boom period.

Even more important in undermining the government's will to tax than the easy availability of customs revenues was its access to development aid. Aid was regularly undervalued by the government, but even the figures that made it into the public records show that it was clearly the most important source of government funding in the 1970s and early 1980s, constituting 30 to 60 percent of total revenues.[19] Throughout the boom decade the Yemeni government displayed a unique genius for soliciting aid simultaneously from the People's Republic of China, the Soviet Union, and Eastern European countries as well as from the United States and a host of Western European countries. The actual amounts are sorely underrepresented in government statistics, for unrecorded gifts from oil-rich neighbors accounted for the entire current budget and much of military spending.

If the incentives behind the Yemeni government's undervaluing of aid and remittances were relatively straightforward, the willingness of foreign donors and international agencies to accept the official figures stemmed from their desire to maintain a presence in the country for political reasons. More than any other country, Yemen was able to utilize superpower rivalries and regional tensions to its economic advantage. Combined with its strategic position as a buffer between the Soviet-backed People's Demo-

[18] Ibid., 18–19, 53–57.

[19] The Yemeni government has a longstanding policy of undervaluing aid. See IMF, *Recent Economic Developments*, 20; John Cohen and David Lewis, "Rural Development in the Yemen Arab Republic," Development Discussion Papers no. 52 (Cambridge, Mass.: Harvard Institute for International Development, 1979), 25; "North Yemen Has Many Reasons" (*Christian Science Monitor*).

cratic Republic of Yemen (PDRY) and Saudi Arabia, Yemen's proven capacity for accommodating any country willing to donate funds meant that exiting donors faced the very real specter of being replaced politically. In the Cold War context, in fact, Yemen was an object lesson for how LDCs could gain resources by presenting themselves as strategic arenas for superpower competition.

Yemeni reliance on aid, however, created a serious dependence on foreign donors. Development economists criticize foreign aid for distorting domestic policies; few, however, have commented on the effects of aid on domestic extractive capacities or emphasized the relative volatility of aid compared with domestic sources of revenue. The United States and the Soviet Union were both willing to provide funding for the Yemeni government largely because of the Soviet interest in expanding the influence of socialist PDRY and the American interest in protecting Saudi Arabia's political elite. Not surprisingly, the withdrawal of both countries from large-scale funding was simultaneous. Similarly, bilateral aid receipts from oil-rich Gulf states were motivated by regional power politics and focused on preventing a rapprochement between the Yemen Arab Republic and the People's Democratic Republic of Yemen. Thus, what appeared by normal LDC standards to be a wide base of aid sources was in fact quite volatile. When the underlying political calculation motivating one donor collapsed, as happened in the 1980s, so too did the motivation driving the others.

To be sure, the decline of agricultural taxes can be at least partially attributed to the shrinkage of agricultural production itself; even had there been absolutely efficient tax collection under the old regime, revenue yields would still have declined with production levels. Moreover, to the extent that it created labor shortages in the civil service, migration itself indirectly undercut agricultural tax efforts by making it harder to recruit and more expensive to pay tax collectors. Being inherently labor-intensive (especially given Yemen's geography), agriculture was a highly impractical tax source for a "least developed, capital-surplus, labor short" country.[20] These factors explain the decline in agricultural taxation; they do not account for the wholesale abandonment of all extractive efforts. The government's diminished interest in taxation was a political decision taken in light of administrative constraints and the availability of alternative revenues. Development aid and trade taxes enabled Yemen to increase the size of the bureaucracy and the military and to spend heavily on the army and on government buildings while avoiding the disruptions of direct taxation. Even more important, external capital flows sustained

[20] Migrant agents estimate that Yemeni migrants in 1981 numbered approximately 1.8 million, over three-fourths of the male work force. Official figures from the Yemeni Union of Migrants places the number at 1.3 million; while YARG and the World Bank rely, presumably by agreement, on the figure of 1 million.

the pact of noninterference between the private sector and the state. Thus, although the role of the Yemeni government expanded in some areas—particularly in planning, real estate contracting, and employment—it could abandon regulation of the private sector only because of available aid and customs duties.

Structurally, remittances were a substitute for social welfare programs. Because of the way they entered and flowed through the economy, taxing remittances was not only administratively impossible but politically undesirable for the central state. To export labor was to export unemployment, and as political-military elites were only too aware, labor was a potential political problem as well. In extreme cases such as Yemen, the political opportunities embodied in labor export have the additional political bonus of enabling the government to rely on politically opaque forms of taxation, such as import duties, rather than on income, land, or profit taxes.

The Yemeni state's growing dependence on aid and customs had an almost immediate impact on the relative strength of different segments of the extractive bureaucracy. Customs duties and development aid reshaped the government's fiscal strategy and transformed the extractive bureaucracy. As a result of its tax policies, the government lost access to information about the staggering economic changes sweeping the country during the boom.[21] Unlike property, income, or value-added taxes, customs do not generate a data base for landholdings, income distribution, and sectoral changes. As a result, planners had little basis on which to build regulatory policies in the economic crises of the 1980s. When the recession came, the Yemeni state was forced to begin economic restructuring in an informational void where the state had formally ceded its right to tax.

If remittance-funded imports and the resultant rise in customs duties allowed the government to contract its extractive institutions, development aid encouraged the centralization of planning and spending institutions.[22] In organization theory terms familiar from the discussion of Saudi Arabia in the boom, resource dependence directly shaped agency relations in a clear and observable fashion, rearranging the relative hierarchy of the bureaucracy. Whereas earlier the Ministry of Finance (MOF) had been the central organization, in the boom the Customs Department and the Central Planning Organization (CPO) assumed paramount importance. The sequence of organizational change is a telling one: First the Customs Department was administratively separated from the MOF; shortly thereafter MOF, consisting of the extractive agencies of the state, minus Customs, lost its independent status and was relocated under the

[21] Othaman Mohammed Othman, "Planning in the Context of Incorrect Information," *Finance and Industry* 6 (1985), published by the Kuwait Industrial Bank.

[22] By far the best work on the subject is ʿAbdulʿAziz Al-Saqqaf, "YAR Government Budget Planning, Implementation and Trends," USAID paper (Washington, D.C.: USAID, 1985).

CPO.[23] As MOF branches were closed down across the country the CPO became a powerful "superministry" governing the Ministries of Finance, Supply, National Economy. The Central Bank was relocated under the CPO director, Muhammad Attar.[24] Much as in Saudi Arabia, the allocative decisions of the CPO took place in a sphere separate from the regulatory institutions entrusted with specific sectors.[25] As a symptom of this shift, the Budget Office, rather than the Tax Department, became the core of the Ministry of Finance when it was reorganized in 1973 by merging the Ministry of the Treasury and the Budget Office.

Aid and customs duties severed the link between taxation and spending in Yemen. As domestic taxation declined, government spending soared, especially in military procurement and construction. Between 1974 and 1980 the government's capital expenditures grew at an annual average rate of 109 percent and current expenditures by 44 percent per year. But this high rate of growth in capital expenditure actually reflects very low initial levels, not the relative balance between current and capital expenditures.[26] Because the government had no industrial policy during the boom, reliance on customs duties from unrestricted imports did not present decision-makers with the usual set of tradeoffs. At the onset of the oil boom the government lowered customs duties, deliberately moved away from regulating the economy through price fixing, import quotas, and so on, sanctioned the free import of foreign labor, lifted all restrictions on imports, and freely granted licenses for domestic investment in industry.[27] In the absence of revenue-seeking motives, Yemen, like Saudi Arabia, did not use its new-found resources to develop new sources of economic information.

Remittances and aid together permitted the government to relax all kinds of economic regulation; the resulting gaps in the state's information about the domestic economy were not dissimilar to those in the Saudi case. The success of the government's fiscal strategy and the "free market" approach that marked the boom years, however, were contingent upon the continued flow of aid and labor remittances. The hazards of heavy dependence on customs emerged in the fiscal crisis of 1986, when the fragmentation of the bureaucracy's administrative agencies was the main barrier to carrying out austerity programs.[28] Deregulation of industry and unrestricted agricultural imports during the boom had created incentive

[23] Ministry of Finance officials, interviews with author, San'a, October 1986–May 1987.

[24] On the role of the Kuwait Fund and the IMF in setting up the CPO as a "superministry," see Richard Gable, "Government Institutions in the YAR," USAID paper (Washington, D.C.: USAID, 1982), 18–19.

[25] See "Administrative Development," in IBRD, *Mobilizing Domestic Financial Resources in the Yemen Arab Republic* (Washington, D.C.: World Bank, 1982); and Gable, "Government Institutions."

[26] Zabara, "Impact of External Financial Resources," 71, 73.

[27] See IMF, *Recent Economic Developments,* 17.

[28] On the penalties for excessive reliance on customs duties, see Due, *Indirect Taxation.*

structures in the economy that could not be sustained without the inflow of foreign exchange and the outflow of labor. The decline of agriculture meant that the largest source of domestic employment had been demolished; in industry, entrepreneurs had responded to labor shortages and unrestricted imports by investing in highly capital-intensive, import-dependent, low value-added plants. These facts would later hobble the ability of the domestic economy to absorb returning migrants and cripple industry unable to function without unrestricted imports.

The administrative changes of the boom also had a political dimension. For in purely political terms, customs revenues and aid permitted the government to roll back its institutional presence in the countryside, withdrawing an administrative and legal presence established at great cost and though much conflict. For Yemen, with its long history of internal conflict, these institutions had represented not just functional responses to local disputes or to revenue imperatives but also an emblem of national belonging: a concrete embodiment of uniformly accessible and universally shared rights. The institutional changes of the boom period were destructive in a variety of ways. The extractive and regulatory apparatus of the Yemeni state and its information-gathering agencies shrank at precisely the historical moment that the central state had an unprecedented opportunity to expand services, promote national integration, and buttress its administrative capacities: The 1970s were not just an interlude when the state could craft an alternative to the tyranny of the northern tribes but also the chance to present a concrete alternative to the predatory organization the state had been, historically, and would be again, all too soon. Administrative withdrawal lost the hard-won gains of the civil war period and rolled back the fragile peace bought in the Republican Pact, for two very different forms of regionally distinct organizations replaced the retreating agencies of the central state. In the north, the government ceded the maintenance of law and security to tribal elites whose large armies were equipped with modern weaponry, thanks to state subsidies and independent revenues from their covert supporter, Saudi Arabia. In the south, Local Development Associations (LDAs) took over the collection of taxes and the development of infrastructure. These two forms of organization not only generated their own sets of elites with strong incentives to resist reforms later on; they also recreated, in even more dramatic form, the differences between north and south that had historically divided the country.

Replacing the State from Below

The most striking effect of remittances was the emergence and growth of the LDAs: over two hundred democratically elected grassroots organizations.[29] As the central administration receded from the countryside, these community cooperatives undertook the development of infrastructure, education, and public health[30] funded by local donations from surpluses created by labor remittances (see Tables 5.4 and 5.5).[31] Development expenditures by cooperatives outstripped government project spending by over 300 percent from 1973 to 1980.[32] Initially focusing on road construction, schools, and clinics, the LDAs later branched out into irrigation projects, farming cooperatives, poultry farms, and even local lending.

The cooperative movement began and grew in the south, the home of the vast majority of migrants. According to the most authoritative study, the first LDAs had been formed in the southern cities of Taiz and Ibb and the port city of Hudaydah during the civil war, when rapid economic expansion was accompanied by a virtual hiatus in government services.[33] These pre-boom cooperatives were founded and led by returning members of the absentee merchant class to provide municipal services in the urban areas, but by the early 1970s the urban cooperatives had all but disappeared. Migration to the Gulf gave rise to a very different pattern of institution-building: the remittance-funded cooperatives of the 1970s

Table 5.4. Some Local Development Association projects in Yemen

	1973–76	1977–78	1979–81
Roads	5,100 km	6,520 km	17,298 km
Schools	581	—	1,730
Water projects	684	643	967

SOURCE: Sheila Carapico, "The Political Economy of Self-Help," Ph.D. diss., SUNY Binghamton, 1984.

[29] The cooperative movement in Yemen captured the attention of many aid donors; see IBRD, *Yemen Arab Republic* (Washington, D.C.: World Bank, 1981). On the movement in general, see James Green, "Local Initiative in Yemen," (USAID, Washington, D.C., 1975, mimeograph); ‘Abduh ‘Ali Uthman, *Al-Harakah al-Ta'awuniyah al-Yamaniyah wa-al-Tanmiyah* (The Cooperative Movement of Yemen and Development) study prepared for the CPO (San'a, 1982); Barbara Samuels II, "Local Development Associations in the Yemen Arab Republic," (USAID, Washington, D.C., 1979, mimeograph).

[30] See Sheila Carapico, "The Political Economy of Self-Help" (Ph.D. diss., SUNY Binghamton, 1984), for an excellent historical account; 'Abdallah Hamid al-'Ulafi, "The Role of Remittances on the National Economy of the Yemen Arab Republic," Department of Research, Central Bank of the Yemen Arab Republic, San'a, 1985; 'Abduh 'Ali Uthman, "The Cooperative Movement in Yemen and Development," report for the Council of Ministers and the CPO, San'a, 1985; and Muhammed al-'Ulafi, "Development of Local Administration in the YAR" (master's thesis, National Institute for Public Administration, San'a, 1985).

[31] Cohen, "Capital-Surplus, Labor-Short Economies"; and Cohen et al., "Development From Below." The most comprehensive coverage of the phenomenon is in Carapico, "Political Economy of Self-Help."

[32] Confederation of Yemeni Cooperative Associations, Financial Accounts of the Cooperatives of the YAR, (Sana'a, 1970–83); and IBRD, *Mobilizing Domestic Financial Resources.*

[33] See Carapico, "Political Economy of Self-Help," 174–81.

Table 5.5. Cost sharing in cooperative projects in Yemen

	1973–76			1978–81			Five-Year Plan (1976–1981)
	% from citizens	% from LDBs[a]	% from government	% from citizens	% from LDBs	% from government	% from citizens
Roads	72	28	—	62	37	1	67
Schools	54	45	1	39	41	18	42
Water	32	68	—	52	29	10	54
Health	31	69	—	32	63	5	29
Misc.	17	78	—	23	63	14	41
TOTAL	64	35	1	52	38	8	59

SOURCE: Sheila Carapico, "The Political Economy of Self-Help," p. 263.

[a]Local Development Board (LDB) revenues from *zakat* (in rural areas) and 2 percent customs tax (in urban areas). Although useful, the distinction between donations from citizens and rural LDBs is a technical one, as *zakat* was collected from citizens on a voluntary basis.

were rural, not urban, and were concentrated in the southern regions around Taiz and Ibb. Although other areas of Yemen also experienced migration, LDA activity in the south was not matched by similar developments elsewhere. The northern provinces of San'a, Jawf, Marib, and Sa'da, for example, experienced an actual increase in tribal organization and affiliation. As an organizational response to remittances which distinguished the south from the north, the cooperatives took on an overtly political character in the late 1970s, accentuating the longstanding differences between the northern and southern provinces of Yemen.

Initially, the government tried to create links between the central administration and these divergent patterns of local development. The different bases of local authority were given institutional expression by the division of rural development programs between two separate state agencies: the Department of Tribal Affairs for the north, and the Ministry of Social Affairs, Youth, and Labor for the south. As the southern cooperative movement developed independent of the initiatives of the central government, however, the expected role of the Ministry of Social Affairs never materialized. Similarly, instead of becoming a mechanism to assert control over tribal leaders, the Department of Tribal Affairs facilitated and legitimized expanded elite control in the northern areas.

The drama of the organizational changes wrought by remittances is captured by the fact that the LDAs took over a state prerogative so basic as to be part of the definition of what the state *is*: in 1975 the government ceded the LDAs the right of taxation. Law 35 of 1975 empowered them to collect and allocate first 50 percent and then 75 percent of *zakat* and *all* indirect taxes.[34] Cooperatives also elected representatives to a national

[34] CYDA, "Proceedings of the First Conference of Local Development Associations" (San'a, 1978) (in Arabic), and Carapico, "Political Economy of Self-Help," 220.

congress of LDA leaders, which directly advised the government on development issues and mediated relations between foreign donors and the local groups. The right to collect local taxes supplemented but did not displace voluntary donations to LDAs: through 1981 more than 64 percent of project expenditures continued to derive from "unspecified citizen and local resources," and government contributions to local development projects after 1978 continued to hover at less than 10 percent (see Table 5.5).[35]

Layered onto politically significant differences between north and south, the organizational and institutional changes of the boom years reinforced ascriptive cleavages in Yemeni society, adding an occupational and economic dimension to historically constituted differences. The divergent forms of organization fostered by shrinking extractive and regulatory branches of the central state have already been highlighted, as has the importance of aid and remittances as sources of external capital controlled respectively by the state and the private sector. Migration to the Gulf, like earlier waves of migration to East Africa and Aden, was heaviest from the southern *Sunni* agricultural areas of Ibb and Taiz, where landlessness made such a move attractive. Remittances found their way back to the remote villages of Yemen through informal bankers and their retinue of subcontracting migrant agents.[36] In the 1970s, as high wages in Saudi Arabia and in the private sector attracted southern segments of the population, the now less lucrative positions in the civil service, the army, and the police became the preserve of the less-educated northern tribal populations. (These factors are reflected in statistics on the educational background of civil servants, although no published material shows their regional origins).[37] Although military leadership and key parts of the political power structure had always been the preserve of northern elites, the functioning of the boomtime economy made divisions of power between northern and southern elites characteristic of the private and public sectors in general: sectoral placement differences between elites became

[35] Carapico, 262. See also Richard Verdery, "LDA Finances and Their Borrowing Potential," Institutional Report no. 2, Local Resources for Development Project, YAR (Washington, D.C.: Chemonics International Consulting, 1982).

[36] Lee Ann Ross and John M. Cohen, "An Informal Banking System," Working note no. 12 (Ithaca: Center for International Studies, 1981).

[37] A study of middle- and top-level civil servants showed that 5,160 were completely illiterate; 1,284 had secondary school degrees, 256 had some postsecondary education, and only 691 held college degrees (Cohen and Lewis, "Review of Literature and Analyses," 8 n. 22). The government's efforts to create a Civil Service Commission to train and increase the productivity of civil servants died in the 1960s after three separate institutional incarnations failed to achieve their aims. At the end of the 1960s the commission acquired four departments: the National Institute for Public Administration, the Committee for Foreign Appointees, Government Assignments, and Training and Retirement. In the absence of regulations on migration, the government found it impossible to overcome the market incentives against state employment. See Ahmed Al Abiadh, "Modernization of Government Institutions, 1962–1964," in Pridham, *Contemporary Yemen,* 150–51.

quite literally, divisions within the general public. Remittances not only changed consumption patterns but also created the capital resources that allowed returned migrants and their families to invest in commerce and service industries. Unlike Saudi oil revenues, the distribution of which created a new class of large commission entrepreneurs and toppled the old, Yemeni remittances created opportunities for new small- and medium-scale entrants into urban and rural business communities, without displacing the larger merchant houses. Thus, at the top, the Yemeni private sector continued to be dominated by returnees from Aden, but with the migrations of the 1970s, southerners came to control even the middle and lower segments of the commercial and service sector. The government and military, down the organizational ladder, came to be staffed by northerners.

Business-Government Relations

In the boom, Yemen's private sector expanded exponentially relative to the public sector. Investment targets set by the CPO were more than met: private-sector investment exceeded government goals by over 60 percent (in constant prices) in the First Five-Year Plan. In contrast, public and mixed-sector ventures were unable to meet their quotas because of the private sector's reluctance to participate in joint projects with the government. Who and what was the private sector?

Unlike the early migration to East Africa and Aden, migration to the Gulf did not spawn a highly skilled and wealthy business elite. Whereas earlier patterns of remittance transmission gave merchants control of large tranches of foreign exchange, the boomtime system capped the amount of capital held by any one individual. The shifting financial mediation of labor export meant that, unlike the absentee bourgeoisie who came back from Aden, returnees from the Gulf became small-scale retailers, wholesalers, and workshop and restaurant owners, rather than industrialists and importers.[38]

The growth of a rural merchant class that handled at least as many luxury goods as urban merchants, if not more, is perhaps the most striking change wrought by remittances. The emergence of a new merchant class introduced market relations in rural areas where trade had once been the province of wealthy landlords who dominated the weekly markets. As they were not dividing their time between farming and trade, the new migrant class of merchants created permanent markets, capturing the customer base of the older merchant class and forcing the landed elite back onto agriculture as its main source of income. In areas such as

[38] See Mohammed Cassam and Dickinson Miller's paper, "Private Sector Assessment," San'a, February 1985.

Udayn, where the incidence of migration reached 85–90 percent among young men, the size of the merchant community grew several-fold.[39] In Mahwit, a market town in the western highlands, a community of 600 traders established permanent shops and serviced a vibrant permanent market in food and consumables.[40] In contrast, weekly and seasonal markets continued in the northern tribal areas of Marib and Jawf.[41]

Industrial investment jumped in the 1970s, but the growth of trade and service-sector business groups occurred largely in the lower echelons of the business community.[42] The membership of the San'a Chamber of Commerce swelled from a few hundred members in 1973 to over 9,000 in 1986.[43] The only comprehensive data on the growth and structure of the business community are contained in the records of the Taiz Chamber of Commerce. Although limited to Taiz members, these show a nineteen-fold increase in the business community and reflect the growth of retail and wholesale enterprises between 1975 and 1986 (see Table 5.6).[44] The lower tier of retailers was made up almost exclusively of returned

[39] Survey conducted by the author in rural areas of Udayn, Ibb province, 19 May–10 June 1987.

[40] 'Abd al-'Aziz Al-Shahadi (director, Mahwit Chamber of Commerce), interview with author, Hudaydah, 2 February 1987.

[41] The business community grew even in the northern tribal areas, but the majority of new entrants were southerners who moved north after the completion of the Marib dam and the discovery of oil on the northeastern border promised more agricultural and service-related opportunities. Mahfud al-Shuaybi (director, Marib Chamber of Commerce), interview with author, Marib, 19 January 1987. In 1986 (after the law for mandatory participation in the chambers came into effect), the Marib chamber had only 250 members.

[42] In 1971, on the eve of the boom, there were 351 industrial firms employing five or more workers, encompassing a total work force of 6,706. In the First Three-Year Plan (1976–80), 167 new factories or expansions were authorized, mostly in food processing and construction materials.

[43] Jamal al-Mutarib (assistant director, San'a Chamber of Commerce), interview with author, San'a, 1987.

[44] The center of commercial and industrial activity shifted from Hudaydah, where most returning merchant families opened offices immediately after the revolution, to San'a and Taiz during the late 1970s. The Hudaydah chamber had 3,000 members in the mid-1970s, mostly importers and wholesalers. By 1981, however, the membership had declined to 687, and by 1985 the number of importers was only 300 (data provided by 'Abd al-Qawi Al-Humayqani, administrative director, Hudaydah Chamber of Commerce). In 1985, after the government made registration with the chamber compulsory for retailers, the membership grew to 1,206: industries, 18; importers, 306; wholesale merchants, 314; retailers, 406; contractors, 2, other, 160. Fifty percent of the Hudaydah community was made up of wholesalers and importers, compared with only 22 percent of the merchant group in Taiz, where the incidence of migration was extremely high; there retailers constituted 56 percent, in contrast to only 34 percent in Hudaydah. The Hudaydah community shrank as importing was concentrated in a few large firms. Similarly, although most modern industries were initially constructed in Hudaydah, where access to imported raw materials was easiest, during the mid-1970s many large southern industrialists set up in Taiz. Despite the considerably higher transportation costs of raw materials from the port, that location gave easier access to the large southern markets and provided a more disciplined and educated labor force for increasingly complex, capital-intensive plants.

migrants or their relatives, who had used remittances and savings to enter trade. In Sanʿa, for example, over 80 percent of the retail shops in the new market areas in 1987 were owned and managed by migrants from the southern regions of Taiz, Ibb, and Hujariyah.[45]

Despite the magnitude of economic and social change fueled by labor remittances, the new entrants into the private sector did not affect the composition of the upper echelon of businessmen and industrialists: big business in Yemen remained concentrated in the hands of *Sunni* southerners who had made their fortunes in Aden. Consumption-fueled imports and initial investments in light consumables created opportunities for the old business elite to expand their sphere of operations and make further industrial investments.[46]

Although the southern merchants continued to dominate the private sector, increased government expenditures in the 1970s encouraged some of the old Sanʿani families to reenter the service sector, take on government contracts, and manage government imports. These families reinitiated their activities mainly by getting exclusive agencies for heavy agricultural and construction machinery. Many, such as the ʿAgil family, actually had collaborative ventures with top-level executives and army officers; others, such as Haj Muhammad al-Withari and the house of al-Thawr, supplied machinery for the government and the Agricultural and Cooperative Credit Bank. So complete was southern control of industry that with the exception of single-product plants set up by the houses of ʿAgil and al-Rammah, no major industrial investments were undertaken by the northerners.[47] The industrial center of Yemen remained in Taiz.

The southerners' domination of all echelons of the private sector was partly related to their propensity to favor co-sectarians in their business ventures, offering them shares particularly in the more strikingly capital-intensive industries in food processing.[48] They also had a tendency to recruit distributors of locally produced goods and even to choose wholesalers on the basis of common origin and sect. By the mid-1980s, as transport and distribution networks for locally produced goods became established, all levels of the market were almost exclusively controlled by southerners. The northern merchants by contrast, since most of their ac-

[45] Survey of traditional and modern market areas of Sanʿa, conducted by author, December 1986–June 1987.

[46] My 1986–87 survey of market areas in Sanʿa showed that although the old local merchant families retained control of traditional markets in the old city, eight of every ten retailers in the new shopping areas were former migrants to the Gulf.

[47] The only known industrial project in which al-Withari and al-Thawr participated was a brick factory, which failed in the early 1980s because of mismanagement.

[48] The three industrial families that regularly financed investments by share sales reported that they regularly sold to the same twenty merchants. All emphasized the importance of ties of trust and collaboration, deriving from shared experiences in Aden, in choosing business partners.

Table 5.6. Membership distribution, Taiz Chamber of Commerce

Year	Importers	Wholesalers	General Merchants	Retailers	Jewelers	Crafts and Produce	Companies	Corporations	Factories	Shops	Hotels	Total
1975	50	15	—	150	5	30	—	—	2	8	—	260
1976	79	28	8	200	18	51	1	—	4	15	1	405
1977	85	36	18	375	41	65	2	2	6	23	1	654
1978	90	60	25	417	60	81	2	2	7	45	1	790
1979	110	87	40	800	81	101	3	3	9	59	2	1,295
1980	120	98	58	992	108	130	5	5	9	71	2	1,598
1981	180	140	67	1100	116	152	5	6	20	95	2	1,883
1982	205	170	94	1500	135	176	6	8	29	110	2	2,435
1983	240	230	120	1835	160	225	9	8	32	125	3	2,987
1984	300	300	125	1901	179	247	10	10	40	151	4	3,267
1985	500	370	140	2210	200	291	22	13	47	170	5	3,968
1986	680	425	160	2807	251	387	38	5	51	202	5	5,021

SOURCE: Data compiled from the records of the Taiz Chamber of Commerce and Industry, 1987.

tivity involved the provision of services and bulk goods to the government and state banks, did not develop links with the lower echelons of the business community.

Despite the growing economic and occupational polarization between the north and the south, the boom years in Yemen were marked by a nearly complete absence of conflict between either business and government or business and labor. The role of the state in production was limited to a handful of industries set up in the early 1970s, minimizing direct competition between state-owned enterprises and private concerns. The Military Corporation, the Grain Corporation, and the Foreign Trade Corporation, designed to provide low-priced commodities to civil servants and members of the armed forces, did not manage to capture even these markets and had a very limited base, even among the fixed-income groups they were designed to serve. Like attempts to encourage cooperation between the private and public sectors in the early 1960s, the government's halfhearted efforts to create a "mixed" sector of industrial and service enterprises failed for lack of private-sector interest. In striking contrast to the Saudi case, the Yemeni business class was organizationally and financially independent from the state, its market comprising not state contracts but consumer goods and services. The unregulated economy, coupled with virtually no taxation and low tariffs, minimized the potential for conflict between business and the state.

The absence of conflict between Yemeni business and labor would be perplexing were it not for the fact that most of the labor force lived and worked abroad during the boom. The unionist movements of the prerevolutionary days, having failed to reconstitute in Republican Yemen, were altogether missing from the political arena. Paradoxically, the only labor unions to emerge after business interests voted down the legalization of unions in the People's Assembly of 1970 were located in the public and mixed-sector enterprises. Boomtime industrial investments, undertaken in a period of capital abundance and labor scarcity, were so capital-intensive that private-sector concentrations of labor were too small to permit effective organizing. The free flow of Yemeni labor across the border to Saudi Arabia and the secondary flow of imported labor into Yemen forestalled labor organization and business-labor confrontation.[49]

The overall result was that both the business elite and labor were depoliticized during a time of rapid social and economic change. High

[49] Most successful in Yemen in the 1980s was the transporters' union, which combines collective insurance funded by donations with a strict organization of the industry. This union has no links with the state or business and is unregulated. It fills a gap left by the two local insurance companies (United Insurance, owned by the Hail Said family; the Red Sea Insurance Company, owned by the Thabit family) which focuses exclusively on shipping and maritime insurance) and the government-owned Marib Insurance Company, which confines its activities to state-owned enterprises and the national airlines.

growth in consumption plus the virtual absence of import restrictions, foreign currency restrictions, and taxation limited the country's underground political parties to middle-level state employees and landless peasants in the agriculturally rich Ibb province.[50] The political apathy of the business elite marked a radical departure from its previous activism, which had included funding and leading the overthrow of the imam. Notwithstanding the entrepreneurs' long abstinence from politics, however, the composition of the group had long-term implications for the success or failure of economic adjustment and political accommodation during the lean years of the mid-1980s.

The importance of sectarian and regional ties and the absence of conflict with the state forestalled the development of formal organizations to express business interests. As in Saudi Arabia, these emerged only when collective bargaining with the government became necessary or when the government sought to use such organizations to perform regulatory functions. For example, the Hudaydah Chamber of Commerce was formed in 1961 during Imam Ahmad's reign, in response both to the government's need to centralize storage of imports bought by the state monopolies and to the merchants' desire to exclude the overland merchants from the Tihamah market. In Republican Yemen the Hudaydah, San'a, and Taiz chambers were created almost exclusively in response to the government's need to collect information on the origin of imports and to issue import permits. Once these tasks were allocated to various government agencies, there was little business interest in the chambers during the 1970s and early 1980s.

Apart from the Taiz Chamber of Commerce, which played a significant role in dispute mediation and historically had participants from all levels

[50] The five Communist parties that make up the National Democratic Front ('Amal, 'Ummal, Dimuqratiyin, al-Sha'biyah, al-Hizb al-Ishtiraki al Yamani) had made headway in the southern regions of Taiz and Ibb, capitalizing on highly unequal land distribution and the abuses of the entrenched landed elite. In 1976–78, outlying areas of Ibb were militarily controlled by the NDF. In 1983, the government reestablished control in these areas following a coup attempt by the Nasserites which had resulted in the execution of at least 300 army officers and more than 500 civilians. Other underground parties included the Iraqi and Syrian Ba'th, the Nasserites, and the Ikhwan al-Muslimin. The last grew rapidly in the 1980s in uneasy coalition with the northern sheikhs—both in the pay of Saudi Arabia. The Ba'thists have long received financial support from Iraq; the Communist alliance relied on funding from Aden. Although political parties were banned in the period under review recruitment in the People's Assembly (*Majlis al-Sha'b*) and the powerful Permanent Council (*Lajnah al-Da'imah*) cleaved along party lines; that is, at any given time, known leaders of the parties were included in these bodies as a means of offsetting the power of any single group. The leaders of al-Sha'biyah, the Ikhwan al-Muslimin ('Abd al-Majid Al-Zindani) and the Ba'th ('Abd al-Wahid Hawwash) all had posts. Other groups are represented as well: students, teachers, land-owners, and so on. The most powerful members of the two councils, however, have always been either tribal elites ('Abd Allah al-Ahmar has been the head of both since their inception) and the *Shafi'i* merchants. The latter tend to express only opinions relating to their economic interests; al-Ahmar appears to involve himself in all aspects of decision-making.

of the tightly knit southern business community, business organizations were weak, precisely because of the lack of state regulation. Few issues arose that concerned the collective interests of business, and individual contacts sufficed to make the occasional necessary demands on the ministries entrusted with economic affairs. Moreover, traditional crafts declined in response to the phenomenal rise in imports in the 1970s, eroding craft and trade guilds. The ancient and previously vibrant guilds of both San'a and Taiz declined in proportion to the diminution of the traditional markets, which had been organized around collecting, transporting, and distributing local goods.[51]

Once aid and remittances had created parallel public and private economies in boomtime Yemen, the pact of noninterference on which their separation rested was viable only as long as the state made no effort to regulate the economy. In late 1982, a decline in aid precipitated a minor tightening of import permits. The origins of private-sector organizational change can be seen in the consequent struggles between business and government over the regulation of the economy. At that time, not unlike other Middle Eastern states, Yemen preempted demands from the business community by creating a formal corporate group aggregating the chambers of commerce under a newly created Union of Yemeni Chambers of Commerce, whose laws limited direct contacts with the government by individuals and separate chambers by channeling private-sector demands through the union. The government directly created and added six new chambers, all from northern tribal areas in which the political leadership had strong support.[52] As each chamber had a single vote, these six tipped the balance against the ascendant southern merchants. Haj Muhammad al-Withari, a northern San'ani merchant with strong government ties, presided over the newly created corporate group. Even the mild set of import regulations introduced in 1982, in short, precipitated a

[51] The guild system of San'a, for example, had historically been among the most encompassing and complex in the Middle East. The guilds' functions had included urban tax collection training, storage, and collective purchasing; they also dispensed justice, resolved disputes, and guarded the market areas. R. B. Serjeant and Ronald Lewcock, eds., *San'a, an Arabian Islamic City* (London: World of Islam Festival Trust, 1983), includes a translation of *Qanun San'a* (the law of San'a), a fourteenth-century document that codifies the organization of the market, and describes the contemporary organization of traditional urban markets. In Taiz, the collection, transportation, and distribution of local produce was highly centralized under an elected guild master who held documents signed by farmers, transporters, and retailers to govern economic transactions and prices. The *'agil* of the market controlled prices, settled disputes, and was a source of finance for both farmers and merchants. After the influx of imports, the *'agil* began to provide additional services such as cold storage. Ahmad al-Warafi (*'agil,* produce market), interview with author, Taiz City, 1987.

[52] The new chambers were created in the towns of Hajjah, Dammar, Baydah, Marib, Sada'a, and Mahwit. See "Dirasah hawl al-Ghuraf al-Tijariyah al-Sina'iyah al-Yamaniyah wa-Ittihadiha al-'Am wa-al-Qanun allati Yahkumuha," Legal Department, Union of Yemeni Chambers of Commerce and Industry, San'a, 1983; and Republican Decree 27, "On the Chambers of Commerce and Industry and Their General Union" (in Arabic), 1982.

major top-down reorganization of the mechanism through which business and government formally bargained. The state thus managed to erect an institutional barrier to filter the demands of the business groups at the very moment of, and indeed in response to, nascent organizational efforts by the largely southern business community to oppose trade restrictions.

Like the Saudi state that created the Confederation of Chambers, the Yemeni government shaped the institutional structure of business by establishing an organization that circumscribed opposition to state policies and subordinated independent groups to others with strong dependent ties to the state. Thus, as group interests were formed in the course of the economic downturn, and collective bargaining became necessary, the government reacted by channeling demands through a body that formally "aggregated" interests but in fact was organizationally biased against the majority of southern businessmen.

SUMMARY: INTERNATIONAL FORCES AND DOMESTIC CHANGE

For Yemen and Saudi Arabia the 1970s ushered in a fundamental set of institutional, economic, and social transformations. These basic reconfigurations, I have argued, were not simply a more rapid or a differently weighted version of earlier patterns of institutional change but a causally and procedurally distinctive set of processes. Their sources and sequences, moreover, were different enough from those in the preceding period that they are best understood through a different analytical lens.

Although new *mechanisms*, born of a different relationship between the domestic and international political economy, were operative in both Yemen and Saudi Arabia during the oil boom, oil rents and labor remittances produced substantially different *forms* of institutional change. In both countries external capital flows precipitated the atrophy of extractive and regulatory institutions, undoing evolving political economic relationships centered on basic questions of where the boundaries of political and economic community were to be drawn, who was to pay for collective goods, and who would control the construction of basic institutions. The decline of the pre-boom tax bureaucracy is critical to an understanding of the obsolescence of attendant social struggles, because taxation was at once the node around which these broader issues clustered, a basic indicator of the expansion and consolidation of the central state, and an arena where conflict occurred.

The decline of the extractive and regulatory bureaucracy affected government capacities (information, enforcement, penetration, authority) and shaped a host of business-government and social relations. Specifically, it had the unintended effect of eroding the state's reservoir of information about the economy, which in turn made distribution, regulation, monitoring, and property rights enforcement very difficult. The effects of this institutional change in the Yemeni and Saudi cases over the boom decade were quite different, however, because of the radically different role played by the state in the domestic economy. Where the Yemeni government's lack of administrative and information capacities became an important issue only in the recession of 1986, as the state's fiscal crisis deepened, the Saudi state's lack of information shaped distributive policies that completely rearranged the social and economic structure of the country during the boom decade. Moreover, two very different organizational patterns replaced the extractive-regulatory state. In Saudi Arabia, a formal distributive bureaucracy emerged to deploy oil revenues in the domestic economy. In Yemen, agencies responsible for managing aid and for trade taxes became ascendant in government, while local institutions independent of the state arose in society.

The organizations, groups, and mechanisms through which oil revenues and labor remittances shaped society were radically different. Where oil revenues empowered the Saudi state to destroy and reconstruct entire classes, to create entirely new sectors in the economy, and to demolish local institutions in the urban service sector and in agriculture, remittances flowed directly to local Yemeni communities where large numbers of nongovernmental local institutions in labor-exporting regions took over the provision of infrastructure and collective projects in place of the state.

The domestic deployment of oil revenues profoundly changed the social and economic landscape of Saudi Arabia. The distributive state created and controlled access to resources through financial institutions and gifts: indirectly through the laws that governed the entry of foreign capital and workers; directly through setting prices, allotting subsidies, and granting interest-free loans. International integration, measured as a high level of interaction with the world economy, coincided with massive domestic price manipulation intended to achieve domestic growth. The fact that Saudi Arabia had no domestic labor force or tradable commodities other than oil but was, at the same time, entirely dependent on the international economy resulted in a very special pattern of relationships between the state, foreign capital, and Saudi nationals: the laws that governed economic transactions were designed to insert Saudi nationals as interlocutors between foreign labor and foreign companies on one hand, and the domestic economy and the state on the other. The fact that state spending for contracts was *designed* to flow through Saudi nationals was both a way of involving the Saudi population in the economy and a way of devolving substantial regulatory functions onto individuals. The character of the business class that resulted demonstrates that Saudi integration into the international economy came through the service sector; finance, imports, construction, and maintenance—not industry—were the mainstays.

The mechanism through which the Saudi state tried to connect the oil sector to the rest of the domestic economy relied, in other words, on rules that in theory gave universal access to Saudi nationals as interlocutors between the foreign and the domestic.

In Yemen, by contrast, remittances flowed into the domestic economy not through state banks and state contracts but through informal banking channels, circulating among and providing capital for private business groups without the interference of the state. No distributive apparatus emerged in Yemen to replace the regulatory and tax bureaucracy. Rather, private cooperatives, fed by remittance earnings, undertook many functions previously provided by the state. Whereas in Saudi Arabia the heavy hand of the central state eliminated preexisting civil groups, and patterns of state spending forestalled the emergence of new organizations outside the nexus of state spending and societal clients, in Yemen a flurry of associational activity occurred in rural areas, outside and independent of the state.

Just as state distribution molded economic classes in Saudi Arabia, remittances changed the composition and structure of rural markets in Yemen, creating a new group of rural merchants and consumers.[53] But whereas the distributive policies of the Saudi government fostered unequal incomes and generated kinship and financial links between business and the state, labor remittances equalized incomes in the labor-exporting regions of Yemen's southern provinces and generated a merchant group completely independent of the state. Distribution patterns in Saudi Arabia concentrated wealth in the cities; the most dramatic change in Yemen was the expansion of resources available to the rural poor. One remarkable feature of income distribution in Yemen compared with other LDCs is that rural communities in the south were generally richer than urban ones. Income distribution data do not exist, but it is well known that common social expenditures such as bride prices were higher in the rural areas than in the cities during the 1970s.[54]

In Yemen, the flow of development aid in the 1970s allowed government spending to rise at the same time that the tax bureaucracy was declining. The government and the private sector grew along parallel lines, each supported by a different source of external capital, and each increasingly dominated by a distinctive religious and regional group. The atrophy of links between the public and private sectors—the decline of taxation, regulation, and state provision of infrastructural, enforcement, and adjudicatory needs—thus undergirded a profound social separation of the northern and southern halves of Yemen. This separation remained

[53] Most of the new merchants in the rural areas of the south had been migrants and became migrant agents (Udayn survey conducted by author, April 1987).

[54] Migrant communities in Ibb and Udayn, interviews with author, April 1987; comparative data from Taiz and San'a.

uncontested, and perhaps even went unnoticed, during the prosperous years of the 1970s but became deeply divisive in the economic crisis of the 1980s when both aid and remittances plummeted.

On the eve of the bust, relations between state and private elites were thus radically different in the two countries. Whereas oil revenues united the new Saudi business classes and bureaucrats through kinship and financial collaboration, aid and remittances further divided business and government along ascriptive lines in Yemen. The union of business and government in Saudi Arabia and the emergence of separate and institutionally unconnected realms in Yemen would be critical to reform efforts in the recession—but not in expected ways. As Chapter 6 will show, it is in the formation and functioning of domestic *financial* institutions that the direct influence of different kinds of capital inflows can be most clearly observed.

Quite unlike the pre-boom period, when gains in the establishment of a uniform legal and economic system weakened the categories of region, tribe, and sect, the boom reinfused ascriptive categories with economic and social significance. In Saudi Arabia a large new class of largely Nejdi commission entrepreneurs replaced the old commercial classes of the Hijaz. The arguably universalistic, legalistic distributive mechanisms of the oil state replicated in the private sector the preexisting regional and kinship networks that were already dominant in the pre-boom bureaucracy. In Yemen, remittances generated a new class of southern rural entrepreneurs and small-scale retail, service, and wholesale operations in the urban areas while simultaneously expanding the influence and wealth of the old *Sunni* commercial classes; at the same time, employment in the bureaucracy and military became increasingly the preserve of the *Shiʿa* northerners. Oil revenues united Saudi kinship and regional networks across business and government lines; labor remittances divided Yemeni business and government along regional and sectarian lines.

Patterns of institutional change in the two countries in the 1970s illustrate not only the power of international economic forces to shape fundamental domestic processes but also the enormous variation produced by different kinds of international influences. These influences, moreover, shape domestic outcomes only in how they interact with social, institutional, and political legacies. Understanding institutional change in any one conjuncture of local and global time requires an appreciation of these legacies, for the construction and contextual operation of rationality occur in the changing contexts of these historically specific institutional conjunctures. But the institutional constructions themselves cannot be explained by recourse to uniform causal factors from one conjuncture to the next.

In stressing the historical specificity of the interaction between domestic legacies and international changes, it is important to point out that my analysis does not support the underlying framework employed by historical institutionalists. To describe state-society relations in the language of "strength" or "autonomy"—two pet terms of the historical institutionalists—fails to capture two critical aspects of the cases discussed here. First, institutional capacity—generally used as a proxy for "state strength"—is, contrary to common usage, not a quality that lends itself to aggregation. For example, while the size and the distributive capacities and organs of the Saudi state were expanding rapidly, its extractive and regulatory organizations were dismantled. And while the planning and aid-related agencies of the Yemeni bureaucracy were flourishing, the Yemeni state not only stopped taxing but ceded large swaths of its former regulatory and developmental mission to a host of social groups. The same argument holds for business groups or "civil society" in general. The effects of state-controlled oil revenues and privately controlled remittances on different parts of the bureaucracy, different kinds of state capacities, and different segments of the business group, in short, were not uniform. They varied; and not in trivial ways.

Second, the state's "autonomy" or "embedded autonomy" in relation to domestic social groups can and does obsolesce rapidly, not just in response to fundamental changes in the domestic economy but also in response to changes in external conditions. One recent revisitation of theories popularized by the historical institutionalists of the 1980s recognizes that state-society relations must be periodically renegotiated, especially after passing some threshold of industrial achievement, but this view fixes us so firmly on successful development as an indicator of embedded autonomy that one forgets the class nature of the state itself.[55] Thus, although public control of oil revenues and private control of labor remittances might have led one to predict the boomtime autonomy of social groups in Yemen and of the state in Saudi Arabia, and although the power of the Yemeni private sector and the Saudi government in the boom confirmed the notion that resources enhance autonomy, *the idea that this autonomy represented something more permanent than the resources that created it cannot be supported.* In the recession, relationships between business and government would reverse in both countries—but not because some developmental goal had been achieved. "Strength" and "autonomy" thus not only meant different things for different segments of state and private institutions; they also changed rapidly at different junctures of domestic and international time; and changes in crude economic resources were the critical components. Constructing the analysis of Saudi Arabia and Yemen around the process of institutional origination and change instead of around developmental outcomes or "success" makes it possible to highlight the extent to which neither the existence nor the

[55] Peter Evans, *Embedded Autonomy* (Princeton: Princeton University Press, 1995), 15–16.

effects of "autonomy" can be predicted, absent a predetermination of developmental outcomes.

Since the sources of institutional change differed radically in the boom, I have argued that method should follow. The mechanisms that produced the institutional outcomes of the boom period—and therefore the analytical focus most appropriate for studying them—were different from those of the pre-boom period. Then, institutional change was largely internally driven; key institutions—the bureaucracy, the army, the national market—originated in social struggles at local and national levels. During the boom, in contrast, institutional change occurred through changes that capital flows introduced in existing organizations and through new institutions that emerged in response to the challenges and opportunities created by remittances and oil revenues. The organizations through which capital flows entered and were allocated in the domestic economy were different in the two cases—the state bureaucracy itself in Saudi Arabia, and networks of informal bankers, businessmen, and the rural cooperatives in Yemen—but in both cases, organizational change preceded and shaped social responses. As resources became independent of domestic contests, preexisting lines of conflict, competition, and cooperation between business and government in Saudi Arabia and between business, tribal, and state elites in Yemen eroded. In both countries the boom removed the most critical sources of contention from the political agenda.

As they had before the boom, the government's sources of revenue still shaped what the state was, knew, and did. But aid, oil revenues, and labor remittances altered both the mechanisms through which institutions changed and the political coalitions undergirding prior institutional arrangements. The locus of institutional change, and therefore the most useful focus of analysis, lay not, as before, in social struggles attending the creation of national institutions but within the organizations spawned by forces *outside* the domestic context. Exogenous resources, by their sheer volume and momentum, rearranged the existing calculus, reoriented organizations, and built new constellations exclusively on the existence of the capital flows of the 1970s. In only a decade, state and social institutions and indeed the very structure of Yemeni and Saudi society were thus rearranged on the basis of an impermanent and unstable change in international prices.

The primary struggles during the boom years were no longer between would-be centralizers and resisting social groups. In fact, the decade of the 1970s was a period of remarkable depoliticization in both countries: with the exit of Yemeni labor and the elimination of Pan-Arab and Hijazi claimants in Saudi Arabia, economic policy could rest on an overt celebration of the market without debate about distributional consequences. The ease with which distributional issues were shelved was no doubt related to the sheer pace at which both economies were growing, but this hiatus also meant that the political terms in which economic change would be described *after* the boom had no links to the pre-boom era. The groups that would join the new contests in the recession of the 1980s were, in short, created almost from whole cloth during the 1970s.

With the decline of taxation and regulation, domestic groups developed qualitatively different relations to government: the politics of distribution and noninterference that typified the Saudi and Yemeni cases, respectively, differed markedly from the politics of extraction and regulation. First, conflicts over resources were conspicuous by their absence. In political terms the abandonment of taxation was part but not the whole of this change. Equally important was the fact that the entire realm of state regulation—from industrial policy to import quotas—was undone: taxation, regulation, economic policy—the concrete nodes of competition among social forces and between groups and segments of the state—moved entirely to the distributive sphere in Saudi Arabia, and in Yemen they ceased, in substantial measure, to exist.

Second, these changes meant that state organizations, or private-sector institutions, or social groups could change without coming into substantial friction with one another. Not only did the boom substantially rearrange the ability of different groups to shape their environment—catapulting, for example, the inexperienced Nejdi commission entrepreneur ahead of the established Hijazi businessman and the successful migrant ahead of the landed elite—but the nature of the claims made on the state by social groups and on groups by their members was dictated largely by the new resources of the 1970s.

Third, and finally, resources independently changed the organizational characteristics of public and private institutions. In the Saudi bureaucracy, successfully adapting organizations established links with and adopted the operating procedures of the all-powerful Ministry of Finance; in Yemen, state organizations did the same in relation to the Central Planning Organization. Rural communities in Yemen replaced previous patterns of lobbying for state resources and protection with local organizing and resource pooling through the LDAs. The erosion of direct lines of conflict, cooperation, and accommodation between the extractive-regulatory state and the social groups that served as its revenue base generated patterns of institutional and organizational change that cannot be comprehended by the social conflict models that sufficed to explain the pre-boom period.

That new forms of institutional change were created in the boom does not suggest that institutional legacies played no part in the specific form these changes took. The capital flows of the 1970s, entering highly charged domestic political arenas, accrued to groups in control, by some combination of history and accident, of sectors of the state or the economy. Existing domestic coalitions influenced the restructuring of business-government relations. This transformation occurred without overt struggle, but patterns set in the boom were crucial to the shape of struggles that took place in the bust. Oil revenues and labor remittances created radically different business classes. The Saudi bureaucracy deployed oil revenues and the legal apparatus of the state to create a new Nejdi business class and a new landed elite. Labor remittances in Yemen fueled private-sector growth that strengthened the traditional southern merchant and industrial classes at the same time that aid enabled the government to function without taxing or regulating the economy. Aid and remittances, the sources of Yemeni public and private finance, influenced national economic policy not, as did oil revenues in Saudi Arabia, by recreating social classes but by enabling separate public and private spheres to coexist without conflict—for the duration of the boom decade.

Chapter Six

Informal and Formal Banking

As the conduits through which the capital flows of the 1970s entered the domestic economy, financial institutions were the first to be affected, and nowhere were the divergent effects of labor remittances and oil revenues more clearly evident. From very similar beginnings, labor remittances and oil revenues produced two very different financial systems in Yemen and Saudi Arabia over the boom decade. In Saudi Arabia a heavily statist financial system centered on four state development banks, through which state bureaucrats determined private-sector access to finance. In Yemen a highly complex and sophisticated informal banking system collected and allocated foreign exchange, not only without the intervention of the state but entirely outside the sphere of state regulation. These two financial systems assumed different functions in the domestic political economy, funneled resources to two different groups of domestic entrepreneurs, shaped different investment patterns, and, when the boom was over, posed radically different regulatory dilemmas for government officials.

This chapter compares the way financial organizations were transformed by the capital flows of the 1970s, supplementing the arguments presented in Chapters 4 and 5 about the effects of remittances and oil revenues and about the social outcomes of the boom period. It shows the precise mechanisms through which two kinds of resource flows directly shaped domestic organizations, influencing access to resources in novel ways unconnected to preexisting struggles over the rules that governed the domestic political economy. Most important, the single sector of finance illustrates the different regulatory pressures created by state and privately controlled capital flows in the boom and the recession. Whereas the composition of business, private associations, and the state bureaucracy influenced the politics of recessiontime reforms in the realm of extraction and distribution, the financial structure set the stage for the success or failure of *regulatory* efforts. Because finance became thoroughly internationalized in both Yemen and Saudi Arabia during the 1970s, asset mobility made the task of regulation a uniquely delicate issue in the 1980s. The politics of financial reform thus differed from that in other sectors, as did the capacity of state institutions to implement reforms. The administrative, political, and economic changes wrought by the oil boom, in short, did not affect all sectors identically. Because of its links to international markets, finance persisted as an independent realm long after immobile assets had met their fate in the fiscal and political exigencies of the recession.

After the first set of responses to the recession played out, it was the relative ability of the two governments to manage the demands of mobile capital against those of other domestic claimants that set longer-term patterns of conflict and accommodation in place. Finance thus constitutes a sphere in which one can observe the concrete effects of structural changes in the international economy. The alacrity with which money moved across borders in the 1980s represented a sea-change in the international economy that presented regulatory challenges to national governments at once reliant on holders of mobile assets for investment and taxes but also held accountable to a landbound domestic constituency that all too often shoulders the cost of collective institutions. Finance puts an additional constraint on regulatory and extractive efforts which is particularly, if not uniquely, relevant in the contemporary context. Efforts to regulate highly mobile assets highlight the problems of applying a single theory of the tax state across different conjunctures of global time, marked by very different technological characteristics. Moreover, the reaggregation of interest groups that occurred in the recession is reflected in responses to financial changes in the system during the 1980s. Finally, this integrated discussion of changing financial institutions vividly depicts the different origins of financial institutions in the pre-boom and boom periods. Empirical material is presented first, followed by analytical discussion.

From Similar Beginnings

At the onset of the oil boom in the early 1970s, Yemen and Saudi Arabia had virtually identical financial systems. In both countries the unification of currency and the development of central banks came late—in the 1950s for Saudi Arabia and 1960s for Yemen. Until 1950, both countries had partially monetized economies in which a variety of currencies circulated. In the 1960s, formal commercial banks were established, displacing parts of the informal sector and mirroring the pattern of progressive formalization and regulation associated with modernization theory. These initial patterns of financial development were broadly similar to those that typified early modern Europe: trade and the state's preference for uniform tax measures were the primary forces behind the unification of currency, the consolidation of finance, and the formalization of banking.[1]

Sequences of formalization were also broadly similar in the two cases. In Saudi Arabia, after a shaky beginning in the 1930s, commercial banking expanded at a steady rate. The merger of the two largest money-changing houses to create the National Commercial Bank in 1939 signaled the consolidation and expansion of formal banking into areas formerly controlled by money-changers in the Hijaz.[2] The regulatory efforts of the state led to a contraction in the number of money-changing houses. Although a few expanded their operations, the profession, once described as "the most important and lucrative occupation" in the western province,[3] was being replaced by formal, privately owned commercial banks. For most of its early history the Saudi state was bankrupt, and thus public lending was virtually nonexistent even in the 1960s except for small seasonal loans from the Agricultural Development Bank established in 1962.

In conformity with the modernization paradigm that they appear to validate, the forces behind the expansion of commercial banking in Saudi Arabia before the 1970s were domestic. The creation of a unified national

[1] See Charles Kindleberger, *A Financial History of Western Europe* (London: Allen & Unwin, 1984), 35; Robert Lopez, *The Commercial Revolution of the Middle Ages, 950–1350* (Cambridge: Cambridge University Press, 1976), 6–7, 14–15; Thomas W. Blomquist, "The Dawn of Banking in an Italian Commune," in *The Dawn of Modern Banking* (New Haven: Yale University Press, 1979), 53–76.

[2] The most comprehensive text is Adnan M. Abdeen and Dale N. Shook, *The Saudi Financial System* (New York: Wiley, 1984); the most up-to-date is Peter Wilson, *A Question of Interest* (Boulder, Colo.: Westview Press, 1991). See also Rodney Wilson, "The Evolution of the Saudi Banking System and Its Relationship with Bahrain," in Tim Niblock, ed., *State, Society, and Economy in Saudi Arabia* (London: Croom Helm, 1982); Wilson, *Banking and Finance in the Arab Middle East* (New York: St. Martin's Press, 1983), esp. chaps. 1, 4; Ragaei El Mallakh, *Saudi Arabia* (Baltimore: Johns Hopkins University Press, 1982), chap. 9; Ali Johany, Michel Berne, and J. Wilson Mixon Jr., *The Saudi Arabian Economy* (London: Croom Helm, 1986), chap. 13; Said H. Hitti and George T. Abed, "The Economy and Finances of Saudi Arabia," *International Monetary Fund Staff Papers* 21 (July 1974): 290–98; and most recently, Abdulaziz M. al-Dukheil, *The Banking System and Its Performance in Saudi Arabia* (London: Saqi Books, 1995). Two texts on Islamic banking include substantial case material from Saudi Arabia and Egypt: Rodney Wilson, *Islamic Business*, rev. ed., Special Report no. 221 (London: Economist Intelligence Unit, 1985); Ahmed Abdel Fattah El-Ashker, *The Islamic Business Enterprise* (New Hampshire: Croom Helm, 1987). My own detailed account is Kiren Aziz Chaudhry, "The Price of Wealth: Business and State in Labor Remittance and Oil Economies" (Ph.D diss., Harvard University, 1990), chap. 10.

[3] From "Jeddah Report," 1916, PRO, FO 371/2781, vol. 77029.

market, the consolidation of the commercial sector, and the government's rising demand for credit all played a part in the process. The expansion of the state's regulatory and extractive apparatus in the 1930s, 1940s, and 1950s promoted larger private enterprises in the commercial and financial sectors and drove out smaller traders and money-changers who were harder to tax and regulate. This expansion was met, as I argued in Chapter 2, by the concerted resistance of the economically dispossessed, which found full expression in the opposition of the Hijazi money-changers to the establishment of the National Commercial Bank and, later, to the creation of the Saudi Monetary Agency (SAMA). Formal banks, whether those of foreign concessionaires such as Gellately Hankey or domestic entrepreneurs such as Bin Mahfuz, were anathema to the Hijazi money-changers, not only because they were bankers to the consolidating state but also because by allying with the state they undercut the main source of money-changers' profits: monetary instability.

In Yemen, a similar process was under way. Before the revolution of 1962, commercial elites relied mainly on Adeni banks. The National Commercial Bank (NCB) of Saudi Arabia established a Yemeni branch in 1959,[4] but it failed to replace the Adeni banks, which by then had developed longstanding relationships with the top tier of Yemen's commercial class—especially the absentee bourgeoisie.[5] The absence of commercial banking before the revolution reflected not a general lack of economic activity but the historical antipathy between the autocratic imam and the southern commercial classes. The political origins of financial institutions are nowhere clearer, then, than in the establishment of the first commercial bank in Yemen, the Yemen Bank for Reconstruction and Development (YBRD), in 1963. Created one year after the coup that deposed the imam, the YBRD was designed specifically to manage the nationalized monopolies the imam had owned in the name of "the state" and to undertake a variety of commercial and developmental functions.[6] It was the new Republican government's holding company and an embodiment of

[4] The al-Kaki family had the minority share of some 20 percent and also controlled Al-Kaki Exchange House, the second largest in Saudi Arabia.

[5] A more important group of competitors for the Saudi bank were the up-and-coming exchange houses and remittance agents. The failure of NCB was ordained by its lack of local networks of remittance agents and inability to cultivate links with the merchants of the overland trade routes; in all, it was largely ignored. Neither the NCB nor Indosuez cracked the influence of Adeni commercial banks: "The Saudi Bank never became a major influence in the commercial life of Yemen; it could not overcome the traditional tendency of Yemen's merchants to deal with bankers in Aden, nor their even more traditional habit of dealing informally among themselves in extending credit to each other" (American Institute for Yemeni Studies, San'a, Documents Section, "Economic Survey for Yemen [with July 30, 1964 balance sheet of the Yemen Currency Board]," Joint State Department/USAID dispatch from the American Embassy in Taiz, 1963).

[6] The state monopolies included Yemen Airlines, Hudaydah Electric Co., Yemen Fuel Co., National Cigarette and Tobacco Co., and Yemen Foreign Trade Company.

the alliance between Republicans and the absentee bourgeoisie.[7] In cooperation with the new regime's supporters in the commercial classes, it financed construction projects to house hundreds of thousands of migrants and businessmen who returned from Aden and elsewhere after the revolution.[8] In 1967 it took over Bank Misr, the financial arm of the departing Egyptian army, which had minted both silver Republican thalers and paper currency during the civil war. Soon afterward the YBRD expanded into branch banking in urban and rural areas, making rapid progress in trade finance as well.

Despite—in some cases because of—the tumultuous events of the 1960s, the network of Adeni banks and money exchangers which had dominated the Yemeni financial sector was being displaced by formal commercial banks. With the hasty departure of the British from Aden, the government of the newly independent People's Democratic Republic of Yemen nationalized trade, commercial banks, insurance companies, and commercial property. An exodus of North Yemeni bourgeoisie, and the termination of their financial ties with Aden, followed. A number of foreign banks opened branches in Yemen beginning in 1971 in response to opportunities for import financing and currency exchange profits.[9]

The oil boom of 1973 brought this seemingly evolutionary process to an abrupt halt in both countries, initiating an entirely different sequence and pattern of institutional change. Immediately after the oil price hike of 1973, labor remittances and oil revenues began to reshape the relative importance of informal, state, and commercial banking institutions.[10] Both Yemen and Saudi Arabia diverged from the classical "path" enshrined in the modernization paradigm, generating two distinctly different financial systems by the turn of the decade. These changes paint a vivid picture of the influence of external capital inflows on the structure of domestic finance.

[7] YBRD acted as banker to the government until 1971, when the Central Bank was created. The government had a controlling interest in the YBRD, but private Yemenis—almost exclusively returnees from Aden—held around 40 percent of the shares.

[8] On the role of YBRD, see ʿAbd al-ʿAziz Ahmad Saʿid Haydarah al-Muqtari, *Al-Nuqud wa-al Siyasah al-Naqdiyah fil Iqtisad al-Yamani al-Hadith* [Money and monetary policy in the contemporary economy of Yemen] (Beirut: Dar al Hidathah, 1985), 67–92.

[9] These included the Habib Bank and United Bank (both Pakistani, 1971), the Arab Bank (Jordanian, 1972), the Banque de l'Indochine (French, 1975), the Bank of Credit and Commerce International (Saudi, 1975), and a latecomer, the Iraqi Rafidayn Bank (1982). Three joint ventures followed with the establishment of the Yemen-Kuwait Bank for Trade and Investment (1979), the largest of all commercial banks, capitalized at YR 50 million and jointly owned by Kuwaiti and Yemeni businessmen; the International Bank of Yemen (1980), a joint venture of YBRD (25 percent), NCB (25 percent), Bank of America (20 percent), and private Yemeni shareholders (30 percent). In 1986 Bank of America sold its shares to Bin Mahfuz of NCB, thereby increasing the Saudi holdings to 45 percent.

[10] "Informal" banking can include lending, deposit-taking, money-changing, remittance systems, commenda arrangements, etc.; the distinguishing feature is the absence of state regulation or supervision. Black markets are informal markets that circumvent the law.

By the middle of the boom decade, state lending institutions in Saudi Arabia, coffers bursting at the seams with oil revenues, had taken over virtually all medium- and long-term lending in construction, agriculture, and industry. In some lending areas state banks—through the Agricultural, Industrial, Real Estate, and Saudi Development Funds—displaced the commercial banks, which could not compete with the funds' concessionary terms. On the other hand, branch networks of money-changers, long in retreat, swiftly expanded across the country until they controlled virtually all retail and deposit banking. Wedged between state banks and exchangers, the activities of commercial banks in Saudi Arabia shrank to short-term trade finance, construction guarantees, and overseas placements. Even within this limited sphere, SAMA's policies discouraged commercial banks from financing the largest construction projects. Low domestic interest rates, high reserve requirements, and other limitations pushed the most lucrative syndications abroad to overseas banking units (OBUs) in Bahrain.

In Yemen a very different set of changes occurred. Labor remittances from migrant workers in Saudi Arabia fueled the growth of complex informal banking networks outside the regulatory control of the government. Informal bankers overtook both the YBRD and commercial banks in providing a range of financial services to the expatriates. Commercial banks and even the Central Bank of Yemen began to rely on informal bankers for access to foreign currency.[11] In contrast to the swift growth of state lending institutions in Saudi Arabia, the Industrial Bank of Yemen (1976), the Housing Credit Bank (1978), and the Agricultural Cooperative Bank (1979) played only minor roles in promoting private-sector investments. All three were set up by donors from the oil-rich Gulf states, but lacking the resources of their counterparts in the oil states these banks remained on the margins of the financial system.[12] State lending in Yemen was limited to public-sector construction and agricultural projects.

The contrasting financial systems that developed in Yemen and Saudi Arabia reflected the different challenges and opportunities in deploying

[11] For transfers going to formal banks, Baghlaf and Sholaq used YBRD, where, by common agreement, they neither received interest on their deposits nor paid fees for services rendered. Al-Rajhi and the National Commercial Bank of Saudi Arabia both used the International Bank of Yemen, in which Bin Mahfuz, owner of the Saudi NCB, was a major shareholder. Although the al-Kaki family was a minority shareholder in NCB, it transfered funds to Yemen through the Pakistani United Bank Limited, which also handled their transfers from Pakistani migrant workers and pilgrims. In contrast, second-tier informal bankers—al-Hadda, al-Mutawaqqil, and al-Mujalli—used a variety of local banks: Indosuez, Arab Bank, and YBRD. As only a small fraction of their business involves transfers from the Gulf and Saudi Arabia, they constantly switch from bank to bank to accommodate the preferences of their merchant clientele.

[12] International Bank of Reconstruction and Development, *Mobilizing Domestic Financial Resources in the Yemen Arab Republic* (Washington, D.C.: World Bank, 1982), 52. For a breakdown of lending by state banks in Yemen, see IBRD, *Recent Economic Developments in the Yemen Arab Republic* (Washington, D.C.: World Bank, 1984), 66–67, Tables 32–33.

widely dispersed remittances on the one hand and centralized, state-controlled oil revenues on the other. These new financial structures in turn shaped important relationships in the domestic political economy. To be sure, other factors—historical patterns of capital accumulation and investment, religious prohibitions, communications, and commercial law—mattered as well. But the financial systems were shaped most by the different requirements of channeling widely held remittance assets and distributing highly centralized oil revenues.

Although labor remittances and oil rents generated very different "leading sectors" in the Yemeni and Saudi financial markets, they had one remarkably similar effect: commercial banking suffered a relative decline. Thus, although the number of commercial banks and their activities expanded during the boom in both countries,[13] commercial banks occupied an increasingly narrow niche in the domestic market. Around them, remittances and oil revenues generated elaborate and distinct institutions that were the main sinews of boomtime finance. In the recession, the weakness of commercial banks would become a critical factor in shaping adjustment strategies.

Banking on the Bureaucracy

Proponents of industrial planning ranging from Alexander Gerschenkron to John Zysman have emphasized the long-term benefits of credit-based banking systems in overcoming the disadvantages of backwardness and achieving international competitiveness. Although in the 1960s commercial banks were important sources of both investment and trade credit in Saudi Arabia, in the 1970s these functions were taken over by the Saudi state banks. Commercial banks were left with specialty market niches, and lending functions significant to long-term development were performed almost exclusively by the Saudi state banks and by Bahraini OBUs. The state lenders were unequipped to play the role of monitor or guardian to the new commercial and industrial classes of Saudi Arabia, suggesting that something more than a credit-based financial system is required if industrial planning is to succeed. Squeezed by the state banks and OBUs, commercial banks also rapidly lost their retail banking customers to money-changers specializing in deposit-taking and remittances. The rise of state banks and money-changers had enormous implications for the regulatory climate, the quality of investments, and responses to post-boom reforms. These sudden changes in the financial structure underscore the ways in which resource flows shape organizations. The rise of the state banks and the money-changers, therefore, presents important

[13] Combined Saudi commercial bank assets grew from SR 4 billion in 1973 to SR 110 billion in 1982 (Abdeen and Shook, *Saudi Financial System*, 69).

evidence of the organizational origins of the transformations of the 1970s.

The phenomenal expansion of money-changing branch networks in the 1970s, which followed a pattern of formalization and centralization typical of other institutions in Saudi Arabia during the 1960s, is not a well-appreciated fact even in the robust literature on banking in the kingdom. Although in the 1920s there were 700 to 800 money-changing houses, in 1972 there were only 50 left—yet by 1979, six years after the boom began, the number of exchange houses exceeded 224.[14] Money-changers controlled 30 to 35 percent of total bank deposits, generally on behalf of individuals of limited means.[15] They also provided remittance services through their large branch networks: by the late 1970s, the two largest money-changing establishments alone had 280 branches in remote areas.[16] The influx of 6 to 8 million foreign workers during the boom created a rapidly rising demand for retail banking and remittance services, which was captured almost completely by the money-changing houses. The pervasive Saudi state, especially SAMA, which controlled commercial banks closely, did not feel compelled to regulate the organizations that held deposits of such large numbers of individuals. Of the 224 money-changing houses, 128 were not licensed by the Ministry of Commerce, and 91 of those had no commercial registration.[17]

Oil revenues affected the organization of commercial banks. In contrast to most other countries, where a large number of small savers provide the deposit base for loans, Saudi commercial banks had few incentives to make inroads into retail banking; put simply, it was too much trouble.[18]

[14] Michael Grinsdale, "Money Changers in the Kingdom of Saudi Arabia" (paper, Saudi Investment Bank, Riyadh, 1985), 6.

[15] According to one study commissioned by the Saudi American Bank in 1981, of a potential Saudi consumer market of 520,653 for current accounts only 130,163, or 25 percent, used banks. The percentages using saving accounts and fixed-term deposits were 22 percent and 1 percent, respectively. Consulting Center for Finance and Investment, *Market Study for Banking Products,* conducted for the Saudi American Bank (Riyadh, 1981), 1–12 and 1–13, tables 1 and 2.

[16] Middle-level houses averaged 30 to 40 branches each. In the recession, the al-Rajhi firm's entry into formal banking prompted massive expansion of branches among the commercial banks as well. See "Al-Rajhi Rings the Changes," *Arab Banking and Finance* 2 (September 1983); and "Saudi Branch Battle Looms Over al-Rajhi Entry," *Arab Banking and Finance* 3 (October 1984). The long-awaited float of the Al-Rajhi Banking and Investment Corporation, the first "Islamic" bank in the kingdom, was finally issued on 19 March 1988 after no less than five years of negotiation; by that time, it had 230 branches and held SR 4 billion in non-interest-bearing accounts. Fifty percent of the bank's shares were held by the four al-Rajhi brothers who owned the exchange company; 5 percent were held by the original shareholders and 2 percent by employees; 43 percent were floated to the public through the Consulting Center for Finance and Investment. Upon opening formally, it became the largest bank in the kingdom in number of branches and paid-in capital, although NCB's customer deposits, at SR 46 billion in 1986, were much higher. See *Middle East Economic Survey* 31 (21 March 1988), B2.

[17] See Chaudhry, "Price of Wealth" (1990), 512, table 10.2.

[18] See J. S. G. Wilson, *Banking Policy and Structure* (New York: New York University Press, 1986), 289–90.

Only 30–40 percent of the population used retail banking services of any kind, and most of the demand was for remittance services in the expatriate communities.[19] In 1977 the two commercial banks had only 71 branches and the nine foreign banks just 27 branches among them.[20] By the time it applied for a license in 1988, al-Rajhi, the largest money-changing house, had 230 branches. Initially, the expansion of retail banking for the foreign and joint venture banks was restricted by SAMA to favor the two Saudi banks, the NCB and Riyadh Bank. After Saudization—a 1977–82 project of expanding Saudi ownership and employment in the banks with foreign partners—commercial bank branches quadrupled, from 80 to 362; 222 of these belonged to NCB and Riyadh Bank, 140 to the remaining seven newly Saudized banks. Despite this spurt of growth, commercial banks never broke the monopoly of money-changers on retail banking.

The money-changing branch networks set up in the 1970s were owned by relative newcomers such as al-Rajhi, who began his operations in the 1940s and expanded them rapidly in the 1970s. By 1983, Al-Rajhi Company for Foreign Exchange and Commerce had 178 branches, some 20 percent more than NCB, the kingdom's largest commercial bank. In the early 1970s the larger exchange firms became international enterprises, developing correspondent relationships in Beirut and in Bahrain, the two successive financial centers in the Middle East. Throughout the decade the large exchange houses simplified their system of drafts and established stable institutional relationships with American and other banks in international financial centers around the world. By the mid-1970s these relationships were sturdy enough that money exchangers could remit money overseas or make international investments with the alacrity of a regular international bank.[21] Some of the exchange houses had strong links with commercial banks, giving them access to international banking relationships and networks.[22]

Unlike commercial banks, which narrowed their range of operations in the boom, the services provided by money-changing houses expanded to

[19] "Saudi Branch Battle Looms," 39.

[20] By 1982, all commercial banks together had only 460 branches. See Abdeen and Shook, *Saudi Financial System,* 60–61.

[21] Grinsdale, "Money Changers," 2. Details on the al-Rajhi family and other Saudi exchange houses and their role in traditional markets are from Michael Grinsdale (Chief Accountant, Saudi Investment Bank), interview with author, Riyadh, December 1985; and R. Wilson, *Banking and Finance,* chap. 2.

[22] For example, the al-Kaki family, a minority shareholder in NCB, also owns the second largest exchange house network in the kingdom. Another example is the formation of the Bank of Investment and International Commerce in Luxembourg, capitalized at $16.5 million and designed to handle exchange and investment for Saudi and Gulf clients. Khalid bin Mahfuz, the majority shareholder of NCB, and Sulayman al-Rajhi, the largest money-changer, owned 35 percent of equity each. Shaykh ʿIsaʿi, another money-changer, owned 20 percent, and the al-Kaki family the remaining shares. See *Quarterly Economic Review of Saudi Arabia,* no. 3 (1979): 13.

include non-interest-bearing deposit accounts, foreign exchange services, and lending in the form of overdraft facilities. Deposit-taking grew with the influx of migrant workers.[23] Yet even in this flurry of innovation, entire financial industries such as insurance services, a stock market, and formal securities markets failed to evolve, despite the obvious affinity between a stock market and Islamic banking principles.[24]

The Saudi state banks, whose virtually inexhaustible resources were lent interest-free, came to control both long- and medium-term lending during the boom. By doing so, they dominated those areas of the financial markets that determined the creation of permanent assets and the future shape of the domestic economy. In the 1970s the massive injection of credit into the private sector through state banks gave the government complete control of fixed investments in industry, agriculture, and construction. The Saudi Credit Bank provided personal loans to Saudi citizens for personal consumption, marriage expenses, and consumer purchases. Between 1977 and 1983 the state banks made long-term, interest-free loans totaling more than SR 96.5 billion. By 1984 the state had disbursed over SR 168 billion in long-term industrial, construction, and agricultural loans.

As Table 6.1 shows, commercial banks played a marginal role in funding fixed capital investment. Squeezed by their competitors in the boom, Saudi commercial banks, famous for their exceedingly healthy capital ratios, increasingly specialized in low-risk, short-term lending, mostly in the form of contract guarantees, letters of credit, and currency exchange.[25] This specialization strategy would put them at a severe disadvantage in the recession, because these particular forms of finance are exceedingly difficult to trace and do not reflect default immediately.[26] The overall domestic component of commercial bank operations shrank, with both the Saudized and indigenous banks becoming little more than conduits for

[23] Saudi exchange houses lent in the domestic market in return for "fees" that disguised high interest rates. The links between their domestic deposit-taking and international currency markets are similar to those described for Sholaq later in this chapter.

[24] *Mudarabah* denotes long-term finance, usually equity stakes in ventures, involving profit- and risk-sharing among investors and financiers. *Murabahah* and *musharikah* arrangements are essentially futures sales for projects to institutional and individual investors. Stock and equity sales through a formal market would be the obvious way to create these forms of finance. For the proximity of Islamic banking and investments through stock exchanges, see R. Wilson, *Islamic Business* El-Ashker, *The Islamic Business Enterprise*; Traute Wohlers-Scharf, *Arab and Islamic Banks* (Paris: Development Center of the Organization for Economic Cooperation and Development, 1983).

[25] See Abdeen and Shook, *The Saudi Financial System*, 77, 84, for debt-to-equity ratios in 1978–82.

[26] The emphasis on short-term lending in Saudi Arabia is similar in form to the British banks' preferences for minimizing formal long- and medium-term commitments. But whereas in Britain this preference grew out of the historical reliance of industrialists on self-financing and the early wide-spread use of inland bills of exchange to cover business transactions, (see J. Wilson, *Banking Policy and Structure*, 280–85) in Saudi Arabia it was the result of state credit.

Table 6.1. Sources of loans for fixed capital investments (FCI) in Saudi Arabia (in million SR)

Year	Total SLI* lending	Commercial bank loans for FCI	Total loans	Total FCI	SLI lending as % of total loans
1977–78	16,588	2,804	19,392	18,354	86
1978–79	13,243	8,522	21,765	19,401	61
1979–80	15,042	9,501	24,543	23,207	61
1980–81	17,783	11,012	28,795	28,691	62
1981–82	15,499	6,320	21,819	35,830	71
1982–83	18,381	2,825	21,206	38,336	87

SOURCES: CCFI, *The Private Sector in Saudi Arabia*; Saudi Industrial Development Fund, *Annual Report, 1403–1404*; Real Estate Development Fund, *Seven Year Review: 1395/96–1401/02*, and *Annual Reports*, 1402/03 and 1403/04; Agricultural Development Bank, *Annual Reports*, 1966–85. All published by the Ministry of Finance and National Economy, Kingdom of Saudi Arabia, Riyadh.
*State lending institutions.

overseas investments made by a narrow commercial elite. High reserve ratios at home and domestic interest rates that averaged half of those available in international capital markets encouraged capital flight. By 1980–82 only about half the deposits of Saudi firms and individuals were being placed locally.[27] Moreover, the ready availability of credit from the state banks further reduced the commercial banks' impact by making potential clients reluctant to accept the latter's customary project design, disclosure, and accounting requirements.

State lending was a way to allocate oil revenues directly in the domestic economy, and the four state banks created immediately after the boom were intended to serve as a direct conduit through which the Ministry of Finance could funnel investment capital into the local economy. The state banks controlled long-term lending and therefore were the only organizations with the capacity to influence long-term investment decisions. In an otherwise unregulated "capitalist" economy, the funds, in principle, empowered government planners to shape the domestic economy. This potential for guiding development went unrealized, however. Born of the singular goal of rapid sectoral development, the organizational infirmities of the state banks reflected the same lack of information and planning goals that characterized the distributive state in general. Between the institutional weaknesses of the state banks and the broader political context

[27] The average net foreign assets-to-deposits ratio of seven commercial banks for which figures are available was 46.5, while the loan-to-deposit ratio was 53.2 in 1978–82. These figures exclude Saudi French Bank, which had special trading agreements with several European countries, and Saudi Cairo Bank, which published no figures for 1982. See Abdeen and Shook, *The Saudi Financial System*, 86.

in which they operated, the distributive agenda easily eclipsed the developmental one.

The Real Estate Development Fund (REDF) and the Saudi Industrial Development Fund (SIDF), responsible for the construction and industrial sectors, respectively, represented opposing poles of institutional coherence.[28] Unlike the Agricultural Development Fund (discussed in Chapter 5), which was designed to fund the investments of a small group of Saudi notables who had already benefited from the land grant programs of the pre-boom years, the REDF had the broadest lending base, the SIDF had the narrowest. Together, these two organizations were responsible for whatever non-state fixed national investments were undertaken in the 1970s in infrastructure and industry.

The REDF, the largest of the state funds, had the broadest impact on Saudi citizens. Like the other funds, its main directive was to distribute as many loans as quickly as possible; between 1974 and 1984, 82 percent of private housing loan applications were approved.[29] During the boom years when urban rents rose rapidly, fed by inflation and the influx of foreign labor, the REDF had a mandate to promote real estate development. A cursory review of its lending record and organizational structure reveals the priority it accorded to distributive over planning functions. The REDF injected more than SR 44.9 billion into the construction sector without ever codifying its lending priorities and procedures.[30] Internal control problems were brought to the attention of government authorities when a 1978 World Bank report noted that the REDF lacked any information on existing housing units or target groups and extended credit in ways that ". . . misallocated resources, disrupted social structures and needlessly fed inflation." The World Bank reported massive misallocation to wealthy applicants who were not in need of housing or government assistance and were using loans to finance commercial building projects. Throughout the 1970s, REDF's organizational difficulties were reflected in its use of commercial banks to process its loans and external consultants to draw up yearly reports based on information that was fragmentary and at least partially fabricated. Observing that the REDF had over 79,000 active accounts "of which no comprehensive record exist[ed]," the World Bank recommended a cessation of loans until the fund gained a better sense of its previous commitments and transferred files kept in various banks to a

[28] If the Saudi state banks were arranged on a spectrum of institutional development, no doubt the Saudi Credit Bank (SCB) and SIDF would mark the two poles. Since virtually nothing is known of the SCB's internal organization and lending, however, the REDF, which would fall about in the middle of the spectrum, is discussed instead.

[29] Ministry of Finance, *REDF: Annual Report for 1403–4* (Riyadh: Government Printing Press, 1986).

[30] Ahmad al-'Ajil (director-general, REDF), interview with author, Riyadh, 31 December 1985.

central data base—although the report correctly recognized that "political considerations" would prevent the kind of lending hiatus necessary for a thorough reorganization.[31] The year after the World Bank submitted its report, the REDF granted loans to 7,000 new applicants.[32]

The REDF introduced borrowers to few, if any, of the procedures and controls that characterize formal banking systems. Most loans were distributed in cash. Since housing was one of the perquisites of Saudi citizenship, approval of home building loans was virtually automatic. According to the REDF director general, "To acquire a loan, a person must prove that he is a Saudi national, have a building permit, and be over twenty-two years of age. There is no evaluation team and we make no checks on the borrower. We don't care if the applicant is a crook or an escaped convict."[33] This approach to lending extended into collections as well. In the recession, as loans became due, REDF farmed out collections to individuals on a commission basis.[34]

It is unnecessary to emphasize the potential for corruption in an institution with these organizational characteristics. Large tranches of cash simply disappeared.[35] The absence of either a policing or even a consultative relationship between the REDF and its borrowers resulted in widespread abuses. Multiple loans to families for the same project were common, and housing loans were regularly used for investment, consumption, or commercial buildings.[36] These weaknesses were catastrophic for the real estate sector in the long run. As neither the fund nor its borrowers had any knowledge of the real estate market's medium-term needs, by 1985 there was an excess capacity of 60 and 40 percent in commercial and residential buildings, respectively.

In contrast, the Saudi Industrial Development Fund (SIDF) was, argua-

[31] International Bank for Reconstruction and Development, *The Real Estate Development Fund Report*, study for REDF (Riyadh: Ministry of Finance, 1978), 1.

[32] Ministry of Finance and National Economy, *REDF: Annual Report for 1980* (Riyadh: Government Printing Press, 1982).

[33] The only check on the wholesale misuse of funds was a loan installment schedule instituted in 1981: an initial 10 percent, a second installment of 45 percent after the skeleton of the building was in place, and the final payment when the building was almost ready for occupancy—but no on-site visits were conducted. Ahmad al-ʿAjil interview, Riyadh, 31 December 1985.

[34] In 1985 the REDF had nearly 100 people working on this basis. Their success varied by region and urban/rural distinctions: collection rates were below 10 percent in the outlying areas of the central province, close to 90 percent in the urban areas of the eastern and western provinces. Ahmad al-ʿAjil interview, 31 December 1985.

[35] The aggregate figures of the REDF in its own reports show an unexplained discrepancy of SR 8.508 billion in loans distributed in the 1975–84 period.

[36] Private housing loans constituted 95–96 percent of total loans but were limited to SR 300,000 per applicant. Commercial loans had a limit of SR 10 million and could be used to fund up to 50 percent of the cost of building. From 1975 to 1984, 277,058 private housing loans and 2,077 investment loans were distributed. Investment loans averaged almost SR 2 million; private housing, SR 200,000 (calculated from *REDF: Annual Reports* 1976–1986).

bly, the most likely to foster learning and skills among entrepreneurs. Like the other state banks, SIDF began with a mandate to lend as much as possible, but it was saved from the early organizational collapse that characterized the other funds because from 1974 to 1977 it was run by a management team on contract from Chase Manhattan of New York. In this three-year period the fund made independent feasibility studies of investment proposals, and its early investments, most of which were managed by experienced Saudi businessmen, were highly successful. After local management took over in 1977, however, SIDF simultaneously stopped participating in project evaluations and began to lend to inexperienced, aspiring industrialists with strong political and kinship connections to the political and bureaucratic leadership.[37] Between 1977 and 1985 the fund was reorganized five times, putting different procedures and priorities in force each time. SIDF vacillated between organizing itself by sector, by province, and finally by the phase of project completion.[38] Internal policies shifted between efforts to improve efficiency and efforts by internal fund factions to gain control of the allocative process. In any event, these organizational changes coincided with management's retreat from close supervision of projects, encouraging applicants to fabricate feasibility studies with the help of foreign consultants. According to a senior loan officer, SIDF was often aware that the typical Saudi applicant was simply a middleman whose status as a well-connected citizen was used to secure interest-free loans for projects to be constructed and run by foreign companies.[39] Like the Agricultural, Real Estate, and Credit Funds, SIDF became a conduit to the commission entrepreneurs of the boom years.

The result of mismanagement was massive overcapacity in many indus-

[37] Tajammul Hussein (senior loan officer, SIDF), interviews with author, Riyadh, January–May 1986.

[38] Under the 1974–77 Chase contract there were no evaluation teams, project departments, or officers; a small group of management people undertook all aspects of studying and following the project. In 1977 three teams were created for chemical, engineering, food, and other sectors. Building materials were separate and divided by province. In 1978 the teams were organized into four divisions, each with two teams: one for the central province and one for all the other regions. In 1983 a new division was created for problem sectors, mainly for failing investments in building materials. In 1985 the fund strengthened its coordination with the Ministry of Finance. One division was abolished and its duties divided between two others, each of which had six project teams: the first specialized in cement, gases, paper, chemicals, and petrochemicals; the second in food, engineering, steel, paints, and construction chemicals. The third division processed small investors' applications, dealt with all the construction projects, and managed all unpaid loans and collections. Tajammul Hussein interviews, January–May 1986.

[39] Widespread abuses of this sort eventually led SIDF to add bank credit checks to its procedures and to make loans conditional on letters of credit in the Saudi applicant's name. The fund could do very little to insure that the Saudi partner was not simply a figurehead. It could, however, force the foreign party to rely on the Saudi sponsor for the duration of its contact with the industrial project. SIDF thus eventually became a guarantor of the long-term involvement of local businessmen in projects managed and controlled by foreign companies, a goal that many of the distributive policies were intended to achieve. Tajammul Hussein interviews, January–May 1986.

trial goods. In 1986 the Riyadh Chamber of Commerce, an organization not known for its candid evaluation of the private sector's weaknesses, estimated that over 35 percent of the projects funded by SIDF were in default; many had already been abandoned in various stages of completion, and those that remained were functioning below capacity.[40] Not surprisingly, the problems of SIDF-funded projects were the problems of Saudi industry as a whole: of the 723 factories built between 1979 and 1983 in the kingdom, 627 of them, or 87 percent, were funded by SIDF.[41]

Despite the heavy role of SIDF in funding industry, industrial "policy" was nonexistent. The structure of state organizations as they emerged in the boom was a large part of the problem. The state banks fell under the Ministry of Finance, not the ministries responsible for sectoral development. Overlapping jurisdictions in the bureaucracy responsible for industrial policy made the collection of comprehensive information on market size, protection, and existing productive capacity virtually impossible.[42] The most destructive expression of institutional rivalry was the Ministry of Industry's deliberate withholding of information on the industrial sector as part of its turf battle with the Ministry of Finance.[43]

In the political contests over policy during the recession, the collective mistakes of the state banks came back to haunt the government. The state banks had played a pivotal role in creating an entirely new and inexperienced groups of entrepreneurs who blamed their ill-advised investments on the state funds' irresponsible management to argue for additional government subsidies and support. Spokesmen for the Nejdi elites who were the primary beneficiaries of state lending put it quite bluntly in a study they commissioned through the Riyadh Chamber of Commerce:

> State banks put investment capital into the hands of unqualified and inexperienced investors. Plentiful loans that far exceeded the needs of investors were distributed without study, and large government subsidies led to the emergence of new establishments to the fullest extent possible, including the

[40] Consulting Center for Finance and Investment, *The Present Condition of the Saudi Private Sector and Its Role in the Saudi Economy*, report for the Riyadh Chamber of Commerce (Riyadh, 1986), 80, 137 (hereafter cited to as *Saudi Private Sector*).

[41] Ministry of Finance, *SIDF Annual Report: 1402–03* (Riyadh: Government Printing Press, 1984).

[42] *Saudi Private Sector*, 95, 173–74.

[43] Like all the state funds, SIDF was under the supervision of the Ministry of Finance. The Ministry of Industry and Electricity, nominally responsible for industrial policy, deliberately sabotaged SIDF as part of its ongoing rivalry with the Ministry of Finance for control over industrial policy. It was common, for example, for the Ministry of Industry to approve and license projects sponsored by well-known defaulting borrowers, or to license new projects in precisely the subsectors that SIDF had marked as overdeveloped. The most flagrant result of such sabotage was that between 1975 and 1983, SR 6.4 billion of a total 11 billion lent by SIDF was in building materials; when the construction boom leveled off in 1982, the enormous capacity of these industries was suddenly deprived of a market (*SIDF Annual Report: 1402–03*, 31).

expansion of existing factories and the invention of a large number of industrial projects that had no economic basis. Thus, the economy grew rapidly on an unsound foundation, creating a large number of peripheral suppliers and retailers who demanded profits despite the fact that they were doomed to fail in the long run.[44]

The state funds had the resources to promote sound domestic investments, plan for the development of different sectors of the economy, and fund the most appropriate industrial technologies. Control of credit by the government raised at least the possibility of eliminating duplication, waste, and shortages. Yet the Saudi state banks accomplished none of these goals. Even through they specialized in long-term finance, a relationship that gives lenders considerable leverage, the state lending institutions did little to foster management, accounting, and marketing skills among local entrepreneurs. So glaring were the failures of projects funded by the state banks that, in the recession, the private sector successfully used them to justify a new set of demands for government assistance.

Between the Mattress and the Bank

The financial system produced by labor remittances differed entirely from that spawned by oil revenues, with one important qualification: in Yemen, as in Saudi Arabia, although the number of commercial banks in operation grew in the 1970s, they were increasingly peripheral to the most dynamic sectors of the economy and constituted only a tiny proportion of the financial sector's activities.[45] The most striking feature of finance in the remittance economy was the virtual absence of deposit-taking institutions. Only 8 percent of the Yemeni population used banks, and the fact that most currency was held outside banks created almost insurmountable barriers to the effectiveness of monetary policy.[46] For a country with an unusually even distribution of wealth, the lack of branch banking was anomalous. Even more striking is the fact that the ratio of bank branches to population in Yemen was the lowest in the Middle East.[47]

The almost complete lack of deposit banking was not unrelated to gov-

[44] *Saudi Private Sector,* 144–45.

[45] In the late 1980s, the largest bank, the Yemen-Kuwait Bank for Trade and Investment, was capitalized at only YR 50 million, or about $8 million; the smallest, Rafidayn Bank, had paid-up capital of only about $1 million; and most of the others were capitalized at $3 million.

[46] Lee Ann Ross, "Informal Banking in Yemen" (USAID papers, 1980); and IBRD, *Mobilizing Domestic Financial Resources.*

[47] IBRD, *Mobilizing Domestic Financial Resources.* Between 1966 and 1973 an average 83 percent of banknotes and currency was held outside the banks; the figure improved slightly between 1974 and 1982 for an average of 73 percent (Al-Muqtari, *Al-Nuqud wa-al-Siyasah,* 184–85).

ernment policies. During the 1960s and early 1970s, in efforts to promote the YBRD—flagship of Republican pride—the monetary authorities restricted branch banking by other banks. Having given YBRD monopoly rights to deposit banking, the government neither encouraged it to expand its branch network nor forced it to accept the deposits of small savers, and as the 1970s wore on, YBRD agents in the rural areas were displaced by money-changing networks.[48] Like Saudi commercial banks, those in Yemen began to specialize in trade finance and construction projects.[49] It is testimony to the complete dominance of the informal bankers, however, that even in the sphere of import financing the role of commercial banks was marginal at best: between 1974 and 1984 commercial banks financed an astoundingly low average of only 16 percent of total imports (see Table 6.2). Their loans for industrial ventures were even lower, averaging a negligible 1.2 percent of total credit to the private sector.[50]

Nevertheless, the profitability of formal banks in Yemen was reported to be 30–40 percent higher than elsewhere—close to that enjoyed by banks in the oil-rich countries.[51] The main sources of these profits were commissions from letters of credit and speculation in foreign currency in the informal market. Smaller banks—in particular, two Pakistani banks, neither of which had been granted permission to set up in Saudi Arabia—specialized mainly in remittances of Indian and Pakistani workers in collaboration with al-Kaki's offices in Saudi Arabia.

[48] YBRD had 38 branches in 1985 and controlled 78 percent of deposits and 72 percent of advances and loans among commercial banks: World Bank, *Yemen Arab Republic* (Washington, D.C.: World Bank, 1979), 104 and annex V-1. The Agricultural Development Bank (ADB) had 21 branches in 1985: *Central Bank of Yemen: 14th Annual Report* (San'a, 1985), 105. Foreign and joint venture commercial banks had a collective total of fourteen branches. Although foreign banks had an initial interest in expanding their branch networks, import finance after 1973 provided such expanded possibilities for profit that their enthusiasm waned. Even YBRD and ADB, both designed to encourage small depositors in the outlying areas, were often reluctant to open accounts for small depositors, reflecting ADB's aversion to high administration costs and the cheaper funds placed at its disposal by international lending agencies and the Central Bank.

[49] For such a young formal banking business, there have been numerous failures and closures. The failure of Indosuez's first Hudaydah branch in 1959 and NCB's failure followed by a quiet nationalization have already been mentioned. Citibank's branch in San'a closed after one year (1975), and BBME's branches in San'a, Hudaydah, and Ibb, after six years, in 1979, because of overextension in agricultural loans and collection problems in Ibb.

[50] In this context, the IBRD team's statement that ". . . commercial banks have been the major channel for credit from domestic financial institutions to the domestic private sector" either applies only to those transactions that flowed through the formal sector, in which case the statement is irrelevant, or to all transactions, in which case it is simply inaccurate. IBRD, *Mobilizing Domestic Financial Resources*, 53.

[51] 'Ali Salami (controller-general, Central Bank of Yemen); 'Ali Riza (managing director, Industrial Bank of Yemen); and Azmat Jamshed (managing director, Habib Bank Limited), interviews with author, San'a, 1987.

Table 6.2. Proportion of Yemeni imports financed by commercial banks (in million YR)

Year	Total Imports	Amount Financed by Commercial Banks	% Financed by Commercial Banks
1974	1,251	126	10
1975	1,866	226	12
1976	3,506	322	9
1977	4,483	1,065	24
1978	6,774	996	15
1979	8,465	1,243	14
1980	9,636	2,564	26
1981	10,397	1,257	12
1982	9,575	1,319	14
1983	8,955	1,541	17
1984	7,696	2,201	28

SOURCE: IBRD, *Yemen Arab Republic: Current Position and Prospects* (Washington, D.C., 1986); *Statistical Yearbook of the Yemen Arab Republic* (San'a: Central Planning Organization, 1986).

Of itself, the marginal role of commercial banks in providing industrial credit is not unusual. In England, which shared the Yemeni characteristic of a relatively even distribution of wealth, commercial banks concentrated on trade finance; their role in providing capital for industrial expansion was minimal. Fixed capital investments of the eighteenth and nineteenth centuries were funded, instead, by reinvested profits.[52] Unlike their counterparts in continental Europe, state authorities in England did not need to channel resources to industry. Historically, commercial banks have provided industrial finance in late developers only in response to deliberate government policy—efforts conspicuous by their absence in Yemen, where industrialists and businessmen had access to ample foreign exchange through the informal banking sector. The informal bankers' ability to meet the specific needs of migrants and merchants was undoubtedly the key factor in the marginal role of commercial banks, though government policy was important as well. Squeezed out of retail and trade finance, Yemeni commercial banks, like their Saudi counterparts, became conduits for capital flight. Lacking domestic outlets for their profits, foreign banks and joint venture banks in Yemen—classified as a "least developed country"—actually became net exporters of foreign exchange in the 1974–83 period.[53]

Soon after the mass migrations of labor in the early 1970s, informal bankers and money-changers displaced the rural agents of commercial banks, gaining control of what increasingly became the main source of

[52] Rondo Cameron, "England, 1750–1844," in Cameron et al., eds., *Banking in the Early Stages of Industrialization* (New York: Oxford University Press, 1967).

[53] IBRD, *Mobilizing Domestic Financial Resources,* 64.

capital aggregation in the country.[54] When the volume of remittances soared to about three times the size of official GNP, the informal banking system expanded rapidly into the remote rural areas of Yemen.[55] During the boom period the remittance business was completely unregulated. But since there were no exchange controls or restrictions on the movement of currency, the informal currency markets of Yemen were not "black" markets.

Despite the large volumes of foreign exchange they handled and their enormous importance to the Yemeni economy, the informal bankers specialized in limited kinds of transactions. They (a) collected remittances from Saudi Arabia through their branch operations there; (b) made foreign exchange available to the Central Bank of Yemen, commercial banks, merchants, and industrialists in Yemen; and, most important, (c) transmitted local currency to the migrants' families in the remote rural areas of Yemen. Because of their location in the regional economy, informal banks never took deposits in Yemen and therefore, unlike some of the larger Saudi exchange houses, did not evolve into deposit-taking banks.

It is difficult to overemphasize a pivotal fact of the Yemeni developmental trajectory: informalization and internationalization of finance went hand in hand. Yemen's informal banking system centralized during the 1970s, reaching down into the remote rural communities of Yemen and out into international capital markets. The importance of links with international capital markets and financial institutions becomes clear in a stylized review of the overall structure of the informal banking system. As Figure 6.1 shows, Yemeni workers in Saudi Arabia and the Gulf earned about $4.8 billion dollars annually during the peak years of 1978–82. Less than a fourth of this amount was sent through formal banks and eventually found its way into government accounts. About 10 percent was brought home by migrants or small informal bankers in the form of hard currency or goods. Roughly 70 percent of total Yemeni earnings were deposited with the two Yemeni exchange houses that had branches in Saudi Arabia, Sholaq and Baghlaf, to be remitted to migrant's families in Yemen.

From the Saudi offices of Sholaq and Baghlaf, the money took one of

[54] ʿAli al-Thawr (director of the state-owned Yemen Cement Manufacturing and Marketing Company, former board member of YBRD), interview with author, Sanʿa, 3 April 1987.

[55] The Yemeni government regularly undervalues remittances in order to support requests for foreign aid. This affects GNP figures. In fact, remittances outstripped the entire state budget by an average of 500 percent from 1973 to 1976. My figure, about four times the official one, is based on interviews with money-changers and bankers in Yemen. My estimates derive from extensive interviews with migrant agents and money exchangers (representing 80 percent of total transactions) and interviews with ʿAli Salami, 1986–87. Similarly, agents estimate the total number of Yemeni migrants at approximately 1.8 million, more than three-fourths of the work force.

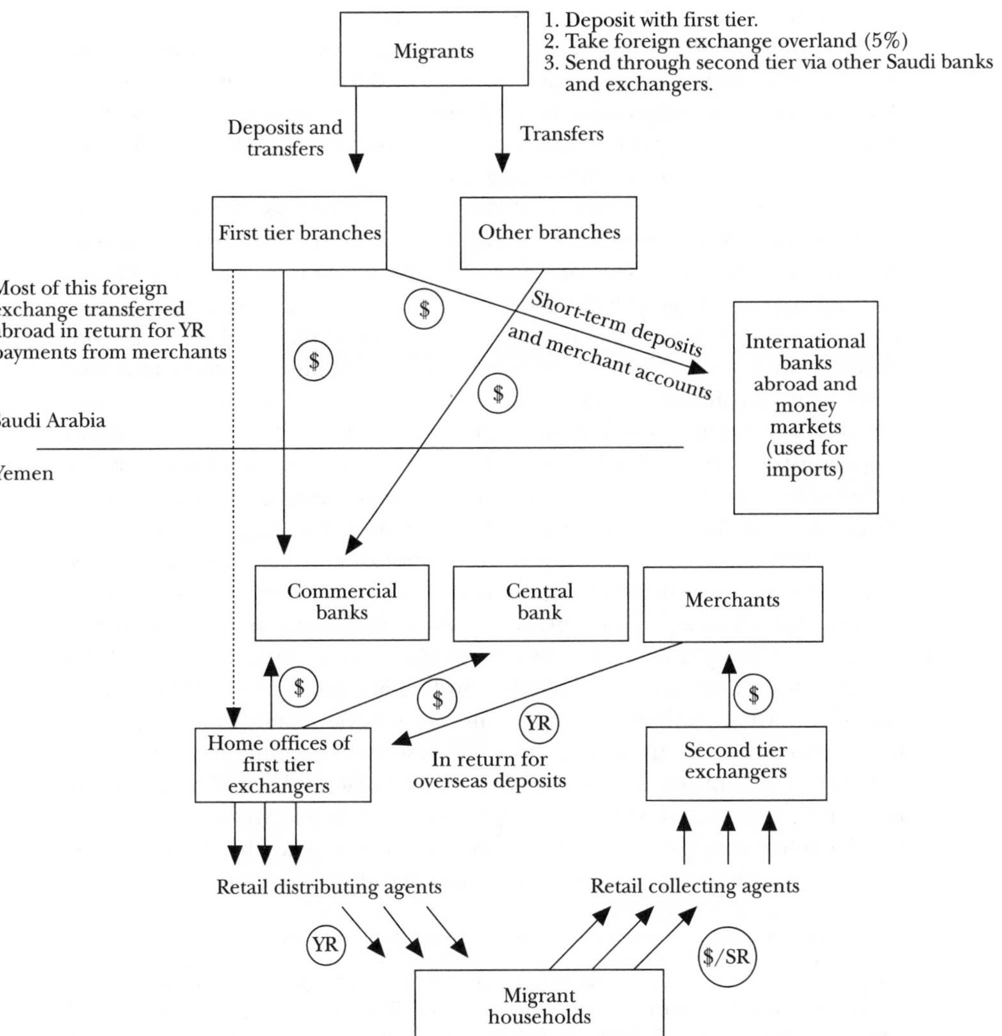

Figure 6.1 The Yemeni informal banking system in the boom period

two routes. Some of it was transferred, in hard currency, to the foreign accounts of Yemeni businessmen and industrialists, who used it to finance imports or investments. In return, these private-sector elites made Yemeni riyals available to the Yemeni offices of Sholaq and Baghlaf; these funds were transported to migrant households in the rural areas through a complex system of rural remittance agents. Alternatively, the deposits were placed in international capital markets. After a lag, usually of about a month, the foreign currency was either transferred back to Yemen or sold to Yemeni institutional and private buyers of foreign exchange in return for Yemeni riyals deposited directly with Sholaq's agents in Yemen.[56] From the money-changers' perspective, this second route was more lucrative than the first. The informal system of the 1970s could not have existed or been profitable in a purely local context. The informalization of finance was thus a product of internationalization.

The informal financial system of Yemen had three sets of players, distinguished not only by the volume of currency flow they handled but also by the particular function they performed in funneling remittances to clients and destinations inside and outside of Yemen. The first tier of informal bankers, comprising the two exchange houses of Sholaq and Baghlaf, controlled over 70 percent of the total deposits of Yemeni workers and specialized in transfer and aggregation functions. Sholaq was by far the bigger player, holding most Yemeni deposit accounts and controlling about 70 percent of the transfer business. The dominant position of the first tier rested solely on the fact that they were the only banking institutions with offices in both Yemen and Saudi Arabia. Sholaq and Baghlaf themselves were of Yemeni origin, but both acquired Saudi citizenship in the 1950s, before the enactment of stringent laws against permanent migration to the kingdom. Sholaq's Saudi branches alone had deposits of between $80 million and $213 million per month in the boom years.[57] The Saudi exchange houses of al-Kaki, al-Rajhi, and al-Suayni, despite their larger branch networks in Saudi Arabia, could not compete because they did not have branch offices in Yemen, massive reserves in Yemeni riyals, and a network of subcontracting agents that gave Sholaq and Baghlaf their competitive edge. Because they could not control networks inside Yemen, the Saudi exchangers lacked the flexibility required to place hard currency in overseas interest-bearing accounts for any significant period.[58]

[56] The percentages of remittances transferred to YBRD as opposed to the personal offices of Baghlaf and Sholaq varied according to the migrants' preferences but remained relatively stable throughout this period: some 70 percent of Sholaq's migrant customers and about 60 percent of Baghlaf's preferred their Yemeni offices to YBRD. the migrants' reasons included speed of delivery, longer working hours at Sholaq's and Baghlaf's offices, their provision of free services in their Saudi offices, and their network of rural agents, for which the banks had no counterpart.

[57] Although other money exchange houses in Saudi Arabia have a diversified business and serve many different nationalities, 100 percent of Sholaq's depositors in Saudi Arabia were Yemeni. Baghlaf diversified into retailing and imports in Saudi Arabia, but his exchange operations were much smaller. Husayn Al Saqqaf (general manager, Sholaq Foreign Exchange), interviews with author, San'a, 1986.

[58] Until 1983, the profits of Sholaq and Baghlaf, in descending order of importance, were windfalls from manipulating exchange rates between YR and U.S. dollars, and YR and SR (physically transporting massive amounts of currency across the border); interest payments and other investment profits from short-term deposits in foreign banks; "normal" exchange rate differentials between foreign exchange prices paid by merchants and market prices in Saudi Arabia; sales to commercial banks, Yemen Bank for Reconstruction and Development, and the Central Bank of Yemen; and the actual 1–4 percent commission on transfers charged to migrants. Husayn Al Saqqaf interviews, 1986.

The second tier, composed of Yemeni exchangers who did not have Saudi branches, specialized in buying and selling foreign exchange domestically, dealing mostly with middle-level merchants. Apart from the differences in volume (in 1982 the turnover of the largest second-tier exchanger, al-Mujalli, was only $149 million, compared with Sholaq's $3 billion), there were functional and organizational differences between the first and second tier of informal bankers.[59] The second tier emerged in the urban areas during the 1970s, dominated by three Sanʿa-based exchange houses: al-Hadda, al-Mutawaqqil, and al-Mujalli.[60] Unlike Sholaq and Baghlaf, who controlled the remittances of the large migrant populations from the south, the second-tier exchangers and their comparatively small client base were from the northern part of the country. Their strong connections with the tribal leaders of the Hashid confederation would become important in the recession, when government regulation drove the bankers underground. Unlike the agents of Sholaq and Baghlaf, whose function was to transport remittances in Yemeni riyals to the countryside, agents connected to second-tier exchangers specialized in buying foreign exchange from migrants and foreigners in the local market. They were, in a word, "collectors" of foreign exchange rather than distributors of remittances.

Informal bankers in the third tier were what one might call retail agents.[61] There were two kinds, "distributors" and "collectors." "Distributing" retailers worked for first-tier exchangers in getting cash to migrant families. By the mid-1970s, subcontracting informal bankers associated with Sholaq had 50 to 60 retailers each. Although the ties between Sholaq and his handful of informal bankers resident in Yemen were exclusive, the structure of the partnership at the lower level was loose: loyalty to Sholaq

[59] Unlike Sholaq and Baghlaf, who employed full-time Yemeni general managers, no second-tier informal bankers had a formal organization but conducted all transactions themselves. Sholaq's offices in Saudi Arabia have a hierarchy of employees, and he had three main managers in Riyadh, Jeddah, and Dammam. According to the rules and regulations governing "category A" exchange houses in Saudi Arabia (see Michael Grinsdale, "Money Changers"), there is a regular accountant, but the largest deals remained outside the books and were usually known only to Sholaq and one other manager. Both Sholaq and Baghlaf provided such services as a *katib* (letter writer) for illiterate migrants, telex facilities for emergencies, convenient hours, and sometimes legal advice concerning local labor laws. Even though expediency has led Sholaq and Baghlaf to choose Saudi nationality, their employees are, without exception, *Shafʿi* Yemenis from Taiz, Hujariyah, Hadramout, and Ibb. Husayn al-Saqqaf interviews, 1986.

[60] A fourth, al-Hariri, went bankrupt in 1978 when his Saudi associate, an al-Rajhi brother, lost their collective funds in speculation on the international silver market.

[61] The information in this segment is based on a detailed survey of migrants in Udayn and interviews conducted in April–May 1987 in Ibb city, Udayn, Hadabah, and Qusah with the following remittance agents: Hassan Aynayn, ʿAbd al-Qadir al-Amin, ʿAli Ahmad Murshad, ʿAli Dahwash, ʿAbd al-Qawi Hadabi, ʿAbd Allah al-Marakah, Qasim ʿAbdul Aymad, Muhammad ʿAbd al-Wahid, ʿAbd Allah Muhammed Mahdi, Hassan Moaz, Ahmad Muqbil, and esp. Qasim al-Mansub, the chairman of the Ibb Chamber of Commerce and the largest agent in Ibb province.

did not prevent retail agents from acting on their own behalf or for other exchange houses.[62] Sometimes two or three agents, in the order of their increasing proximity to the migrant's village, were listed on the transfer authorization sent from Saudi Arabia.[63] The payment time lags for the agents at the lowest end of the rural system were two to three weeks, those for Sholaq regularly one month. Some distributing agents worked independently, but most were employed by the first or second tier of informal bankers. "Collecting" agents, on the other hand, worked mainly in urban areas, gathering small tranches of foreign exchange in markets and remitting it to the second-tier exchange houses. Relatively unimportant in the boom, they were to become central to the financial system in the recession of the 1980s.

Rural remittance mechanisms were diverse, depending largely upon the composition of the migrant community, the migrants' professional specialization, and their host country. It has often been observed, in support of the hypothesis that migration takes place through networks, that entire clusters of villages in Yemen not only migrated to the same area or region but also took up the same work. Migrants from the southern regions of Udayn, Hadabah, Surrah, Qaidah, Yarim, Usfal, Qusah, Jiblah, Dalil, Sanuban, and Hubaysh, for example, and from the Ibb province in general, were construction workers, laborers, merchants by proxy, drivers, and farmers in Saudi Arabia. Here, all levels of "wholesale" and "retail" agents were found, with the two groups working together for small margins of profit.[64] Most of the "retail" agents in Ibb used Qasim al-Mansub, Sholaq's primary associate in Ibb city, as their intermediary between the money-exchanging houses, the banks, and their own activities.[65] For migrants

[62] This flexibility is best demonstrated in the career of Qasim al-Mansub, the most prominent of Sholaq's collaborators in Yemen, who handled transfers also from Baghlaf, ʿAbdallah Salih al-Rajhi, al-Subahi, al-Thalihi, al-Ula'i, al-Kaki, and Khulaydi—all competitors of Sholaq in Jeddah and Mecca. Of Qasim al-Mansub's total business, however, these other exchangers remitted only 10 percent. In addition, in 1967 he acted as an agent for the Yemen Bank for Reconstruction and Development, handling remittances from the United States and Europe. Apart from the collaborators, no independent sub-agents emerged. Qasim al-Mansub and his counterpart in Taiz, Ahmad Qasim Sufyan, used frequent travelers to transport the remittances to rural households.

[63] For example, a transfer might originate in Riyadh and be sent to Qasim al-Mansub in Ibb with instructions to pay al-Amin from the town of Udayn. Al-Amin might receive further instruction from Sholaq's office in Ibb city, or have a regular arrangement of remitting the money to a third subagent in Qusah, a village near Udayn. The lags in this system are often used to advantage by the agents, who may use funds to make short-term investments in precious metals or to issue loans to farmers or rural entrepreneurs at high interest rates.

[64] These systems are described systematically, if somewhat inaccurately, in Lee Ann Ross and John M. Cohen, "An Informal Banking System," Working note no. 12 (Ithaca: Center for International Studies, 1981); and Muhammad al-Ulufi, *Dawr Tahwilat al-ʿAmilin bi-al-Kharij fi al-Iqtisad al-Watani lil-Jumhuriyah al-ʿArabiyah al-Yamaniyah* [The role of migrant workers' remittances in the national economy of the Yemen Arab Republic] (master's thesis, National Institute for Public Administration, Sanʿa, 1985).

[65] The region of Udayn, for example, has a migrant population in excess of 75,000, served by fifteen major remittance agents.

from areas such as Shayr, al-ʿAwd, Damt, and Baʿdan, however, who worked in the United States and the United Kingdom, remittances were sent directly to banks or home by mail order—an option made available by the early willingness of these migrants to invest in roads, automobiles, electricity, and telephones. Farther north, in areas such as Bani Awwam, Saʿda, and Barat, migrants did not use agents at all, relying instead on the regular traffic over the northern border.[66] The informal remittance systems in their fully developed incarnation were thus typical of the southern regions of the Yemen Arab Republic, not of the north, where proximity to Saudi Arabia provided other, quicker ways to send money home.

The vast majority of rural remittance agents were shopkeepers who used their profits to establish themselves early on.[67] In Udayn and other parts of Ibb, almost all the agents were former migrants themselves. The rural agents had the closest contact with the migrants and their families, and the scope of their services was broad, from providing capital for initial migration (which was repaid out of remitted earnings in increments—at a disguised interest rate of up to 200 percent) or lending money for home construction, personal disaster, or bride price payment to acting as a liaison between the migrant and his family or making investments for the migrant in his absence.[68]

The informal banking system was not simply an expanded version of pre-boom money-changing. In both what its practioners did and how they did it, it was an entirely new phenomenon. The old exchange houses had depended on rate differentials for their profits; the informal bankers of the boom capitalized on economies of scale. Their profits depended on the stability of the Yemeni riyal, a condition that was achieved only through the enormous rise in temporary migration during the 1970s. The money-changers' interest in a stable exchange rate was itself an artifact of the boom; in the absence of rate stability and parity of official and black market rates, migrants would have preferred to send their remittances home in the form of hard currency rather than as transfers made through the first-tier exchangers. Lower volumes of deposits and transfers would cut into the volume of hard currency available to Sholaq and Baghlaf to send to interest-bearing accounts and short-term investments abroad.

Baghlaf and Sholaq not only had a keen interest in a stable and strong Yemeni riyal; they were actually much more important than the Central Bank of Yemen in achieving this desired result. Their interest in currency

[66] For migration and remittance patterns in Bani Awwam, see Sheila Carapico and Richard Tutwiler, *Yemeni Agriculture and Economic Change* (Sanʿa: American Institute for Yemeni Studies, 1981), esp. 47–50.

[67] The remittances handled by the more prominent group of rural agents in 1975–78 was between $650,000 and $750,000 a year per agent; others controlled $55,000 to $100,000 per year. The cycle for the larger agents was almost one month; for the smaller ones, only a week.

[68] Ross and Cohen, "Informal Banking System," 5.

stability was thus an administrative bonus for the Central Bank. Indeed, it is no exaggeration to say that throughout the boom years, the informal bankers performed the function of a central bank, flooding the market with Yemeni riyals when they were scarce in Riyadh or Jeddah and buying them up when there was a glut. The aim was to stabilize the exchange rate to prevent a large spread from developing between the rate charged for transfer funds and the rate of the Yemeni riyal in the market. If the market rate rose too far above the transfer rate offered by Sholaq, migrants preferred to take cash across the border instead of using transfers. The efficiency of the informal bankers, in large part, accounts for the stability of the Yemeni riyal against the dollar and the Saudi riyal from the early 1970s until about 1985. The importance of stable exchange rates for the viability of the boomtime financial system became evident during the recession, when the decline of the riyal's value led to the collapse of the boomtime financial market.

Sholaq's and Baghlaf's long-term interest in a stable Yemeni riyal did not prevent them from manipulating exchange rates in the short term. Sholaq in particular held enough Yemeni riyals to create short-term fluctuations in the currency's value, sometimes accomplished by physically transporting bales of currency over the border.[69] In the two- or three-day lag between glut, scarcity, and normalization, Baghlaf and Sholaq were well placed to make windfall profits. This sort of behavior was the exception rather than the rule, however; more often the informal bankers worked with the government and the Central Bank as proxies to stabilize the riyal, aggregate the earnings of migrant workers, and allocate foreign exchange. Two points deserve emphasis: the first is the connection between informalization and internationalization. The second is the informal bankers' interest in and promotion of interest rate stability. The harmony between the economic interests of a completely unregulated group of informal bankers and state officials in boomtime Yemen calls into question the commonly assumed conflictual relationship between informal markets and governmental aims.

Boomtime Regulation and Regulatory Instruments

The increasingly marginal role of commercial banks in both Yemen and Saudi Arabia during the boom period, and the attendant rise of informal and state banks, respectively, in the two countries had a profound influence on the regulatory capacities of the two governments. At one level the boom brought an administrative bonus to the central banks of both countries. Just as Sholaq and Baghlaf stabilized the Yemeni riyal, state lending

[69] Sholaq's Saudi offices had the ability to buy up to YR 60 million per day to bring about these desired changes. Husayn al-Saqqaf interview, 1986.

gave SAMA an easy way to influence the domestic economy without developing other monetary tools; thus a host of conflictual relationships that are usually resolved through regulation temporarily disappeared during the 1970s. At another level it created future problems, for this happy confluence of interests was founded on impermanent economic conditions. Ignoring regulation during the boom not only affected the quality of investments in Saudi Arabia but also meant that the central banks of both countries would enter the recession without the normal range of tools to shape economic and financial transactions. Moreover, the burdens of waiting were clearly cumulative: state regulatory institutions that emerge in the course of customary commercial banking practices were missing in both countries precisely because abundant resources had made them unnecessary in a critical period of growth.

The marginal status of commercial banking was particularly problematic for SAMA, because the American advisers who designed the organization had created SAMA with a view to controlling a financial system comprising formal commercial and deposit banks—a vision entirely different from the system that actually developed in Saudi Arabia in the 1970s. SAMA had little control over the state banks, which were directly supervised by the MFNE. Recycling petrodollars may have propelled SAMA and the Saudi Investment Bank into the upper reaches of international finance, but the boom years created a financial system that was at once highly politicized and virtually impossible to learn about, let alone regulate.[70] Because the boomtime system had drawn few into the formal banking, an important source of centralized information was unavailable to the government when it tried to reintroduce taxation during the recession. Because of the resources at its disposal during this period, SAMA failed to develop the regulatory capacities normally associated with central banks, relying instead on state lending, reserve requirements, and infusions of capital as the exclusive constituents of monetary policy.

Regulatory weakness had important political implications as well. The unregulated growth of deposit banking in the money-changing industry, based on a large clientele of foreign laborers, created both political and financial risks for the government. In the 1970s, money-changers held the funds of millions of depositors in unregulated, non-interest-bearing accounts, yet their establishments often had no corporate identity distinct from that of individual owners. Specifically, there was concern about the Al-Rajhi Foreign Exchange Establishment, the largest exchange house, whose assets in 1972 were equal to all deposits in the British Bank of the Middle East (BBME) and Citibank and second only to those of NCB.[71] Al-

[70] On Arab financial institutions after the oil crisis and their role in recycling petrodollars, see Naeim Sherbiny, "Oil and the Internationalization of Arab Banks" (manuscript, Oxford Institute for Energy Studies, 1985); and Wohlers-Scharf, *Arab and Islamic Banks.*

[71] Grinsdale, "Money Changers."

Rajhi in particular and money-changers in general were known to speculate heavily in international silver markets, real estate, land development, and commodities and to place deposits in interest-bearing accounts abroad. These investments, made in the name of individual owners, were impossible to trace or, in the event of bankruptcy, to seize.[72]

Strikingly, SAMA's control over money-changers actually declined during the boom. In contrast to Ibn Saud's summary treatment of money-changers (he often fined them heavily for exploiting the market and then threw them in jail for good measure), SAMA's responses were meek. The collapse of silver prices in 1972, which resulted in the failure of one of the al-Rajhi brothers' establishments, prompted a mild regulation absolving the government from responsibility for deposits placed with the exchangers.[73] In 1974, after King Feisal refused to issue a stringent law designed by the Finance Ministry, SAMA settled for another conciliatory piece of legislation that created a license requirement and limited the exchangers' activities to remittance transfers, check drafts, and currency exchange. Aimed specifically at regulating deposit-taking activities, the 1974 law gave exchangers three years to return deposits to their clients or to transfer deposited funds to commercial banks regulated by SAMA.[74] Both sets of regulations were quietly ignored; money-changers continued to take deposits. When SAMA tried to review the accounts of the exchange houses, they complained to the king, who promptly issued pronouncements preventing the agency from interfering with their activities: "In response to the strong opposition expressed in reaction to this [1974] resolution by this powerful sector of the community, it was decided not to implement the resolution at that time."[75]

The king's tolerance of the repeated failures of the al-Rajhis stemmed in some measure from their support by the ulema. Perhaps more important, the al-Rajhi family came from the politically strategic area of Buraydah in al-Qasim and had on several times helped the government overcome monetary crises.[76] One such crisis occurred at a time when SAMA had misplaced its accounts in the process of moving its central office from Jeddah to Riyadh.[77]

[72] The potential problems of the money exchangers' bankruptcy are illustrated by figures on the reputed personal net worth of partners in two leading firms: Sulayman, Salih, 'Abdallah, and Muhammed al-Rajhi, U.S. $7 billion; 'Abd al-'Aziz Kaki, U.S. $0.50–1 billion (Grinsdale, "Money Changers," app. B).

[73] Ministry of Finance Circular 11135/12, 1393/6/21 (1972).

[74] Council of Ministers Decree 1012, "On the Profession of Money Changing," 1394/7/12 (1973), prohibits deposit-taking, gives the exchangers three years to draw down existing deposits, and states that no new licenses for the industry would be issued.

[75] Grinsdale, "Money Changers."

[76] For the history of the al-Rajhi establishment and its subsequent problems see Grinsdale, "Money Changers"; and R. Wilson, *Banking and Finance,* chap. 2.

[77] In late 1978, when a tight international market in riyals was not alleviated by three devaluations, Al-Rajhi Company for Currency Exchange and Commerce stepped into the

The 1974 law remained unenforced until 1981, when ʿAbdallah Saleh al-Rajhi lost everything in the silver market. His debts were estimated at $300 million, and his depositors lost an average of SR 20,000 each. Despite its disclaimers, in 1985 the government stepped in to guarantee payments to all his creditors owed $2,740 or less.[78] It was only in response to this rather dramatic event that SAMA generated the political capital to have the king resurrect the unenforced 1974 regulations and issue implementing rules.[79] These rules took the exchange houses out of the jurisdiction of the Ministry of Commerce, a stronghold of the new Nejdi commercial class, and put them under SAMA's regulatory control. Notably, those who drafted the implementing rules felt obligated to cite as legal authority the agency's 1957 charter, which stated that one of its aims was to control the exchangers.[80]

Although the 1981 regulations proposed to close all exchange houses that had not completed licensing, reserve, and other formalities by September 1984, as of 25 June 1984 only one of the eight leading exchange houses had begun the process of applying for bank status and only thirty others had obtained licenses.[81] Effective regulation of money-changers was not to occur until 1986, when the recession forced fundamental changes in the regulatory environment governing all financial institutions in the kingdom.

In Yemen, the ability of the money-changers to stabilize the riyal had similar effects on the Central Bank. The bureaucratic machinery that had performed the functions of a central bank between 1964 and 1971 had been exceedingly fragmented; competing institutional structures created at various junctures during the civil war shared overlapping jurisdictions.[82]

---

market with massive riyal-denominated funds, pushing short-term interest rates from 17 percent back to 10 percent in one day: *Quarterly Economic Review of Saudi Arabia,* no. 1 (1979): 11.

[78] Michael Grinsdale (chief accountant, Saudi Investment Bank), interview with author, Riyadh, 2 December 1985. Although initially the more successful members of the al-Rajhi family did not step in to bail out the failed business, in June 1985 they took over the management of the smaller debts. Up to that time, no arrangements had been made for the institutional creditors of ʿAbdallah al-Rajhi, a list that included international borrowers such as Kredietbank, Lloyds Bank International, and Thomas Cook: *Quarterly Economic Review of Saudi Arabia,* no. 3 (1985): 23.

[79] Ministry of Finance and National Economy Resolution 3/920, "Money Exchange Regulations" (December 12, 1981).

[80] SAMA's charter was issued by Royal Decree 23, 23/5/1377 (5 December 1957).

[81] The net result of the 1981 regulations was that eight category "A" and twenty-two category "B" exchangers had acquired SAMA licenses. Of some 180 others, most survived the regulations of the early 1980s (Grinsdale, "Money Changers," 9).

[82] Monetary authorities included the Yemen Currency Board, the Yemen Bank for Reconstruction and Development, and later, the Foreign Exchange Control Board. The purpose of the board was to manage foreign aid and loans and to set the multiple rates for foreign exchange. In 1970, when the YAR joined the IMF, it followed the fund's advice and replaced multiple rates with a free exchange rate system, thereby accepting by law the de facto exchange regime that already existed.

In 1971 these were consolidated in the Central Bank of Yemen, which, reflecting the country's reliance on aid and on the informal bankers, performed only three functions: printing money according to the directives of the political leadership, distributing financial aid from donor countries among government agencies, and fixing the interest rates of commercial banks. The deficiencies of state regulation in Yemen directly affected commercial banking. For example, inadequate land registration during the real estate boom of the 1970s produced highly confused and contested property rights, which prevented commercial banks from using real estate as collateral for loans.[83] Since 70–80 percent of commercial bank loan portfolios were 100 percent collateralized against foreign reserves held by clients, lending was narrowed to an already entrenched commercial and industrial elite.[84]

For believers in the free market, Yemen's experience in the boom period poses some basic questions about the utility of regulation. Informal bankers, they might argue, met the foreign currency requirements of merchants and the transfer needs of migrants with alacrity. Deposit banking did not develop because it was not necessary. Where there was no motive to protect depositors, why regulate? The short answer is somewhat mechanical: the windfall on which the precarious structure of the Yemeni economy rested was impermanent. The informal financial system that emerged in the boom depended on two specific conditions: stability in the exchange rate of the Yemeni riyal, and parity between official and market rates. From 1975 to 1982 the official and market rates of Yemeni currency held steady at YR 4.6 per U.S. dollar, a remarkable record for any country, and it held steady because it was in the interest of the moneychangers that it do so. In these unusual circumstances, migrants were willing to relinquish control of their Saudi riyal earnings, thereby allowing their wages to enter the informal financial system. The partnerships between second- and third-tier "collecting" and "distributing" agents were predicated on this stability. With any downturn in remittances or any attempt at regulation, the whole structure would have tumbled.

This is exactly what happened in the recession. Once the economy was in crisis, controlling the sophisticated and entrenched informal market even temporarily meant deploying draconian measures that were ultimately ineffective (see Chapter 7). In short, what appeared to be felicitous conditions for regulators during the boom curtailed the state's regu-

[83] Ali Reza (general manager, International Bank of Yemen), interview with author, San'a, 1987. Land registration: director, Land Registration Department, and Husayn al-Hubayshi (director, Legal Office of the President), interviews with author, San'a, 1987.

[84] The remaining 20–30 percent of the portfolios, in which local real estate and corporate assets were used as collateral, had been problematic assets. Ali Reza and Mansur al-Adimi (accountant, IBY), interviews with author, San'a, 1986.

latory capacities and undercut the governments' ability to adjust to new pressures in the economic climate of the recession. In the boom, excess liquidity made regulation unnecessary. In the recession, both governments faced sudden and cumulative pressures to implement reforms in their domestic financial systems and the regulatory regimes that governed them.

There are, however, even more basic connections to be made here. The core argument for regulation is, at base, a political one. Yemen's complete reliance on imported foods meant that any shift in the exchange rate would be immediately reflected in the prices of basic goods. The informal system of the boom period made consumers, and therefore political authorities, vulnerable in the recession. The economic jolt of the 1980s forced the administratively weak Yemeni state to regulate the informal market in order to protect consumers. But by then, divisions between the bureaucracy, the army, and the private sector were deep. Regulation, particularly of the sort that the Yemeni government resorted to, was interpreted through the lens of regional and sectarian hostilities, with profound implications for the political system—not to mention general welfare—as a whole.

Access to Finance

As they evolved in the boom period, the structure of the financial systems in both countries conditioned the abilities of particular groups to gain access to investment capital. In Saudi Arabia the state's control over credit was complete, and contacts with the government determined who could obtain long- and medium-term credit. In Yemen, where the government had no control over remittances or the informal banking sector, resource allocation was managed by an experienced group of informal bankers and entrepreneurs. The structural properties of the two financial systems thus had a profound impact on the composition of the business class, domestic patterns of investment, and the development of entrepreneurial skills. In Saudi Arabia, state lending was one of the primary mechanisms through which the government created an entire class of businessmen and speculators who entered and exited business ventures without learning much about what they (formally) did. In Yemen, investments in highly capital-intensive and import-dependent industries reflected real shortages and accurate calculations of opportunity costs *at the time they were made*, but these industries were utterly inappropriate to the country's resource base when the labor force came home and foreign exchange dried up.

The Saudi government did not use its control over lending to channel resources into productive investments.[85] Instead, state lending institutions dominated by Nejdi bureaucrats allocated funds to their inexperienced kinsmen, creating a new class of merchants, contractors, and industrialists. Legal assurances to both bankers and savers were minimal, as commercial banks and domestic savings were largely peripheral to the state-dominated financial system. The state banks also failed to encourage improvements in the skills of entrepreneurs. On the contrary, they neglected to enforce the standards of disclosure, marketing, and evaluation normally associated with large-scale credit extension by commercial banks. The strong links that developed between bureaucratic bankers and their relatively unskilled clients would prove highly resilient in the recession.

In Yemen as in Saudi Arabia, the structure of the financial system influenced access to capital, affecting the composition of the private sector. Because access to credit depended on personal contacts between the top echelon of informal bankers and entrepreneurs, until the recession the old Yemeni business classes continued to dominate the largest ventures. Returning migrants who entered the retail and service sectors used their savings to make investments. Because commercial banks were so weak, credit for aspiring investors in medium-sized projects was virtually nonexistent, regardless of their qualifications or the viability of their projects.

This concentration stemmed directly from the centralization of the informal banking system in the 1970s. Before Sholaq's service agency separated the control of remittances from the merchant class, merchants themselves had had direct access to capital to finance trade. That pattern broke down in 1967, when the border was closed between the People's Democratic Republic of Yemen and the Yemen Arab Republic. When merchants from Aden, Somalia, and Ethiopia returned to Yemen in the 1960s, they brought adequate savings to finance the volume of trade and the small industrial projects that typified private investments before 1973. Remittance agents and exchange houses facilitated access to foreign currency, but as the volume of industrial and trade finance was small, they did not completely control foreign exchange. In the boom period, by contrast, when imports soared and bulky fixed investments became common, informal bankers became the key links between migrants and merchants, foreign exchange and industrialists. The top tier dealt with large investors, the Central Bank, and commercial banks; the second tier dealt with middle-level merchants. Those merchants too small to use overseas accounts to buy currency directly from Sholaq and Baghlaf were forced to

[85] This finding implies that John Zysman's positive evaluation of state control of finance (his case is Japan) must be modified. To use financial resources in the service of adjustment and productive investments, the government must have an agenda for industry and the institutional/informational capacity to carry it out. Zysman recognizes this fact in the conclusion of his book but does not address the issue in detail; see his *Governments, Markets, and Growth* (Ithaca: Cornell University Press, 1983), 314–15.

rely on the middle tier of "collector" exchange houses and the middle-level managers affiliated with Sholaq.

Throughout the 1970s the upper echelon of the private sector—from the *Sunni* south—never wanted for investment capital. Most industrial investments in Yemen were controlled by a dozen families who financed their largest projects by selling equity shares or bonds to a select group of merchants. In the absence of a formal stock market, this method of financing had important consequences for the size and composition of investors in fixed capital. Ownership was concentrated in a small number of Hujarri commercial families linked by shared experiences in Aden and regional, sectarian, political, and kinship ties. The vast majority of large exchangers, merchants, and industrialists came from the southern *Sunni* areas of Ibb, Taiz, Hujariyah, and Hadramout. Cooperation, trust, and longstanding business contacts among them facilitated ready access to capital but forestalled development of the marketing, accounting, and investment skills normally fostered by commercial banks in the course of their lending activities. This explains the resilience of family organization in business and industry even in the top echelon of the Yemeni business community. The control of major industrial and commercial families extended into the boards of formal financial institutions.[86] For prominent commercial families, default was a convenient method of indefinitely extending the period of a loan. The fact that the top echelon of the commercial and industrial elite was not among YBRD's 20,000 shareholders made this an attractive option.

At the lowest level of wholesalers and retailers, migrants themselves—also largely from the southern provinces—were able to make small-scale investments. The group that had virtually no access to capital were those wishing to make medium-sized investments in industry, imports, or processing and packaging. Here, at the bottom of the private-sector pyramid, the weakness of the commercial banks stymied the entry of new entrepreneurs into the domestic market. The organizational structures of boom-time finance directly produced class formations in Saudi Arabia and reproduced them in Yemen. The causal dynamic of the pre-boom period was turned on its head.

Summary: Beyond Gerschenkronian Economics

From similar beginnings, oil revenues and labor remittances generated two very different financial systems in Saudi Arabia and Yemen. In Saudi

[86] Houses like the Hail Said Group, Muhammad Sayf Thabit, and the Thabit Brothers have members of their families on the boards of IBY, YBRD, and Kuwait Bank. The Hail Said Group and Muhammad Sayf Thabit defaulted on YBRD loans of YR 140 million and YR 80 million, respectively. Ali Reza interview, 1987.

Arabia, oil revenues fostered the establishment of huge state lending institutions that displaced the emerging commercial banks in construction, industry, and services. State-owned banks took over the provision of credit in the agricultural, real estate, industrial, and construction sectors and even came to dominate personal credit. Unlike state banks in European late developers, however, Saudi state banks were funded exclusively by oil rents. Their rise was not coupled with the mobilization of domestic savings, and they did not perform the planning, coordination, and mentoring functions normally associated, in the Gerschenkronian tradition, with state-dominated banking systems. Simultaneously, the influx of foreign workers prompted the growth of branch banking among unregulated money-changing houses, which specialized in deposit-taking (on a non-interest basis), transfers, and exchange activities. With the state lending institutions dominating fixed capital investments and the money-changing houses in control of retail banking, commercial banks were confined to providing short-term credit for imports, construction guarantees, and overseas placements. Credit from other sources undercut the bargaining position of commercial banks in relation to both the government and business.

In Yemen, labor remittances generated a complex informal banking system—completely unregulated by the government throughout the boom years—which displaced existing bank branches and commercial bank agents. In the 1970s the informal system became the primary source of industrial and commercial capital. Increasingly specialized and centralized, it tied the earnings of Yemeni laborers in Saudi Arabia to global financial markets. Unlike the Saudi state funds, state lending institutions set up by aid donors in Yemen remained insignificant, specializing in financing government construction projects.

In both countries, excess foreign exchange fostered a lopsided and weak commercial banking system geared almost exclusively to financing imports. This concentration threatened the solvency of the commercial banks' portfolios during the recession because the bulk of their business was in transactions that were difficult to monitor. The marginality of commercial banks also limited their ability to introduce management, marketing, and project design skills into the domestic private sector. In both countries, these characteristics of the financial systems had a significant impact on the development of entrepreneurial talent, the structure of the private sector, rural and urban investment patterns, and not least, the ability of the government to control credit, interest rates, and the overall quality of private investment. In Yemen, access to foreign exchange depended either on longstanding business relationships between informal bankers and the old merchant class or on the individual and family savings of migrants. In Saudi Arabia, contacts with the bureaucrats that staffed the development funds were crucial in acquiring investment funds.

In Yemen, the financial system facilitated the expansion of the traditional *Sunni* merchant elite's dominance in trade, contracting, and industry. In Saudi Arabia, state lending created a new industrial, contracting, and agricultural elite composed of prominent Nejdis with strong kinship ties to top bureaucrats; by the middle of the boom decade this new class, fed by state bank funding, had displaced the traditional Hijazi commercial and industrial elite.

Financial institutions are the nexus of a host of relationships between business and government. The structure of the financial system affects a government's ability to influence the behavior of industrial managers, firms, and sectors. The decisions of bankers and the regulatory environment affect the size, form, and direction of entrepreneurial investments, define the barriers to entry in particular industries, and ultimately influence the sectoral configuration of the economy and the composition of the business class. John Zysman summarizes this position succinctly:

> The particular arrangements of national financial systems limit both the marketplace options of firms and the administrative choices of government. That is, financial markets in each country are one element that delimits the ways in which business and the state can interact. The structure of those markets at once influences a government's capacity to exert industrial leadership and the nature of political conflicts that arise from its economic objectives. Very simply, in market economies where freely moving prices allocate goods and services, money is not only a medium of exchange but also a means of political and social control: it is one way of deciding who gets what.[87]

The theoretical literature dealing exclusively with financial institutions testifies to the wide acceptance of this view of finance as a key determinant of political economic outcomes. The sources of the changes that shape financial institutions have generated debates on the degree to which institutional change can be explained as a result of external, international factors. To say that finance is a key determinant of political-economic outcomes does not say much about why financial systems differ from one another, or why they change. Indeed, the Gerschenkronian view, adopted in broad form by Zysman, emphasizes the persistence of national structures or institutional "traditions" at the expense of providing clues to how change may be explained. As capital-abundant LDCs that went from virtual isolation to complete immersion in the international system, Saudi Arabia and Yemen contradict many accepted precepts of historical institutionalist theory which emphasize the persistence of "national" styles of financial evolution and regulation. The emphasis of Michael Loriaux and others on the importance of international pressures

[87] Zysman, *Governments, Markets, and Growth*, 16; see 11–80 for the full argument.

and the related shifting opportunities for domestic elites is a useful starting point.[88]

Anyone interested in finance as a window into political economy cannot help observing that most of the scholarship on the subject is based on countries that have stable institutional settings and constituted national regulatory systems. If we probe the question of how different kinds of financial systems come into being, two rather unsatisfactory propositions emerge from the literature on the role of financial institutions in development: they are characterized either as passive agents that grow out of and respond to economic change or, alternatively, as dynamic innovators.[89] According to the first view, following the broad precepts of modernization theory, financial institutions evolve in uniform patterns that match the trajectories followed by early industrializers. Economic growth generates financial assets, which are increasingly held in formal, regulated banks and banklike institutions. Raymond Goldsmith summarizes this position:

> Apart from the different path taken since World War I or II by the countries that have a centrally planned economy in which the government owns most of the means of production, the existence of clearly different paths of financial development is doubtful. The evidence now available is more in favor of the hypothesis that there exists only one major path of financial development, a path marked by certain regularities in the course of the financial interrelations ratio, in the share of financial institutions in total financial assets, and in the position of the banking system, deviations being primarily connected with war finance and with inflation; a path on which different countries have started at different dates, in the two-fold sense of different calendar dates and of different phases of their nonfinancial economic development; a path along which they have traveled at different speed, again in the sense of both calendar time and the phases of economic development; and a path from which they have deviated only to a minor extent.[90]

The second view rejects the notion that all countries retrace the same evolutionary pattern, suggesting that international conditions and timing influence the structure and functions of financial institutions in late developers. In Gerschenkron's classic formulation, backward countries must make bulky investments to achieve the economies of scale already present in their advanced competitors. "Catching up" requires special financial institutions to assume leadership in identifying and funding investments.[91]

[88] Michael Loriaux, *France after Hegemony* (Ithaca: Cornell University Press, 1991).

[89] See Rondo Cameron, ed., *Banking and Economic Development* (New York: Oxford University Press, 1972), 3–25; and Cameron et al., *Banking in the Early Stages*, 1–14, 290–321. The most prominent proponent of the latter position is Alexander Gerschenkron; see his *Economic Backwardness in Historical Perspective* (Cambridge, Mass.: Belknap Press, 1963).

[90] Raymond W. Goldsmith, *Financial Structure and Development* (New Haven: Yale University Press, 1969), 40.

[91] See Gerschenkron, *Economic Backwardness*; Cameron et al., *Banking in the Early Stages*;

The more backward a country, relative to its competitors, the more prominent the role of the state both in industrial policy and in aggregating and allocating savings through direct or indirect means.[92] Sylvia Maxfield offers a third perspective, arguing that differences in the structures of financial institutions in several Latin American countries reflect the relative political and institutional strengths of competing coalitions—each composed of state and non-state actors—that have different economic interests.[93]

The changes in the structure of financial markets in Saudi Arabia and Yemen, however, cannot be completely explained by these theories. To restate bluntly a central thesis of this discussion, no single theory of the origins and evolution of financial institutions explains the patterns of development at the three different conjunctures of domestic and international change covered here. In the pre-boom era, the development of formal commercial banks and state regulatory organizations at the expense of the money-changers and merchants specializing in long-distance trade was largely an internal process connected to the creation of a central state and a national market. The rise of commercial banks reflected the ascendant interests of the Hijazi elite and the Saudi crown in the one case, of the returning Aden-based bourgeoisie and the Republican state in the other. And both were resisted, however unsuccessfully, by the groups and coalitions they displaced. In the boom, however, an entirely different dynamic of institutional change made irrelevant the commercial banks and the state regulatory apparatus centered on controlling them. The impetus for organizational change was generated outside the domestic economy and severed from ongoing domestic conflicts. Change took place in the 1970s because of the opportunities and costs that labor and oil export created for organizations. That classes or groups were beneficiaries or losers in the new political economy became a source of political tension only as the boom drew to a close.[94] Meanwhile, domestic classes were themselves shaped by the organizational transformation of state and

---

Stanley Chapman, *The Rise of Merchant Banking* (Boston: Allen & Unwin, 1984); Cameron, *Banking and Economic Development.*

[92] The former intervention might include the creation of state lending institutions or direct government investment in industry. The latter involves designing appropriate incentives for saving, soliciting outside assistance, and fostering through regulation and legal guarantees a hospitable environment for savers and financial institutions alike.

[93] Sylvia Maxfield, *Governing Capital* (Ithaca: Cornell University Press, 1990).

[94] On its face, the explanatory power attributed here to oil revenues and labor remittances contradicts Maxfield's contention that Mexico's windfall oil revenues cannot account for differences in the economic policy-making capacities of Mexico and Brazil (*Governing Capital,* 188). But there are obvious distinctions between the cases: in Saudi Arabia and Yemen, financial institutions were only first being consolidated at the onset of the oil boom, and these revenues represented a far greater proportion of GDP in the Middle East cases than they ever did in Mexico. Moreover, Maxfield's argument is made in the spirit of much historical institutionalism, and it is thus very hard either to prove or to disprove the causal primacy of institutional change or "coalitional interests."

private financial institutions. The sheer volume of remittances independently created incentives for the expansion of informal banking networks that Yemeni money-changers were best able to exploit, and oil revenues generated state banks within the Ministry of Finance to shape investment through interest-free loans to Saudi citizens. In both instances, struggles over regulation ceased at precisely the moment when parts of the domestic private sector were establishing strong links with the international system through ostensibly local financial institutions. In the recession, these legacies of institutional development and regulatory neglect presented both regulators and entrepreneurs with an entirely new set of circumstances.

There are relatively clear reasons why Yemen and Saudi Arabia do not fit the standard story. But these reasons also illustrate some general conceptual problems in a literature that is important to the extent that it informs policy on newly forming financial systems in countries embroiled in liberalizing their economies. The earlier formulations of the role that financial institutions play in late developers are based on cases where the impact of external economic pressures is mediated by already entrenched institutional and regulatory structures. The financial systems of Yemen and Saudi Arabia in the boom were not spawned by fundamental change in the domestic economy, nor did they emerge as dynamic and efficient allocators of resources in the course of structural changes brought about by industrialization. Despite the radically different financial systems that responded to the influx of remittances and oil revenues, the two cases together attest to the common effects of large volumes of external capital on financial development. The functions that Gerschenkron associated with financial institutions in late developers—aggregating and deploying domestic savings—were irrelevant here. Resources born of global flows of commodities and labor, not the financial requirements of late industrialization in a national regulatory context, defined the context of competition between formal commercial banks, state banks, and informal banking and set the parameters for the regulatory tools available to the central banks of Saudi Arabia and Yemen.

The financial systems that developed in these countries in the 1970s were products of capital abundance, not scarcity. Unlike most countries in the initial stages of economic development, they both had massive excesses in investment and commercial capital during the boom, which obviated the necessity of aggregating domestic savings. This unusual condition delinked processes that have, historically, been inextricably connected: in Yemen and Saudi Arabia, growth in investments and consumption had little to do with domestic savings and productivity. Capital abundance stymied the development of important ancillary institutions, such as a formal insurance industry and a stock market. Moreover, it forestalled the emergence of effective regulatory mechanisms, resulting in the growth of informal and unregulated financial markets in both cases. Where investment capital is made up of local savings, governments have a political interest in protecting savers and entrepreneurs by regulating financial institutions.[95] Capital abundance meant that neither country grappled with the problems common to capital-scarce LDCs. For example, surpluses in foreign exchange allowed the formal commercial banking systems of both countries to function without government controls on import financing, capital flight, and domestic credit. Capital surpluses opened up alternatives to regulation: the Saudi government used the distribution of its oil revenues as a substitute; the Yemeni government relied on the unregulated informal banking sector to perform functions normally associated with central banks.

The experience of capital-abundant LDCs such as Saudi Arabia and Yemen suggests an amendment to Gerschenkron's argument about high levels of integration in contemporary international financial markets. Gerschenkron pictured the international arena as a mirror in which backward countries could measure their profile against that of their competitors, find themselves lacking, and self-consciously chart a course of rapid achievement. He assumed that international competition in *commodity markets* in constituted nation-states determines the role of financial institutions. For late developers to compete with established producers, their volume of savings needs to be both larger and increasingly centralized.

Countries situated in contemporary international *capital markets*, in contrast, are subject to a number of constraints and opportunities disconnected from domestic economic activities. Domestically, integration into these markets is possible through informal financial arrangements. As a result, regulatory institutions in capital-abundant developing countries that are suddenly integrated into global capital markets must innovate in ways quite different from those specified by Gerschenkron, for the problem is not to aggregate savings but to create a means of tying capital to actors in the domestic economy. The informalization of Yemen's entire financial sector and the growth of Saudi Arabia's informal sector in the retail banking industry were directly dependent on one index of sea changes in the international economy: the internationalization of the banking industry in general. The remittance business of money-changers would not have been lucrative or even organizationally possible without the structure of integrated international finance to build upon; globalization and informalization reinforced each other.

In the context of capital flows and the higher mobility of investment capital, earlier models of national financial development such as those put forth by Gerschenkron appear to need revision. Not only are processes of financial innovation no longer necessarily connected to the pro-

[95] See P. J. Drake, *Money, Finance and Development* (New York: Wiley, 1980), 34.

cess of late industrialization, but under conditions of global financial market integration the absence of regulatory institutions at the national level might actually be an advantage for entrepreneurs in the financial sector. In countries such as Saudi Arabia and the Yemen Arab Republic, where the process of defining the regulatory and legal context in which domestic financial institutions would function coincided with the overall erosion of effective national regulation, meeting the changing needs of finance requires regulatory regimes different from those in financial markets formed at an earlier period. In contrast to late developers whose elaborate exchange rate and currency control regimes associated with import substitution might be particularly disadvantaged in contexts requiring innovation, countries that never achieved financial regulation adjust more easily to changes in international markets but at the same time spin out a virtually unmanageable set of regulatory problems for national governments still presiding over national constituencies.

The Yemeni case provides clear evidence that sudden influxes of foreign exchange can at once promote the growth of informal finance with direct links to international capital markets and stymie the development of formal financial institutions. The growth and expansion of informal banking in Yemen belies the view that economic development is coupled with the growth of formal financial institutions in the Third World, suggesting a much more complex set of contingencies.[96] Yemen's experience supports the growing body of evidence for resilience and growth in the informal sector of LDCs in response to international integration.[97] The particular banking needs of migrants and the wide distribution of remittances gave rise to a complex informal banking system that even the most efficient regime would have found difficult to regulate. In Yemen, where regulatory institutions were weak, the sudden infusion of wealth into the informal sector during the boom period enabled informal bankers to develop links with international financial markets while simultaneously undercutting economic and political incentives for new regulatory institutions. A remarkable feature of this entire system—or one that would at least surprise the institutional economists—was that no clear-cut set of contractual relationships governed these transactions. Perhaps the close personal contacts between rural retail agents and migrants account for the fact that of 2,000 cases of abuse reported to the Union of Yemeni Migrants per year, only about 15 were complaints against remittance agents.[98]

[96] See ibid., 5.

[97] For a good review of this literature, particularly on the rise of informal labor markets in both developing and developed capitalist economies, see Alejandro Portes and Saskia Sassen-Koob, "Making It Underground," *American Journal of Sociology* 93 (July 1987): 30–61.

[98] Data collected from the legal department of *Ittihad al-Mughtaribin al-Yamaniyin* [Union of Yemeni Migrants], San'a, 1987.

Political elites in developing countries could charitably be thought of as simultaneously facing two tasks: defining the domestic regulatory environment in which financial institutions function, and generating incentives for investors. Combining these tasks is today more daunting than ever before. The internationalization of capital and labor markets during the 1970s made it increasingly difficult for developing countries to achieve regulatory objectives.[99] Some informal financial arrangements at both the apex and the base of the intenational economy directly contradict the goal of generating national regulatory regimes. Large volumes of illegal trade, labor remittances, recycling of loans and oil revenue, commodity and currency swaps, massive transfers of funds between branches of multinational corporations, and other aspects of international finance put entrepreneurs a step ahead of regulators. In many ways, international capital markets reward the efficacy of the informal in LDCs, which respond to international opportunities with as much alacrity as do specialized investment houses in the developed world. Not surprisingly, a growing informal sector increasingly dominates credit systems in newly industrialized countries, as much in Singapore and Hong Kong as in Saudi Arabia and Yemen, through exchange houses that bear little resemblance to formal deposit-taking banks. Similarly, haute finance is increasingly outside the national regulatory scope—not only politically, as may have been the case in the past, but *technically*. Although governments have a vital interest in imposing and enforcing national regulatory regimes on financial transactions, doing so is difficult enough under conditions of "normal" development. When opportunities to link domestic holdings in hard currency to international markets suddenly multiply, as they did in the oil boom, the soundness of regulatory regimes is a likely casualty. Alternative means of affecting accumulation and investment—distribution in Saudi Arabia; government reliance on informal bankers to perform the functions of the central bank in Yemen—were adequate only for a limited time. With the recession regulatory demands changed: distribution became untenable, and the same informal bankers who had stabilized the Yemeni riyal became the source of monetary instability. The regulators' dilemma in the recession involved a complex set of administrative and political balancing acts. International links precluded harsh treatment of the financial elites, yet the maintenance of political authority ultimately depended on providing regulatory checks on their behavior.

[99] See Chapter 1 n. 30.

Part III

The Bust

Chapter Seven

Beyond the Paradox of Autonomy

In 1986 the international price of oil fell by half, plunging Middle Eastern oil exporters into crisis and shattering the stability of the regional economy. For Saudi Arabia and Yemen, the economic downturn of the 1980s was no ordinary recession: Saudi oil rents dropped from over $110 billion in 1981 to $17 billion in 1986; Yemeni foreign aid fell from over 90 percent of the current budget to 2 percent and remittances plummeted to 40 percent of the 1981 high.[1] The boom was decisively over.

The economic crisis of the 1980s and 1990s slashed the resources that had generated the organizational changes of the boom years and initiated new patterns of social transformation. At one level, for Yemen and Saudi Arabia the difficulties of restructuring the economy were similar, involving nothing less than the creation of national regulatory, legal, and extractive institutions and enforcement agencies. More important, however, the recession sparked a reshaping of boomtime coalitions under conditions of scarcity, generating struggles over who would pay for public goods and under what terms. As similar as these issues were to those surrounding the creation of the national market and central state following World War I, the recession did not replay processes of institutional change from the preboom era. Not only had the capital flows of the prosperous 1970s

[1] *Middle East Markets* 14 (19 January 1987) gives the official amount of $17.4 billion for Saudi 1987 oil revenues. The "lost year"—March 1986–January 1987—had a $16 billion budget, according to a source at the Ministry of Finance, but budget figures for this period were never released. In 1987 the Saudi budget began to be issued in accordance with the Gregorian calendar year, reflecting the degree to which state revenues were increasingly tied to international financial and commodity markets. See *Saudi Economic Survey* 20 (12 March 1986) for a text of the king's "budget speech" and the statement of the Council of Ministers.

reshaped the domestic arena, but the international economy had itself been transformed by the debt crisis, the ascent of the new economic liberalism, and new technologies of communication and production.

For Yemen and Saudi Arabia these international changes had very specific consequences. Reform efforts in both countries were pegged not only to domestic political relations but also to seemingly contradictory aspects of the new internationalization of the 1980s. On one hand, governments were more reliant on domestic sources of finance than at any time since the 1950s; on the other, the parameters of extractive and regulatory capacity were severely bifurcated, with different logics at work for fixed and mobile assets. Robust ties between domestic and foreign financial markets, generated in the boom, thus severely constrained the state's regulatory reach in the recession. The international economy into which Yemen and Saudi Arabia descended in crisis was a capital-scarce one in which the political strategies available to LDCs during the cold war had been substantially eroded. New efforts to tax and regulate thus took place on the ground: the sustainability of domestic coalitions was tested largely against domestic resources. At the same time, the new internationalization of the 1980s and 1990s created ever more direct links between domestic actors and international prices.

Institutional change in the recession was a fluid, multi-dimensional process, suggesting the impermanence as well as the non-transferable nature of state and group capacity. For, with the recession, not one but two distinct dynamics of change were generated in sequence. The first was located in organizations born of the boom; the second took form in the new social movements of the 1990s. At the onset of the recession, mechanisms of institutional change differed little from the boom: nose-diving capital flows first changed the organizations through which they entered the economy; the distributive organs of the state in Saudi Arabia, and the informal financial system of Yemen. In contrast to the 1970s, however, where capital abundance made possible the uncontested wholesale restructuring of society through these mediating organizations, the parameters of institutional change in the recession were set by business-government relations established in the boom, *but not as we might expect.* Both governments responded to the fiscal crisis of 1986–87 in similar ways: reinstituting taxes, cutting government spending and regulating financial institutions, but with radically different outcomes. In Saudi Arabia, the dependent state-created business class successfully opposed state austerity measures and succeeded in gaining even more robust entitlements. In Yemen, the independent business elite was unable to block the state from carrying out a broad-based reform program that all but closed down the private sector. Efficacy and independence co-varied in counter-intuitive ways that belie the historical institutionalists' assumptions of continuity, suggesting, instead, the highly task-specific and contextual nature of institutional capacity and social efficacy. Moreover, it was not simply the chimerical nature of political alliances or "politics" that explained the outcomes: under identical political conditions, institutional capacities varied by *sector.* Thus, however powerful the political determinants of state capacity, a part of the economy—finance—was functionally immune. Efforts to regulate fixed and mobile assets in the recession produced very different results. This fact reflected not just strong links between domestic and international finance but also qualitative changes in what the international economy had become. For domestic actors and organizations, these changes meant that the same set of business-government relations would generate one set of regulatory possibilities for holders of fixed assets—land, commercial property, industry—and another for holders of financial assets.

Reform measures at the onset of the recession shaped the texture of longer-term responses to continuing economic decline, setting the stage for a new conflict-driven pattern of institutional genesis in the 1990s. Yemen's draconian anti-business reforms and Saudi Arabia's economic support for a progressively narrowing group of the wealthiest new business elites meant that through very different processes, the vast majority of domestic consumers would suffer rapidly declining standards of living. The substantive texture of the economic crisis was as important as absolute levels of decline. In the context in which it occurred, organizational responses to the recession essentially undid the complex bundle of entitlements and expectations that had attended the construction of the national market in both Yemen and Saudi Arabia. With the reforms of the first phase of the recession, the distributive bureaucracy in Saudi Arabia and the LDAs and informal banks in Yemen—the organizations that had mediated the impact of the flux of international prices on domestic constituencies and concretely defined the "national" for Yemeni and Saudi citizens in the boom decade—became inoperable. The Yemeni government's reforms drove the informal banking system underground, shattering private-sector incentives in maintaining stable exchange rates and sending the riyal into a dizzying downward spiral. With Yemen importing over 70 percent of its food, inflation and shortages ravaged consumer savings at the same time that capital-intensive boomtime investments foreclosed the possibility of generating domestic employment. The Saudi government's withdrawal of consumer subsidies and the termination of the most broadly based distributive measures similarly introduced higher prices and economic uncertainty into a society characterized by its dependence on the state as the puissant provider. So central had been the flow of capital from abroad in defining domestic relationships that its ebb left not just an economic but also an ideational void in which the very real consequences of economic change in the boom stood as stark emblems of elite failure.

As the recession wore on in the 1990s, an entirely new second dynamic of institutional change began in both countries with very different aggregative proclivities than either those of the boom or the pre-boom period. In both Yemen and Saudi Arabia movements based on the politics of identity—religion, region, tribe—arose in opposition to the government. In Yemen, where the private and public sectors were divided along regional and sectarian lines, the economic decline of the 1990s created a host of tribal and religious movements led by regional elites proposing a variety of sub-national programs ranging from secession to autarkic re-centralization. In Saudi Arabia, where the new business elite and government were united, and where oil still constituted the only viable sector, clandestine Islamist groups organized to overthrow the Al Saud and re-shape a different kind of community. In response to these movements, both governments adopted a number of organizational strategies, often in rapid succession. Many of these changes—the creation of the Saudi Majlis al Shura, Yemeni elections, the Yemeni reunification and subsequent civil war—can rightly be described as fundamental.

The social movements of the 1990s and the responses they elicited from governments signaled an open-ended return to the politics of scarcity after a prolonged period of political stasis. Far from being contests within the rules of an established political system, these movements have sought to re-shape membership and community, rearrange borders, and effect revolutionary change in the geographical scope of the economy and the ideational foundations of politics. Clearly, the transition from the elite politics of the late 1980s to the raw social struggles of the 1990s cannot be understood using organizational theory, for the primacy of political alliances or divisions between business and governments in shaping outcomes in the initial stages of the recession was indisputable. Instead, a closer look at the membership of these movements locates their origins in the deconstruction of the national economy and the subsequent transformation of the life chances of groups located in specific sectors or regions. The recession and subsequent austerity and liberalization programs re-valued endowments according to a new logic that assumed the absence of distribution, prompting domestic actors to realign. The substantive content of these realignments is explored after a review of the politics of the early recession.

EARLY RESPONSES TO RECESSION: 1984–1989

The first impact of the recession was felt in the organizations through which oil revenues and remittances entered the domestic economy. In Saudi Arabia the crisis started in the Ministry of Finance and then filtered out to society. In March 1986, when King Fahd appeared on Saudi television to announce that falling oil prices precluded the possibility of designing a national budget, the disarray of the Saudi fisc became public.[2] Journalistic accounts illuminated the dimensions of the economic downturn, but few observers knew what had happened to the Saudi budgetary process and state spending in the crisis of the early 1980s. Starting in 1982, repeated changes in the budget format made it impossible to compare allocations across sectors.[3] By 1985–86 the private sector was experiencing the full force of the downturn.[4] Real estate prices and rents dropped as the foreign work force departed, generating a 60 and a 40 percent overcapacity in office space and housing, respectively.[5] Commercial banks held substantial doubtful assets; a full 35 percent of the factories funded by the Industrial Development Fund declared bankruptcy.[6] Share prices for major joint stock companies and banks plummeted.[7] In 1983–84 alone, 300 limited liability partnerships were involuntarily liquidated.[8] The effects of the recession were felt most in Riyadh, where state spending had most shaped private investment. According to one knowledgeable source, the number of merchants, retailers, commission-holders, agents, and industrialists in Riyadh declined by 80 percent in the mid-1980s.[9]

In Yemen not the fisc but the informal banking sector was first to be affected. Starting in late 1984, the Yemeni riyal began to fluctuate after a decade of stability. Then, as aid receipts declined in 1985–86, the government paid local bills by deficit spending, putting downward pressure on the Yemeni riyal and creating inflation. By the time the fiscal crisis peaked in 1986–87, the black market rate of the riyal was already setting domestic prices.

When oil prices softened in 1983 the Saudi government imposed some

[2] See, e.g., Emma Duncan, "GCC Survey: Down to Earth," *Economist,* 8 February 1986, 5–40; and Bob Hagerty's series in the *International Herald Tribune* (22, 29, 30 November and 3 December 1985).

[3] The mysteries are fleshed out in "Saudi Budget: Examining the Figures," *Middle East Markets* 14 (19 January 1987); *Country Report: Saudi Arabia,* no. 2 (1987): 12–13; "New Budget," *Economic Review of the Arab World* 22 (January 1988): 17; "Statement of the Ministry of Finance and National Economy on the Budget for Fiscal Year 1408–1409," *Middle East Executive Reports,* February 1988, 25.

[4] *Saudi Private Sector,* 136.

[5] On overcapacity in service industries, see *Country Report: Saudi Arabia,* no. 3 (1987): 22.

[6] According to the Consulting Center for Finance and Investment survey of 1986, 25–30 percent of all private establishments had difficulty with loan payments to commercial banks and reported an inability even to pay the salaries of their workers. See *Saudi Private Sector,* 96, 137.

[7] The share price of the Saudi American Bank, for example, fell from SR 1,300 in 1983 to SR 450 in 1985. CCFI data base; and Mohammad Ramadi (senior vice-president, Saudi American Bank), interview with author, Riyadh, January 1986.

[8] Report issued by the Ministry of Commerce and quoted in *Country Report: Saudi Arabia,* no. 2 (1985): 12.

[9] *Saudi Private Sector,* 166. Saleh al-Toaimi (secretary general of the Riyadh Chamber of Commerce, Industry, and Agriculture) estimated that the size of the upper echelon of the business community in Riyadh had shrunk from 21,000 to less than 10,000 by the end of 1985: interview with author, Riyadh, 5 November 1985.

fees on services, including passports, vehicle registration, document verification, visas, airport use, sponsorship transfers, and mailboxes as well as fees on pilgrims.[10] Comprehensive reforms began in 1985–86, when both governments attempted three broad categories of reform: direct taxation, regulation, and financial reform. In response to broadly similar government efforts to tax and regulate, very different outcomes ensued. In late 1985 the Saudi government reinstated profit taxes on foreign companies and *zakat* taxes on Saudi companies and individuals.[11] The new legislation caused initial concern among foreign businesses, but since the state lacked both the administrative apparatus and the information to assess and collect direct taxes, it was largely ignored. Sporadic attempts to tax foreign companies embroiled the government in legal disputes concerning the juridical status of those registered locally under Saudi owners and resulted in the DZIT's decision to postpone *zakat* collection.[12]

Later efforts to tax incomes likewise failed, because of politics, before the ability of the state to collect taxes was tested. Then, in 1988 the Saudi government announced taxes on both public- and private-sector salaries. Unlike the profit taxes and *zakat,* the government had substantial information on wage earners through the General Organization for Social Insurance. In fact, throughout the boom period, the government had assumed GOSI payments on behalf of both public and private employees. The response of the private sector to this much more credible threat of taxation was immediate: public criticism and private lobbying compelled the oil state to rescind the income tax *within three days of its announcement.*[13]

Saudi extractive efforts failed from a combination of organizational weakness and political resistance, but the state's defeat in efforts to trim distributive programs was exclusively a result of protest from business

[10] *Resolution of the President of the Council of Ministers* 254, 1403/11/14 (1983–84); Resolution of the Council of Ministers 14, 1400/2/26 (1979–80) for airport fees on foreign carriers; Resolution of the Council of Ministers 105, 1405/6/24 (1984–85) for the port fees increase; Resolutions of the Council of Ministers 107, 1405/6/24 (1984–85), and 5, 1406/1/13 (1985–86), for travel and passport fees, respectively. Stamp fees were raised by Decree of the President of the Council of Ministers 291, 1403/12/3 (1982–83); post office box fees were raised from SR 25 to SR 300 in Decree of the President of the Council of Ministers (no number), 1405/1/26 (1984–85); fees for the verification of documents were raised in Council of Ministers Decree 254, 1403/11/14 (1982–83), and Royal Decree M/53, 1403/11/23 (1982–83). On 30 March 1985, the fee for changing sponsors was raised to SR 1,000–3,000; car taxes, for registration, from SR 75 every five years to SR 100–700 per year (depending on value of car): *Country Report: Saudi Arabia,* no. 2 (1985): 12.

[11] See Bruce Palmer, "Tax Exemption Revoked," *Middle East Economic Review,* December 1985, 7; Council of Ministers Decree 103, 1405/6/24 (1984–85), sanctioned by Royal Decree 40, 1405/7/2 (1984–85). The 1985 announcement of the *zakat* collection referred back to the Royal Decree issued by Ibn Saud in 1950.

[12] Saleh Al-Shoaibi interview, February 1986.

[13] The personal income tax for foreigners, up to a maximum of 30 percent, was announced by Royal Decree M/13 (30 December, 1987) and withdrawn 1 January 1988, as reported in "Taxes Imposed on Foreigners in Saudi Arabia" and "Saudis Rescind Plan of Tax on Foreigners after Wide Protests," *New York Times,* 5 and 6 January 1988. For the reaction of both foreign workers and Saudi businessmen, see *Middle East Executive Report,* January 1988, 4–5.

elites. Unlike taxes, cuts in subsidy, loan, and support programs were real threats. Thus, when the government announced its intent to slash subsidies for electricity, water, gasoline, and agricultural production and reduce the 15 percent guaranteed return to shareholders in utility companies, it met with the immediate opposition of the affluent business classes. In response, each measure was unceremoniously withdrawn.[14]

Much more important than taxation and subsidy cuts were the Saudi government's failed attempts to regulate the labor market. Following a boomtime yearly population growth of 3.6 percent and an open regime of labor import, unemployment among Saudi citizens emerged in the 1980s as a major social and economic problem. The contraction of the private sector in 1986 coincided with the government's decision to suspend guaranteed public-sector employment for Saudi high school graduates.[15] For the first time since the 1960s the government tried to introduce protective labor laws and to reactivate programs for placing Saudis in the private sector. Three interlocking sets of regulations aimed to replace foreign workers with Saudis, including a strict review process for new labor imports, new "Saudization" laws, and new social insurance laws requiring businesses to pay 8 percent of the social security previously covered entirely by the government.[16] In response to the new labor regulations, the Saudi business community launched an immediate and successful campaign through informal contacts, the press, and the chambers of commerce. Apparently convinced by private-sector assessments of the expense and nonproductivity of Saudi labor, the transfer, sponsorship, and insurance laws were revoked.[17] The Saudization law was neither repealed nor enforced.[18]

[14] The government statement upon withdrawing the new tariff on electricity users lists its desire to ensure profits for stockholders as the primary motive for the power subsidy of SR 1.7 billion in 1985, and estimated that the total subsidy for 1986–90 would be 2.5 to 3 billion (*Saudi Gazette,* 19 December 1985, 3). Actually, the subsidy for the General Electric Corporation (in billion SR) was 5.2 in 1984–85; 3.3 in 1985–86; 2.3 in 1987–88 and 2.1 in 1988–89: *Middle East Executive Reports,* February 1988, 26. In 1985, the electrical companies had net losses (including guaranteed payments to shareholders) of SR 1.74 billion; in 1986, SR 1.77 billion: *Country Report: Saudi Arabia,* no. 2 (1987): 22. See "Government Reduces Tariff Burden," *Middle East Economic Digest,* 23 January 1988, 21.

[15] See statement of Turki Al-Sudairi (president, Bureau of the Civil Service) in *Saudi Gazette,* 14 March 1986, 3.

[16] Royal Decree M/451/8, "New Regulations for Transfer of Sponsorship" (14 December 1985). The Saudization law required that within five years, 60 percent of private-sector employees be Saudi citizens (*Saudi Gazette,* 11 March 1986, 3). The new GOSI law required that the employer pay his legal share of the insurance. Essentially, the law withdrew a direct subsidy that had covered the entire share of insurance paid by the employer since 1978. For reactions from the merchants, see, "The Future of the Private Sector" and "The Eight Percent GOSI Payment," *Al-Tijarah* 28 (November 1985).

[17] The GOSI payments for foreign laborers due from private-sector employers were withdrawn retroactively from March 1987: *Middle East Markets* 14 (8 June 1987); and *Country Report: Saudi Arabia,* no. 2 (1987): 12–13. The only response was a series of queries by foreign laborers in a column of the *Saudi Gazette* reserved for clarification of legal issues: e.g., "For the Record" column in *Saudi Gazette,* 28 December 1985; 7 January, 4 February, and 11 March 1986.

[18] Wages for Saudi labor in the construction industry were SR 5,000 per month; those for

In stark contrast to the Saudi experience, the Yemeni government successfully carried out retroactive direct taxation of personal and corporate incomes and profits, and imposed a variety of new taxes in 1985. Collections were stepped up in 1986, with the result that receipts for the *first quarter* of 1986 were twice the yield for the entire previous year.[19] Profit, personal income, and *zakat* taxes were collected from the commercial class for the previous six years. These taxes fell inordinately on the southern merchant classes based in Ibb, Hudaydah and Taiz.[20] The impunity with which the Yemeni state pursued its extractive goals is reflected in the number of legal conflicts that occurred on tax-related issues: in 1985 there were 8,001 disputes concerning commercial, professional, consumption, and real estate taxes; in the first quarter of 1986 alone, there were 37,865.[21]

As the crisis deepened the government adopted even more drastic measures. In late 1986 all private-sector imports, including raw materials for local industries, were banned. The government reserved 60 percent of all imports for the newly merged Foreign Trade, Grain, and Military Corporations; instated a strict regime of permits for the remaining 40 percent; and took over 100 percent of basic goods imports. Administrative centralization accompanied the government's direct entry into the economy. State corporations set up during the civil war of the 1960s were revived and reorganized under the Ministry of Supply.[22] Monopolies on trade gen-

Filipinos, SR 1,000 a month. Indian and Bangladeshi labor was even cheaper: Khalid al-Hamidi (chairman, Construction and Contracting Committee, Riyadh Chamber of Commerce; owner, Hamidi Contracting and Trading Establishment), interview with author, Riyadh, 13 November 1985. Businessmen and bankers reported that Saudis were also less disciplined than foreign labor and more difficult to fire: Abdulrehman al Jeraisy (chairman, Committee for Trade, Riyadh Chamber of Commerce), interview with author, Riyadh, 16 December 1985.

[19] According to the director of the Department of Income Tax, direct tax revenue in 1986 exceeded that of the previous year by over 300 percent: directors of Departments of Income Tax and *Zakat*, interviews with author, *San'a*, 1986–87; and a review of Ministry of Finance accounts for all years.

[20] In *San'a*, for example, only 7,000 private-sector enterprises paid taxes, compared with 17,700 from Hudaydah, Ibb, and Taiz. According to the director general of the Department of *Zakat*, there was a 200 percent increase in the *zakat* collected on commercial profits. Information collected from the Department of *Zakat*, San'a; Ahmad Zaid al-Radhi (president of the Department of *Zakat*) and Muhammad al-Rammah (director general, Department of *Zakat*), interviews with author, San'a, 1–7 June 1987.

[21] Kiren Aziz Chaudhry, "The Price of Wealth: Business and State in Labor Remittance and Oil Economies" (Ph.D. diss., Harvard University, 1990), 605, table 11.3.

[22] In the Foreign Trade Corporation (FTC), created in the early 1970s, shares were divided between government agencies and private entrepreneurs (25 percent YBRD, 25 percent government, and 50 percent private shares). In 1976 the company, facing bankruptcy, was made a state corporation by *Qarar Majlis al Qayadah* 146 (1978). The unification of the four corporations was undertaken in two stages: in September 1985 they were put under one board of directors but retained autonomous managing directors, etc.; in 1987 all state corporations were unified to take advantage of common marketing and transportation resources. Abdallah al-Barakani (former general director, Grain Corporation, San'a; director, Agricultural and Cooperative Bank), Muhayyudin al-Dhabi (deputy minister of economy,

erated substantial profits for the government. For example, the same Grain Corporation that had netted a *loss* of over YR 13 million in 1981 had a YR 26 million net *profit* in 1986.[23] The Foreign Trade Corporation, unprofitable during the boom, had a net profit of YR 10 million in 1986.[24] The Ministries of Economy, Supply, and Trade and Industry were merged and made independent of the previously powerful Central Planning Office.[25] For the first time since the early 1970s the unified ministries crafted a single set of priorities for industrial investment and at the end of the 1980s initiated a strict import substitution regime favoring the use of local raw materials, the provision of essential needs, and investments in high value-added goods.[26]

The Special Case of Mobile Assets

Outcomes in the realm of extraction and regulation differed entirely from those in the financial sector. Here, the Yemeni government's efforts to reform the informal banking sector were catastrophically unsuccessful. The Saudi regime, however, after a series of policy reversals, managed to craft an effective set of legal reforms governing relations between businessmen, bankers, and money-changers.

The Saudi economic downturn had reached the financial system in earnest by 1985–86. Commercial banks, specializing in trade finance and construction guarantees, were especially hard hit: the profits of seven commercial banks for which accurate data are available dropped by more than 70 percent, from SR 1.8 billion in 1982 to SR 535 million four years later.[27] The combined profits of the two largest, NCB and Riyadh Bank,

San'a), and Muhammad Saleh Obaad (branch manager for San'a, FTC), interviews with author, San'a, 10 June 1987.

[23] An internal memorandum (n.d.) of the Yemeni Public Corporation for Grains, lists losses and profits for various years (in million YR): 1977, 1.44 (loss); 1978, 2.68 (loss); 1979, 5.58 (loss); 1980 13.75 (loss); 1981 13.54 (loss); 1982, 7.20 (profit); 1983, 3.80 (profit); 1984, 10.77 (profit); 1985, 17.00 (profit); 1986, 26.00 (profit).

[24] Abdallah al Barakani (former director general, Grain Corporation, San'a, interview with author.

[25] These ministries were unified by Presidential Decree 17 (July 1986) and confirmed by Republican Decree 5 (January 1987).

[26] Muhayuddin al-Dhabi and Abbas al-Kirshi (president, Yemen Bank for Industry), interviews with author, San'a, 8 March 1987.

[27] The figures—for Saudi British Bank, Saudi Investment Bank, Saudi American Bank, Saudi-Fransi Bank, Saudi-Hollandi Bank, Arab National Bank, and Riyadh Bank—are from various sources, including CCFI, "Memorandum on Six-Month Reported Profits for Saudi Arabian Banks," January 1986; "Riyadh Bank Reports Fall in Earnings, Total Assets," *Saudi Gazette,* 21 July 1985; "Saudi-French Profits Decline," *Saudi Gazette,* 12 August 1985; "SAMBA Earnings Drop," *Saudi Gazette,* 18 August 1985; "Bank Al-Jazira Profits Decline," *Arab News,* 22 August 1985; "Saudi-Cairo Mid-way Earnings Fall by 39%," *Saudi Gazette,* 3 September 1985; "United Saudi Commercial Bank Loss Mounts to SR. 6.6 m in Six Months" and "Saudi British Bank Earnings Drop," *Saudi Gazette,* 4 September 1985; "Al Hollandi Earnings Fall

fell by 77 percent between 1982 and 1986, plummeting from SR 1.16 billion to SR 267 million. For the three years from 1985 through 1987 six banks, not including the two largest ones, put SR 1.5 billion in loss provisions.[28] As of January1986, it was estimated that commercial banks held at least SR 4.5 billion in nonperforming assets.[29] By the end of 1985 the foreign partners of several Saudized banks were seriously considering selling off their shares. Three foreign banks divested shares in the Saudi Investment Bank and United Saudi Commercial Bank, the two smallest and least profitable commercial banks.[30]

The economic downturn jostled boomtime alignments in the Saudi financial system. Conflicts between bankers and borrowers had appeared by early 1985 and deepened throughout 1986. Although the main clash was undoubtedly between the commercial banks and Saudi businesses, the recession also divided segments of the financial community itself. Foreign and Saudi board members of commercial banks disagreed on the disposition of doubtful loans, the former advocating uniform policies for all and the latter supporting a case-by-case approach with debt rescheduling for Saudi companies. The Saudized banks, in turn, were united against the preferential treatment that SAMA afforded to the two wholly Saudi-owned banks, including non-interest-bearing deposits and less stringent regulation.[31] The recession also sharpened competition between government lending agencies, commercial banks, and their rivals in the retail sector—the money-changers.

These conflicts were resolved in ways that consistently favored the interests of large domestic businesses and contracting firms. Business interests took three positions on the banking issue during the 1980s—each marked by shifting alliances between business, the Islamic jurists, regulators, and

17%" and "Arab National Bank's Earnings Fall," *Saudi Gazette,* 5 September 1985; *Country Report: Saudi Arabia,* no. 3 (1987): 23–25; "Arab National Announces Profit," *Middle East Economic Digest,* 20 February 1988, 30–31; "Profits Rise for Samba" and "Saudi French Reports Profit Fall," *Middle East Economic Digest,* 27 February 1988, 24–25; *Middle East Economic Survey,* 29 February 1988, B2–B3; "Small Profits for Saib," *Middle East Economic Digest,* 12 March 1988, 28–29; and Adnan M. Abdeen and Dale N. Shook, *The Saudi Financial System* (New York: Wiley, 1984), 91.

[28] The six were Saudi British, Investment, Dutch, Fransi, American, and Arab National.

[29] *Saudi Gazette,* 24 January 1986.

[30] West Germany's Commerzbank sold its shares in Saudi Investment to National Investment Company, a diversified Saudi holding company—managed by Mohsin Jallal—with both institutional and individual shareholders: *Saudi Arabia: Country Report,* no. 3 (1987): 25. Chase Manhattan had earlier sold its shares in Saudi Investment after disagreement with the Saudi board of directors regarding action to be taken on doubtful loans to Saudi businessmen. Lebanon's Banque du Liban et d'Outre Mer sold its 10 percent stake in USCB, a partnership of Bank Melli of Iran and United Bank of Pakistan: *Saudi Arabia: Country Report,* no. 2 (1987): 26.

[31] Abdeen and Shook, *Saudi Financial System,* 123. Cash inflows from SAMA were on a non-interest-bearing basis and could be invested abroad at considerable profit.

the banks—and with each shift, government regulations changed to match the articulated interests of Saudi business. The first such alliance was struck in early 1982, when major construction firms and their banks experienced delays in government payments for state projects. Suddenly, a banking activity that had been virtually risk-free and highly profitable became a major liability for commercial banks. In the first phase, banks demanded closer supervision of contractors, including disclosure of profits, assets, and balance sheets.[32] Contractors, in turn, blamed not the government but the banks for their failed projects. As delayed payments and defaults became commonplace, banks initiated legal action against borrowers and began to foreclose on the pledged real estate assets of local companies.

At the first juncture, in alliance with other local businessmen and Islamic jurists, contractors extracted two key concessions from regulatory agencies. First, they successfully lobbied the government to issue a decree prohibiting foreclosure on real estate assets.[33] Second, they won the right to have their cases heard not in the secular Committee for the Resolution of Commercial Disputes, but in the Shariʿa courts, where Islamic jurisprudence was practiced. In the religious courts, evidence of even a single interest-based transaction guaranteed a ruling against banks, for legally, interest did not exist in the kingdom.

The protection afforded by the laws of 1982 soon became a liability for the private sector. Lacking legal guarantees, the banks simply stopped lending. If the first demand of the Saudi private sector was protection from their creditors, the second was for clearer government policies on stalled state projects. By late 1985, Saudi business was turning its attention to the single most important source of the construction and services sector's sudden decline: delays in government payments and the shelving of projects already contracted.[34] In phase two, banks and borrowers vied for first claim to government payments; the banks lost.

As liquidations of local companies, joint ventures, and partnerships continued, the weakest members of the private sector exited the market.[35] This partially explains the change in demands made by business in 1986–87, when banks and borrowers united in favor of broad-based legal reform of the financial system. In December 1985, commercial bank managers and leaders of the Confederation of Saudi Chambers met to construct a mutually agreed-upon set of recommendations to be presented to SAMA. By 1985–86, business elites that had survived the first three years of the recession appeared to have recognized that their long-term survival depended on a stable and cooperative commercial banking system.

[32] Khalid al-Hamidi, interview, Riyadh, 13 November 1985.

[33] High Legal Council Decree 81/8/8/291 (1981).

[34] For a rare published note to this effect, see *Quarterly Report of Saudi Arabia: Annual Supplement*, 1985, 21–22.

[35] *Quarterly Economic Review of Saudi Arabia*, no. 2 (1985): 12; and no. 4 (1984): 18–20.

The new business perspective was reflected in an influential document written under the instruction of the Riyadh Chamber of Commerce and submitted to the government in 1986: "Just when the private sector needs more credit to survive the economic downturn, commercial banks have stopped lending because the necessary guarantees have been taken away. . . . [Banks] need strong legal protection to be able to lend again. Thus banks must be allowed to register real estate as collateral again." The report recommended the registration of mortgages by a government agency, and the acceptance of fixed capital investments and inventory as a legal form of collateral. In unusually bold terms it demanded that the government delays follow explicit policy and be limited in duration to allow businesses and contractors to present banks with credible rescheduling proposals. Arguing in favor of "long-term legal reform to enable banks to lend," the report continued: "It is more important to expand the role of banks than to adhere to the strictest interpretation of Shari'a. . . . We must have a stable legal system governing the long-term loan market, commercial papers, and securities."[36]

Four years into the recession, the business elite of Saudi Arabia had developed, perhaps for the first time, a sense of their stake in uniformly applied laws to govern the financial system. For a third time, and again in accord with new private-sector demands, policy changed. In 1987, in direct contradiction to Shari'a rulings, the prohibition on the use of real estate as collateral and the foreclosure on land was lifted.[37] Between 1986 and 1988 the government issued an important series of laws defining the jurisdiction of different courts and clarifying procedural issues, with the support if not at the instigation of business elites.[38] The implementing rules for arbitration; the civil rights regulations, defining enforcement procedures; the relocation of the inefficient Committee for the Settlement of Commercial Disputes under the jurisdiction of the Grievance Board; and the creation of a new, secular Banking Committee under the auspices of the Saudi Arabian Monetary Authority were the result.[39]

With the establishment of these new rules, rapid changes occurred in the institutional structure of SAMA, in the commercial banks, in the money-changing community, and in the legal system that adjudicated disputes relating to financial transactions. These changes suggest that capital

[36] *Saudi Private Sector,* 202–3, 193, 209, 216–17.

[37] Ibid., 197–200.

[38] See Nancy Turck's descriptive account in "Dispute Resolution in Saudi Arabia," *International Lawyer* 22 (Summer 1988): 415–44.

[39] The Implementing Rules of the Arbitration Law were issued by Council of Ministers Decree 7/2021/M, 1405/9/8 (1984–85); the arbitration rules themselves had been issued by Royal Decree 46 (25 April 1983). See "Saudi Police Court Rules Codified," *Middle East Executive Review,* November 1985, 9; "Grievance Board to Take Over Business Litigation," *Middle East Executive Reports,* August 1987, 7.

scarcity may be a necessary prerequisite to the health of the financial sector. Commercial banks shifted their profit centers from construction and trade guarantees to retail banking and overseas investments.[40] Rapid branch expansion brought consumers into the formal banking system, and deposits increased at an unprecedented rate.[41] Revolving lines of credit were almost uniformly turned into structured term loans, and new overdraft facilities were granted only to the most creditworthy customers, usually in the form of back-to-back lending secured by deposits in overseas accounts. The overall move out of construction and trade lending into retail banking, overseas investments, and currency trading led commercial banks to expand into new overseas markets and prompted structural shifts in the internal organization of the banks.[42]

Similar organizational changes took place in the state banks, although at a slower pace. Moreover, SAMA's efforts to regulate money-changing houses, so unsuccessful in the boom, were more effective in the recession.[43] As a result, the structure of the informal banking sector changed radically: middle-tier money-changers with 20 to 50 branches began to shut down, and on SAMA's prompting the four largest exchange houses applied for banking licenses.[44]

Contrasted with the narrow financial institutions of the boom period, the capital scarcity that emerged in the recession generated renewed efforts to expand and improve the financial services system. After the initial vacillation of the regime between shifting coalitions, state monetary authorities issued a series of reforms that expanded the monetary tools available to the government and recreated a healthy legal environment for lenders. These reforms included the first issues of short- and long-term debt by SAMA, an activity prohibited by its charter and deeply opposed by the religious elite. The creation of debt gave SAMA direct influence over domestic interest rates and liquidity. Higher interest rates expanded the

[40] Wellington Yee (senior credit officer, NCB), interview with author, Riyadh, 16 January 1986. See also "Riyadh Bank Plots New Strategies," *Middle East Economic Digest,* 19 March 1988, 54.

[41] The total number of commercial bank branches grew from 88 in mid-1976 to 524 in mid-1984; see *SAMA Annual Report:* 1403–1404 (Riyadh: Government Printing Press, 1985). Saudi Dutch Bank was able to treble profits in 1987 largely because of staff and salary cuts and a rise in deposits. See "Saudi Dutch Trebles Profits," *Middle East Economic Digest,* 19 March 1988, 54–55.

[42] Peter Wilson, "Banks Treasuries Take Strategic Shift," *Saudi Gazette,* 12 May 1986; Michael Grinsdale and Mohammad Ramadi interviews, December–January 1985–86. On internal organizational changes in commercial banks, see Chaudhry, "Price of Wealth" (1990), chapter 10.

[43] *Country: Saudi Arabia Report* no. 4 (1987): 11.

[44] The new bank was named Al-Rajhi Banking and Investment Corporation; 50 percent of its shares were sold to the public. Its initial paid-up capital was $200 million. The bank took over Al Rajhi's 230-branch network, which had accumulated customer deposits of over $4 billion; see "Al-Rahji Bank Ready for Business," *Middle East Economic Digest,* 6 February 1988, 40–41.

domestic liquid assets of banks, which provided a source of funds for local lending and prevented the outflow of funds to the European market. Previously, the only method of injecting liquidity into the domestic market had been government spending and lending through the state banks, but repayment of the bills with interest gave SAMA an additional method of boosting the money supply at the same time that it forced both deposits and borrowing to be channeled through commercial banks. Interest rates, which had stagnated at about half the levels common in international capital markets, were raised to prevent the flight of capital abroad to Bahrain and to more favorable markets in Europe.

In stark contrast to the Saudi experience, Yemeni efforts to regulate the informal banking system not only failed to achieve the aim of stabilizing the riyal but fragmented the informal system, effectively foreclosing the possibility of future stabilization. The collapse of informal banking vividly depicts the problems of regulating finance by force. In the boom period three large informal bankers had determined exchange rates. Even when the riyal might have appreciated in the mid-1970s, the exchangers had kept the rates stable to protect their reserves, which were held in hard currency. The stability of the Yemeni riyal from 1975 to 1982 was a direct result of the actions of a handful of informal bankers. When reserves were adequate, the free flow of currency across the northern border was actually a stabilizing force on the value of the Yemeni riyal. The government offset its holdings in hard currency by issuing new currency, and remittances and aid flows ensured that new currency issues were covered by deposits with the Central Bank. As the charter of the Central Bank prohibited it from selling foreign currency on the international market, the rise in remittances led immediately to an equivalent rise in money supply.[45] Until early 1983, inflationary pressures were offset by capital outflows for imports.[46]

In the recession, as declining aid and remittance receipts put downward pressure on the riyal, the government made its first efforts to regulate the informal banking system by issuing a largely ineffective set of restrictions on money exchangers and commercial banks.[47] A 5 percent import tightening initially failed as well, because the commercial banks entrusted with issuing permits were both uncooperative and largely pe-

[45] Abdallah Hameed Al-Ulofi, "Al-Dawr al-Tahweelat al-ʿAmileen bil Kharij fi al-Iqtisaad al-Watani lil Jamhuriyyah al-Arabiyyah al-Yemaniyyah" [The role of migrant workers' remittances in the national economy of the Yemen Arab Republic] (internal memorandum, Research Department of the Central Bank of Yemen, Sanʿa, 1987), 12.

[46] See International Bank of Reconstruction and Development, *Recent Economic Developments in the Yemen Arab Republic* (Washington, D.C.: World Bank, 1984); and Ulofi, "Al-Dawr al-Tahweelat," 34–35, on the boomtime equilibrium and the eventual emergence of the black market.

[47] Ali Salami interviews with author, January–March 1987.

ripheral to the financial system.[48] On 2 May 1984, in response to volatility in exchange rates, the government tried to restrict transfers and the flow of currency across the border by requiring approval of transfers in excess of $15,000.[49] This measure, too, proved ineffective, leading in 1985 to a slight devaluation of the Yemeni riyal.[50]

In 1986, as the crisis deepened, large-scale hoarding and smuggling of foreign currency across the northern border became common practices. As the spread between black market and commercial rates grew in late 1986, the government initiated policies that reflected in their bluntness the powerlessness of regulatory authorities. In October 1986, owners of the second-tier exchanges and the managing directors of Baghlaf and Sholaq were imprisoned, immobilizing the apex of the informal banking sector. Administrative reform followed. The Central Bank thereafter issued import permits, and commercial banks were strictly prohibited from dealing with informal bankers.[51]

Unable to restrict the flow of goods and currency across the northern border or to keep pace with the ingenuity of smugglers, the state initiated truly heavy-handed policies on 31 December 1986.[52] All imports of goods and raw materials were banned, and previously issued licenses were revoked. Basic imports, including foodstuffs and petroleum products, were taken over by newly revitalized state trading enterprises. Severe punishment of black market speculators and new restrictions on the activities of the formal banks had the desired result: the Central Bank became the sole purchaser of foreign currency. The complete ban on private imports reduced local demand for foreign exchange. The government itself became the mediator of remittances: in early 1987 the Central Bank made six purchases of foreign exchange from Sholaq, totaling $700 million, exchanged for Yemeni riyals used to cover remittance payments.

To force foreign currency into the formal banking system, the High Economic Commission decided to stabilize the rate of the Yemeni riyal at

[48] IBRD, *Recent Developments,* 35; Azmat Jamshed (managing director, Habib Bank Limited), interview with author, Hudaydah, 1986.

[49] Ali Salami interviews, January–March 1987.

[50] After the devaluation of 1985, the official rate of the Yemeni riyal was 6.48 to the U.S. dollar; the black market rate was 8.00. See IBRD, *Current Economic Position of the Yemen Arab Republic* (Washington, D.C.: World Bank, 1986), 23.

[51] "Minutes of the Meeting of Commercial Bank Managers held on November 25, 1986, under the Chairmanship of the Governor of the Central Bank Mohammad Ahmad al Junaid" (English translation of internal memorandum of Central Bank of the YAR, San'a, November 1986).

[52] Among the most ingenious methods was suspending weighted bags of currency from fishing boats to conceal them from customs officials. Hard currency and Yemeni riyals were thus transferred to Somalia and Ethiopia and thence flown to Jeddah. The riyals were destined for Sholaq's and Baghlaf's offices; dollars were deposited by middlemen in formal bank accounts. This was a method used by southerners who lacked strong links with the northern tribal sheikhs and were unable or unwilling to solicit their cooperation.

11.88 to the U.S. dollar[53] by unilaterally raising the rate of the dollar from 9.0 to 11.88 YR in the first two weeks of March 1987. By mid-March the black market rate for the U.S. dollar was lower than that set by the Central Bank.[54] Hoarded currencies, in particular those held by less sophisticated members of the business community, found their way into the Central Bank seeking the more attractive rates: in those two weeks the Central Bank purchased over $300 million in foreign exchange from Yemeni nationals and gained control of $2–3 million per day in remittances now sent through the YBRD.[55]

These heavy-handed policies were not a sign of strength but a direct reflection of the weakness of the economic and monetary tools available to the government. The texture of the reforms was a sign of administrative weakness, but the political capacity of the government to carry them out signified the political expendability of commercial elites and informal bankers. Moreover, the brute manipulation of currency values was possible only because Yemen had no material exports. Economic weakness, paradoxically, became the basis for decisive, if ultimately unsuccessful, monetary reform: the Central Bank's policies of 1986 would have been suicidal had Yemen had exports other than labor.

The reforms controlled the informal market for less than three months. Even this limited success was the result of uncertainty created in the financial system and the harshness of the policies more than of any real formalization of banking. Temporary control of remittances was made possible by the fact that Sholaq's offices were closed and his functionaries in prison. Banks were forced to remit all foreign exchange purchases to the Central Bank immediately and were compensated in newly issued Yemeni riyals. The resulting excess liquidity of Yemeni riyals actually undercut the government's aim of driving the riyal into formal banks: on May 7 commercial banks stopped giving interest on riyal-denominated accounts, and two weeks later they stopped taking riyal deposits altogether.[56]

Effective in the very short term, then, the reforms destroyed the possibility of future financial reforms in Yemen. The highly centralized informal banking system of the boom period fragmented completely, driving

[53] Yemen Arab Republic Banking Control Department Circulars 38391, "Taʿmeem ila Kafaat al Banook al Tijariyyah al ʿAmila fi al Jamhuriyyah" [To all commercial banks operating in the Republic] (31 December 1986), and (no number), "Taʿmeem ila Kafaat al Banook al Tijariyyah al ʿAmila fi al Yemen" [Circular to all commercial banks operating in Yemen] (13 January 1987).

[54] On the theoretical possibility of this phenomenon, see Sanjeev Gupta, *Black Market Exchange Rates* (Berlin: J.C.B. Mohr, 1981), 7–17.

[55] See "YAR Government Centralizes Foreign Exchange Purchases," *Middle East Economic Digest*, March 14, 1987.

[56] The government tried to alleviate the pressure on the banks by offering commercial banks a deposit rate of 7 percent for riyal deposits in the Central Bank. Anticipating the failure of state regulatory strategy, commercial banks refused.

the remittance system and private imports underground. In the new environment of mid-1987, the second-tier informal bankers based in Yemen developed strong ties with northern tribal sheikhs to facilitate the smuggling of truckloads of Yemeni currency to Saudi Arabia, where it was sold to Sholaq, Baghlaf, and other money exchangers.[57] Retail exchangers specializing in purchasing small amounts of locally held foreign exchange on behalf of merchants grew from about 20 persons in 1983 to over 260 in 1987 in the capital city of San'a alone. The reforms created strong incentives for individual migrants to bring their earnings home (in goods or currency) instead of remitting them at the officially fixed transfer rate; according to one knowledgeable source, this method of transfer had expanded to encompass 80 percent of remittances by mid-1987. Regulation undertaken without the cooperation of the informal bankers had failed completely: the days of monetary stability were over.

Explaining the Outcomes

In the boom period, the flow of oil revenues and remittances to Saudi Arabia and Yemen generated outcomes in broad conformity with the argument that access to resources produces efficacy and independence. Oil revenues empowered the Saudi bureaucracy to reshape the economy and society; labor remittances, aggregated through the informal banking system, fueled the rapid expansion of a powerful and independent private sector in Yemen. If the balance of business and state power at the end of the boom decade could be used to predict outcomes in the recession, one could reasonably expect the financially autonomous Saudi government to implement austerity measures over the objections of the dependent, state-created business groups. Similarly, one might have predicted that the wealthy and independent Yemeni business class would be able to protect its interests, if not influence the overall course of economic policy. Beginning with similarly undeveloped extractive and regulatory capacities, Saudi Arabia and Yemen varied markedly in the effectiveness of the austerity measures they pursued during the recession. Outcomes in the first phase of the recession differed in three categories: institutional innovation, political capacity, and regulation of fixed or mobile assets.

Government capacity to implement policy and the ability of business to resist or influence economic policy varied by case and by sector. Not only was the relationship between boomtime state capacities reversed between Yemen and Saudi Arabia, but the wide variation between outcomes in

[57] Saudi riyals, bought at YR 2.94/SR, were smuggled back to the Yemeni market and sold at YR 4.53/SR. For their services the smugglers received YR 10,000 for every million SR or YR taken across the border. Husayn al-Saqqaf and several anonymous smugglers in Jawf, interviews with author, 1986–87.

different sectors keenly illustrates the poverty of monolithic views of state capacity and political autonomy. State capacities are not, as these two cases show, transferable across different functional tasks: the regulation of fixed and mobile assets requires radically different capacities, both administrative and political. Moreover, alliances struck in prosperity did not persist in crisis. The ability of both governments and social groups to affect policy in the recession depended, rather, on a host of factors. Important among these were, first, the strength and vitality of civil organizations in society. In Saudi Arabia, where the distributive policies of the boom period had destroyed local associations, little social infrastructure existed to redeploy the regulatory and extractive apparatus of the state. In Yemen, by contrast, local institutions formed an important basis for institutional innovation. Second, different patterns of business-government relations were critical to producing the two outcomes. In Saudi Arabia, where business and state were united by kinship and financial ties, austerity reforms failed; elite pressure forced the government to abandon its reform package. In Yemen, deep ascriptive divisions between the powerful *Sunni* private sector and the *Shiʿa* bureaucracy and military empowered the government to impose austerity measures with impunity. Where the political will existed—where business and state were divided—tax institutions were enormously resilient.

An entirely different set of political prerequisites for policy success prevailed for mobile assets. The regulation of finance—unlike trade, industry, and real estate—required the consent if not the active participation of private-sector elites. In finance, the same links between the top echelon of private-sector elites and the state which forestalled austerity and taxation enabled the Saudi government to implement broad institutional changes that withdrew important concessions from the domestic business classes but extended legal protection to solvent borrowers and banks. Similarly, Yemen's ability to override private-sector elite interests in fixed asset sectors rested on the very same set of relationships that doomed financial reforms to failure. Sectoral variation in state capacities and business efficacy was not just a measure of the social basis of the two regimes; it was also a primary index of the rapid internationalization of the Yemeni and Saudi economies during the boom decade. Finance linked both economies to international markets, generating a new kind of policy dilemma for governments and dividing business interests.

The clearest difference between the Saudi and Yemeni experiences was in the relative ability of the two governments to revitalize extractive institutions. In Yemen, where the government had abrogated administrative and extractive tasks to locally controlled civil institutions, the bankrupt state was able to expand its extractive and information-gathering agencies by co-opting the leadership and organizational structure of the Local Development Associations. The LDAs had been collecting local and service taxes since the central government ceded them this right in 1975. In 1986 the expansion of the state's presence into the remote rural areas of the south was achieved through the reorganization of the LDAs, which were then entrusted with collecting and remitting to the government the agricultural, *zakat,* and commercial taxes and land transaction fees. Through the Confederation of Yemeni Development Associations (CYDA), the central government appropriated the services of an existing cadre of local leaders at little cost. Equipped in San'a with newly acquired knowledge in accounting and reporting procedures and accompanied by police, LDA leaders went back to assume posts as administrators in their home regions.[58] Stripped of their independence, they became the mayors, administrators, and tax collectors in the remote rural areas of the south.[59]

The Yemeni tax and *zakat* departments were completely restaffed and reorganized.[60] The number of branches of the Central Tax Department grew from 6 in 1980 to 21 in 1986; DZIT's provincial branch employees went from 409 in 1980 to 1,059 in 1986.[61] Information collection expanded with DZIT's first survey of commercial establishments. The reorganized Land Registration Department initiated the first cadastral survey.[62] In the traditional urban markets of San'a, Ibb, and Taiz, the heads of craft and trade guilds and domestic produce associations were identified and employed by the state to perform a variety of regulatory and taxing functions which, predictably, met some not inconsiderable local resistance.[63]

Whereas the Yemeni reforms were made administratively easier and less expensive by the government's adaptation of existing institutions in civil society, the Saudi state—having deliberately destroyed civil institutions in the boom period, substituting the sinews of the distributive bureaucracy

[58] Director of financial and administrative departments, General Union for Local Councils (formerly CYDA) Ahmad Zaid al-Radhi and Muhammad al-Rammah interviews, August 1986–July 1987. See also Republican Decree 12, "Establishment of Local Councils" (1985).

[59] See General Union of Local Councils, "The New Administrative Structure for the Local Councils" (internal memorandum, San'a, 1986); and Abdul Aziz al- Saqqaf, "Redirecting the Cooperative Effort in the YAR" (manuscript, San'a University, 1986).

[60] Information on the reorganization of the Tax Department was collected by the author in numerous interviews with Sheikh Al Hajarri (director, Department of Income Tax) and his staff, San'a, August 1986–July 1987.

[61] Data collected from Department of *Zakat* and Income Tax, San'a, 1987. For details, see Chaudhry, "Price of Wealth" (1990), 606, tables 11.4A–11.4C.

[62] "The Registry Department Law," *Qarar Jamhurri* 34 (1987).

[63] Most resistance took the form of quiet noncompliance. I witnessed an interesting case involving the government's attempts to force *qat* sellers in Taiz to sell in the official government market, where assessment of the 10 percent *qat* tax was easily imposed. Many of the vendors were women from the Jabal Sabr region, where, for reasons that remain unclear, females rather than males are responsible for cultivating and marketing the narcotic leaf. The head (*agil*) of the *qat* market, entrusted with moving vendors to the newly built and state-supervised market outside the city but prevented by custom from physically removing the female vendors, finally arrested male members of the vendors' families in their homes and held them hostage until the women complied. Vendors and Said Abdallah Khalid (*agil suq al-qat*), interviews with author, Taiz, 24–29 March 1987.

for local organizations—was ineffective in redeploying its tax apparatus. Variation in the Saudi and Yemeni patterns of institutional innovation suggests the importance of civil institutions for the success of the state's extractive and regulatory efforts. The task of reshaping the huge distributive bureaucracy in Saudi Arabia was, moreover, qualitatively different from that of creating institutions anew.

Institutional inertia is clearly central to any explanation of the oil state's inability to tax and regulate; however, the origins of these failures were as much political as institutional. Where the political will existed, as in Yemen, organizations were remarkably resilient. Finding the answer to divergent institutional outcomes, then, ultimately thrusts the analysis back onto differences in business-government relations as they had evolved in the boom. In both cases, state efficacy and the relative strength or weakness of business elites can be explained by examining patterns of social and occupational stratification during the boom years. Between 1973 and 1986 the composition of the business classes and the bureaucracies in Yemen and Saudi Arabia was conditioned by the distribution of economic opportunity in the public and private sectors, reflecting variations in the control that the state and the private sector had over oil rent and remittances.

In Yemen, remittances expanded private-sector opportunities for the more educated southern *Sunni* groups; the less lucrative positions in the bureaucracy and the armed forces were staffed by northern *Shi*ʿ*as* and tribesmen. Occupational divisions, as I showed earlier, predated the boom period. In the 1970s, however, the dramatic expansion of the private sector had added stark income disparities to existing divisions between the public and private sectors. Over the boom period, local capital and the bureaucracy were separated by a variety of regional, economic, and sectarian cleavages, allowing the northern state to override the interests of southern entrepreneurs in the recession. Because it divided business and state, both of which had functioned in parallel spheres of mutual noninterference, the replication of sectarian and regional cleavages in the public and private sectors in the boom became a source of state strength in the recession. The regime's commitment to a free economy lasted only until the recession, after which the interests of the northern tribal elites, the army, and the bureaucracy merged with the state's pressing need to replace diminishing aid revenues with local taxes. Precisely because state regulation was virtually absent in the boom, the independent and affluent Yemeni merchant class had not cultivated institutionalized ties with the state bureaucracy.

By contrast, the Nejdi business class and the bureaucratic elite of Saudi Arabia were linked by kinship *and* economic ties.[64] During the recession

[64] On the tribal basis of the state, see Mordechai Abir, "The Consolidation of the Ruling Class and the New Elites in Saudi Arabia," *Middle Eastern Studies* 23 (April 1987): 150–71.

these ties allowed the Saudi private sector to block government policies and reverse the dictates of the financially autonomous oil state. Saudi spending policies over the boom decade married tribal privilege with economic dependence, embroiling the state in patronage relationships that prohibited economic reforms in the lean years of the 1980s.

If political distance built on ascriptive and occupational divisions explains the outcomes of regulatory and extractive policies, these same links provide the key to understanding the differences in the two governments' abilities to regulate the financial sector. Whereas coercion and corporatism enabled the Yemeni government to tax and regulate fixed private assets, they did not empower the state to restructure the domain of mobile assets. Redesigning the institutional context governing finance, as is frequently observed, requires the cooperation of mobile asset holders.[65] Thus, the blunt instruments of Yemeni regulation had entirely different effects in the financial sector than in trade, industry, and services. The Saudi financial regulations, occurring as they did with the support if not under the direction of the domestic business elite, eventually succeeded in eliciting the cooperation of both banks and business.

Business Rebuilt

As the 1980s wore on, distinct changes in the Yemeni and Saudi private sectors signaled the consolidation of links between the upper echelons of the Nejdi business class and the emergence of a new state-sponsored tribal business group in Yemen. In Saudi Arabia, even as the lower tiers of the state-created Nejdi business class were pushed out of private-sector activities, business leaders gained even more concessions from the government. That prominent businessmen successfully promoted policies in opposition to foreign businesses, retailers, wholesalers, and Saudi labor revealed the consolidation of the private-sector elites. These elites sponsored broad-based protective measures against foreign competition in commodities and contracts.[66] To achieve the protection intended under the "Buy Saudi" laws, Riyadh's businessmen successfully lobbied to create a centralized government agency, made up of representatives from the Confederation of Saudi Chambers, to promote government use of locally produced supplies.[67] In 1984 the government issued strict guidelines requiring government contractors to use only local products, if available,

[65] Cf. Robert Bates and Da-Hsiang Lien, "A Note on Taxation, Development, and Representative Government," *Politics and Society* 14, no. 1 (1985): 53–70.

[66] For a general (and excessively optimistic) review see "The Investment Climate," *Middle East Executive Reports*, October 1985, 9.

[67] *Saudi Private Sector*, 173–74, 176. According to local industrialists, the "Buy Saudi" rules requiring state agencies to procure as many supplies as possible from domestic producers are inadequate because of gaps in the state's knowledge about locally produced goods, weak systems for exchanging information, and the inability of local industrialists to interpret the rules in their favor. Khalid al-Hamidi interview, 13 November 1985.

and only local services, transport, insurance, food, and banking. In response to contractors' demands, the 30 Percent Rule was expanded, and the government agreed to split all contracts into small portions appropriate for local contractors.[68] Broad policing powers were delegated to the Confederation of Saudi Chambers, now utterly dominated by Nejdi business elites, to investigate complaints of local suppliers against government agencies and to link up suppliers and subcontractors with specific government projects.[69] In December 1985 an export promotion agency was set up, with the participation of 160 businessmen, to study and distribute export subsidies to local manufacturers.[70] Local industry was granted increased protection in the form of higher tariffs, against the interests of both consumers and Saudi importers. Business elites gained in negotiating the status of delayed government payments by the expansion of the Grievance Committee designed to hear private-sector cases against government agencies.

The recession increased the businessmen's awareness of their collective interests in relation to other actors such as labor, foreign companies, consumers, and the government, yet it also heightened competition between subsectors of the business community, each seeking to influence government policy to accommodate its specific interests. Consequently, policies vacillated, favoring first one group and then another. Importers complained that tariffs, which were at once a source of revenue and protection for local industry, were raising prices on imported goods at a time when domestic demand was shrinking. Local industries began to employ new marketing devices that undercut the market shares of traders in imported goods. Some even argued that government promotion of domestic exports was an unnecessary bonus for local industries, strengthening them at the expense of traders in imported goods. Conflict also emerged between small traders who catered to low-income urban groups and large retailers who had high overhead costs.[71]

The demands of the Saudi business elite were increasingly expressed through the institutional medium of the chambers of commerce. The changing role of the Riyadh Chamber, and of the Saudi Confederation of

[68] *Quarterly Economic Review of Saudi Arabia: Annual Supplement,* 1985, 21. An earlier ruling issued 6 August 1984 had required foreign contractors to include the names of local contractors who would receive 30 percent of the contract work: *Quarterly Economic Review of Saudi Arabia,* no. 4 (1984): 10–11.

[69] Rules on standard forms for public-sector contracting, consulting, and supplies were issued in the daily newspaper *Al-Riyadh,* 6 November 1984, 7. The implementing rules for revised "buy Saudi" regulations and subcontracting were issued in Ministry of Finance Circular 5767/404 (6 August 1984).

[70] *Arab News,* 10 December 1985. The Export Promotion Committee was to work in conjunction with a newly created Exporters' Association created in 1985 in the Riyadh Chamber of Commerce; Abdulrehman al-Jeraisy (Chairman, Committee for Trade, Riyadh Chamber of Commerce), interview with author, Riyadh, 16 December 1985).

[71] Abdulrehman al-Jeraisy interview, 16 December 1985; *Saudi Private Sector,* 147.

Chambers in general, reflected the rise of a peak organization empowered to articulate business demands. The chambers, moreover, were unique in their collective access to decision-makers; no comparable organization existed for labor, consumers, traditional farmers, small businessmen, or, indeed, any other group.

While the state-created business elite consolidated control in Saudi Arabia, traditional private-sector elites in Yemen were in the process of being displaced by the new economic policies of the 1980s. In essence, the austerity measures signaled the Yemeni government's abrogation of the republican pact of noninterference, struck at the end of the civil war in 1971, between the northern dominated state and the southern private sector. As in Saudi Arabia, the direct entry of the state into the economy went hand in hand with patronage for politically significant ascriptive groups. In Yemen the patronage flowed mainly to militarily powerful northern tribal leaders, who had been the beneficiaries of direct subsidies from Saudi Arabia in return for their opposition to unity talks between the Yemen Arab Republic and the socialist People's Democratic Republic of Yemen. Through control of the upper ranks of the army and the powerful Permanent Council, tribal leaders had also developed substantial influence in the military and the executive during the 1970s.[72] In the recession, Riyadh began to withdraw its financial and military support for Yemeni tribal leaders, creating scarcities that undercut the patronage networks through which they had maintained control over the rank and file. Nevertheless, state regulation of the financial sector and the ban on private imports enriched the northern tribes through two mechanisms. First, by dominating the northern territories, the tribes gained control of the buoyant smuggling trade over the Saudi border.[73] Collaboration among kinsmen in the army and the tribes facilitated the flow. In addition, state-controlled imports were largely subcontracted to influential northern tribal sheikhs, many of whom had personal or political connections with President Ali Abdallah Saleh, himself a member of the Hashid tribal confederation. The new tender system for government imports involved intermediaries who contracted with foreigners for imports and were entitled to a share for local distribution. The rules stipulated that the tender winners would import 100 percent of the country's requirements and then allocate 60 percent of these to the government for sale through state-owned corporations and wholesalers chosen by these corporations. In 1986, for

[72] Yemen's President Ali Abdallah Saleh is a Hashid but does not have a position of tribal leadership. Major tribal leaders who sit on the council include Abdallah al-Ahmer, leader of the Hashid confederation and president of the Permanent Council, and Sinaan Abu Lahoom, sheikh of the Nahim tribe in San'a province.

[73] Interviews conducted by the author with leading merchants and industrialists in San'a Hudaydah and Taiz, January–February 1987. See also Special Political Announcement on the Current Economic Conditions, (internal memorandum, drafted for the People's Assembly, San'a, 1986), and *Qarar Majlis al-Wuzara al-Iqtisadiyya* (no number) (9 August 1986).

example, state tenders were awarded *exclusively* to northern tribal elites, who thereby gained monopolies on basic goods.[74]

The government's new trade monopolies eliminated the activities of large segments of the Yemeni commercial elite and made significant private-sector investments in industry, cold storage, repackaging, and transportation redundant. When the Taiz and Ibb Chambers of Commerce were placed under the north-dominated Confederation, the government blocked institutionalized channels for traditional southern business seeking to influence state policy. Thus, the benefits of independence in the boom became a crippling liability in the recession. In the context of politicized ascriptive divisions, the expansion of government agencies into the southern rural areas during the recession reflected and magnified a growing social polarization in Yemen, even as the use of existing local institutions made the sudden reintroduction of government taxation possible. In the larger context of Yemeni politics, then, the government's reform measures were deeply divisive, particularly in light of the renewed alliance between the state and the northern tribal chiefs and their subsequent takeover of key import and wholesale sectors.[75]

The outcomes of the 1985–86 reforms could hardly have been predicted by using a deductive method. Institutional change occurred in both cases but reflected neither the apparent strength of government and business groups nor higher efficiencies prompted by scarce resources. Rather, changes in the extractive and regulatory regimes of both countries followed a logic based on the political constraints imposed by groups and relationships that had emerged in the preceding period of the boom. State autonomy, efficacy, and capacity varied by case, by sector, and over time—as did the preferences and the efficacy of the different segments of the private sector. More important, sectors based on fixed assets—trade, industry, agriculture—were shaped by a logic quite different from that which applied to mobile assets. Yemeni success in implementing a regime

[74] Figures for grain imports, which became 100 percent government controlled in 1986 and were managed by the Grain Corporation, a state-owned enterprise, show the following distribution of total subcontracts (all but one to prominent tribal sheikhs): Sheikh Al Roayshaan, 17 percent; Sheikh Abu Lahoom, 39 percent; PL 480 aid, 34 percent. The figures for sugar import, also government controlled since 1986, are equally revealing: al-Faahim (old Sana'ani merchant family), 20 percent; Sheikh Musallim, 23 percent; Sheikh al-Ahmer, 20 percent. For flour, all the contracts went to Sheikh Al-Roayshaan of Kholan. Grain Corporation of the Yemen Arab Republic, internal memorandum, San'a, 1986.

[75] Because of the social organization of the tribes and the fact that their leaders were in military control of the northern regions of Jawf, Marib, and Sa'da, the government organizations set up in these regions in the mid-1980s were directly dependent on the tribal leaders for their authority. The clearest example involves the method by which land titles are recognized and the evaluation process for loans for the extensive agricultural developments in Marib after construction of the dam. Loans required formal title, which was guaranteed by the leader of the tribe; tribal leaders were also guarantors of loans to farmers. Director of the Marib branch of the Agricultural Development Bank, interview with author, Marib, 1987.

of taxation and regulation bespeaks the political capacity of an impoverished state to force compliance from a powerful and affluent private sector. The Saudi case reveals the political fragility of a powerful oil state confronted with resistance from a dependent, state-created private sector. In regulating finance, however, the opposite outcomes ensued. In Saudi Arabia the financial system was effectively stabilized and a comprehensive system of legal mechanisms was created to mediate disputes between the government, the banks, and borrowers. In Yemen the government's efforts to eliminate the black market, control the informal banking system, and stabilize the riyal led to a fragmentation of the informal banking structure and, ultimately, to a complete loss of government control over money and finance. The Yemeni state's political independence from the private sector, in short, was not effective when deployed to regulate finance. The contrasting experience of Saudi Arabia suggests that regulating mobile assets requires the cooperation, if not the direct involvement, of private-sector elites. The formulation of policy and response to policy in the early phase of the recession was confined to business, bureaucratic, and tribal elites. Support for financial reform among elites in Saudi Arabia stabilized an increasingly narrow business-government coalition, but the Yemeni government's initial reforms led to a complete break with the private sector and foreclosed the possibility of business-government cooperation.

The Second Phase: Unmediated Prices and Social Change

As the 1990s opened, substantial domestic opposition to economic conditions had developed in both Saudi Arabia and Yemen. In the second phase of the recession (1990–95) both countries experienced a deteriorating economy, coupled with the emergence of social movements centered squarely on issues of redistribution and the reconstitution of politics on a new ideational and organizational level. This reconstitution produced a strong religious opposition in Saudi Arabia and a plethora of regional, tribal, and sectarian groups in Yemen. In both cases the composition and political claims of these groups were responses to new opportunities and costs generated in the recession. The rebirth of politics centered on economic issues and articulated in the language of identity was a response not to scarcity alone but to a very specific set of economic conditions that were, arguably, peculiar to the late twentieth century. For rank-and-file Saudis and Yemenis, the second phase of the recession initiated a period of economic uncertainty associated with an institutionally unmediated economy. In both countries, the organizations and institutions that had protected domestic populations from price fluctuation, foreign exchange uncertainty, and scarcities during the rapid internationalization of the 1970s—the government in Saudi Arabia; the informal financial system in Yemen—had become dysfunctional. In Saudi Arabia the state borrowed heavily in domestic and foreign markets while cutting welfare, education, and subsidy programs that had reached the largest number of citizens. In Yemen the government's inability to stem the free fall of the Yemeni riyal had a similar effect on a population heavily dependent on imports of basic necessities. In both instances, unemployment rates were high, and underemployment was ubiquitous.

The progression from the elite politics of the early recession period to the social movements of the 1990s marked the advent of political movements on the part of groups unable to contemplate exit as an option. Whether as responses to the flux and insecurity of world prices, or to genuine scarcity, or to differences in subnational endowments thrown into sharp relief by the deconstruction of the national market, identity-based religious, regional, and tribal movements sprang up in both countries. In the wake of profound changes wrought by the regional economic crisis, failed economic liberalization programs, and the Iraqi invasion of Kuwait, these movements deployed the language of identity and morality to reconstitute the borders of economic community on lines different from existing national units. Their proposed solutions ranged from withdrawing from the international economy (by, for example, canceling the national debt and instituting a system of Islamic finance that prohibits interest), to secession, to novel forms of governance and distribution based on reconstructed regional and subnational networks.

In both countries the economic measures of the late 1980s actually terminated many of the mechanisms that had stabilized consumption in two economies that were exceptionally vulnerable to exogenous shocks, intimately tied to international economic forces, and virtually devoid of domestic productive capacities. These mechanisms—the state in Saudi Arabia, the informal bankers in Yemen—became dysfunctional at the same time that the regional oil-based economy collapsed. In both countries, by the turn of the decade, the economic policies of the early recession period had generated a secondary set of responses that reaggregated social forces at the mass level.

The new politics of scarcity *and* uncertainty were hardly unique to Saudi Arabia and Yemen. The oil price changes of the 1980s had plunged each country in the region into crisis and severed the exchanges of labor and capital that characterized the regional economy of the boom decade. Most important, the fiscal crises and liberalization policies pursued by heavily indebted or aid-dependent countries had undone national coalitions that had stabilized over the 1970s, in some cases threatening the life chances of brutal regimes whose weakening could only presage massive violence. Poverty was not a unique experience for the Arabs, but the experience of poverty in the overcrowded urban areas of the region in the late twentieth century was quite unlike that associated with rural poverty in the pre-boom era, when local markets and subsistence farming were the lifeblood of the majority. The deconstruction of the national market injected the uncertainties of world prices directly into now atomized urbanized communities that had enjoyed very high levels of protection even from domestic market forces, in the form of guaranteed state-sector employment, higher education, and subsidized food, housing, and utilities. In Arab countries with domestic labor forces—Syria, Iraq, Algeria, Tunisia, and Egypt, in particular—labor's bargaining power for economic benefits had far outpaced its actual importance to the domestic economy precisely because of its political significance for regime stability. In fact, the exceptionally long-term truncation of political rights in most Arab countries had rested, to a large extent, on social acquiescence bought through market protection—through the distribution of economic entitlements.

Regional alliances changed rapidly as Iraq began simultaneously to rebuild and to liberalize its economy. The end of the Iranian threat undid the military justification for the Gulf Cooperative Council but did not generate the will for economic integration. Refused membership in the GCC, Iraq embodied a deeply threatening return to the language of Pan-Arabism and regional redistribution. The 1970s had been a decade of economic integration and mutual political reinforcement among national leaders, but at the end of the 1990s—as in the heyday of Nasserism—swiftly changing regional alliances reflected a reopening of the perennial questions of Arab nationalism, accompanied by wide-scale interference by leaders in the internal affairs of other countries. The Pan-Arab rhetoric of the 1990s, however, had a distinctly economic twist focused on the arbitrary nature of national borders, questions concerning the ownership of oil wealth, and regional entitlements. Under the Arab Cooperative Council, Iraq reinitiated a debate about the shape and boundaries of the Arab community that had enormous resonance at the popular level. Not just Iraq and Kuwait but the two Yemens, Saudi Arabia and Yemen, Saudi Arabia and Iraq, and Jordan and Saudi Arabia all reopened disputes about undefined national borders and territorial control.

The destruction of the regional economy meant that the flows which had equilibrated national endowments in capital and labor were coupled with what turned out to be the enormously disruptive effects of economic liberalization. The withdrawal of subsidies and the end of government services and guaranteed employment, the emergence of highly visible economic inequality, the dual impact on employment of returning migrants and open trade regimes, inflation-managed fiscal crises, and subsequent devaluations all coincided with the rise of identity politics—movements based on regional, religious, sectarian, and tribal associations—in virtually every country in the region. In Yemen and Saudi Arabia, as elsewhere, these movements pitted themselves against governments dedicated to their destruction.

Struggles to redefine identity, reshape economic borders, and redesign the state are difficult to characterize as "institutional" change, but they certainly signaled the collapse both of the arrangements that emerged in the 1970s and of the reactive policies and elite struggles of the mid-1980s. At the same time, the immersion of all countries of the region in the international economy and the increasingly wide swath of the national market in which world prices prevailed suggests that the mechanisms by which the state could hope to attract adequate financial support narrowed considerably. The form taken by internationalization in the 1990s undercut alliances that had existed either in periods of isolation or in the internationalization episode of the boom era. Emerging patterns of institutional change in the 1990s are radically different from those of both the pre-boom and the boom period. In contrast to the pre-boom period, would-be state-builders in Yemen and Saudi Arabia can no longer offer control over the national market in return for elite support of the state.

Under conditions of easy exit, the rise of popular opposition movements in both countries generated a new politics of survival among state elites. Leaders changed political coalitions repeatedly and rapidly. Measures that superficially appeared democratic actually coincided with the deployment of an increasingly brutal and arbitrary security and surveillance apparatus designed to identify opposition leaders and eliminate sources of dissent. Genuine oppositional movements from below resulted in a new narrowing of actual power behind increasingly elaborate facades of decentralization, reform, and inclusion.

The advent of the new internationalization was not automatic. Within constraints, elites in both Saudi Arabia and Yemen made decisions that eventually undercut old mechanisms of governability at the top and of survival at the bottom. By the early 1990s, these decisions had undercut bargains struck in the early recession period.

The Saudi government's inability to withdraw elite entitlements resulted in a mounting deficit that became more acute as payments for the Gulf War came due in the 1990s.[76] The war itself resulted in a mini-boom in which entitlements and subsidies that had been cut heavily through 1988 were briefly restored almost to boomtime levels.[77] Subsequently,

[76] The main items included in off-budget spending are stipends to royal family members and arms purchases; off-budget revenues derive from oil sales outside the purview of the OPEC price and quota system and earnings on international holdings. For the annual deficits, 1983–95, see *Middle East Markets* 14 (16 March 1987); Peter W. Wilson and Douglas F. Graham, *Saudi Arabia* (Armonk, N.Y.: Sharpe, 1994), 192; and "Special Report—Saudi Arabia," *Middle East Economic Digest*, 10 March 1995, 28. Total deficit spending from 1983 to 1995 was approximately $183 billion.

[77] Between 1984 and 1988, for example, domestic (not including agricultural) subsidies went from $2.3 billion to $0.8 billion, then rose to $1.9 billion in 1990 and 1991. Cf.

however, distribution became even more skewed: while fees on services used by the entire population were raised, and subsidies to consumers were cut, ever larger amounts of state resources flowed to ever more concentrated groups of large companies and politically prominent persons.[78] Financing the military effort against Iraq and a constant level of defense spending of about $20 billion a year from 1987 through 1993 generated a looming debt problem by the mid-1990s that drew criticism from domestic banks and businesses.[79] Business elites and bankers, for their part, lamented the government's practice of not paying its bills.[80] Legal reforms designed to address disputes between public and private sectors remained ineffectual, lacking adequate enforcement powers against powerful government agencies.[81] In short, by the decades' turn the bottom of the distributive pyramid was already in shambles: as government schemes repeatedly failed to force private-sector companies to employ Saudis instead of imported labor, unemployment among Saudi males reached a remarkable 46 percent.[82] By the mid-1990s, the government was in danger of losing even its most well-placed supporters in the business community.

Opposition groups were not initially as fragmented and violent as they were to become by the mid-1990s. As the Gulf War progressed, two distinct opposition movements emerged: one comprised the Westernized elite; the other, Islamist groups with broad-based non-elite membership and leadership that included the government's allies in the religious establishment. Their first public statements, issued in late 1990 and early 1991,

---

Ministry of Planning, *The Achievements of the Five Year Plan: 1984–1989* (Riyadh: Government Printing Press, 1990), 228; and Wilson and Graham, *Saudi Arabia*, 194.

[78] For example, although agricultural subsidies were lowered steadily starting in 1986, they remained well above international prices. In 1991 the government began issuing permits allowing companies to sell wheat back to the government at subsidized prices and spent $2.12 billion that year on the wheat repurchase program—more than all other subsidies combined; see Wilson and Graham, *Saudi Arabia*, 222–25. Subsidies as well as loans continued to flow to large Nejdi agribusinesses. Average values of loans remained comparable to boomtime levels, though fewer loans were distributed to more select companies: in 1988–98, 83 percent of the Agricultural Bank's lending went to the Nejd, compared with 72 percent at the height of the boom. See *Saudi Arabian Monetary Agency Annual Report: 1409–10* (Riyadh: Government Printing Press, 1991), 201, table 249.

[79] Until 1990 the deficit was financed largely by drawing down reserves—estimated at $115–120 billion in 1981—to only about $6 billion in 1993 (Wilson and Graham, *Saudi Arabia*, 192). By 1993, net outstanding internal debt was $78 billion, and external debt was estimated at $4.5 billion. Together, net external and internal debt made up 67 percent of GDP in 1993; see "Special Report—Saudi Arabia," citing IMF Article 4 Report, 1994.

[80] By 1994 a $5 billion backlog in government payments was recorded among domestic contractors. See "Banks Propose Securitised Payments Plan to the Central Bank," *Middle East Economic Digest*, 6 January 1995, 35.

[81] Mitri J. Najjar, "Dispute Resolution in Saudi Arabia," *Middle East Insight* 8 (May–June 1992): 47–51.

[82] According to a Ministry of Planning study, unemployment rates were as high as 46 percent for Saudi males in 1990 and 94.7 percent for women (Wilson and Graham, *Saudi Arabia*, 254).

were remarkably similar, but the secularist group's emphasis on social freedoms ultimately led to a decisive split between the two movements in 1991, ostensibly over the issue of women's rights.[83] Government reaction superficially addressed the commonly stated demands put forth in the two petitions by announcing three reform bills in 1992: the Basic Statute of Government, the Statute of the Provinces, and the Statute of the Consultative Assembly. Following these "reforms," Islamist criticisms of the regime became more strident, focusing on government corruption, lack of accountability, economic redistribution, moral laxness, and the close connection between the Al Saud and Western powers. In 1992 the religious hierarchy split under pressure from the government to rein in its dissident members.[84] Thereafter, groups quite unconnected to the official religious hierarchy organized in various parts of the kingdom: discontented veterans of the Afghan war, such as Osama Binladen; frustrated former beneficiaries of the regime, such as the population of Buraydah; hijackers demanding the release of political prisoners; religious Hijazi college students; and a host of others based abroad. Khomeinist techniques of distributing sermons by tape, clandestine meetings, and, very occasionally, demonstrations after prayer occurred in the urban centers. Islamist organization was not randomly distributed in the population at large but centered on the regions of the Nejd that had been the key political bases of the Al Saud and thus the primary beneficiaries of state largess in the 1970s, such as Al Qasim in general and the politically important city of Buraydah in particular.[85]

In 1995 a number of austerity measures affecting low-income families—including higher charges for visas, petrol, refined products, utilities, domestic airfare, and domestic telephone service—were announced as part of a general effort to stem the deficit.[86] These were accompanied by a new round of political changes that signaled another centralization of power and a possible shift away from the Nejdi coalitional base toward the self-sustaining economy of the Hijaz and the oil-based region of al-Hasa. In contrast to the Nejd, which had suffered most from the economic decline of the 1980s, ARAMCO's new corporate strategy of internationalization had generated a sustained growth spurt in the east; similarly, the underlying strength of the *haj*-based economy in the Hijaz had cushioned the

[83] For texts of the secular and religious petitions published in December 1990 and February 1991, respectively, see Middle East Watch, *Empty Reforms* (New York: Human Rights Watch, 1992), 59–62.

[84] For the various phases of this fragmentation and the Al Saud's reaction, see Wilson and Graham, *Saudi Arabia*, chap. 2.

[85] See R. Hrair Dekmejian, "The Rise of Political Islamism in Saudi Arabia," *Middle East Journal* 48 (Autumn 1994): 627–43.

[86] See "Taxing Times for the Saudi Economy," *Middle East Economic Digest*, 13 January 1995, 30; and "Special Report—Saudi Arabia," 25–48.

western province from the worst effects of the recession.[87] An overhaul of the domestic client base has been a standard political strategy for non-GCC oil states. Indeed, in Iraq, the constant cycling of state clients is one way the regime maintains itself and manages to rest on new constituencies of support as each old alliance crumbles.[88] Lacking substantial populations, it has been possible for GCC oil exporters to develop more enduring client bases, but the new alliance between the Hijazi elite and the Al Saud suggests a change in the life cycle of the oil state in Saudi Arabia related to higher population levels, lower revenues, and class antagonisms among nationals. Both the cabinet reshuffle of 1995, which replaced sixteen of twenty-eight ministers and reassigned two portfolios, and highly publicized gestures of reconciliation by the king toward the eastern province's *Shi'a* communities could be interpreted as evidence that such a shift is occurring. Although important cabinet positions remained in Al Saud hands, the technocratic bent of the rest of the cabinet, the virtual absence of other Nejdis, and the high representation of Hijazis of non-Arabian origin are significant changes; whatever their longevity, they are unlikely to go unnoticed as a political message from the regime to its boomtime Nejdi clients.

Changes in Yemen were considerably more dramatic: where the Gulf War brought Saudi Arabia new financial obligations and substantially higher oil earnings, the regional tensions of the late 1980s only added to Yemen's economic crisis. In 1988 a major oil discovery in the Shabwa-Marib region reignited disputes over undefined national boundaries of Saudi Arabia, the former People's Democratic Republic of Yemen, and the Yemen Arab Republic. At the time, both Yemens were in a state of acute economic crisis for substantially similar reasons. In the PDRY the decline of Soviet and Eastern bloc aid and a fall in labor remittances had plunged that nation of two million into severe crisis. An economic liberalization program starting in 1985 generated tensions within the ruling party hierarchy that fractured the military and the government along sectoral-institutional lines which, because of the way state organizations had been constructed in the 1960s and 1970s, aligned with provincial-tribal divisions as well. Owing in large part to the very different natural endowments of the regions that made up the PDRY and the way the experience of British colonialism in Aden had transformed these divisions into factions that came to be represented in the National Liberation Front at independence, even low levels of liberalization were deeply disruptive to the domestic political balance. The liberalizations of 1985–86, which

[87] See "Eastern Promise for Saudi Business," *Middle East Economic Digest,* 10 February 1995, 2–3.

[88] See, e.g., data on Iraqi contractors in Kiren Aziz Chaudhry, "On the Way to the Market," *Middle East Report* 22 (May–June 1991): 14–23.

opened the PDRY to foreign investment, tourism, construction projects, and the sale of fishing rights, inordinately benefited Aden and Abyan at the expense of the resource-poor internal regions. These had never been part of the British colony but had led both the labor movement and the forces that won independence from the British; hence, members of the poorer regions of the hinterland were heavily represented in the national army and security services.

Liberalization also meant that the mechanisms through which PDRY's disparate regions and populations had been knit together into a national unit would cease to function. During the Cold War the PDRY, heavily supported by the Soviet Union, had developed an extensive set of internal distributive measures that equalized resources and services among regions with radically different economic endowments and competitive potentials. These measures provided not just low-cost basic goods, housing, and utilities to citizens but also excellent educational and health services. The government was substantially involved in sustaining the national market, and rightly boasted a highly competent and exceptionally honest bureaucracy. But the liberalizations of the Ali Nasir period highlighted the vastly different futures that awaited the regions of the PDRY after socialism and created incentives for segments of the bureaucracy to develop aims that accounted for these differences. Such divisions fragmented the party along regional lines and in 1986 resulted in a brief but bloody civil war in which approximately 10,000 south Yemenis were killed, in the main because of their regional origins.[89] The faction that took over after the fighting ended was reputed to be led by old-style socialists, and it was perhaps a measure of the depth of the economic crisis that Ali Salem al Bid, the new leader of PDRY after the civil war, continued to liberalize the economy.

Also important in the politics of liberalization were the absentee bourgeoisie of the PDRY, composed largely of members of old landed classes and merchants of Aden, Hadramout, and Lahj who had migrated to Saudi Arabia at independence (1967), when the radical faction of the National Liberation Front triumphed over the moderate liberal leadership of the Front for the Liberation of South Yemen and expropriated the properties both of the indigenous business and Sultans and of Adenese involved in the British colonial entrepot trade. Many of the wealthiest Hijazi families were of Hadrami origin, and the prospect of expanding into a new liberalized PDRY was attractive to them. The PDRY government, not unlike that of Syria, Iraq, and Iran in recent years, had been embroiled in sending delegations to overseas communities to solicit in-

[89] See Fred Halliday, "Catastrophe in South Yemen," *Middle East Report* 16 (March–April 1986): 37–39; and Jean Gueyras, "The Last Days of 'Ali Nasir," *Middle East Report* 16 (July–August 1986): 37–40.

vestment on promises of returning properties confiscated in the 1960s and 1970s.

Meanwhile, the Yemen Arab Republic, having failed to stabilize the exchange rate of the Yemeni riyal or control the informal financial market, was solving its fiscal crisis by printing money. The effect on a domestic economy highly dependent on imported food and basic goods was devastating. The reinstitution of private-sector imports in late 1988 had solved supply problems but did little to bridge the gap between domestic wages and the cost of imported foods. As projects in the Gulf dried up, laborers developed a pattern of rotating home every few months in search of opportunity but found no employment. Meanwhile, tensions between the *Sunni* merchants and northern tribal elites continued to intensify with the government's failure to stem smuggling across both the southern and northern borders.

The choices facing the two Yemeni governments in 1988 were, in short, stark: either go to war for control of the Shabwa-Marib oil field, or find a way of sharing the oil wealth.[90] Both Saleh and Bid lacked popular support, and the decision to step back from armed confrontation in 1988 was not unrelated to the enormous popularity of the idea of unity—*al wahda*—in both countries. Following brief scrimmages in 1988, the two governments agreed on the establishment of a 2,200-square-kilometer area for a joint investment project. In addition, they opened their borders to civilian travel in June 1988, presumably as a gesture of good will. For those interested in what a national market is, responses to the end of travel restrictions are revealing. Heavily subsidized South Yemeni goods were bought up by North Yemeni merchants, transported to the north, and sold at prevailing prices. The southern system of subsidies, procurement, and distribution, designed for a population of 2 million, was suddenly serving a combined market of 11 million, with predictable results: hoarding, price inflation, shortages, and panic. Unity, planned for late 1990, was pushed up to May 1990 following the collapse of the PDRY fisc. Although many observers credited the speed-up to the upcoming ACC meeting and Iraqi leader Saddam Hussain's desire to see a united Yemen, economic facts too were no doubt important in shaping the southern leadership's willingness to implement the hastily concluded unification.

For the North Yemeni government, the creation of the new Yemeni Republic, which added some 2 million *Sunnis* to the country's heretofore equally divided population, signaled the potential for an army capable of controlling the northern tribes. Following the regime's close association with the northern tribal leaders in 1985–86, Ali Abdallah Saleh's government had become increasingly unable to control them and was shifting

[90] Robert D. Burrowes, "The Yemen Arab Republic's Legacy and Yemeni Unification," *Arab Studies Quarterly* 1 (Fall 1992): 48, 58–59; and Charles Dunbar, "The Unification of Yemen," *Middle East Journal* 46, no. 3 (1992): 457–59.

back to a position of cooperation with the traditional *Sunni* merchant classes in an effort to stabilize the economy. The Shabwa-Marib oil find was in Hashid territory, and without the cooperation of the south the central government's control over the area was tenuous at best. Moreover, the Saudi government, a traditional ally of the Hashid tribal confederation, was also laying claim to the disputed border area, making it all the more important to roll back the privileges extended to the tribes in the early recession era.

The organizational and institutional problems facing the unification agreement are well known and documented. Postponement of the merger of the military, the ad hoc combination of the southern and northern bureaucracies, the maintenance of two currencies with different values, the different price and property structures and legal systems of the two countries, and the glaring cultural differences that deeply divided attitudes and practices toward the social status of women were just the major issues. More important for our purposes was the fact that unification precipitated tooth-and-nail struggles between the absentee bourgeoisie of the former PDRY—located largely in Saudi Arabia and the Gulf states—and the southern *Sunni* capitalist classes of the former Yemen Arab Republic. At stake was the best property in Aden, controlled by the local bureaucracy since its nationalization in 1967: ocean-side resorts, industrial plants and investments, and agricultural and commercial land. Resistance from the PDRY's bureaucracy and labor unions was a third and independent aspect of the struggle.

Then, to punish Yemeni's position on the Gulf War, Saudi Arabia expelled 800,000 to 1,000,000 Yemeni workers and investors resident there and stepped up its campaign to disrupt oil extraction plans in the Yemeni republic. Yemen's absentee labor force, theretofore a group absent from domestic politics, came home to an economy utterly incapable of accommodating them.[91] For the third time in Yemen's modern history, the transnational movement of an entire class rearranged the social and political structure of the country. The labor force returned, moreover, as primary property rights were being reallocated in the former socialist south in a context of renewed labor organization among public-sector workers in Aden. The entry of a million unemployed workers into the unified economy foreclosed the possibility of success for the southern workers.

In May 1994, a series of disputes centered on economic policy and on power sharing among the three main parties that emerged in the 1992 national elections—the Socialist Party, the conservative Reform Party led by tribal and religious leaders, and the General People's Congress (GPC) led by Ali Abdallah Saleh—erupted into a bloody civil war in which the

[91] Dunbar, "Unification of Yemen," 471. The Economist Intelligence Unit reported that the exodus resulted in a loss of $1.8 billion per year in remittance earnings; see *Country Report: Oman, Yemen,* no. 3 (1991): 23.

northern and southern armies, having failed to merge after 1990, destroyed the combined infrastructure of the country, including airports, the Aden oil refinery, military bases, and bridges.[92]

Between 1991 and the onset of the war—quite separate from the realm of electoral politics, the new press freedoms, and the play of constitutional struggles—a remarkable transformation was occurring in the organization of Yemeni political life.[93] One aspect can be described as a regionalization and tribalization of political associations and identities, especially among urban educated groups from the *Sunni* south who had in the past been deeply critical of ascriptive politics. Now, prominent businessmen, bankers, and professionals not only spoke of but also associated and schemed with others from their own specific region or tribe. In this fashion the tribal confederation of Madhaj, to which the traditional professional and business classes of Yemen belonged, became not only a common referent but also a political and military force that laid claim to the "central regions" of the country and spoke of revitalizing the ancient port of Mocha. The Bakil tribal confederation, larger and more spread out than either the Hashid or the Madhaj, held several formal meetings to organize, choose its leadership, and establish contingency plans against both the government and the Hashid. Each group justified its particularities in the language of nationalism: the tribe was necessary to preserve the Yemeni nation; ascriptive organization was a necessary basis for citizenship. The PDRY had already had one devastating experience with regional and tribal antagonisms in 1986, but from 1991 to 1994 tribal and regional organizations became openly secessionist.

The regional dynamics of this reaggregation of interests was connected not to long-lost identities subsumed under socialism but to what the advent of world prices and the collapse of the national economy did to regions and individuals with very different endowments. For example, in Hadramout, the discovery of a major new oil field and the persistent show of interest by Hadrami business elites long established in Saudi Arabia, combined with Saudi funding of local anti-unification groups, resulted in the creation of tribal leadership structures that in many cases hardly matched their pre-socialist predecessors. Saudi Arabia, having asked the Republic of Yemen for and been refused pipeline access to the Indian Ocean through the Hadramout, had an interest not only in more regional autonomy there but, according to some, in incorporating both the province and the oil field into the kingdom. These new interests affected

[92] See Chuck Schmitz, "Civil War in Yemen," *Current History* 588 (January 1995): 33–36.

[93] These observations are based on my field trip to Yemen in December 1991–February 1992 to study the causes and consequences of the collapse of its socialist economy. I interviewed business and political leaders in the former PDRY and YAR, and conducted an intensive survey of privatization of commercial property in Aden and of agricultural property in the southern province of Lahj.

government policy as well. For example, in 1991–92 the socialist segment of the unity government and the GPC made valiant efforts to return confiscated agricultural land to former owners in the Hadramout in order to attract their investments as well as their political support for a unified Yemen. Other regions such as Aden had endowments of location—the port, the refinery, natural beauty—which encouraged them to revive their cosmopolitan past as a British free port. Colonialism and the colonial past was recreated, this time in nostalgic tones, as a golden era. Professionals and businessmen from old Adenese families spoke glowingly of the potential of Aden to be another Hong Kong—if only the hinterland could be severed from the dynamic enclave. The groups that had been prominent in the Socialist Party and the army, in contrast, came from poorly endowed regions and understandably had a keen interest in reconsolidating the national market and crushing secessionist tendencies. Unlike the Islamists who formed the major opposition movement in Saudi Arabia, in Yemen the Islah party was simply one among many factions, sitting in uncomfortable association with the Hashid tribal confederation.

Alliances and counteralliances, both secret and public, shifted repeatedly throughout the economic and political crisis that led to the civil war of 1994 and, indeed, shaped the last-minute outcomes of the war itself. As these social forces and identities took form and changed, the state itself was reshaping its coercive machinery to meet the challenges of the institutional reforms that accompanied unity. Most important among these was a centralizing process of primitive accumulation of power that was quite unlike previous efforts: before, during, and after the war Ali Abdallah Saleh and his faction were purging the key organizations of all opposition groups, arranging for mass and individual assassinations of dissidents and Socialist Party supporters and setting up a brutal security state constructed on the model and, by many informal accounts, with the advice of the Iraqi Ba'th.[94]

SUMMARY: IDENTITY POLITICS AND INSTITUTIONS IN THE MAKING

Like the boom, the international economic changes of the 1980s and 1990s transformed domestic institutions in Yemen and Saudi Arabia. Starting in the organizations that mediated the capital flows of the 1970s, the crisis introduced new dynamics of institutional change which transmuted as the recession wore on. In the beginning stages, business-government relations constituted in the boom shaped policy and circumscribed institutional change, but in ways completely contrary to the boom period. Moreover, under the same political dynamics, institutional capacity varied

[94] See Amnesty International, *Yemen* (New York: Amnesty International, 1994).

broadly in different sectors: the same political relationships produced diametrically opposing outcomes in different sectors. Thus, the same regional cleft between business and state that enabled the Yemeni government to tax and regulate fixed assets was also responsible for the government's complete failure in regulating finance. Similarly, the very same ties that paralyzed Saudi reforms in industry, agriculture, and contracting, were responsible for a relatively successful reform of the commercial banking sector.

As the recession continued, an entirely new set of causal patterns emerged as the elite politics of the 1980s were subsumed by radical social movements from below. Not unlike the social struggles attending the creation of national institutions in the earlier part of the century, these movements opened up fundamental questions centered on the purpose and scope of economic community. However, both the international context in which these struggles were initiated and the local societies in question had been utterly transformed by the events of the 1970s. At the domestic level, the groups that engaged in new contests over economic goods were entirely the creation of the 1970s: not guilds and tribes, farmers and notables, but highly urbanized participants thrust together by the economic changes of the boom. Moreover, the fundamental economic relationship that shaped their connection to the domestic economy was not that of *production* but of *consumption.* As the recession wore on, the economic shocks to which these populations were subjected not only intensified but also underwent qualitative changes. Where the internationalization of the boom had filtered through organizations that in effect protected the broad mass of domestic populations from the instability and flux of international prices, in the 1990s, no such organizations remained. Meanwhile, large-scale unemployment meant that relations of work were increasingly eroded, leaving only relations of consumption. At the same time, however, this new form of international integration also gave financial elites unprecedented mobility, undercutting not only their desire to dominate the national market but, even more, their willingness to participate in the domestic political economy at all. From the perspective of Saudis and Yemenis unable to contemplate exit, the unmediated impact of international prices was a qualitatively different experience of internationalization from that of the 1970s, and the calculations of economic elites were radically different from those that had shaped their earlier support for national regulatory regimes.

I have argued that the new internationalization produced patterns of local institutional change causally distinct from that which occurred in the 1970s, and that the analytical framework best suited to understand this new mechanism of aggregation is not class analysis or organization theory but methodological individualism. This does not, however, suggest that there is a convergence of domestic institutional outcomes; quite the opposite. The new internationalization may mean the unmediated advent of international prices into domestic structures, but endowments, their local distribution, their overlap with local groupings, and their influence in shaping the reaggregation of groups will vary radically from one situation to the next. Political movements based on cultural identifications unconnected to the apparatus of the modern national state can thus be seen as outgrowths of the new internationalization. A closer examination of domestic institutional structures suggests how: what changed between the 1970s and the 1990s were not simply economic conditions but the substantive links between the domestic and the international economy. In the 1970s, both Yemen and Saudi Arabia had undergone a period of rapid internationalization *mediated* by domestic organizations that protected domestic groups from the flux and uncertainty of global prices. The distributive state in Saudi Arabia and the LDAs and the informal bankers in Yemen stabilized exchange rates and prices and provided public goods. In the 1990s, in contrast, domestic groups experienced the *unmediated* effects of international integration in the form of international prices. This does not mean that they were paying the same amount for different commodities, or that prices, in the abstract, exist without institutional mediation, but that the social mechanisms to tame the late-twentieth-century version of Polanyi's "Satanic Mills" had collapsed without being replaced with an alternative. The fact that Yemen and Saudi Arabia were dependent on imported commodities for virtually everything, including 70 to 80 percent of their food, hints at the dramatic material implications of the problem. Rapidly fluctuating exchange rates, sudden influxes and outflows of capital, shortages, scarcities in basic goods and the demise of organizations that protected individuals from these uncertainties all combined to produce not only a poorer population, but a fundamentally insecure one as well. The economic shocks of the 1990s thus introduced very different aggregative processes at the local and subnational levels that replaced incentive systems previously lodged in national institutional frameworks.

These uniquely local economic experiences are a useful starting point in trying to understand both the form that the social movements of the 1990s have taken and their potential to shape new institutional outcomes. The role of the new internationalization in disaggregating and rearranging social groupings rooted in the old national economy is clearly visible in the form that the new social movements took. For example, Islamist movements in Saudi Arabia are concentrated in those regions of the Nejd that benefited most from the boom, but, because of a combination of environmental degradation associated with the agricultural programs of the 1970s and the paucity of other resources, these regions have also had a severe experience of the recession. In contrast, groups with a history of antigovernment activism that were not primary beneficiaries of the boom but have relatively robust "natural" endowments in location or in skills—the Hijazi commercial classes and the *Shi'a* of the eastern province—have largely disbanded. Similarly, the demands and organizational strategies of groups claiming tribal and regional entitlements and identities are vividly connected to the vastly different endowments of Yemen's diverse regions. There, elites from areas with good chances of economic solvency—Aden, the Hadramout, Abyan, Taiz—mobilized for more autonomy from the central state while those with no resources sought to recentralize and recreate national regulatory systems. When this was not possible, these groups, lodged in the military, directly used force to appropriate control over resources.

To the extent that these social movements are generated in symbiosis with newly constructed identities and economic opportunism, the question of how groups aggregate devolves onto individual responses to new economic circumstances: there are no "traditional" groups to return to; no "traditional" identities; economic and political identities are thus created in tandem even though the primacy of the economic in the causal chain is beyond dispute. In other words, the deconstruction of key national economic institutions that mediated international economic changes does not predetermine what new aggregations will emerge, how alliances will form, or how material incentives will shape individual choices. In many instances cross-national alliances and resource flows have already influenced local struggles not only in Arabia but in the broader region as well. It is thus hardly surprising that the new social movements are not plainly class-based. Explaining the origins of institutions in the 1990s, in contrast to the pre-boom era or the boom years, requires an understanding of the incentive structures on which groups still in formation are acting. Rationalist individualism, so rightly criticized for ignoring institutional influences, allows such an analysis to proceed without prejudging the shape these groups will take; it also allows us to trace the formation of nonclass-based movements composed of consumers that mobilize identities in response to rapidly changing economic conditions. It does not, however, permit us to predict how new institutions will form, but guides us, only, in crafting a description of pre-institutional struggles.

Chapter Eight

Worlds within the Third World

Economists, political scientists, and sociologists are in increasing agreement on the importance of institutions in shaping political and economic outcomes. Yet where institutions come from and why they differ from one case to the next are questions that have remained relatively unexplored. This analysis has sought to explain the origins of institutions in three distinct nexuses of local and world-historical time as a way of reopening the issue afresh. As extreme cases of reliance on external capital flows in the 1970s, Saudi Arabia and Yemen are clearly unique in some ways. Yet the political economy of institutional origination in these two countries before, during, and after the period in which their economies became tightly linked to international economic forces has broader implications. As two countries with high levels of dependence on two very different kinds of market-regulated exports—labor and oil—these cases illustrate the fitful and reversible process through which institutional change occurs in late, late developers that have strong links to the international economy. Rapid changes in the domestic political economies of the two countries during the oil boom of the 1970s and the recession of the 1980s support three interrelated arguments about the formation of state and market institutions in late developers.

First, the sources of institutional origination and change are not constant over time and cannot be explained by recourse to one, universally applicable theory. The relative importance of domestic social struggles and international economic opportunities in shaping institutions varied in the three junctures covered in this study. In contrast to lines of argument put forth by institutionalists with either economistic or historical inclinations, these cases reveal shifts in the confluence of domestic and international forces that create, transform, and in some cases destroy fundamental state and market institutions.

The sources of institutional change before the oil boom and during the recession contrasted markedly with what occurred in the boom years. In the pre-boom period, institutions were shaped largely by internal factors centered specifically on local reactions to the extractive efforts of nascent state-builders. During the oil boom, domestic conflicts were far less important in determining institutional outcomes; the strategies pursued by state and business elites were more strongly conditioned by the flow of labor remittances, aid, and oil revenues through state and civil organizations. Institutional change was to a substantial measure disconnected from domestic struggles as state and private institutions responded to opportunities quite unrelated to the balance of domestic social forces and interests. Then, in the recession, when capital flows declined, domestic politics once again became exceedingly important in shaping both policy and institutional change, but in a context thoroughly transformed by the previous decade of economic expansion. Local history shapes context, but at particular moments, ongoing struggles at the domestic level are arrested and transformed by international economic forces.

The first point, then, is that the origins of domestic institutions vary at different conjunctures of world-historical and local time, each conjuncture requiring analytical foci appropriate to the moment. In the oil boom, social, institutional, and political outcomes in two countries enmeshed in a new world of international economic changes were shaped by capital flows in ways barely related to ongoing contests for political and economic power. This observation contrasts with the assumptions of both the NIEs and dependency theory. The former ignore the importance of world-historical time altogether and completely neglect international influences, with important consequences for methods of historical comparison. The search for broad universal generalizations does not just obliterate the particular but does away with the entire tier of theorization that occupies most social scientists. Whereas early dependency theorists assumed the constant and unchanging involvement of international influences in shaping domestic outcomes in late developers, structural Marxists neglected the extent to which local contingencies, born of international or social organizational factors, precluded a union of political and economic power. Recent arguments about the relative autonomy of the state represent efforts to undo this ironclad assumption, but they neither offered a satisfactory definition of "autonomy" nor successfully explored the highly contingent ways that autonomy in one set of material circumstances can become its functional opposite in another. When autonomy and dependence are directly related to international economic influences, as in the two cases discussed here, these issues become ever more complicated.

In times of relative insularity from international economic forces, institutions originate as the result of intense social struggles. These struggles produce coalitions of domestic groups which obsolesce as the conditions that cemented alliances erode. The process is not necessarily incremental: even fundamental institutions can change quite rapidly.

Tracing the process through which a centralized extractive and administrative bureaucracy was born in Saudi Arabia and forestalled in Yemen exposes the importance of domestic contingencies. Locating institutional outcomes in domestic struggles does not, in short, guarantee similar outcomes. In Saudi Arabia, the creation of a national army that controlled the production of order and violence and the unification of the currency laid the ground for a stable coalition between traditional private-sector elites and political leaders in support of a centralized administrative power governing an increasingly united national market. In Yemen, the inability of the political leadership to acquire a monopoly on violence, coupled with the revenue-gathering strategies to which military weakness gave rise, led to fragmentation of the national market and the flight of traditional merchant classes beyond the juridical reach of the increasingly predatory tax state. The military context in which taxation was stepped up determined social responses and led to very different initial experiences in state- and market-building in the two cases. Even in the pre-boom period, different parts of "the state" were differentially developed, and there was little correlation between its capacity to tax, produce order, or regulate.

In periods of relative insulation from the international economy, the synergies and tensions between state- and market-building processes become clear. Institutional outcomes in pre-boom Yemen and Saudi Arabia illustrate these connections with particular clarity. State-building and market unification are mutually reinforcing processes. Yet in cases such as Yemen, where the tax state expands but tax authorities do not gain control of the production of violence, the revenue-gathering activities of the state can fragment rather than unify the would-be national economy. These enclaves, in turn, produce exchange patterns that later become even stronger barriers to the unification of the national market. In Yemen, the predatory ruler's revenue-gathering efforts generated three geographically distinct Yemeni bourgeoisie operating in separate economic spheres. The initial success of the Saudi state in creating institutions to cut transaction costs and facilitate exchange over a large contiguous territory set the stage for a stable business-government coalition; the Yemeni government's failure to achieve a similar military outcome created fissures in the commercial classes, resulting in a violent struggle between the local and absentee bourgeoisie. With the creation of the Yemen Arab Republic, this conflict defined the protagonists in the civil war of 1962–1970. Capitalists, disunited, can undo the efforts of nascent state-builders. Struggles over who makes the rules governing the national market can lead to its demise.

In the oil boom of 1973–83, processes of institutional creation and decay were deeply influenced by the inflow of two very different kinds of capital flow. The oil boom interrupted the wrenching, ongoing processes of state-building and national integration that had been under way in both Yemen and Saudi Arabia since the early 1930s. Both societies were split by regional and sectarian cleavages which overlapped with divisions between the military-political and the economic sphere. Both governments were embroiled in the disruptive process of expanding the extractive and regulatory capacities of the central state—a process which, teased apart, gets to the common core of local pressures for constructing centralized states and national markets. In a fitful and discontinuous way, urban demands for protection generated taxing bureaucracies. Neither country had a colonial experience, and as a result no "overdeveloped" bureaucratic and military organization existed; political entrepreneurs began, as it were, from scratch. Hence, the process of constructing a national market and the expansion of the state's extractive and regulatory institutions were entwined with intense conflicts as local elites resisted centralization.

The boom recast ongoing struggles by adding a stark economic dimension to divisions already imbued with political significance. Oil revenues and labor remittances were controlled by two very different groups. In Saudi Arabia, oil revenues flowed directly to the state fisc, decisively expanding the resources of the Nejdi elite that controlled the bureaucracy, the army, and the political leadership and quickly disenfranchising the historically powerful economic elites of the Hijaz province. In Yemen, labor remittances controlled by about 1.8 million migrants, mostly from the southern *Sunni* provinces, bypassed the formal banking system and the government. Entering the country through a complex informal banking system, remittances fueled the growth of a prosperous and independent private sector dominated by traditional commercial and financial elites from the *Sunni* south.

The second major argument in the analysis is that both similarities and differences in institutional outcomes were produced by the two kinds of capital inflow. The structure and functions of state institutions in both Saudi Arabia and Yemen were transformed by the prosperous 1970s. Access to extraordinary sources of foreign exchange had one surprisingly similar effect on the two bureaucracies: in both countries the government abandoned its prior project of creating extractive institutions and the ancillary legal, fiscal, and information-gathering bureaucracies associated with them. Rulers, in fact, do not like to tax. When they can, they avoid it.

From this point, however, the effects diverged. High levels of external capital inflows coincided with processes of state-building, creating a disjuncture between the development of regulatory, extractive, and distributive institutions. Extractive bureaucracies declined in both cases, but the two kinds of capital inflow generated very different alternative state structures. Oil rents created in Saudi Arabia a huge, financially autonomous distributive bureaucracy that became the mechanism for governing the domestic economy. In contrast, labor remittance flows to Yemen bypassed both state institutions and the formal banking system altogether, engendering an independent and affluent private sector. Labor migration undercut the state's traditional tax base in agriculture and made tariffs on trade the exclusive source of domestic revenue. The Yemeni government tapped the broadly distributed wealth in society through customs duties, using them to supplement substantial flows of development aid. Fed by import duties and development aid in Yemen, and oil revenues in Saudi Arabia, both bureaucracies grew, albeit at different rates. Yet amid this apparent burst of state-building, the most essential function of the modern state, its power to tax, declined. In Yemen, the growth of the private sector far outpaced that of the government, engendering parallel structures of public and private authority lodged in two distinct subsections of the economy.

State-controlled oil revenues and privately controlled labor remittances not only transformed the balance of social forces struggling to shape political and economic institutions in accord with their interests; they altered the very landscape in which these conflicts were occurring. Economics soon flowed into politics, prompting institutional change in the financial sector and in society. In Saudi Arabia, the government was freed from having to tax its population. Undoing a carefully constructed corporatist relationship with the Hijazi private sector, the Nejdi state used its new wealth to create an alternative base of support in society. Through the deployment of oil revenues the Saudi government created a large private sector in its own image, one that mirrored the ascriptive attributes of the Nejdi bureaucracy and the Nejdi political elite that controlled it. In Yemen, by contrast, remittances reinforced the historical dominance of southern *Sunni* commercial and industrial elites, generating rapid growth in a virtually unregulated private sector with no ties to the bureaucracy, the army, or the political leadership dominated by northern *Shiʿa.*

In both cases, external capital inflows reinforced existing cleavages, but with radically different implications for business-government relations. The Nejdi government in Saudi Arabia distributed oil revenues through a formal bureaucracy designed to allocate contracts, interest-free loans, and subsidies, generating a large state-sponsored private sector that swiftly replaced traditional commercial and service elites from the western province of the Hijaz. These distributive policies created a new private sector from whole cloth, one that mirrored the tribal and regional composition of the bureaucracy, linking business and government through kinship networks, tribal loyalties, and business partnerships. During the recession these primordial ties at once obscured the conflicting interests of business and the state and provided an effective informal framework for opposing austerity measures.

Labor remittances accrued directly to millions of Yemeni migrants through an informal, decentralized banking system that fed the buoyant private sector with virtually unlimited amounts of foreign exchange. Unlike oil revenues, remittances concentrated economic opportunity in the traditional business class, where the southern *Sunni* merchants expanded their dominance. Returning migrants, also from the *Sunni* south, entered the lower echelons of the business community. The northern *Shiʿa* areas were not centers for labor export but had historically staffed the army and the bureaucracy. Labor remittances accentuated longstanding disequilibria in the social composition of the bureaucracy and army on the one hand, and the merchant class on the other, by adding a stark economic dimension to existing cleavages along occupational, sectarian, and regional lines. During the boom years, remittances so divided the interests of business and state elites that when the crisis came to Yemen, bureaucrats were able to override the objections of private businessmen and create new instruments of extraction, regulation, and state monopoly. The Yemeni bureaucracy, because it lacked the financial means to create a system of distribution under conditions of wide-based prosperity, actually augmented its political and social independence from the private sector during the boom and used it to implement its policies in the recession. The weakness of the bureaucracy's ties with business became a source of strength for a state otherwise lacking the organizational capacities and institutional tools to govern the economy. Ascriptive divisions are a substitute for "state strength," conventionally defined.

Evidence from Yemen and Saudi Arabia supports the proposition that large volumes of external capital inflows have a definitive impact on the structure and functions of state institutions. The comparisons of institutional, social, and economic change presented in the paired case material illuminate the effects of international capital inflows in two ways. First, they show the effects of extreme dependence on any kind of unstable, market-regulated external capital inflow. Second, they illustrate the different patterns of change sparked by state-managed versus privately controlled inflows. Either way, large volumes of external capital inflow diminish the extractive and regulatory capacities of the state by creating alternative sources of state revenue and diminishing incentives for economic regulation. In both Yemen and Saudi Arabia, the inflow of external capital—whether aid, remittances, or oil revenues—coincided with the forging of fundamental extractive, regulatory, and redistributive institutions and exerted a strong influence on the structure and functions of state institutions. Extraordinary sources of income transformed the contours of political debate in the domestic arena by separating the resources necessary to maintain a bureaucracy from local taxation.

Even in Saudi Arabia and Yemen, where none of the conditions assumed by dependency theorists were present, international economic forces had a dramatic effect on institutional development. The more extreme the exposure of developing countries to international economic forces at the initial stages of state-building, the more discontinuous we might expect the construction of domestic political and economic institutions to be. When the influx of external capital coincides with the forging of fundamental state institutions, previous gains in institutional entrenchment and state penetration are reversed, resulting in administrative crises in times of economic recession.

These findings challenge conventional views on the relationship between economic and political power, state autonomy and state strength, independence and efficacy. External capital inflows are not of a piece. Their effects depend on a host of historically constituted relationships. Moreover, these cases underscore the importance of viewing different types of external capital as distinct independent variables that have identifiably different effects on business-government relations and state capacity, depending on who controls them and when. The divergent effects of external capital inflows on different clusters of state institutions highlight the importance of desegregating the "state." The administrative and political capacities of the state can co-vary in highly irregular ways that cannot be captured in any formulaic fashion. The strength of the state varies according to what it sets out to do, when, and to whom.

Capital flows had differential effects not just on the state but on society as well, transforming the contours of domestic politics in a variety of ways. The withdrawal of state regulation and taxation transformed the nexus of relationships between the state and society by depoliticizing economic issues and ameliorating conflict between business and government during the boom. To the extent that taxation at once requires the government to justify its expenditures and economic policies and creates incentives for groups to try to influence its programs, state accountability as well as the interest of groups in aggregating and articulating their views atrophied. In the nonconflictual economic environment of the boom, the emergence of ideological politics in both countries was forestalled. In Yemen the virtual absence of any regulation made it possible for economic elites to thrive without any contact with the bureaucracy, and the absence of taxes on profits forestalled demands for political representation from the business community, making it perfectly content to leave governance to the northern *Shi*ʿ*a* groups. Similarly, in Saudi Arabia, where previously the king's need to tax had precipitated the creation of a consultative council dominated by Hijazi merchants, the withdrawal of taxes coincided with the depoliticization of the old merchant elite and led to the abrogation of their hard-won legal rights. The issue of reintroducing taxes in the recession raised thorny issues of civil entitlement and representation which the Saudi government avoided by simply withdrawing its post-boom fiscal reforms. Unable to afford this option, the Yemeni government responded to similar demands by allowing local elections to take place while continuing to choose central parliament members on the basis of corporate representation.

At a more basic level, the flow of remittances and oil revenues had significant effects on social stratification in Yemen and Saudi Arabia, but through very different mechanisms. In Yemen, remittances created new classes of local elites and empowered migrants with the financial resources to enter and dominate the retail, transportation, and service sectors. In Saudi Arabia, unequal access to state revenues precipitated the decline of the old bourgeoisie and the rise of a new Nejdi private-sector elite. Oil revenues empowered the state to destroy local institutions in both rural and urban realms.

Both the speed with which the contours of domestic classes changed and the extent to which these changes were unrelated to other broad processes of development lay bare deficiencies in both Weberian and Marxist conceptions of social change. Not once but twice in its modern history, whole classes of Yemeni society migrated abroad, only to return at a later juncture. The mass exodus to Aden, the return of both the absentee bourgeoisie and labor in 1962, the migration of laborers to Saudi Arabia, and their subsequent homecoming during the Gulf War of 1991 all bespeak a fluidity in social change hardly captured by social scientific analyses. The critical junctures at which either labor or the bourgeoisie exited had an enormous impact on institutional and political outcomes in Yemen. At the end of the twentieth century, Yemen is beginning a project of incorporating labor in an environment radically different from that which characterized other late developers during the same process. Similarly, in Saudi Arabia, state spending rapidly created new social classes in less than a decade. In transforming the composition and political proclivities of the national bourgeoisie, external economic influences did not just alter the role the middle class would play in these societies but created contexts that fall beyond the purview of available analytical tools currently applied in the development field.

The third argument is that economic policy during the recession revealed the relative weight of political and administrative barriers to economic reform. Oil rents and labor remittances had the similar effect of destroying the institutional mechanisms required to carry out economic reforms during the recession, with the result that neither the Saudi nor the Yemeni government was administratively equipped to manage the effects of the crisis of the 1980s. The differences in their post-boom responses, however, suggest that the ability of the state to respond to economic crisis was only broadly constrained by administrative weakness; where the political will existed, institutions were remarkably resilient. Rather, the main barriers to intrusive economic policies were and are political, embedded in broad social and economic changes that altered the nexus of tribal, regional, and sectarian cleavages between the private sector and the bureaucracy during the boom period. Here, state-managed and privately controlled capital inflows had divergent effects, which ultimately determined state capacity during the recession.

The key difference in the impact of oil rents and labor remittances was the way their effect on the balance of economic opportunity in the public and private sectors interacted with the social composition of the bureaucracy and the private sector. Both publicly and privately controlled capital inflows intensified existing primordial cleavages but had very different consequences for business-government relations. It is these divergent patterns of relations that explain both the differential ability of the state to respond to crises and the power of entrepreneurial groups to resist disruptive economic policies. During the boom period the fiscally autonomous Saudi oil state created a client private sector in an effort to build a stable base of political support. Through its distributive policies the bureaucracy replicated its tribal and regional characteristics in the new private sector, which consisted of political and tribal claimants from the central province of the Nejd. The new commission entrepreneurs cultivated strong kinship ties with the bureaucracy by expanding existing tribal relationships to include mutual economic interests. By recreating "tribalism" as a new form of identification, the spending patterns of the autonomous oil state set the stage for continuing demands on the state treasury. Thus, in the post-boom crisis the new private sector successfully resisted state policies through precisely the same kinship links with the bureaucracy that had accounted for its ascendance during the boom years. The Saudi pact persists. Having already drawn down its international reserves, the state would rather borrow than trim, would rather import foreign labor at the expense of a growing stratum of unemployed nationals than confront the business elite.

By contrast, the boom years in Yemen separated private-sector elites and bureaucrats along sectarian and regional lines, affording the state the corporate cohesion and the political will to implement stringent austerity programs in the recession. Unlike those of Saudi Arabia, Yemen's bureaucracy and private sector became divided by regional and sectarian distinctions that embodied a variety of historical differences. During the boom period, the southern *Sunni* population was drawn into the affluent private sector, leaving the army and the bureaucracy to the *Shiʿa* tribal groups of the north. Remittances eroded traditional authority in many rural areas of the south, where they engendered strong local organizations to undertake functions normally performed by the state. Yet during the recession these very associations became the vehicles of state administration and tax collection in rural areas. In urban areas the bureaucracy was able to generate both the will and the institutional capacity to move against the interests of the commercial class in favor of consumers and tribal notables, abrogating the pact that had underpinned the Republican revolution of 1962. At least in the short run, social distance from the private sector strengthened the political resolve of the Yemeni state. Yet gains in institutional entrenchment were bought at the cost of social polarization. Despite reforms that were essentially fiscally sound, policy choices increasingly served the interests of the regional and sectarian groups that dominated the army and the bureaucracy. The Yemeni private sector, though structurally autonomous, was unable to resist state policies in the crisis precisely because its independence had obviated the necessity of cultivating ties with the bureaucracy and the army. The long-term price of "money made in air" was institutional decline and intensified cleavages antithetical to national integration. During the single boom-and-bust cycle covered in this analysis, state and group autonomy based on external capital inflows diminished the efficacy of those that controlled them.

The patterns of state-society relations in Saudi Arabia and Yemen reveal the importance of strong civil groups for effective state action, laying bare the danger of seeing state and civil strength as a zero-sum relationship. In Yemen, strong local groups organized along democratic lines were aggregated at the center. This experience is in stark contrast to that of Saudi Arabia, where previously strong groups in the Hijaz were disbanded and corporate groups were created directly through state spending. The weakness of the latter pattern was that group interests coalesced only as a result of state spending patterns. Rather than forming a loyal political base, continued financial support from the state purchased the private sector's acquiescence. Ironically, opposition to austerity measures was not spearheaded by the disenfranchised Hijazis, or by the impoverished populations of Asir and Al-Hasa, but by the two main beneficiaries of Saudi state spending: the state-sponsored landed elite and the new Nejdi merchant and industrial class.

These findings bear on the utility of "state autonomy" as a useful analytical category, revealing flaws in the current use of the term as a means of defining a condition or of predicting the relationship between the state and social groups. The unrelenting exposition of the virtues of "autonomy" which characterizes the recent interest in state capacity may be appropriate for the study of advanced capitalist economies where the democratic process gives organized social groups institutionalized opportunities to block state policies. It makes less sense in countries where the main impediment to the implementation of policies is the *lack* of central institutions; where the extension of central administrative control over territory coincides with the financial autonomy of the state; where formal mechanisms for the expression of political priorities are weak or nonexistent, and both state and society are divided by tribal and sectarian cleavages. Even the capacities of strictly autonomous states are conditioned primarily by their ability to override social opposition. Agendas generated exclusively by ministries of finance without input from social groups eventually confront the scrutiny of economic elites who test the actual parameters of state power. Similarly, social groups that enjoy high levels of independence may find themselves left out of new coalitions that emerge in response to economic crises. Saudi Arabia and Yemen demonstrate the crucial role of domestic social context in mediating the effects of capital flows to developing countries, the majority of which are divided societies presided over by fragile, emerging bureaucracies. In the initial stages of state-building, state efficacy and national integration do not necessarily reinforce each other. Under certain conditions the narrow primordial basis of the state results in higher levels of efficacy; in the short run, the state is able to realize its aims. In the long run, however, one might expect the renewed emergence of ethnic conflict at a more pronounced level. The costs of waiting are cumulative.

The twin processes of state-building have been, and are likely to remain, discontinuous, marked by fits and starts, backsliding and decay, quick victories and rapid defeats. Advances in technology, communications, and transportation assure that the process of constructing national institutions will be radically different in the future. Yemen and Saudi Arabia's experiences in the 1970s and 1980s are important clues to how different the project of connecting political and economic community will become.

Parallel to the substantive arguments about the cases and the process of institutional change is a methodological point that the preceding text has presented and demonstrated. Put simply, it is this: processes of institutional origination and change differ enough at different conjunctures of the domestic/local and international economy that they cannot be studied through the same analytical lens. A modified class analysis, useful in explaining the process through which the national market and state were forged, was quite irrelevant to understanding institutional changes wrought by the kind of internationalization that Saudi Arabia and Yemen underwent in the boom period. In the 1970s, because of the form that internationalization took, organization theory provided a better explanatory framework than class analysis. Similarly, in the internationalization that occurred in the two countries in the 1990s, when individuals in the domestic arena were exposed to institutionally unmediated world prices, I argue that rational choice frameworks constructed on individual choices made in response to changing economic opportunities would be the most useful starting point for understanding the pre-sociology of contemporary institutional change. I am not certain that such an analysis is actually possible. Certainly, I have not tried to provide it. Yet the identity-based social movements that emerged in both Saudi Arabia and Yemen in the 1990s pose the question of how individual (not group or class) preferences develop and how they influence fundamental political choices and behavior. Only this sort of analysis, which has been largely a theoretical possibility incapable of substantiation through the study of real living societies, might explain why particular constellations of identity-based political groups have taken shape in response to the ongoing economic crisis in contemporary Arabia.

Index

Cornell Studies in Political Economy

Edited by Peter J. Katzenstein

National Diversity and Global Capitalism, edited by Suzanne Berger and Ronald Dore
Collapse of an Industry: Nuclear Power and the Contradictions of U.S. Policy, by John L. Campbell
The Price of Wealth: Economies and Institutions in the Middle East, by Kiren Aziz Chaudhry
Power, Purpose, and Collective Choice: Economic Strategy in Socialist States, edited by Ellen Comisso and Laura D'Andrea Tyson
The Political Economy of the New Asian Industrialism, edited by Frederic C. Deyo
Dislodging Multinationals: India's Strategy in Comparative Perspective, by Dennis J. Encarnation
Rivals beyond Trade: America versus Japan in Global Competition, by Dennis J. Encarnation
Enterprise and the State in Korea and Taiwan, by Karl J. Fields
National Interests in International Society, by Martha Finnemore
Democracy and Markets: The Politics of Mixed Economies, by John R. Freeman
The Misunderstood Miracle: Industrial Development and Political Change in Japan, by David Friedman
Ideas, Interests, and American Trade Policy, by Judith Goldstein
Ideas and Foreign Policy: Beliefs, Institutions, and Political Change, edited by Judith Goldstein and Robert O. Keohane
Monetary Sovereignty: The Politics of Central Banking in Western Europe, by John B. Goodman
Politics in Hard Times: Comparative Responses to International Economic Crises, by Peter Gourevitch
Closing the Gold Window: Domestic Politics and the End of Bretton Woods, by Joanne Gowa
Cooperation among Nations: Europe, America, and Non-tariff Barriers to Trade, by Joseph M. Grieco
Nationalism, Liberalism, and Progress, volume 1, by Ernst B. Haas
Pathways from the Periphery: The Politics of Growth in the Newly Industrializing Countries, by Stephan Haggard
The Politics of Finance in Developing Countries, edited by Stephan Haggard, Chung H. Lee, and Sylvia Maxfield
Rival Capitalists: International Competitiveness in the United States, Japan, and Western Europe, by Jeffrey A. Hart

The Philippine State and the Marcos Regime: The Politics of Export, by Gary Hawes
Reasons of State: Oil Politics and the Capacities of American Government, by G. John Ikenberry
The State and American Foreign Economic Policy, edited by G. John Ikenberry, David A. Lake, and Michael Mastanduno
The Paradox of Continental Production: National Investment Policies in North America, by Barbara Jenkins
Pipeline Politics: The Complex Political Economy of East-West Energy Trade, by Bruce W. Jentleson
The Politics of International Debt, edited by Miles Kahler
Corporatism and Change: Austria, Switzerland, and the Politics of Industry, by Peter J. Katzenstein
Cultural Norms and National Security: Police and Military in Postwar Japan, by Peter J. Katzenstein
Industry and Politics in West Germany: Toward the Third Republic, edited by Peter J. Katzenstein
Small States in World Markets: Industrial Policy in Europe, by Peter J. Katzenstein
The Sovereign Entrepreneur: Oil Policies in Advanced and Less Developed Capitalist Countries, by Merrie Gilbert Klapp
Norms in International Relations: The Struggle against Apartheid, by Audie Klotz
International Regimes, edited by Stephen D. Krasner
Business and Banking: Political Change and Economic Integration in Western Europe, by Paulette Kurzer
Power, Protection, and Free Trade: International Sources of U.S. Commercial Strategy, 1887–1939, by David A. Lake
State Capitalism: Public Enterprise in Canada, by Jeanne Kirk Laux and Maureen Appel Molot
Why Syria Goes to War: Thirty Years of Confrontation, by Fred H. Lawson
Remaking the Italian Economy, by Richard M. Locke
France after Hegemony: International Change and Financial Reform, by Michael Loriaux
Economic Containment: CoCom and the Politics of East-West Trade, by Michael Mastanduno
Mercantile States and the World Oil Cartel, 1900–1939, by Gregory P. Nowell
Opening Financial Markets: Banking Politics on the Pacific Rim, by Louis W. Pauly
Who Elected the Bankers? Surveillance and Control in the World Economy, by Louis W. Pauly
The Limits of Social Democracy: Investment Politics in Sweden, by Jonas Pontusson
The Fruits of Fascism: Postwar Prosperity in Historical Perspective, by Simon Reich
The Business of the Japanese State: Energy Markets in Comparative and Historical Perspective, by Richard J. Samuels
"Rich Nation, Strong Army": National Security and the Technological Transformation of Japan, by Richard J. Samuels
Crisis and Choice in European Social Democracy, by Fritz W. Scharpf, translated by Ruth Crowley
In the Dominions of Debt: Historical Perspectives on Dependent Development, by Herman M. Schwartz
Winners and Losers: How Sectors Shape the Developmental Prospects of States, by D. Michael Shafer
Europe and the New Technologies, edited by Margaret Sharp

Europe's Industries: Public and Private Strategies for Change, edited by Geoffrey Shepherd, François Duchêne, and Christopher Saunders

Ideas and Institutions: Developmentalism in Brazil and Argentina, by Kathryn Sikkink

The Cooperative Edge: The Internal Politics of International Cartels, by Debora L. Spar

Fair Shares: Unions, Pay, and Politics in Sweden and West Germany, by Peter Swenson

Union of Parts: Labor Politics in Postwar Germany, by Kathleen A. Thelen

Democracy at Work: Changing World Markets and the Future of Labor Unions, by Lowell Turner

Troubled Industries: Confronting Economic Change in Japan, by Robert M. Uriu

National Styles of Regulation: Environmental Policy in Great Britain and the United States, by David Vogel

Freer Markets, More Rules: Regulatory Reform in Advanced Industrial Countries, by Steven K. Vogel

The Political Economy of Policy Coordination: International Adjustment since 1945, by Michael C. Webb

International Cooperation: Building Regimes for Natural Resources and the Environment, by Oran R. Young

International Governance: Protecting the Environment in a Stateless Society, by Oran R. Young

Polar Politics: Creating International Environmental Regimes, edited by Oran R. Young and Gail Osherenko

Governments, Markets, and Growth: Financial Systems and the Politics of Industrial Change, by John Zysman

American Industry in International Competition: Government Policies and Corporate Strategies, edited by John Zysman and Laura Tyson